This book is published in celebration of the twenty-fifth

anniversary of the Philadelphia Museum of Art Associates

Program and was made possible by the generosity of the

Museum Associates Co-Chairmen, 1969–96.

Since 1969, the Associates of the Philadelphia Museum of

Art have played an invaluable role in the life of the Museum

through their active participation and patronage. The

involvement and generosity of these individuals are vital

to the continuing growth and well-being of the Museum,

and to its ability to serve the public.

The Museum gratefully acknowledges additional support

from the National Endowment for the Arts, a federal agency.

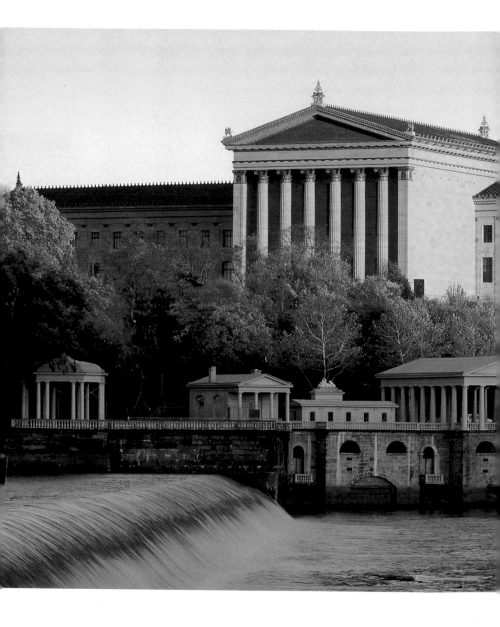

Philadelphia Museum of Art

Handbook of
the Collections

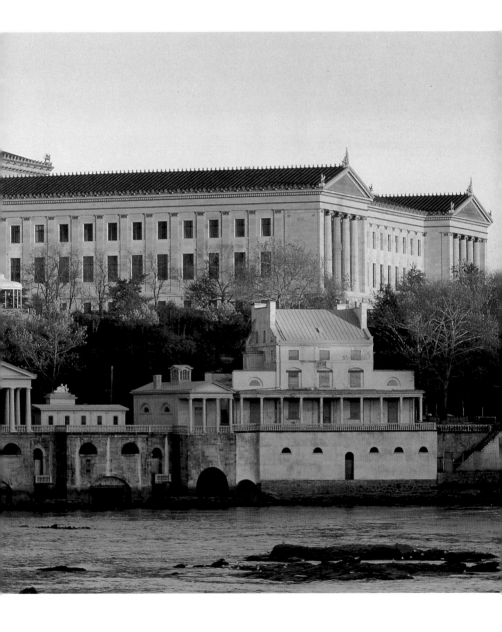

Front and back covers: Detail of the central portico of the Philadelphia Museum of Art (photograph by Graydon Wood)

Details on divider pages: Asian Art, from *Bamboo under Spring Rain* by Hsia Ch'ang (page 29); Costume and Textiles, from a quilt by Rebecca Scattergood Savery (page 91); European Decorative Arts, from a tapestry designed by Peter Paul Rubens (page 130); European Painting and Sculpture, from *The Burning of the Houses of Lords and Commons* by Joseph Mallord William Turner (page 189); Prints, Drawings, and Photographs, from *Still Life with Peonies* by Charles Aubry (page 225); American Art, from *Sailing* by Thomas Eakins (page 285); Twentieth-Century Art, from *The City* by Fernand Léger (page 315); Special Collections, from a Mexican mural fragment (page 348)

Editor: Sherry Babbitt
Designer: Diane Gottardi with Angie Hurlbut, AHdesign
Production Manager: Sandra M. Klimt
Typographer: Duke & Company, Devon, Pennsylvania
Printer: Amilcare Pizzi, S.P.A., Milan

Copyright 1995 by the
Philadelphia Museum of Art
26th Street and the Benjamin Franklin Parkway
P.O. Box 7646
Philadelphia, Pennsylvania 19101-7646

Printed and bound in Italy

Library of Congress Cataloging-in-Publication Data
Philadelphia Museum of Art.
    Handbook of the collections / Philadelphia Museum of Art.
        p.   cm.
    Includes bibliographical references and index.
    ISBN 0-87633-096-0 (alk. paper)
        1. Art—Pennsylvania—Philadelphia–Catalogs.   2. Philadelphia Museum of Art—Catalogs.
    I. Title.
N685.A56 1995   95-23944
708.148′11—dc20   CIP

Contents

Philadelphia Museum of Art Associates Co-Chairmen

Mrs. Walter H. Annenberg Paul M. Ingersoll	*1969–71*
Lorine E. Vogt Raymond G. Perelman	*1971–73*
Ann S. Moyer Benjamin Alexander	*1973–75*
Laura T. Buck Isadore M. Scott	*1975–77*
Hannah L. Henderson Edwin P. Rome	*1977–80*
Helen McCloskey Carabasi Kenneth S. Kaiserman	*1980–82*
Margaret Wright Tilghman Norman U. Cohn	*1982–84*
Dr. and Mrs. Joseph M. Hoeffel, Jr.	*1984–86*
Margaret W. Pew Marvin Lundy	*1986–88*
Christel M. Nyheim Marvin Lundy	*1988–90*
Barbara B. Aronson William M. Hollis, Jr.	*1990–92*
Annette Y. Friedland B. Herbert Lee	*1992–94*
Barbara Eberlein Edward Fernberger, Jr.	*1994–96*

Preface

This is the first comprehensive handbook to the Philadelphia Museum of Art, its more than four hundred color illustrations both presenting masterpieces from all areas of the collections and suggesting the Museum's strengths, idiosyncracies, and distinguishing features.

We were encouraged to make the commitment to the necessarily lengthy and considered process of selection, writing, and production required by such a complex undertaking by the Museum Associates, under the leadership of Barbara B. Aronson and William M. Hollis, Jr., when they served as co-chairmen in 1990–92. It was their timely and propitious proposal that this publication be designated as the group's twenty-fifth anniversary project, and it has been funded by the generosity of the successive co-chairmen of the Associates. During the past two and one-half decades, the Associates have become a mainstay of support for the Museum, and no other project could so aptly have demonstrated their centrality to this institution or so elegantly have expressed our gratitude to them.

Nor has any publication within memory drawn on the talents of so many people in so many of the Museum's departments. The curators, who proposed the objects and wrote the texts, and the photographers, who shot the splendid pictures, were the major participants, and are listed individually on page 9. The Publications staff, who gave the book its editorial and visual form, and many others, from Development to Packing, Conservation, and the Office of the Registrar, also contributed significantly to its success. The role of the support staff in the curatorial departments should especially be mentioned, for without their aid in all aspects of daily operations, this publication would have been nearly impossible to produce.

Virtually every color illustration was newly shot for this book by Graydon Wood and Lynn Rosenthal. Graydon Wood worked tirelessly for over two years to assure that each photograph accurately represented the objects and installations that are to be seen in the galleries. His task was particularly challenging because it coincided with the extensive reinstallation of the European collections, when many of our precious objects were under wraps and when many of the period rooms were inaccessible for months at a time. The resulting complications of scheduling the photography and overseeing its logistics were deftly negotiated by Conna Clark and Terry Flemming Murphy.

In the Publications Department, Sherry Babbitt, Diane Gottardi, and Sandra M. Klimt were responsible respectively for the editing, design, and production of this handsome volume, working with George H. Marcus, whose thoughtfulness about both the concept and detail, and whose intimate knowledge of the collections were invaluable to its realization. They were supported by Angie Hurlbut, Alison Rooney, and Willy Ulbrich, and assisted by Amy Agurkis, Mary Kay Garttmeier, Wendy Kanzler, Carol Meller, Sharmi Patel, and JoAnn Walter.

Individual members of other departments who contributed to specific aspects of the project were Nancy D. Baxter and Gail Maxwell, working with the Indian art material; Clarisse Carnell in the Registrar's Office; and Susan Brown and Julia E. Wood in the Development Office. We are all grateful to Alexandra Q. Aldridge, vice-president for development, for her instant enthusiasm for this idea and her endearing impatience as she watched the book come into existence.

We owe thanks to several scholars outside the Museum for their help in this endeavor: Allen Wardwell and Sherman E. Lee wrote entries, and Joseph Dye reviewed the entries on Indian objects, which were completed after the death of Stella Kramrisch, whose generosity also enriched the contents of this volume with several extraordinary works of art. Above all, the Trustees and staff, and the past, present, and future public of the Philadelphia Museum of Art, are profoundly indebted to each and every one of the donors whose gifts fill the galleries and whose generosity can only be suggested by the selection presented here.

Anne d'Harnoncourt
The George D. Widener Director

Robert Montgomery Scott
President and Chief Executive Officer

	Dilys Blum	DB
	Martha Chahroudi	MC
	Donna Corbin	DC
	Anne d'Harnoncourt	AD'H
	Eda Diskant	ED
Authors	Felice Fischer	FF
	James Ganz	JG
	Beatrice B. Garvan	BBG
	Martha C. Halpern	MCH
	H. Kristina Haugland	HKH
	Kathryn B. Hiesinger	KBH
	John Ittmann	JI
	Stella Kramrisch	SK
	Donald J. LaRocca	DLR
	Sherman E. Lee	SEL
	Jack L. Lindsey	JLL
	Katherine Crawford Luber	KCL
	Emiko Usui Mikisch	EUM
	Miriam E. Mucha	MEM
	Ann Percy	AP
	John B. Ravenal	JBR
	Christopher Riopelle	CR
	Joseph J. Rishel	JJR
	Ella Schaap	ES
	Darrel Sewell	DS
	Innis Howe Shoemaker	IHS
	Julia H. M. Smith	JHMS
	Carl Brandon Strehlke	CBS
	Ann Temkin	AT
	Dean Walker	DW
	Allen Wardwell	AW

Photographers

Principal photography by Graydon Wood.

Additional photography by Lynn Rosenthal. Other photographs by Joan Broderick, Will Brown, Rick Echelmeyer, Andrew Harkins, Joe Mikuliak, and Eric Mitchell.

Introduction

The vast, honey-colored temple housing the Philadelphia Museum
of Art rises majestically at the end of the Benjamin Franklin Parkway,
facing southeast down that broad tree-lined boulevard toward the
splendid late-nineteenth-century structure of City Hall, and to the
northwest commanding a lush green view of the largest urban park in
the United States, called Fairmount Park after the granite hill of Fairmount on which the Museum stands. When the Museum's building
was finally completed in 1928, after nine years of construction, during
which its two side pavilions were erected first to ensure that necessary
city funds would be voted to finish it, a skeptical artist grumbled about
the expense for this "Greek garage," implying doubts that its vastness
would ever be filled, but thanks to an outpouring of gifts and judicious
purchases over the years, the Museum now brims with treasures,
installed with rare character.

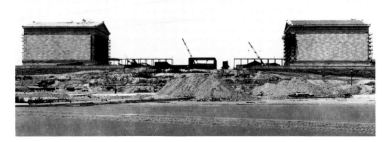

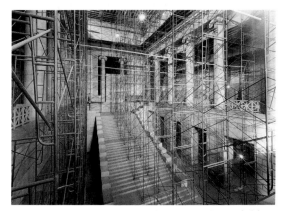

*Construction of the side pavilions of the Museum, 1925 (top), and of the
Great Stair Hall (bottom)*

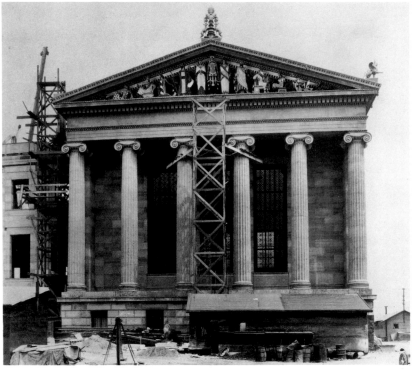

Installation of the polychrome sculpture on the north pediment of the Museum

The building's design was the cumulative work of a number of architects, including Horace Trumbauer and the firm of Zantzinger, Borie, and Medary, and yet gives no hint of indecision or compromise. Notable not only for the painstaking archaeological detail of its glazed ceramic decoration and the alert bronze griffins that patrol its acres of blue tile roof, the Museum's surprisingly adaptable interior is as welcoming to contemporary art as it is to gold-ground paintings or Shaker furniture.

The origins of the Philadelphia Museum of Art precede its current building by over fifty years. In 1876 Philadelphia was host to the first international exposition ever held in the United States, appropriately timed and sited to celebrate the one hundredth anniversary of the country's independence. The fair occupied a huge tract of land in Fairmount Park, and with singular foresight the pavilion built to exhibit the world's arts and industries was intended as a permanent structure that still stands, now known as Memorial Hall. The American public's fascinated response to the diverse assortment of fine arts, crafts, and industrial products exhibited at the Centennial Exposition led directly to the decision of civic leaders in Philadelphia to found their own art

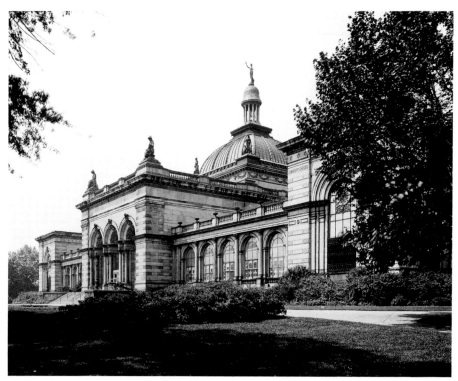

Memorial Hall, the first home of the Philadelphia Museum of Art

museum, which would be housed in the art and industries pavilion once the fair was over. A simultaneous decision created a school for fine and industrial art associated with the new museum, but never housed in the same building. In their commitment to "the improvement and enjoyment of the people of the Commonwealth," the founders of the Pennsylvania Museum and School of Industrial Art, as it was first called, drew upon the same combination of civic virtue and common sense that inspired the creation of public art museums in cities across the United States in the late nineteenth century; it is the unique aspects of each city's history and citizenry that give each of these institutions its own distinctive character.

The character of the Philadelphia Museum of Art is made up of many strands. Perhaps the most notable is the pervasive influence of Philadelphia's active role in American history, from William Penn's first arrival in 1682 and his vision of a "green countrie towne" as the spiritual and commercial center of a vast new domain called Pennsylvania, to the Declaration of Independence a little less than a century later, and the long, arduous process of forging a constitution for the new republic that took place over the hot summer months of 1787. The political vision, commercial activities, and aesthetic tastes of both the leaders of the new country and the citizens they served can be read in the astonishing array of architectural monuments and humbler buildings dating from past centuries that still stand in Philadelphia and in a wealth of works of art in the Museum's collection. Not only do the holdings of the Department of American Art richly reflect these origins but objects from many other countries also find their home in this Museum because of the international interests and connections of eighteenth- and early nineteenth-century Philadelphians.

Another early determining influence on the direction taken by the Museum's collections was the admiration, shared by many Americans in the late nineteenth century, for the model of the South Kensington Museum in London (now familiar as the Victoria and Albert), which devoted itself not to the "fine" arts of painting and sculpture but to

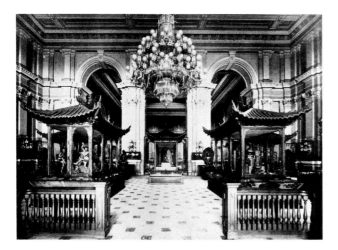

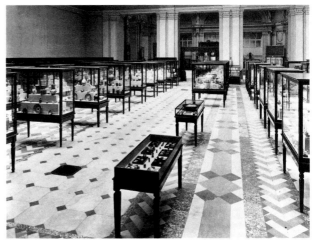

Asian art galleries in Memorial Hall

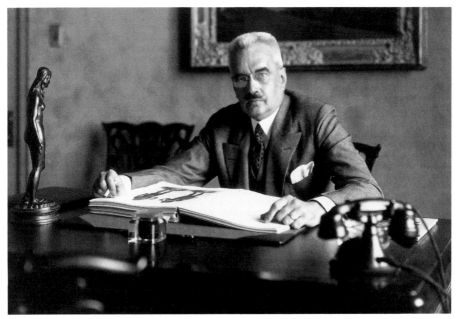

Fiske Kimball, Museum director from 1925 to 1955

an encyclopedic interest in craftsmanship, whether demonstrated by the skilled use of the hand or of the machine. Many of this Museum's earliest acquisitions had been shown in the Centennial Exposition, whose organizers clearly adhered to this conviction of the importance of the "useful" arts. Thanks also to several outstanding curators who were pioneers in their fields, such as Edwin AtLee Barber, whose taste encompassed both Talavera pottery and Tiffany glass, the collections over a century later present a kind of parity between the fine and decorative arts that is rare in American museums.

The third pervasive influence on the character of this Museum and its collections arrived in the energetic person of Fiske Kimball, the distinguished architectural historian who became director in 1925 and served for almost thirty years. Kimball's interests were voluminous, ranging from the Rococo style in Europe to the architecture of Thomas Jefferson, and he had both a demanding standard of quality in works of art and a passion for presenting objects in contexts that would be readily understandable and enjoyable for the public. It was great good fortune that he was hired in time to set a course for the installation of the entire second floor of the vast new Museum building that was then approaching completion, intended to replace Memorial Hall, which had become outmoded and overcrowded as well as seemingly remote from the city as it spread in new directions. Convinced that museums communicated most powerfully if they offered a vivid experience of history, Kimball sent his curators to China and Japan, France and England, Austria and the Netherlands, to find well-preserved architectural interiors of the quality required to stand up to the great works of art that he hoped they would soon contain. Equally determined to give an American audience some sense of where its own background fit in, he acquired a parlor from a great town house in Philadelphia and a kitchen from a Pennsylvania German dwelling to juxtapose with eighteenth-century salons from Paris and London and a snug seventeenth-century Dutch room. As today's visitor to Philadelphia moves from gallery to gallery in the Museum, passing through an Indian temple and a Chinese palace hall to arrive at the spare tranquillity of a Japanese teahouse, Kimball's intended "walk through time" continues to exert a dramatic magic that is surprisingly compatible with the most up-to-date methods of conveying information to the public of all ages about what they are seeing.

Going farther still, beyond the walls of the Museum, Kimball was the moving force behind the careful restoration of a remarkable number of historic houses that survived on their original sites in Fairmount Park,

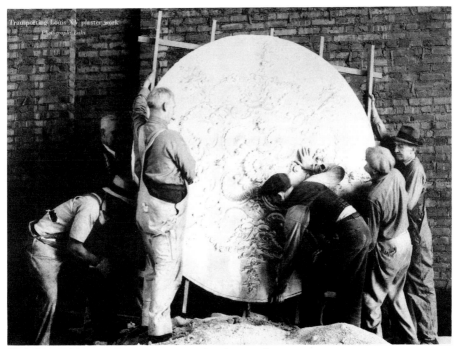

Works Progress Administration workers moving an eighteenth-century plaster medallion for installation in the salon from the Château de Draveil, 1938

built when that gentle river landscape attracted eighteenth-century Philadelphians seeking respite from the summer heat. The superb Georgian proportions of Mount Pleasant, for example, which briefly belonged to Benedict Arnold, place it among the finest houses of its type in the United States; Museum objects installed in its rooms bring it to life today. Period objects also enliven Cedar Grove, an eighteenth-century farmhouse that was continuously inhabited by five generations of a Philadelphia family, moved to the park in the 1920s from its original location in the Frankford section of the city.

The fourth great influence visible in every gallery of the Philadelphia Museum of Art flows from the interests and generosity of the many individuals who gave much-loved family possessions or vast collections

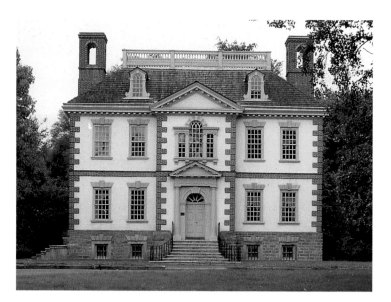

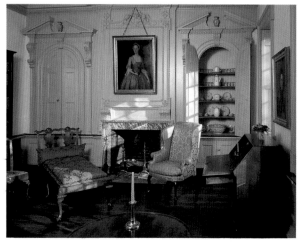

The Georgian-style Mount Pleasant, built between 1762 and 1765, with period furnishings

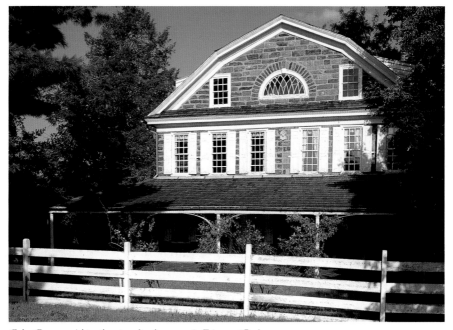
Cedar Grove, an eighteenth-century farmhouse now in Fairmount Park

to the public through their donations to the Museum. The character
of the Museum's holdings was forged by the intense and well-informed
passions of generations of collectors and curators; it must suffice to
cite but three. One of the greatest collectors, widely respected as a
museum man in his day, was the distinguished corporate lawyer John
G. Johnson, whose death in 1917 prevented him from seeing the much
anticipated new Museum building begun, but whose gift to the city of
Philadelphia of a splendid array of European old master paintings now
animates the Museum's grand medieval galleries in a way that surely
would have thrilled him. Without Carl Otto von Kienbusch's extraordinary gift of arms and armor in 1977, the Museum would lack one of
its most popular and distinctive elements—the huge and airy armory
overlooking the park, which contains both a wealth of superbly crafted
objects and the stuff of dreams for generations of children who gasp
at their first sight of a knight on horseback. The single-minded appetite
of Louise and Walter Arensberg for the most rigorous and beautiful
productions of the early modern artists who were their contemporaries, and their particular friendship with Marcel Duchamp, made the
Museum a pilgrimage site for twentieth-century art lovers, scholars,
and students from the moment of the Arensberg Collection's initial
installation by Duchamp in 1954.

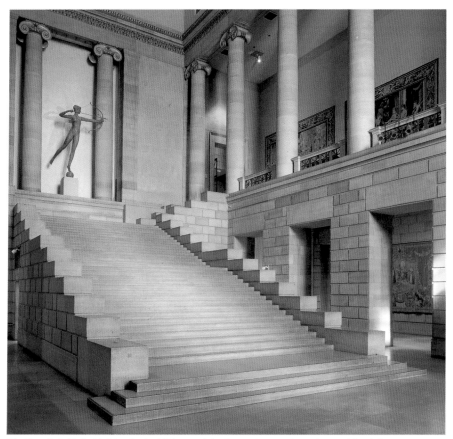

The Great Stair Hall with Saint-Gaudens's Diana *and the Constantine tapestries on the second-floor balcony*

In a city notable as a center for the training of artists over two centuries, generosity has also come from artists' families and descendants: Mrs. Thomas Eakins's gift, together with Mary Adeline Williams, of her husband's estate, established the Museum as the center of studies for this great nineteenth-century American painter, while Philadelphia's early twentieth-century craftsman in iron, Samuel Yellin, found donors to purchase and give his rare collection of European metalwork to the Museum, and it was Carroll Tyson, Jr.'s experience as a painter in France that drew him to the great Impressionist and Post-Impressionist pictures that now shine in the Museum's nineteenth-century galleries.

While the Museum's many deep strengths in a diversity of fields, from Chinese ceramics to Cubist collages, stem from the enthusiasms of collectors whose generosity no acquisition fund could ever match, individual purchases have transformed the collections over the years by adding masterpieces whose memorable quality instantly clarified and focused the objects around them, often attracting other works of art in their wake. One such purchase in 1945 was Charles Willson Peale's trompe l'oeil portrait of two of his sons climbing a staircase, which epitomizes eighteenth-century Philadelphia's blend of matter-of-factness with high artistic ambitions; another, decades later, was Hendrick Goltzius's spellbinding and exquisitely crafted image of awakening love, which found the ideal home in the context of Philadelphia's collections of ornate Northern Renaissance decorative arts and an abundance of Goltzius's own prints.

Some of the Museum's most spectacular holdings are inextricably linked with the experience of the building itself, including the great suite of Constantine tapestries by Peter Paul Rubens and Pietro da Cortona that were the providential gift of the Kress Foundation in 1959 and perfectly fit the walls of the second-floor balcony overlooking the Great Stair Hall in the center of the Museum. Nor are visitors likely to forget Augustus Saint-Gaudens's *Diana* at the top of those stairs or Alexander Calder's mobile *Ghost,* which gracefully inhabits the air above them. When visitors turn from admiring *Ghost* to gaze through

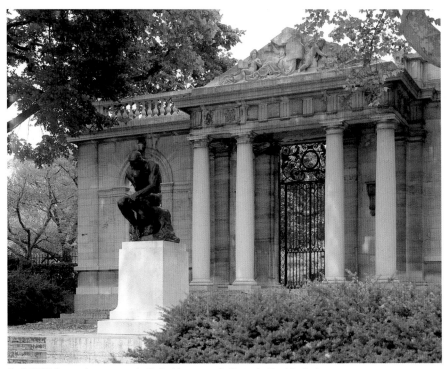

Rodin's Thinker *at the gateway to the Rodin Museum on the Benjamin Franklin Parkway*

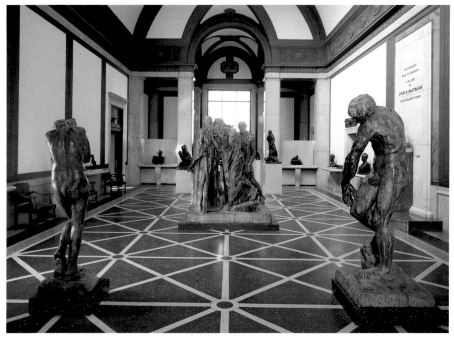

The central gallery of the Rodin Museum with The Burghers of Calais

a window or doorway at the spectacular view of downtown Philadelphia, the close connections between this great international art
museum and the city in which it has grown and flourished are expressed by the fact that the sculpture of William Penn distantly visible
atop City Hall's tower was made by Alexander Calder's grandfather.

Three blocks down the Benjamin Franklin Parkway from the Museum,
the Rodin Museum displays the gift of yet another prodigious collector.
The Philadelphia movie theater owner Jules Mastbaum assembled his
extraordinary holdings of sculpture and drawings by Auguste Rodin in
the space of three years, and commissioned the gifted Beaux-Arts
architect Paul Cret to design a suitable building, but died before he
could see the realization of his dream. Cared for and administered
by the staff of the Philadelphia Museum of Art, the Rodin Museum
opened its doors in 1929, and its treasures include casts of *The Burghers
of Calais* and *The Thinker,* which greets visitors at the entrance on the
Parkway, as well as the monumental *Gates of Hell,* which were cast for
the first time from Rodin's original plaster at Mastbaum's request.

Some of the Museum's most extensive holdings, such as prints and
drawings or costume and textiles, cannot be on permanent view
because they are made of fragile materials, but they are given their
full due in this volume as resources of great quality and breadth that

are rotated in the permanent galleries and special exhibitions. It is another distinguishing characteristic of the Museum that many of its strengths (whether in the art of India or of the Pennsylvania Germans, to cite just two examples) extend to works in numerous mediums, which greatly enhance the Museum's ability to create rich and lively installations.

It is a joy for the entire staff to place this first handbook to the collections of the Philadelphia Museum of Art into the hands of visitors and potential visitors, with the hope that each of you may find herein works of art that exert an irresistible attraction. Since it is happily impossible to predict which of the Museum's over three hundred thousand objects will strike a responsive chord, it seems essential that you all have the opportunity to discover by means of this richly illustrated volume a sampling of what awaits you behind the Museum's exuberant Neoclassical facade, or nearby in the Rodin Museum and the historic houses in Fairmount Park. Welcome!

Anne d'Harnoncourt

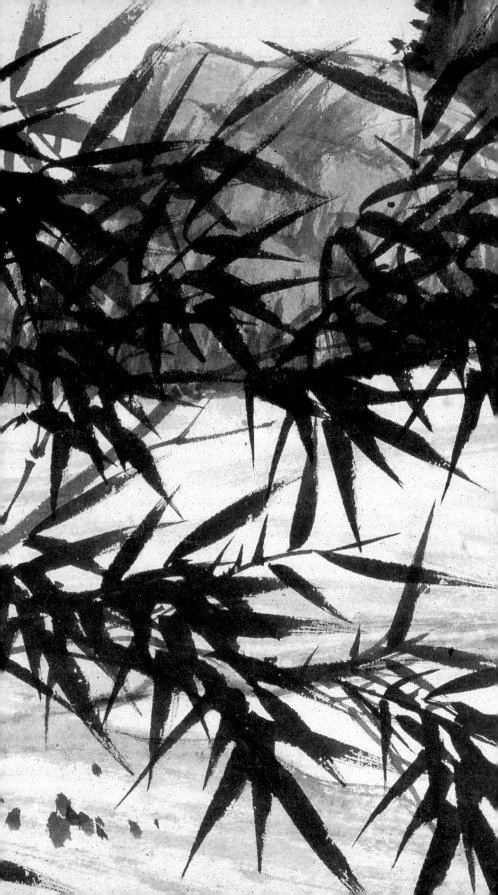

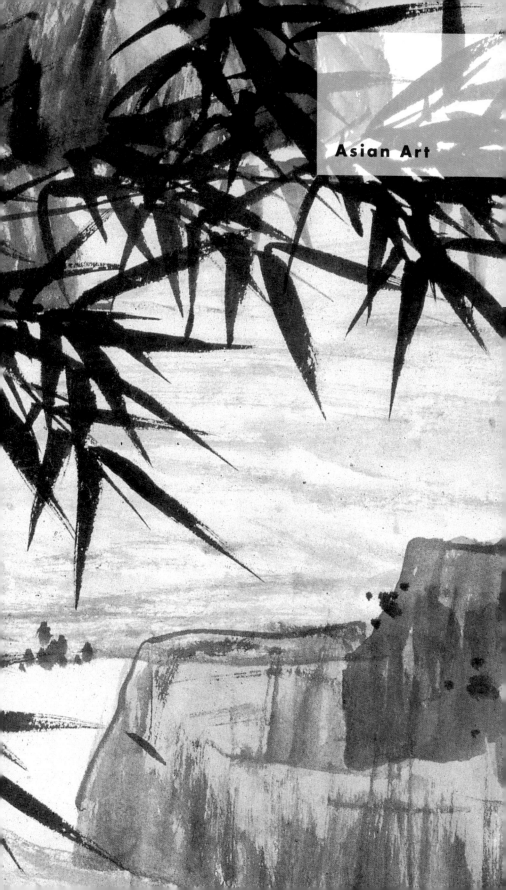

Asian Art

Asian Art

The great interest aroused in things "Oriental" by the displays at the Philadelphia Centennial Exposition in 1876 led to some of the first purchases for the newly established Museum: lacquerware, furniture, ceramics, and other decorative arts from the Chinese, Indian, Japanese, Moroccan, and Persian exhibitors. The Centennial also provided a second group of Japanese ceramics through a later bequest of General Hector Tyndale, one of the jurors at the exhibition and a manufacturer of porcelain in Philadelphia. These early holdings of Asian art were supplemented by important Chinese ceramics given by Mrs. Bloomfield Moore in the late nineteenth century.

After the arrival of the distinguished Orientalist Langdon Warner as director of the Museum in 1917, the Division of Eastern Art was established, and Horace H. F. Jayne became curator of Oriental art in 1923. They worked together to build the Asian collections, the highlight being the acquisition of over 750 Chinese ceramics in 1923, including a group of outstanding tomb figures collected by George Crofts. In 1919 the Museum received what would become its first Asian architectural interior: carved stone pillars and relief panels from a sixteenth-century temple compound in southern India, as a gift from a Philadelphia family. This would eventually form part of the great suite of architectural spaces that now gives such character and distinction to this Museum's Asian galleries. After Warner's departure in 1923, he continued to advise and assist with Museum projects and was instrumental in Jayne's quest for Chinese and Japanese period rooms for the new Museum building that opened in 1928, among which were the evocative Chinese scholar's study and the Japanese ceremonial teahouse. In 1929 a large group of Chinese paintings was purchased, while a comprehensive collection of Sung, Yüan, and Ming dynasty Chinese ceramics and rock crystals formed by Major General and Mrs. William Crozier during their residence in Beijing was donated in 1944. Under the directorship of Fiske Kimball, W. Norman Brown, professor of Sanskrit at the University of Pennsylvania, was named curator of Indian art in 1931. The expansion of the department was augmented through a 1931 expedition to Persia, jointly sponsored by the University of Pennsylvania Museum, where Jayne simultaneously served as director.

Jayne's successor as curator from 1955 until 1986 was Jean Gordon Lee. During her tenure the encyclopedic survey of Chinese ceramics, which remains one of the great assets of this Museum, was rounded out with the bequest in 1955 of the renowned Ch'ing dynasty porcelain collection originally formed by the Englishman Leonard Gow. The gift of the outstanding Persian and Turkish carpets from the Joseph Lees Williams collection the same year, together with those received in 1943 from the bequest of John D. McIlhenny, assured that Philadelphia would be a renowned center of great rugs in the United States. The series of acquisitions of fine Chinese hardwood furniture of the Ming dynasty for which this Museum is also celebrated was undertaken during this period as well.

The Austrian-born scholar Stella Kramrisch, who had been the first Western art historian to teach at the University of Calcutta, succeeded Brown as curator of Indian art in 1954, and remained curator emeritus from 1972 until her death in 1993. Under her aegis, the Museum's major holdings in Indian sculpture and painting were acquired. In 1959 came the first of seventy-one gifts from Natacha Rambova, who was the major benefactor of the Himalayan collections. Dr. Kramrisch's bequest of her own collection in 1993 brought to the Museum distinguished examples of Indian sculpture, painting, and folk art in many mediums, reflecting the full range of her scholarly interests.

In recent decades the holdings of Korean art have been augmented with a choice group of ceramics and lacquer. The Japanese collections have been expanded and given new shape with gifts and purchases of painted scrolls and screens, swords, and decorative arts, including contemporary ceramics, crafts, and industrial design, which came as a result of the Museum's exhibition *Japanese Design: A Survey Since 1950* in 1994.

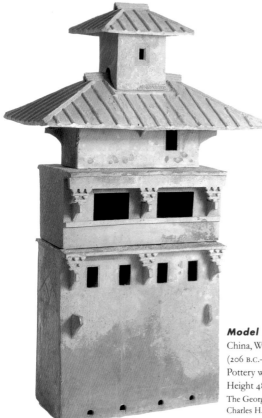

Model of a Building

China, Western Han dynasty
(206 B.C.–A.D. 8)
Pottery with traces of paint
Height 48″
The George W. Crofts Collection, gift of
Charles H. Ludington. 1925-53-9a–f

Since no actual buildings from the Western Han dynasty have
survived, models such as this, which were placed in tombs to
accompany the deceased in the afterlife, provide vital material
evidence of early Chinese architecture. The model clearly illustrates the basic Chinese building scheme used for nearly two
thousand years: post and crossbeam construction, bracketing
to help support the weight of the beams, and tiled roofs with
projecting eaves. The building probably represents the main
house of a large residential complex. The lower story would
have been used for storage and the upper floors for living
quarters, with a watchtower at the top. The various sections
of the model were shaped from molds in a fine-bodied gray
clay and show traces of paint. FF

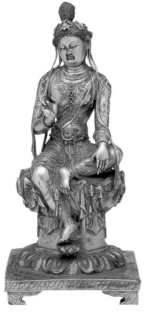

Seated Bodhisattva

China, T'ang dynasty (618–907)
Early eighth century
Gilded bronze with traces of color
Height 9″ (with base)
Purchased with Museum and subscription
funds. 1928-114-24a,b

By the first century A.D. Buddhism had been brought from
India to China, where it became a major source of artistic inspiration, its complex pantheon of Buddhas, guardian deities,
and enlightened saintlike beings, or bodhisattvas, providing a
rich choice of subjects. In representing this bodhisattva, the

artist has followed the traditional iconography as set down in the pattern books used by generations of Buddhist sculptors. The deity is seated in a posture of ease, with his hands in a gesture that signifies reassurance or tranquillity. The youthful face, rounded shoulders, slim torso, elaborate jewelry, and flowing robes, all executed with a crisp definition of line, are examples of the sophisticated modeling attained in the best sculpture and painting of eighth-century China. A masterpiece of bronze casting, this small statue displays particularly fine work in the intricate details of the crown, necklace, ribbons, and hair. The high topknot and undulating waves of hair show traces of a blue pigment (ultramarine), and the eyebrows, eyes, and lips may also have been painted. FF

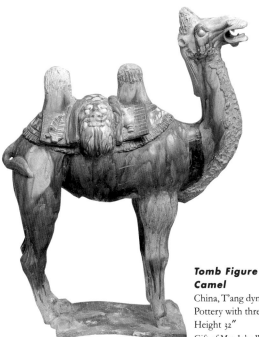

Tomb Figure of a Bactrian Camel

China, T'ang dynasty (618–907)
Pottery with three-color glaze
Height 32″
Gift of Mrs. John Wintersteen. 1964-9-1

This tomb figure of a fully laden camel suggests the flourishing overland trade carried along the Silk Route that stretched from the Chinese capital of Ch'ang-an to its western terminus in Constantinople (Istanbul). The modeling of the ungainly camel is rendered naturalistically and reveals a loving attention to detail, down to the slab of dried meat and water flasks on the saddle. The size of the tomb figures of animals and other representations of daily life that were customarily buried with the deceased was regulated by law. This exceptionally large and impressive piece from the Museum's outstanding group of T'ang tomb figures must have been commissioned for a high-ranking member of the nobility as a testimony of his wealth in this life and a reassurance to his departed spirit in the afterlife. Ch'ang-an was a major center for the production of the tomb figures, and its potters discovered new glazing techniques that produced the rich tones of green, yellow, and brown seen on this camel. FF

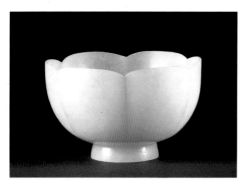

Cup
China, Sung dynasty (960–1279)
Twelfth century
Nephrite
Height 2″
Gift of the Far Eastern Art Committee
in honor of Henry B. Keep. 1978-41-1

This elegant, six-lobed cup in the shape of a flower is made
from nephrite, a type of white jade obtained from the riverbeds
of Central Asia along the ancient Silk Route. Jade had been
venerated by the Chinese from earliest recorded times as an
emblem of both sacred treasure and personal luxury, holding
a place equivalent to that of gold in the West. After the cosmo-
politan exuberance of the art of the T'ang dynasty (618–907),
aesthetic preferences shifted toward restraint and refinement.
The connoisseurs of the Sung dynasty accordingly developed
an appreciation for materials such as jade, especially their tactile
qualities. These are emphasized in this jade cup by its total absence of decoration, which focuses attention on the economy
and purity of the form and the texture of the subtly mottled
surface. FF

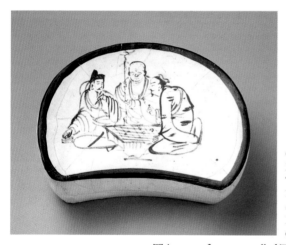

Tomb Pillow
China, Chin dynasty (1115–1234)
Dated 1178 (eighteenth year of the
Ta-ting period, 1161–1189)
Pottery with underglaze decoration
(Tz'u-chou ware)
Height 4″
Gift of Mrs. Carroll S. Tyson. 1957-26-1

This type of pottery, called Tz'u-chou ware after the place in
China where it was made, was a popular type of ceramic made
in large quantities. However, the remarkable scene painted on
this pillow—the three great philosophies of Chinese civilization
as represented by a Confucian scholar, a Buddhist monk, and
a Taoist priest seated at a chessboard—is unique among known
pillows; this is also one of the few ceramic works of the period
that bears a precise date, in this case one that corresponds to
1178. The freely brushed figures are enclosed in a thick brown
outline that follows the crescent shape of the pillow, which
would have been placed with the deceased in the tomb. FF

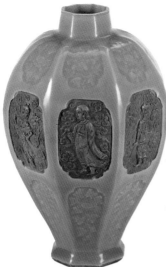

Vase

China, Yüan dynasty (1260–1368)
Fourteenth century
Porcelain (Lung Ch'uan
celadon ware)
Height 10″
Gift of Mrs. S. Emlen Stokes. 1964-58-1

This octagonal vase is one of only a handful of such vessels that combine a lustrous gray-green celadon glaze with unglazed red-brown panels. The process used to produce these wares is very exacting and difficult, which may explain why it was only used on a limited number of works. To achieve the bold contrast of colors and textures, Chinese potters developed a new technique: after the entire vase was formed, eight of the twenty-four molded decorative panels on its surface were covered with wax, and a celadon glaze was applied to the whole piece. When the vase was fired in the kiln, the glaze turned the green color known as celadon, while the wax melted from the panels, leaving them to turn the soft reddish brown hue of the clay itself. The figures on the panels represent the Eight Immortals of Chinese Taoist philosophy. FF

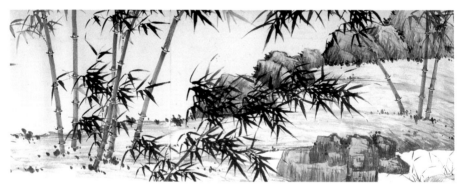

Hsia Ch'ang

Chinese, 1388–1470
Bamboo under Spring Rain
(detail), c. 1460
Ink on paper, mounted as
a handscroll
1′8⅜″ x 31′2⅝″
Purchased with the Joseph E. Temple
Fund and the John T. Morris Fund
1953-51-1

Bamboo was an ideal subject for Hsia Ch'ang to have chosen for displaying his virtuosity with brush and ink, for the thick black brushstrokes of the older stalks contrast with the delicate young shoots that are rendered in a light gray wash, while the leaves appear to sway gently with the breeze. The rock formations are painted with a drier brush to give a sense of their rough texture. In this handscroll Hsia Ch'ang, a scholar and sometime government official who made bamboo painting his specialty, establishes a viewpoint that was daring for his time by depicting the scene from a very low perspective, a sort of "bug's-eye view," as if the artist were floating along the banks of a stream and observing the bamboo forest all around, which extends beyond eye level at the top and bottom of the scroll. Only a small section of the over thirty-foot-long scroll may be seen at any one time as it is horizontally unrolled from right to left, thus offering the viewer a wonderful variety of composition and brushwork. FF

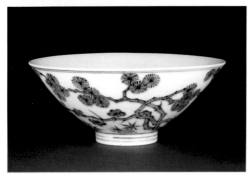

Bowl

China, Ming dynasty (1368–1644)
Early fifteenth century
Porcelain with underglaze cobalt
decoration
Height 3½″
Purchased with the Henry B. Keep
Fund, the Joseph E. Temple Fund, the
Bloomfield Moore Fund, the John T.
Morris Fund, and with funds contrib-
uted by Mrs. Walter H. Annenberg,
The Beneficia Foundation, Mr. and Mrs.
J. Welles Henderson, Mrs. Howard H.
Lewis, Mrs. William F. Machold, Mrs.
Donald Petrie, Meyer P. Potamkin,
Hugh Scott, and Mrs. William L.
Van Alen. 1984-116-1

When the use of cobalt as a pigment for painting ceramics was introduced to China from the Middle East in the fourteenth century, it opened a new world of decorative possibilities. Instead of relying on different colored glazes to create patterns, Chinese artists could achieve pictorial results on ceramics comparable to those found in ink paintings on paper and silk. The subject illustrated on this bowl is the Three Friends of Winter: two plants that remain green in the winter, a sturdy pine branch and a stalk of bamboo, along with the flowering plum, which is the first to bloom as a harbinger of spring. The brushwork is from the hand of a master who met the challenge of working on the curved surface with confidence and dexterity, thereby creating a composition that transcends mere decoration to become the focus for the graceful rhythms of the sloping sides of the bowl itself. FF

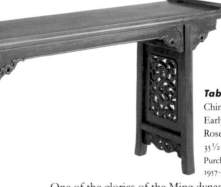

Table

China, Ming dynasty (1368–1644)
Early seventeenth century
Rosewood
35½ x 75 x 17½″
Purchased with Museum funds
1957-99-1

One of the glories of the Ming dynasty, and a distinguished part of the Museum's important collection of Chinese art, is its furniture. In this Ming table the color and finish of the oiled and polished undecorated wood combine with a felicitous balance of mass and line to present a particularly fine example of the furnituremaker's art. The tabletop is made from a single board of rosewood, chosen for the beauty of its rich grain; its long, flat surface is softened by the curved flanges at either side. Likewise, the strong vertical lines of the recessed legs are played off against the delicate carving of the apron at the top and the openwork panels at the sides. The table is constructed with sophisticated mortise and tenon joinery, using no glue or nails and only wooden pegs, which facilitated its disassembly and rebuilding whenever its scholar-bureaucrat owner had to move to a new government post. FF

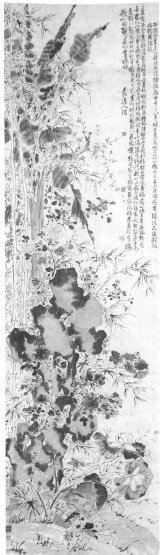

Hsü Wei
Chinese, 1521–1593
Sixteen Flowers
Ink on paper, mounted as a
hanging scroll
10′ 11″ x 3′ 3″
Purchased with the Fiske Kimball Fund
and the Marie Kimball Fund. 1968-29-1

Hsü Wei did not begin painting until he was in his fifties,
after several unsuccessful bids at a career as a bureaucrat, an
attempted suicide, and a seven-year jail term for the murder
of his wife. Best known during his lifetime as a playwright, Hsü
Wei demonstrates his dramatic flair in the staging of the sixteen
flowers on this hanging scroll, accompanied by a poem that he
composed and calligraphed. It was for his calligraphy that Hsü
Wei himself wanted to be remembered, but in China the arts
of poetry, painting, and calligraphy are inexorably intertwined.
This stunning scroll, almost eleven feet long, is a showcase for
his brushwork, depicting in vivid profusion such flowers as the
lotus, narcissus, peony, begonia, and camellia, anchored by a
solid rock formation and counterbalanced by the calligraphy
that falls like rain from the upper right. Ancient legend inspired
Hsü Wei to paint the flowers of all seasons blooming simultaneously, which in his poem he likens to beautiful young women
whose good looks must also inevitably fade away. FF

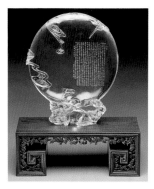

Moon Crystal

China, Ch'ing dynasty (1644–1911),
Ch'ien-lung period (1736–1795)
Rock crystal
Height 10⅞"
Gift of Major General and Mrs. William
Crozier. 1944-20-8

Rock crystal, a transparent form of the mineral quartz, was called "water essence" in early Chinese writings because of its resemblance to ice. It is a difficult medium to work: first the general shape must be sawed and chipped down, and then the detailed carving is done with a bow drill. Here the artist has mastered the technique to create a nearly flawless disk representing the moon. Clouds drift across its face, and it is supported on a base depicting the rabbit of Tao legend who lives in the moon and concocts the elixir of immortality. The fifth-century prose poem incised on the surface tells of an ancient ruler who had parted from his beloved and found solace in moon gazing. It was cut into the crystal by the famous carver Chao P'ing-chung, who dated this work in the last year of the reign of the Ch'ien-lung emperor, a renowned patron of the arts and probably the original owner of this precious object. FF

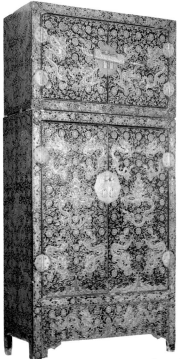

Cabinet

China, Ch'ing dynasty (1644–1911)
Late seventeenth century
Lacquer on wood
114¼ x 56½ x 26⁵⁄₁₆"
Purchased with the Bloomfield Moore
Fund. 1940-7-1a–c

Intended for one of the spacious interiors of the residences of the Chinese nobility, this extraordinary cabinet, one of a pair, was designed to store clothing, with the separate, smaller cupboard on top used for hats. The red and gold lotus and dragon motifs were painted on the black lacquer chest to create a sumptuous effect appropriate to the status of its aristocratic owner. The five-clawed dragon shown here was the symbol of the emperor as the Son of Heaven, mediating between heaven and earth. The use of this image was originally restricted to wares intended for imperial use or commissioned by imperial command. The frontal design of the five-clawed dragon with pairs of smaller confronting dragons above and below is almost identical to that found on imperial robes of the same period, which would have been kept folded flat in such a cabinet. FF

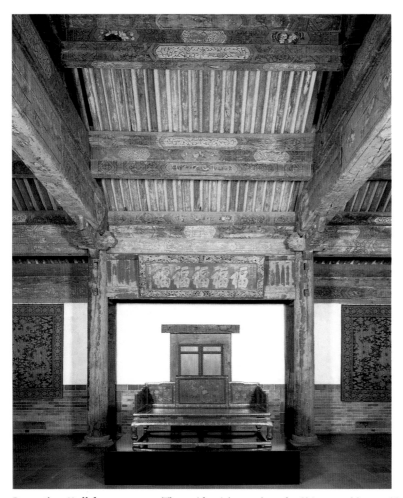

Reception Hall from a Nobleman's Palace

China, Beijing, Ming dynasty (1368–1644)
First half of the seventeenth century
Gift of Edward B. Robinette. 1929-163-1

The residential complex of a Chinese nobleman, like the traditional family compound, was built on a rectangular plan, facing south, and surrounded by a wall. Closest to the south gate was the most formal building, the reception hall, such as this example from Beijing, the only interior of its type in an American museum. It was here that a high-ranking nobleman, seated on his raised lacquer couch, received visitors, who then, as now, would be most impressed by the ceiling, soaring nearly thirty feet high. Its huge beams and rafters are supported by eighteen red lacquer columns as well as the traditional system of interlocking carved brackets. The grandeur of the space is accentuated by the floral, animal, and geometric motifs painted on the exposed ceiling members. Below, the architectural symmetry of the room and the placement of its furnishings reflect the Confucian ideal of order and harmony. FF

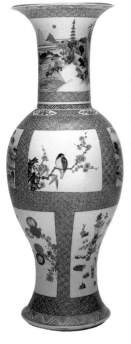

Vase
China, Ch'ing dynasty (1644–1911),
K'ang-hsi period (1662–1722)
Porcelain with underglaze and
overglaze enamel decoration
Height 28⅛″
The Alfred and Margaret Caspary
Memorial Gift. 1955-50-99

During the sixty-year reign of the K'ang-hsi emperor (1662–
1722), Chinese porcelain production reached new heights of
technical perfection. The gorgeous palette of overglaze enamels
on this imposing vase shows landscape and floral panels set
off against a rich, brocadelike ground pattern. Chinese porcelains such as this were long admired by Europeans, who called
this particular color combination "*famille verte,*" which means
"green family," for the predominance of that shade. One of
the most enthusiastic collectors of the time was Augustus the
Strong (1670–1733), elector of Saxony, who amassed a huge
treasury of ceramics at the Johanneum in Dresden, Germany,
where this piece was once housed. The vase is among over four
hundred outstanding examples of Ch'ing porcelain bequeathed
to the Museum by Alfred and Margaret Caspary. FF

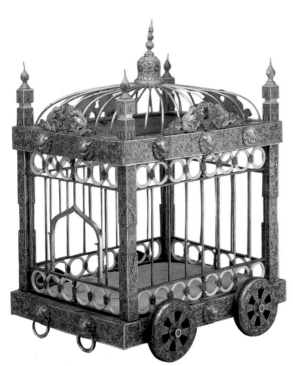

Dog Cage
China, Ch'ing dynasty (1644–1911),
Ch'ien-lung period (1736–1795)
Brass with cloisonné and gilt
decoration and jade fittings
Height 45½″
Gift of the Friends of the Philadelphia
Museum of Art. 1964-205-1

This elaborate dog cage epitomizes the luxurious life of the
imperial court during the long reign of the Ch'ien-lung emperor, when the extravagant display of wealth extended even
to the accouterments of the imperial kennels. The body of the

cage is decorated with the intricate enameling technique known as cloisonné, in which copper wires (or *cloisons*) are used to separate areas of various colors mixed from metal oxides that are then fired at high temperatures to harden. The finials at the top of the cage as well as the five-clawed dragons and lions' heads around the perimeter are gilded, and rows of jade rings complete this miniature palace on wheels. The emperor was said to be especially fond of cloisonné and had workshops that specialized in the process established on the palace grounds in Beijing, where this cage for a favorite pet dog was undoubtedly fabricated. FF

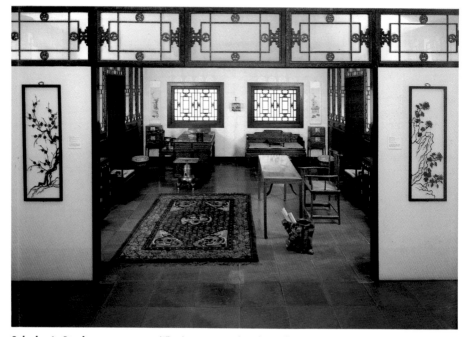

Scholar's Study

China, Beijing, Ch'ing dynasty
(1644–1911)
Late eighteenth century
Gift of Wright S. Ludington in memory
of his father, Charles H. Ludington
1929-30-1

The innermost chamber of the Chinese scholar-bureaucrat's residence was his private study. While retaining the symmetrical arrangement of architecture and furnishings found in the formal, public rooms, the study provided an intimate, congenial space away from official duties. In this late eighteenth-century example from Beijing, two walls are lined with hinged lacquered panels that have silk-covered latticework at the top and delicately painted landscapes at the bottom. The study has been furnished in a style typical of the period. The rosewood desk offered ample room for storing the scholar's books, brushes, and other writing equipment. The brass stove nearby kept hot water ready for tea to share with visitors on the cushioned couch (*kang*). The long, narrow table was designed for painting or looking at scrolls, some of which are kept in the burl wood holder on the floor. A bird singing in the birdcage hanging on the window wall and the sounds from the garden filtering through the paper-covered windows would have completed the peaceful, contemplative setting. FF

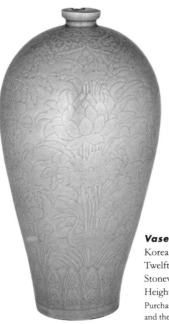

Vase
Korea, Koryŏ dynasty (918–1392)
Twelfth century
Stoneware with celadon glaze
Height 16″
Purchased with the Fiske Kimball Fund
and the Marie Kimball Fund. 1974-133-1

With its small mouth and broad-shouldered body tapering at the foot, this elegant, harmonious vessel is known as a *maebyŏng*, or "plum vase," for the flowering plum branches it was designed to hold. The soft, lustrous blue-green of the celadon glaze is typical of the finest ceramics of the Koryŏ dynasty, and this vase, the largest of its type to survive, must have been made under royal patronage. This masterpiece of the Korean potter's art, with a delicately incised underglaze design of herons amid mallow and lotus blossoms, once belonged to the American financier J. P. Morgan, in whose catalogue it is listed as of Chinese origin. However, although the celadon glaze technique was introduced from China, the vase was undoubtedly made in Korea, probably in the southern part of the peninsula, where the major kilns for pottery production were located. FF

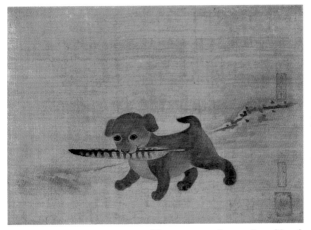

Attributed to
Yi Am
Korean, 1499–after 1545
Puppy with Feather
Ink and color on silk, mounted
as a hanging scroll
12⅛ x 17⅛″
Purchased with Museum funds
1959-105-1

The essence of puppyhood has been captured in the portrait of this charming canine frolicking with his prize feather. The painting is attributed to the artist Yi Am, about whom little is known except that he was a member of the Korean royal family who specialized in animal and flower paintings. The style of paintings such as this was probably inspired by Chinese examples, but Yi Am's ability to communicate the wide-eyed wonder of this particular puppy makes one speculate that he had a live model close at hand. FF

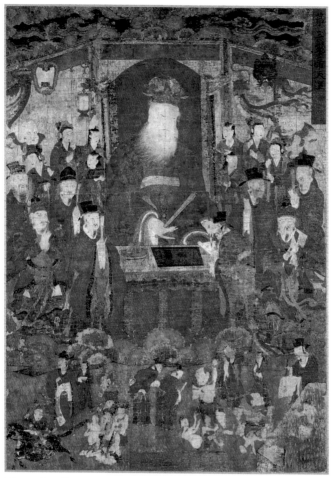

King of Hell
Korea, Chosŏn dynasty (1392–1910)
Seventeenth century
Ink and colors on silk
75 x 50½″
Gift of Mrs. W. James Anderson, Mrs. Samuel Bell, Jr., Mrs. Richard Drayton, and Charles T. Ludington, Jr., in memory of their parents, Mr. and Mrs. Charles Townsend Ludington
1970-259-3

The awe-inspiring figure at the center of this painting is Song-che, one of the ten Buddhist Kings of Hell, who sits in judgment of the deceased, writing his decision on the scroll held by his assistant. At the bottom, below a line of clouds, are scenes of punishments that have been meted out: one man is imprisoned in a stockade, another is about to be impaled by a halberd-bearing demon, while two figures at the right seem to be trapped in a pit of nails. The vivid liveliness of this portion of the image stands in contrast to the stately dignity of the King of Hell, surrounded by his attendants. Such paintings on silk were usually made in sets of ten, one for each of the kings, and were often displayed in the building in Korean temple complexes known as the Hall of the Underworld Courts. The names of the donors and priests of the temple for which this work was made appear in the rectangular cartouche at the bottom. FF

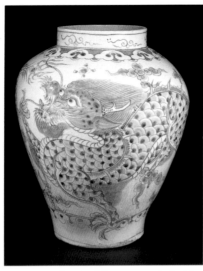

Dragon Jar
Korea, Chosŏn dynasty (1392–1910)
Eighteenth century
Porcelain with underglaze cobalt
decoration
Height 16⅛″
Purchased with Museum funds
1950-106-1

A pair of dragons encircle this robust jar, the swirling curves
of their torsos swelling along the contours of its slightly asymmetrical ceramic surface. In Korea as in China, the dragon was
an auspicious creature, a symbol of the authority and benefi-
cence of the ruler. Traces of the Chinese origins of the motifs
on this jar can be seen in the formal bands of ornament around
the neck, but the sophisticated yet free brushwork used to paint
the dragon has a vitality and dynamism that are hallmarks of
Korean art. Because in eighteenth-century Korea cobalt was a
luxury item imported from the Middle East, its use for decorating porcelain was restricted to items produced for members
of the ruling class. FF

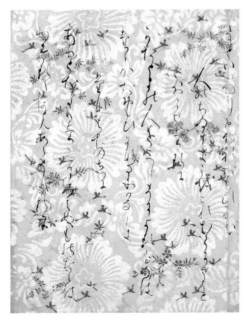

**Leaf from a Poetry
Anthology**
Japan, Heian period (794–1185)
1108–12
Ink and paint over a woodblock
print on coated paper, mounted
as a hanging scroll
8 x 6¼″ (exclusive of mount)
Purchased with the John T. Morris
Fund. 1965-77-1

A design of chrysanthemums and plum blossoms, woodblock
printed in a white ink made of shimmering ground mica, decorates the paper of this album leaf on which an elegant cursive
script is brushed in black ink. The sheet is also embellished with

pine branches, bellflowers, maple leaves, and birds delicately painted and stamped in silver. This page from a collection of poems by Lady Ise, who died about 940, originally formed part of a sumptuous edition of the "Anthology of Poems by Thirty-Six Poets" believed to have been commissioned for the sixtieth birthday celebrations of the emperor Shirakawa in 1112. The anthology consisted of some 190 pages that were separated in 1929, when several leaves were mounted as hanging scrolls. Some twenty of the leading calligraphers of the time worked on the project. The refined brushwork done on richly decorated paper is typical of the entire anthology, which reflects the aesthetic preferences of the ruling class of the Heian period. FF

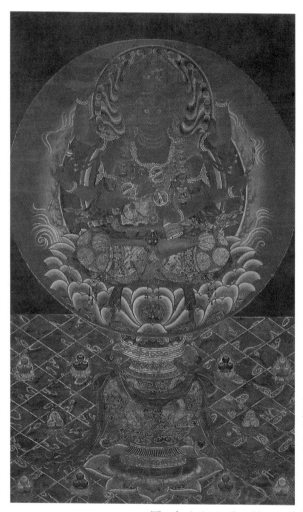

Aizen Myōō
Japan, Nambokuchō period
(1333–1392)
Fourteenth century
Colors and cut gold on silk,
mounted as a hanging scroll
45 x 25¾"
Purchased with the John T. Morris
Fund. 1960-7-1

The depictions of multi-armed deities are among the most impressive works of Japanese Buddhism. Here the central image is Aizen Myōō, one of the five Kings of Bright Wisdom who are the ferocious guardian deities of Esoteric Buddhism. He holds in his richly jeweled arms the symbols of his power—the thunderbolt, bell, bow and arrow, and lotus—as he sits on a lotus pedestal supported by a dragon vase, from which jewels scatter onto the floor. The fine detailing of the robe, jewelry, and vase is done in cut gold. His expression is fierce, and his body is as red as the setting sun, with flames of passion emanating from his head. The red of his body shows gradations in shading, an unusual feature in Buddhist painting. This scroll dates to the fourteenth century, when the worship of the Wisdom Kings was particularly popular as their protection was invoked against the Mongols who were attacking Japan; the ultimate failure of the invasions served to bolster belief in the efficacy of these deities. FF

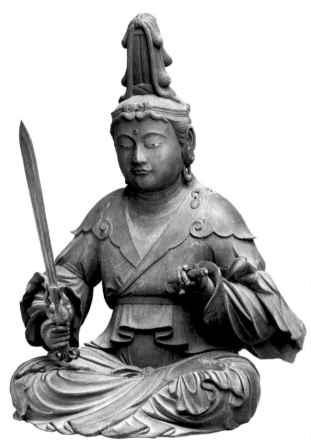

Seated Monjū

Japan, Kamakura period
(1185–1333)
Early fourteenth century
Cypress
Height 14⅝"

Purchased with the Katharine Levin Farrell Fund, the Haney Foundation Fund, the Margaretta S. Hinchman Fund, the Bloomfield Moore Fund, the John T. Morris Fund, the Edgar Viguers Seeler Fund, the George W. B. Taylor Fund, and with funds contributed by Mrs. Rodolphe Meyer de Schauensee. 1979-57-1

In this depiction the typically youthful Monjū, who is worshiped as the manifestation of the wisdom of the Buddha, holds a scroll symbolizing the sacred Buddhist writings in his left hand and an upright sword representing the victory of wisdom over ignorance in his right. Whereas earlier Japanese sculptors carved from a single block of wood, the artists of the Kamakura period worked with several pieces joined together, which enabled them to use a combination of the best woods with the finest grains. Here the use of the grain in the lines of Monjū's jacket and in his face demonstrates the craftsman's sensitivity to his medium. The inlaid eyes, probably rock crystal, were inserted from behind the hollowed-out head before the front and back sections were joined. The deeply cut folds of the figure's drapery and the crisp, delicate carving of the elaborate topknot further reveal the highly developed techniques of the Buddhist sculptors of the time. FF

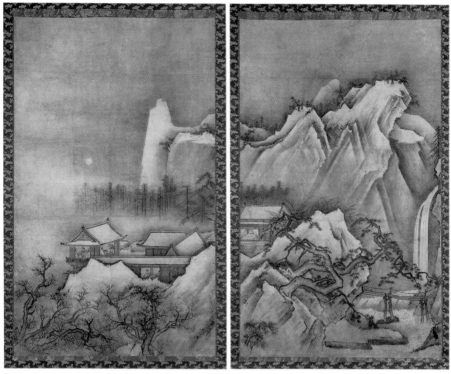

Pavilions in a Mountain Landscape

Japan, Muromachi period
(1392–1573)
c. 1550
Ink and colors on paper, mounted as hanging scrolls
60 x 38″ (each)
Purchased with the Henry P. McIlhenny Fund in memory of Frances P. McIlhenny, the Henry B. Keep Fund, and the Far Eastern Art Revolving Fund. 1990-92-1a,b

Now mounted as hanging scrolls, this pair of ink paintings were originally set into lacquered wood frames to serve as sliding doors in an upper-class Japanese residence or Buddhist temple of the sixteenth century. The artist is not known, but he was well trained in the Chinese-style ink-painting techniques and themes that were popular in Japan at the time. The composition of the scene reads in the traditional manner from right to left across the two panels. The viewer's attention is thus immediately focused on the sharp contours of the mountain cliffs at the upper right and then gradually shifts downward with the movement of the waterfall to the frothy pool of water and narrow bridge. Emerging from behind the hills beyond the bridge is an elegant pavilion where a group of scholars are taking tea. A small grove of pines in the mist is punctuated by the pale moon above, as the scene that began so dramatically ends on a note of harmony and respite. FF

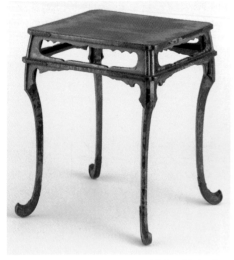

Incense Table

Japan, Muromachi period
(1392–1573)
Fifteenth century
Negoro lacquer on wood with
engraved metal fittings
14½ x 12⅜ x 11¼"
Purchased with the John T. Morris
Fund. 1982-4-1

This table is decorated with the technique known as *negoro*,
which was named after a Japanese temple famous for the production of this type of lacquer. The wood of the carved table
was first covered with multiple layers of black lacquer over
which a final layer of red lacquer was applied. With age and use,
the top red layer would wear through unevenly to the black
lacquer beneath, thus creating an unpredictably mottled pattern.
The slender, curved legs and delicately carved side panels of
this small square table are echoes of its Chinese ancestry in the
eighth century, when lacquer wares were introduced to Japan
by Buddhist monks traveling from the Asian continent. Tables
such as this were originally designed to hold a temple's incense
burners and other ritual implements. In later centuries, the
elegant simplicity of their sculptural form as well as their unadorned red lacquer surfaces appealed to Japanese tea connoisseurs, who began collecting such *negoro* wares for use in
the tearoom. FF

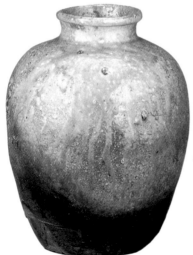

Storage Jar

Japan, Momoyama period
(1568–1615)
Stoneware with ash glaze
(Iga ware)
Height 12"
Purchased with the John T. Morris
Fund, the John D. McIlhenny Fund,
and with funds contributed by the
Honorable Hugh Scott. 1993-66-1

Stately jars such as this example from Iga Province in western
Japan were originally intended as utilitarian wares for storing

tea leaves or grains. Made of rough, unrefined clay, they were stacked tightly together in the kiln for several days. During the firing, ash from the kiln fire would blow up into the chamber and settle down on the pots, where it melted to form a glaze. Debris from the ceiling of the kiln chamber also often fell and stuck to the jars. A felicitous combination of such kiln "accidents" has produced the remarkable surface effects seen on this piece. The transparent, crackled glaze has fired to a soft, moss-colored green that spills over three-fourths of the surface. Its high iron content turned the clay a persimmon brown, with some darker scorch marks where the fire was most intense at the lower third of the jar. The entire body is accentuated with craggy adhesions that give a dynamic energy to the surface texture of this vessel. FF

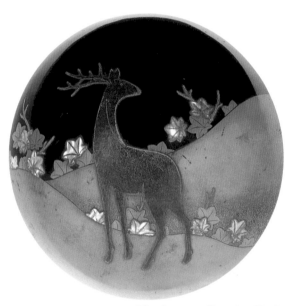

Writing Box
Attributed to Hon'ami Kōetsu
(Japanese, 1558–1637)
Early seventeenth century
Lacquer on wood with lead and
mother-of-pearl inlay
Diameter 11 9/16″
Gift of the Friends of the Philadelphia
Museum of Art. 1992-7-1a–d

The famous calligrapher Hon'ami Kōetsu was also a sword connoisseur, potter, tea master, and lacquer designer. While no piece of lacquer has been definitively assigned to his own hand, Kōetsu's creative inspiration is clearly evident in this elegant writing box. In a theme taken from classical Japanese poetry, the cry of the deer, lonely for its mate, pierces the silence of the hills, whose foliage has turned the brilliant hues of autumn. The sense of solitude is emphasized by the black lacquer of the night sky, with the mother-of-pearl inlay of the autumn leaves reflecting silver in the moonlight against the faded gold of the ground. The motif of scattering autumn leaves is carried over into the interior of the box, which is equipped with a water dropper and stone used for preparing ink for writing. FF

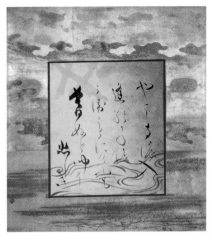

Hon'ami Kōetsu
Japanese, 1558–1637
Calligraphy of a Poem
Early seventeenth century
Gold, silver, and ink on paper,
mounted as a hanging scroll
7½ x 6¾″ (exclusive of mount)
Purchased with the Henry B. Keep
Fund and with gifts (by exchange) of
Mrs. Andrew B. Young, Mrs. Henry W.
Breyer, Sr., and Karen Myrin. 1988-87-1

Hon'ami Kōetsu was one of the most versatile artists of his
time, admired above all for his talent as a calligrapher. His great
achievement was to create a new style of calligraphy through
a synthesis of the Chinese-influenced style with elements of
the classical Japanese writing tradition of the Heian period
(794–1185). The poem on this scroll is from the "Collection of
Chinese and Japanese Poems for Recitation," originally compiled around 1018, and reads: "How melancholy to hear/Today
too has ended/With each ringing/Of the evening bell/At the
mountain temple." The verse is written on paper decorated with
a sparse scene of a silver river under a sky of abstract clouds in
gold wash, most likely also done by Kōetsu. The whole is surrounded by another painted layer of iridescent gold and silver,
lending an opulent effect to this diminutive work. FF

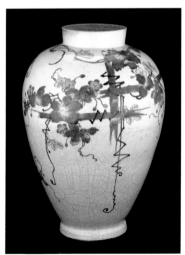

Tea Jar
Japan, Edo period (1615–1867)
Eighteenth century
Porcelain with enamel glazes
(Arita ware)
Height 17¾″
Purchased with the George W. B. Taylor
Fund. 1955-10-1

The quietly elegant mood expressed by this tea jar almost
obscures the bold and experimental nature of its decoration.
Instead of using the conventional approach, strongly influenced by Chinese porcelain, of covering the entire surface with
intricate details to create an effect resembling brocaded cloth,
the decorator of the Museum's jar chose a scheme that recalls
a native Japanese painting style and related developments in
Japanese kimono design. A single subject, a fence with a flower-

ing vine, is dramatically and asymmetrically placed using the entire surface of the jar as its field. The large amount of empty space further establishes a clear opposition between the subject and its background. Although heavy-bodied jars of this sort were made in great numbers during the Edo period for both export and domestic tea storage, this decorative style is rare and perhaps even unique among such pieces in public collections today. EUM

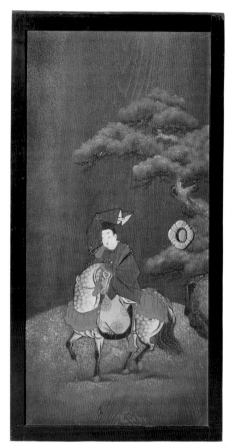

Courtier on Horseback
Japan, Edo period (1615–1867)
Seventeenth century
Ink and colors on cryptomeria, mounted as a sliding door
69¾ x 36¼"
Purchased with the Fiske Kimball Fund and the Marie Kimball Fund. 1966-211-11a

Traditional Japanese interiors are characterized by the interplay of art and architecture. Since columns rather than walls supported the weight of the roof, walls could be movable, and made of either paper or wood. This sliding door, one of a set of twenty in the Museum's collection that would typically have been used to divide and decorate the rooms of a private residence, is painted with an elegant courtier riding his dappled steed through the evening, perhaps returning from a tryst. The long sleeve of his raised arm protects him against the snow that covers the ground and the old pine tree. The wood is left otherwise unpainted, giving the scene a sense of richness and depth, with the beautiful grain itself reading as the falling snow. The gilded door pull features the three hollyhock leaves used in the crest of the Tokugawa family of shoguns. Perhaps these doors were originally designed for a shogunal residence, although their exact provenance is no longer traceable. FF

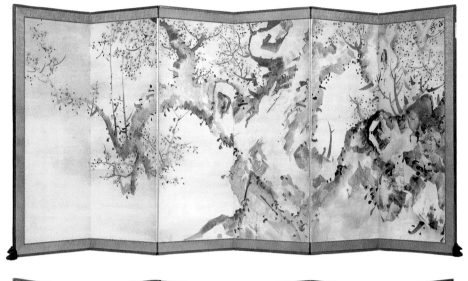

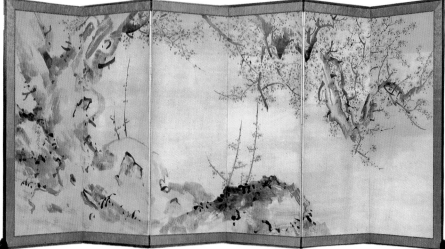

Ike no Taiga
Japanese, 1723–1776
Flowering Plum Trees in Mist
c. 1770
Ink and gold wash on paper,
mounted as a pair of six-fold
screens
5′ x 11′9¼″ (each)
Purchased with the George W. Elkins
Fund. E1969-1-1, 2

The supremely accomplished and individualistic painter Ike no Taiga gives a bravura display of his brushwork in this pair of monumental screens, meant to be seen side by side. Rising from the massive rock formation executed in angular, abstract patches of ink at the right (top) is an immense, rugged plum tree. On its aged, sculptural branches that extend beyond the frame of the screen, Taiga has painted a profusion of new blooms with precise and detailed lines of ink. The blossoming boughs of the gnarled companion tree on the other screen reach over to form an arched bower, while the expanse of empty space is compelling and profound. In the contrast between the unpainted void and the solid forms of his composition, Taiga suggests the dualities of *yin* and *yang,* darkness and light, death and life, found in the natural world. The surface of the painting is highlighted with a pale gold wash that shimmers warmly in the changing light and gives yet another layer of subtle depth to Taiga's masterful composition. FF

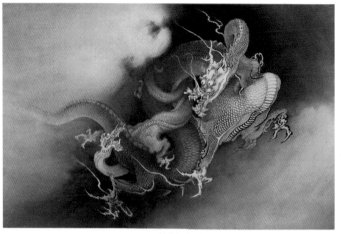

Kanō Hōgai
Japanese, 1828–1888
Two Dragons in Clouds, 1885
Ink on paper
35½ x 53¾"
Gift of Mrs. Moncure Biddle in
memory of her father, Ernest F.
Fenollosa. 1940-41-1

This highly naturalistic rendering of two intertwining dragons
glistening amidst the clouds represents a bold experiment
in adapting Western techniques to traditional Japanese ink
painting. Kanō Hōgai derived the sense of depth and three-
dimensional perspective seen here from the Western oil paintings that were newly introduced in late nineteenth-century
Japan, while the subtle gradations of ink tones and calligraphic
clarity of the lines reflect his training in Japanese brush painting. The subject of dragons was a popular one in Japanese
painting, but the combination of an adult with a young dragon
is unusual and may have been inspired by the mother and child
theme that Hōgai was using in his Buddhist paintings, which
in turn were based on Western depictions of the Madonna and
Child. This dramatic, large-scale work was painted for Hōgai's
friend and patron Ernest F. Fenollosa, an American who encouraged the revival of the Kanō school of Japanese artists in
the late nineteenth century. It is one of an important group of
works from Fenollosa's collection owned by the Museum. FF

Munakata Shikō
Japanese, 1903–1975
No Footprints Show, 1959
Ink on paper, mounted as a
hanging scroll
53 x 13¾"
Gift of Carl Zigrosser. 1974-179-5

Often considered the greatest artist of woodblock prints in the
twentieth century, Munakata Shikō, who in 1956 was the first
Japanese winner of the Venice Biennale, brought the same force
and energy shown in his prints to this six-character ink calligraphy done while he was visiting Philadelphia in 1959. Shikō's
devotion to the folk idiom of his native Japan, as well as to Zen

Buddhism, is expressed in this inscription. The exact source of the line is not known, but it is probably from a Zen aphorism, and may be rendered in English as, "No footprints show where flowers grow deep." The thick, almost abstract lines of the calligraphy seem to burst beyond the surface of the paper, and were executed with slashing strokes of the brush in a furious burst of speed and with the intense concentration and power that distinguished all of Munakata Shikō's work. FF

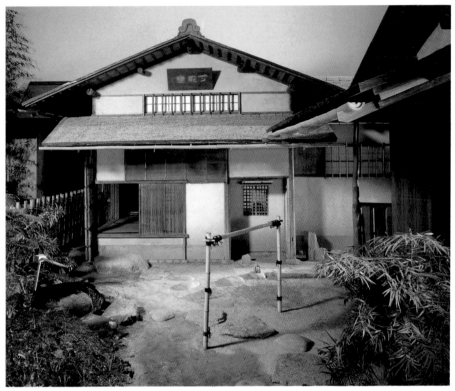

Ceremonial Teahouse: Sunkaraku
Designed by Ōgi Rodō
(Japanese, 1863–1941)
c. 1917
Purchased with Museum funds
1928-114-1

The name of this teahouse, Sunkaraku, or "Evanescent Joys," reflects the spirit of the traditional Japanese tea ceremony as a temporary refuge from the complexities of daily life. The architecture reveals a special delight in natural materials: cedar thatch for the roof, nandina and red pine with the bark intact for the pillars, bamboo stalks for the ceiling and rainspouts, and earth-colored plaster for the walls. The Museum acquired Sunkaraku from Ōgi Rodō, the architect who constructed it using elements from an eighteenth-century teahouse. We know from diaries kept by one of the participants in the tea ceremonies held at Sunkaraku that the guests included leaders of the financial and political world of early twentieth-century Japan, for whom Ōgi Rodō designed country retreats and teahouses. The Sunkaraku teahouse is the only one of Rodō's works outside Japan, where just three of his buildings remain extant. FF

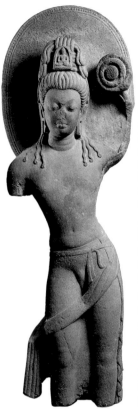

Khasarpana Avalokiteshvara

India, Uttar Pradesh, Sarnath
region, Gupta period
c. 465–85
Sandstone
Height 48½"
Stella Kramrisch Collection. 1994-148-1

Among the great contributions of Buddhism to the universal
ideal of compassion is the bodhisattva, one who delays an
already attained salvation until all other beings are themselves
released from the Wheel of Life. This beautiful sandstone
bodhisattva is a sculptural embodiment of the conception of
compassion, produced at the height of the Gupta dynasty in
the traditional Buddhist heartland of North India. It represents Avalokiteshvara, a bodhisattva closely associated with
Amitabha, the Buddha of the Western Paradise, who is represented in the headdress. The lower legs and arms of the figure
are missing, but the right arm and hand probably hung down,
lightly holding a falling piece of drapery, while the left hand
held the stem of the lotus still remaining on the damaged halo.
The downcast eyes, "bee-stung" lower lip, bow curves of the
upper lip, and smooth, clinging drapery of the elegant and
slender body are all contributions of the Sarnath school to
what became classic Buddha and bodhisattva types, models
that had vast influence in the Buddhist art of East Asia. SEL

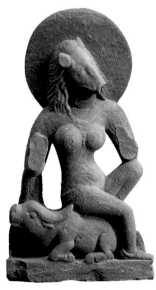

Varahi

North India, Gupta period
c. 550–600
Sandstone
Height 29¼"
Purchased with the W. P. Wilstach Fund
W1977-1-1

Varahi is one of the seven Mothers, the active powers of the
Hindu gods. She is the female aspect of the god Vishnu, preserver of the universe, when he assumed the shape of a mighty
boar to raise the world from the primeval waters; for this reason
she is shown with a boar's head. Subtly modeled and individually conceived, as is apparent despite the intensive weathering
of the richly colored stone, this image is an outstanding example of carving from the Gupta period, which itself represents
the height of achievement of Indian sculpture, although it is
better known for Buddhist than for Hindu images. SK

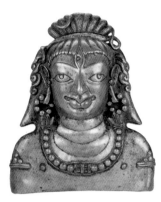

Shiva Bholanatha

India, Himachal Pradesh,
Chamba school
c. 800–900
Brass
Height 11″
Gift of the Friends of the Philadelphia
Museum of Art. 1980-99-1

Groups of gleaming images such as this were—and still are—taken out of Hindu temples in the Kulu Valley region of India and carried in processions during religious festivals. Cast as a kind of brass plaque, this image represents Shiva, the Great God. His young, round, firm face is charged with energy; with full lips, strong, sensitive nose, and wide-open, commanding, demanding eyes (perhaps once inlaid with silver), he gazes from a depth of inner awareness far beyond the world that the nose scents and the mouth relishes. Shiva's third eye boldly cuts across the forehead; in his shaggy hair trimly fitting the dome of the head, a sleek serpent holds his crown of matted hair, an indication of the god's asceticism, while above is the crescent moon, his symbol. The strands of hair are engraved with lines flowing in rapid waves, many rubbed off by frequent worshipful touching over the years. SK

Rama

India, Tamil Nadu, Chola school
c. 1000–1100
Bronze
Height 31⅞″
Purchased with the W. P. Wilstach Fund,
the John D. McIlhenny Fund, and with
funds contributed by the Women's Com-
mittee of the Philadelphia Museum of
Art in honor of their 100th anniversary
W1982-106-1

Bronze images from the eleventh-century Chola dynasty are peak creations of Indian art, and this image of Rama is among the best of them. These bronzes give form to the living, breathing, pulsating quality of the human shape—to the stream of life itself—which in turn becomes the body of the deity. Their naturalism is based neither on description nor on the structure of the human frame, but on the experience of breathing; it is one of rhythm and fluidity—within the bodily shape and the space it creates, and of the space that surrounds it. Rama, an incarnation of the Hindu god Vishnu, the ideal king and hero of the great epic the *Ramayana,* is customarily represented in human form, two-armed and holding a bow and arrow, although as is seen here, the weapon itself is not always shown. When the bow is depicted in sculptures such as this, it is held in the raised left hand and rests on the lotus base, while the arrow is grasped vertically in the right. SK

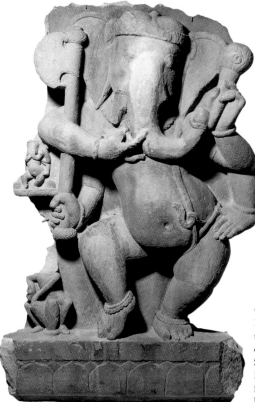

Ganesha Dancing
India, Madhya Pradesh, Gwalior
region, Gurjara-Pratihara school
c. 800–900
Sandstone
Height 50″
Purchased with the New Members
Fund. 1971-154-1

Pot-bellied and elephant-headed, Ganesha is a widely worshiped Hindu god, for to the ordinary person he is the source of all success. As Lord of Obstacles he is extremely powerful; he must be invoked at the beginning of every undertaking. His is the power to put obstacles in the way—and to remove them. Ganesha dancing, as he is shown in this reddish sandstone sculpture from a temple devoted to the Great God Shiva, his father, is the image that most fully conveys the joyous wisdom that he embodies, the knowledge that humans are one with the Absolute. Four-armed, his body sways in a triple bend to the rhythm beaten out by the spirit drummer below him on the left, and his dance reverberates throughout the universe. His main right arm cradles an ax, his most conspicuous emblem, held by the lower hand. His upper left hand holds a radish—a delicacy for an elephant—which symbolizes unity. SK

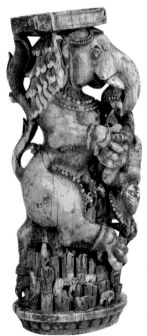

Beautiful Woman of the Gods (Surasundari)

India, Rajasthan, Bharatpur region
c. 1050–1150
Sandstone
Height 21″
Stella Kramrisch Collection. 1994-148-8

Prominent on the buttresses or projections of the walls of Hindu temples are images of *surasundaris,* "beautiful women of the gods." Self-absorbed messengers of divine presence, they are temptresses who attract religious devotees to worship. The female figures, carved almost fully in the round, reveal conceptually as well as visually the power dwelling in the house and body of the god whose image or symbol the temple enshrines. Offering themselves in alluring poses, they represent the eternally feminine, the power that emanates from within the temple in each of the projections of its walls. This *surasundari* standing in a sinuous, triply bent pose shows her left hand in the "bee" gesture, an elongated finger touching her breast. The other hand, resting on her hip, holds a bowl. The provocatively calm oval of her face, bun of hair resting on her shoulder, domes of her breasts, arc of her hips, and circular earrings resemble an arrangement of sweet ripe fruits within her cradling arms. SK

Leg of a Throne

India, Orissa, East Ganga school
c. 1250–60
Ivory
Height 14¼″
Gift of Mrs. John B. Stetson, Jr. 1960-96-1

Ivory carving brought intricacy to the art of Indian sculpture. This composition of an elephant-headed lion seizing a pot-bellied demon in his trunk is animated by an abundance of stylized detail: the curled locks of his grooved mane, repeated on his thighs and legs; his beaded chains with pendants or bells; the bristling hair of the upside-down demon and his dagger and shield; and the trees, boars, antelope, ram, and mounted rider hidden in the dense, craggy landscape. Mountain, beast, and demon constitute one tightly carved volume, its slight forward tilt dictated by the natural curve of the elephant tusk from which it was carved. The hollows between head and chest and tail and back were calculated to give a clear profile to the composite figure of a lion, a royal symbol, which once formed one leg of an ivory throne. SK

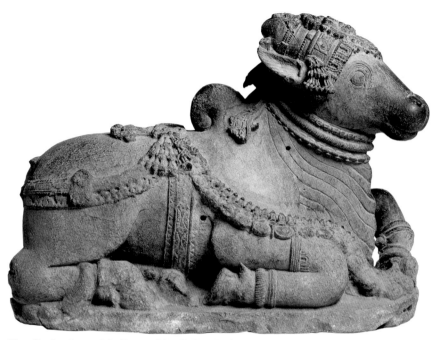

Nandi, the Sacred Bull of Shiva
India, Mysore, Hoysala school
c. 1200–1250
Chloritic schist
Length 31¾″
Purchased with the Joseph E. Temple Fund. 1966-123-1

Nandi (Joy) is the name of the humped, or zebu, bull, which when represented in Indian art conveys the presence of the Hindu god Shiva. Like the anthropomorphic images of divinity, those of the sacred bull are carved in many different styles but are primarily a contribution of the art of South India. Generally these sculptures were placed in a temple facing the sanctuary that held the main symbol of Shiva. The posture of these animal figures is usually the same: they recline in a slightly asymmetrical way, as if having just lowered themselves into this position with their legs and tail tucked under and with the head attentively raised in a noble attitude. Here, intricate garlands of jewelry, bells, and other trappings and linear accents all carved like filigreework enhance this monumental yet sensitively modeled animal manifestation of a god. SK

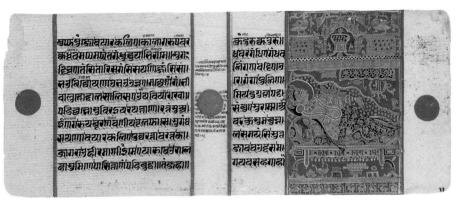

Queen Trishala on Her Couch

India, North Gujarat

1432

Opaque watercolor with gold on paper

5 1/8 x 13"

Gift of Stella Kramrisch

1967-226-1(11)

This painting depicts an episode in the life of Mahavira, the last of the twenty-four saviors of the Jain religion, who are born successively over the ages. Their story, which is the same for each savior, is told in the *Kalpasutra,* a canonical religious text. In this scene, Queen Trishala, who is to give birth to the savior, is on her couch asleep; her fourteen propitious dreams will be interpreted by the king's astrologers and sayers to assure him that the child will be either a universal emperor or a savior. Her full face in three-quarter profile, silhouetted against a halo, has eyes that are wide open although she is asleep. The queen appears in a splendor of color and pattern, with the encircled flowers on the bedstead, wild ganders on the coverlet, and dots on her veil creating a stupendous display of textiles, suggestive of the well-known production of Gujarat, where this painting was created. SK

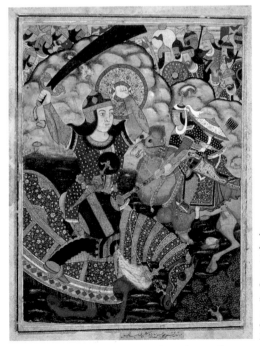

A Follower of Amir Hamza Attacks Tahmasp

India, Mughal school

1562–77

Opaque watercolor with gold and silver or tin on cloth

31 x 25 1/2"

Gift (by exchange) of the Brooklyn Museum. 1937-4-1

Between 1562 and 1577, Emperor Akbar brought scores of painters to his workshop in Delhi to provide illustrations for the *Hamza-nama* (Romance of Amir Hamza). This romantic tale recounts the wild and fantastic adventures of Hamza, an uncle of the Prophet Muhammad. With 1,400 hand-painted illustrations bound in twelve volumes, each about 32 by 25 inches, it was the largest book ever made in India. This remarkable undertaking created a renaissance of Indian painting in a style that melded traditions of both India and Persia. In this dense battle scene, two warriors on contrasting mounts are set off against the foaming curves of fantastic rocks. The tree below establishes the painting's scale; its short trunk seems to bend under the weight of ballooning masses of foliage, which vie with the minute patterns that fill the armor of the falling horse, the saddlecloth of the bulging camel, and the combatants' costumes. The sword of the Persian king Tahmasp, raised high but in vain, is a dominant accent, one of several intersecting diagonals that organize this vigorous painting. SK

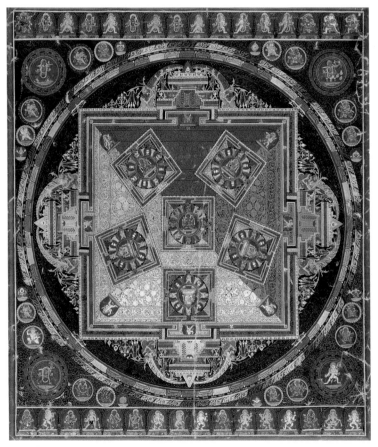

Vajradhara Mandala
Tibet, Nepali school
1400–1500
Opaque watercolor on cotton
32¼ x 28½"
Purchased with the John T. Morris Fund. 1963-154-1

This Nepali painting, compact in design and strong in color contrasts, contains a mandala—a large circle enclosing a square—which is a symbolic diagram of a divine "temple." Such images are used by Buddhist worshipers to help them reach a state of focused concentration through meditation and prepare them for their ultimate encounter with the Absolute, symbolized by the central image of the Buddha. The mandala itself is a sacred circular field bordered on its exterior by a rim of flames, which is separated by a narrow girdle of *vajras*, or "thunderbolts," from an inner rim of lotus petals. These three borders signify the fire of consciousness, which consumes ignorance; supreme consciousness, which is indestructible like the thunderbolt; and spiritual rebirth, which is symbolized by the lotus. Four elaborate gate structures lead into the fortified temple square, which is shown as if in bird's-eye view. Lacelike scrollwork impregnates the ground, and the five images of Buddhas, with their consorts in the smaller mandalas and the main deity in the center, seem to float eerily above it. sk

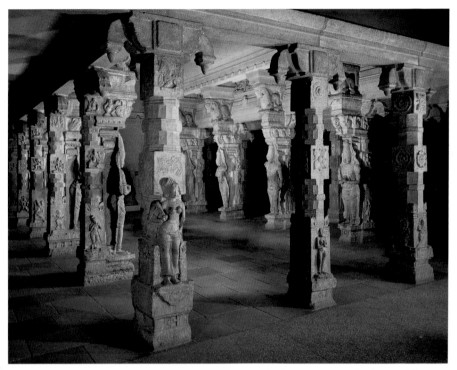

Pillared Hall from a Temple (Mandapa)
India, Tamil Nadu, Madurai, Vijayanagar school
c. 1525–50
Granitic stone
Gift of Susan Pepper Gibson, Mary Gibson Henry, and Henry C. Gibson in memory of Adeline Pepper Gibson
1919-714

This evocative space, which now exists at the heart of the Museum's rich collections of Indian art, is made up of elements acquired by a Philadelphia family traveling in India in the early years of this century. Reconstructed from the ruins of three shrines in South India devoted to the worship of the Hindu god Vishnu, preserver of the universe, this is the only example of Indian stone architecture to be found in an American museum. Its monolithic, highly complex granite pillars are arranged to form an intermediate temple hall, a space where pilgrims might prepare themselves for worship. The door at the end would have led to the innermost sanctuary, where the main image of the divinity was located. Projecting from the pillars are life-size figures of heroes, sages, mythical animals, and divine beings that relate to Vishnu and his appearances on earth in human and animal form. Above, bracketed capitals in the shape of lions support panels carved in relief, which show episodes from the *Ramayana,* the great Indian epic based on the exploits of Rama, one of Vishnu's manifestations on earth. sk

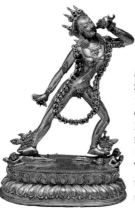

Dakini of All the Buddhas

Sino-Tibetan
1700–1800
Gilded brass with paint
Height 13¼″
Bequest of Natacha Rambova
1964-180-2a,b

This brass image represents a celestial figure, the Dakini of All
the Buddhas, the force of inspirational consciousness who
urges the devout toward the realization of Buddhahood. She
strides to the left upon two four-armed gods, one prostrate,
the other supine, whose upper hands salute the goddess. Naked
except for a garland and crown of skulls and her jewelry, she
has long, flowing hair and a third eye in the center of her forehead. With insatiable elation she drinks blood from the foaming
skull cup held high in her left hand; in her right she grasps a
chopper. Despite the grimness of the image, it connotes universal ideals of deliverance. The blood-filled cup does away with
all ideas of substance and nonsubstance and is a symbol of
oneness. SK

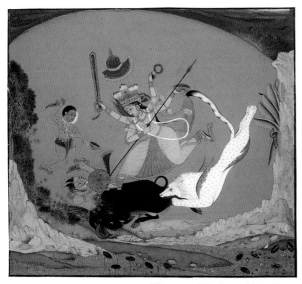

The Great Goddess Durga Slaying the Buffalo Demon

India, Rajasthan, Kotah school
c. 1750
Opaque watercolor with gold and
silver or tin on paper
10¹¹⁄₁₆ x 12³⁄₈″
Stella Kramrisch Collection
1994-148-390

The great Hindu goddess Durga, the demon slayer, keeps the
world free from ills and afflictions. She is formidable; she
fights with weapons of all the gods. Here, in one from a group
of Durga images from the Kotah school that are unrivaled in
Indian painting, she is shown as the slayer of the greatest of all
demons, the buffalo, the embodiment of evil. As Durga leaps
from her lion mount onto the back of the falling buffalo and
spears the beast, his green demon shape emerges from the body
of the dying animal. This is an act of grace that Durga performs
at the edge of the world, where in the turquoise vastness framed
by the glow of a sun that has risen over the nascent vegetation
of the earth this primordial battle takes place. SK

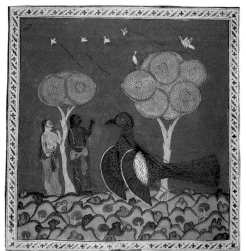

**Dying Jatayus Tells
Rama and Lakshmana
About Sita**

India, Deccan, Rajamundry school
c. 1750
Opaque watercolor on paper
13¾ x 13⅞"
Purchased with the Katharine Levin
Farrell Fund. 1975-149-1

The story of Prince Rama, told in the *Ramayana,* an epic
poem of ancient India, was illustrated again and again in Indian
painting. The episode shown in this monumental but folklike
watercolor is one of many that recount the prince's attempt
to recapture his wife Sita from the demon king Ravana. Here,
atop a patterned landscape and silhouetted against an omi-
nous cinnabar-red sky, Rama, the dark figure, and his brother
Lakshmana come upon the vulture king Jatayus, who was
wounded while trying to stop Ravana from abducting Sita.
Heroically, with his last breath, the mighty bird assures Rama
that Sita is still alive and points toward Ravana's kingdom,
to show him the direction in which the two have fled. sk

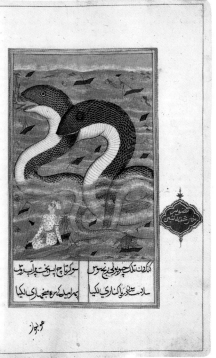

**Pythons Wreck Prince
Manohar's Ship**

India, Deccan school
1743
Opaque watercolor with gold
on paper
14 x 10"
Gift of Mrs. Philip S. Collins in memory
of her husband. 1945-65-22

The Rose Garden of Love, by the seventeenth-century court poet
Nusrati, is one of the major works of the Muslim mystical Sufi

sect written in an Indian language. Through the poem's introduction runs the Sufi theme of the world as a creation of God's love, which is manifest in many forms, including seemingly endless suffering and separation from the source of love. The poem is also imbued with the hope that all earthly obstacles will be overcome and finally union with God in love will be achieved. The story tells of Prince Manohar, who searches the world over for his love, the princess Madhumalati. This painting, one of ninety-seven finely executed illustrations from a complete eighteenth-century manuscript of the poem in the Museum's collection, depicts the episode in which Manohar's ship is besieged by a giant python, but an even larger one comes to do battle with it. In the ensuing melee, Manohar's ship is wrecked, and his raft is tossed on the waves for several days before he reaches shore. SK

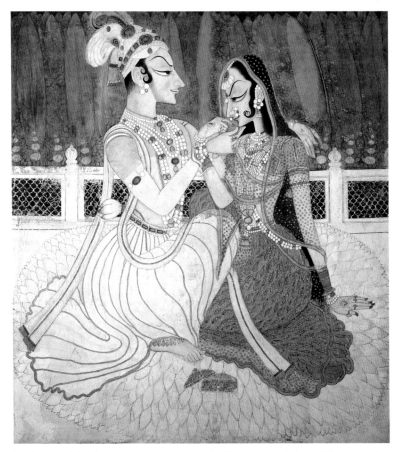

Radha and Krishna

India, Rajasthan, Kishangarh
school
c. 1750
Opaque watercolor with gold
on cotton
40¾ x 37″
Purchased with the Edith H. Bell Fund
1984-72-1

Composed with utmost subtlety of line and color, this unusually large painting of the Hindu god Krishna and his loved one Radha might be the work of Nihal Chand, a master of the Kishangarh school trained at the imperial court in Delhi, to whom only a few paintings can be attributed. On a white terrace, seated on a large lotus flower, a princely figure in a gesture of endearment offers a betel leaf to the lips of his beloved. Like another lotus, the man's garment envelops his seated posture;

in his belt is a lotus bud, as tender as the touch of the woman's hand that rests on the floor. The sharp-featured, slender figures resemble one another; they carry the dream of each other under the eyebrows vaulting high above lowered lids that veil their emotion. Theirs is the intimacy of lovers and the stillness of icons. SK

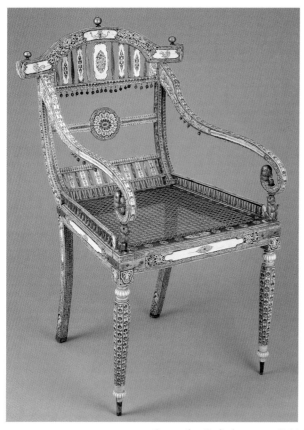

Armchair
Anglo-Indian
c. 1800
Engraved and stained ivory, wood, brass, caning
Height 38¾"
The Henry P. McIlhenny Collection
in memory of Frances P. McIlhenny
1986-26-313

Soon after India became a British colony in the mid-eighteenth century, Indian craftsmen began making furniture to contemporary British designs using local materials and decorative motifs. This armchair, made of hardwood veneered with engraved ivory, has turned front legs, scrolling armrests, saber-shaped rear legs, and a cane seat in the style of the late eighteenth-century English furniture designer Thomas Sheraton. The typically Indian decoration includes the floral engraving, the brass finials along the top of the backrest, and the brass bells hanging from the arm- and backrests. Although such furniture was first commissioned by the British living in India, by the early nineteenth century much of the work that was produced was being bought by wealthy Indians. Vishakhapatnam, a city on the eastern coast of India with a long tradition of ivory work, became the center of the manufacture of ivory-veneered Anglo-Indian furniture. JHMS

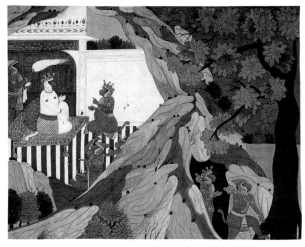

Book four of the Indian epic the *Ramayana* tells of the alliance
of the monkey kingdom with the Hindu god Rama in his quest
to rescue his wife Sita. Seated on the throne, Sugriva, who with
Rama's help has been reinstated as king of the monkeys, in-
structs the monkey chief Hanuman in his mission. Hanuman,
shown again exiting from the cave to lead the rescue party, will
perform such prodigious feats as bridging the sea from India
to Lanka in one leap and setting fire to Lanka in order to rescue
Sita. Together, the great deeds of Hanuman and the valor and
cunning of Sugriva and his army help Rama defeat the demon
king Ravana and bring Sita back to India. This episode is set in
the architecture of the resplendent nineteenth-century princely
courts of northern India and the lush landscape of the Panjab
Hills, a world created of sharply edged rocks and caves dotted
with vegetation and lined with veins of precious metals. sk

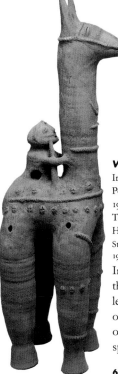

Votive Horse and Rider
India, Gujarat, Sabarkanta,
Poshine, Bhil tribe
1966
Terracotta
Height 40"
Stella Kramrisch Collection
1994-148-296

In rural areas of India today as in the past, sculptures such as
this clay horse and rider are made as offerings to a deity and
left untended where they are placed, under a tree, near a pond
or river, or in a grove. They accumulate, they decompose, and
others take their place. This horse and rider is an image of the
spirit freed from the human condition; it represents a state of

perfection and fulfillment and is credited with the power of granting wishes and desires. The stunning clay figure was made in 1966 by the potters of the Bhil tribe of Gujarat. The verticality of the enormously long neck of the horse and its fiercely held head is made the more striking by the scalloped edges that form the outer silhouette of the high, tubular legs. One of the first exhibitions anywhere in the world to be devoted to Indian folk art, *Unknown India: Ritual Art in Tribe and Village,* was held at the Museum in 1968 and brought sculptures such as this to public attention. SK

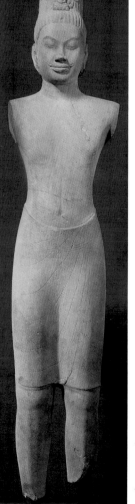

Avalokiteshvara

Khmer Empire, Pre-Angkor period
Late seventh century
Sandstone
Height 69¾"
Purchased with the W. P. Wilstach Fund
W1965-1-1

Originally nearly seven feet tall, this is surely one of the most beautiful and moving images in any medium of Avalokiteshvara, the Buddhist bodhisattva, or saintlike being, of compassion. The sculptor has given the body, which is modeled in the round except for the simple garment that is carved in low relief, a taut smoothness achieved by means of its highly polished sandstone. The small image of the Buddha at the front center of the elaborate chignon identifies this image as Avalokiteshvara, but the spirituality of the deity is transmitted through the face: the high forehead and nose, perfectly arched eyebrows, downcast eyes, and serene smile convey a sense of majesty, wisdom, and repose. One can only imagine the effect the sculpture would have had in its original setting, and even now it allows us a glimpse of the eternal through its subtle, understated monumentality. FF

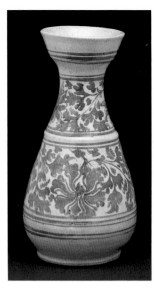

Wine Bottle

Thailand, Kalong
Fourteenth–sixteenth century
Stoneware with underglaze
decoration
Height 10¼″
Gift of Dean F. Frasché. 1967-162-60

Situated along a river valley near rich deposits of high-quality clay, the ceramic center at Kalong, with over one hundred kilns, was one of the largest production sites in northern Thailand from the thirteenth to the sixteenth centuries. In later years, ceramic production moved south along with political power, and the existence of the Kalong site was forgotten until it was excavated in the 1930s. The sophisticated design of this wine bottle testifies to the flourishing and advanced pottery manufacture at Kalong. Its top and bottom were made separately and then luted together at the middle, with the scrolling peony and vine motif appearing in two horizontal bands along either side of the seam. The painting shows characteristically strong brushwork, which was applied with iron pigments and then covered with a transparent glaze. FF

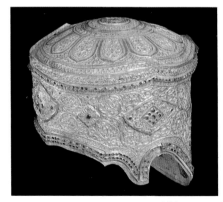

Crown

Thailand, Ayudhya period
(1350–1767)
Fifteenth century
Height 7½″
Gold with inlay of rubies
and pearls
Purchased with the Far Eastern
Art Revolving Fund. 1982-105-1

This rare early example of the Thai goldsmith's art was probably made for a princess by court craftsmen and dates to the fifteenth century, when Ayudhya was the capital of the country. The art of jewelry-making in Thailand reached great sophistication during this period, as demonstrated by this crown with its intricate design inlaid with rubies and pearls. The prestige of gold among the Thai ruling class was such that its usage and ornamentation were strictly prescribed by sumptuary regulations, and gold jewelry was often buried with its wearer in the tombs of members of the royal family. FF

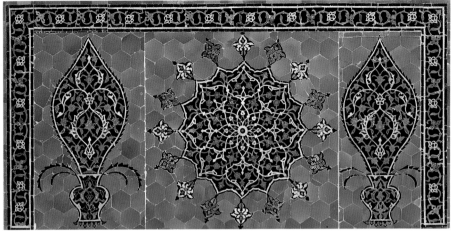

Tile Mosaic Panel
Persia, Isfahan, Safavid dynasty
(1501–1736)
Sixteenth century
Glazed pottery
Height 3′6″
Purchased with Museum funds
1931-76-1

Architecture has provided the most visible "canvas" for Islamic art, achieving particularly sophisticated expression during the reign of the Safavid court at Isfahan in Persia. This mosaic panel is one of a group installed in the Museum that are said to have come from a sixteenth-century monastery of the Sufi branch of Islam, but Persian buildings of all sorts, both sacred and secular, were covered inside and out with such elaborately decorated ceramic tiles. The glazed turquoise, cobalt blue, faun, white, and black colors of this panel are clear and brilliant, and the small ceramic pieces form a mosaic pattern whose predominant motifs are round star medallions that alternate with symmetrical floral palmettes in vases. These abstracted designs are meant not so much to emulate nature as to reflect the infinite perfection and ideal order of the universe. The complex pattern is repeated in the series of tile panels that encircle the room, giving a rich sense of depth to the space. FF

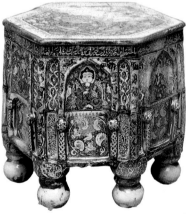

Tabouret
Persia, Kashan, Great Mongols
period (1206–1634)
Early thirteenth century
Pottery with overglaze decoration
Height 12″
Gift of Henry P. McIlhenny in memory
of his parents. 1943-41-1

The hexagonal shape of this ceramic tabouret, which could be used as either a seat or a side table, is modeled on the garden pavilions found on the estates of Persian aristocrats. Between the columns on each of the six molded sides is a recessed niche from which a seated nobleman gazes out over a pond where ducks swim among lotus plants. Every part of the surface is decorated with scrolling vines and birds to enhance the rich effect of the setting, and a poetic inscription surrounds the scene of the lord accompanied by attendants on the top. This is the only known tabouret decorated in the luster technique, a time-consuming and expensive process that required two firings of its silver and copper pigments. The surface was then hand-polished to achieve a high gloss meant to rival bronze and gold. The fine quality of the painting and the evenly controlled glaze bespeak the great skill of the artist, and suggest that this tabouret was a one-time luxury commission for a Persian prince. FF

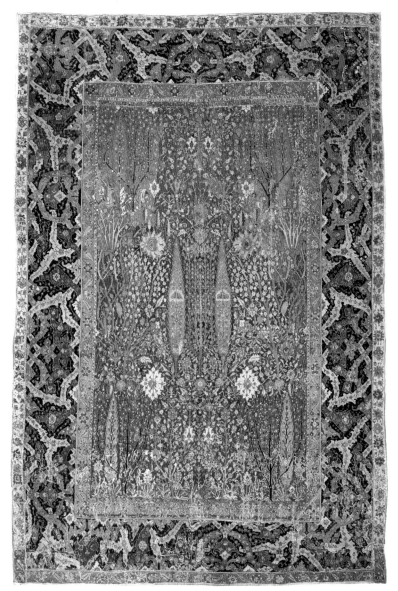

Tree Carpet
Persia
Sixteenth–seventeenth century
Wool, cotton
17′4″ x 11′9″
The Joseph Lees Williams Memorial
Collection. 1955-65-25

Less than half of the original forty-foot length of this Persian tree carpet, one of the showpieces of the Museum's outstanding rug collection, survives, with only the lower section of seven rows of cypress, almond, and other trees remaining. The bottom row is bounded by a blue ribbon of water, and the whole garden scene is surrounded by several "walls." This elaborate and unique carpet pattern was first executed by one of the painters in the Persian court and then woven and knotted by highly skilled craftsmen. The exceptionally high number of knots per square inch (225) produces the subtle variety of colors and the meticulous definition of the trees and blossoms. The Persian word for "walled garden" also means "paradise," and the representation of a garden on this imposing carpet must surely have been meant to summon up visions of an ideal eternal life where luxuriant trees and fragrant flowers bloom year-round. FF

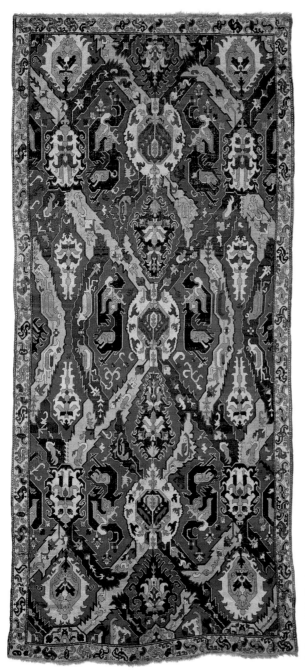

Dragon Rug
The Caucasus, possibly Shemakha,
Shirvan Province
Seventeenth–eighteenth century
Wool
17′ x 7′10″
Gift of the Sharples family in memory
of Philip M. Sharples. 1948-83-1

Dragons and other Chinese motifs were introduced into the ceramics, paintings, and textiles of Islamic countries after the Mongol invasions from Central Asia in the thirteenth century. Monumental showpieces such as this rug were most likely woven on commission at one of the great commercial weaving centers of the Caucasus. This sole example of a complete dragon rug takes its name from the three pairs of dark brown dragons that run along either side of the central column of abstract floral designs. Surrounding the dragons are jagged-edged bands representing phoenixes. Any naturalism in portraying the animal or plant world yields here to the dynamic rhythm and organization of the dramatic overall geometric pattern, shown against a brilliant red ground, which combine to make this the most stunning example of such rugs in any museum. FF

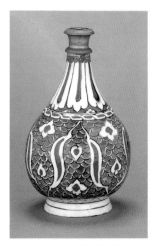

Bottle
Turkey, Iznik
Late sixteenth–early seventeenth century
Pottery with underglaze decoration and metal mount
Height 10¼″
Bequest of Mrs. Joseph V. McMullen in memory of her husband. 1983-84-12

During the reign of the Ottoman Sultan Ahmed I (1603–17), there were some three hundred ceramic workshops at Iznik, a city in northwest Anatolia (present-day Turkey). These potteries, which had been established in the fifteenth century primarily to produce brilliantly colored architectural tiles, also made vessels such as this bottle, one of numerous Iznik objects in the Museum's collection. The palette of cobalt blue, green, and bright red came to define Iznik wares. The gray clay of the body of this piece was first covered with a pure white slip, and the geometrically arranged multicolored design was outlined in black. As seen here, the deep red pigment was usually applied thickly, giving it a raised effect, and then the whole piece was covered with a clear glaze that gave the surface a lustrous, vibrant sheen. The colors and exuberance of their freehand patterns made the Iznik wares popular throughout the Ottoman Empire as well as in Europe, where they were in turn imitated by Italian and English potters. FF

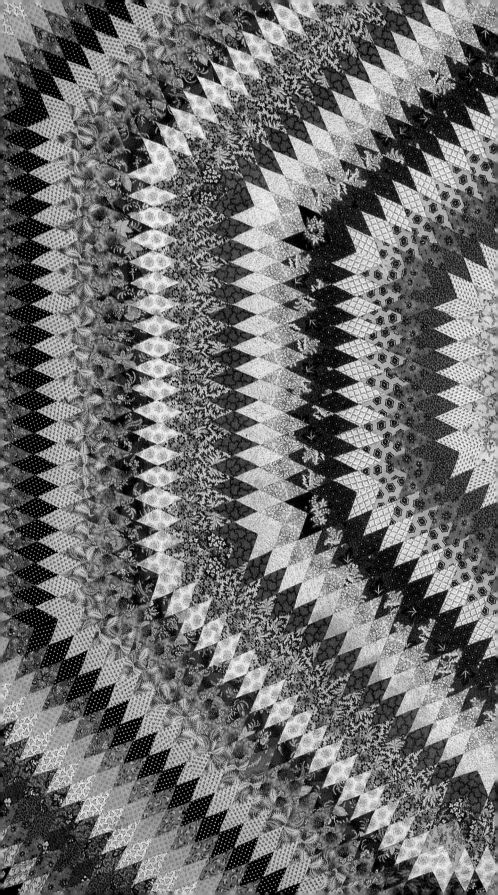

Costume and Textiles

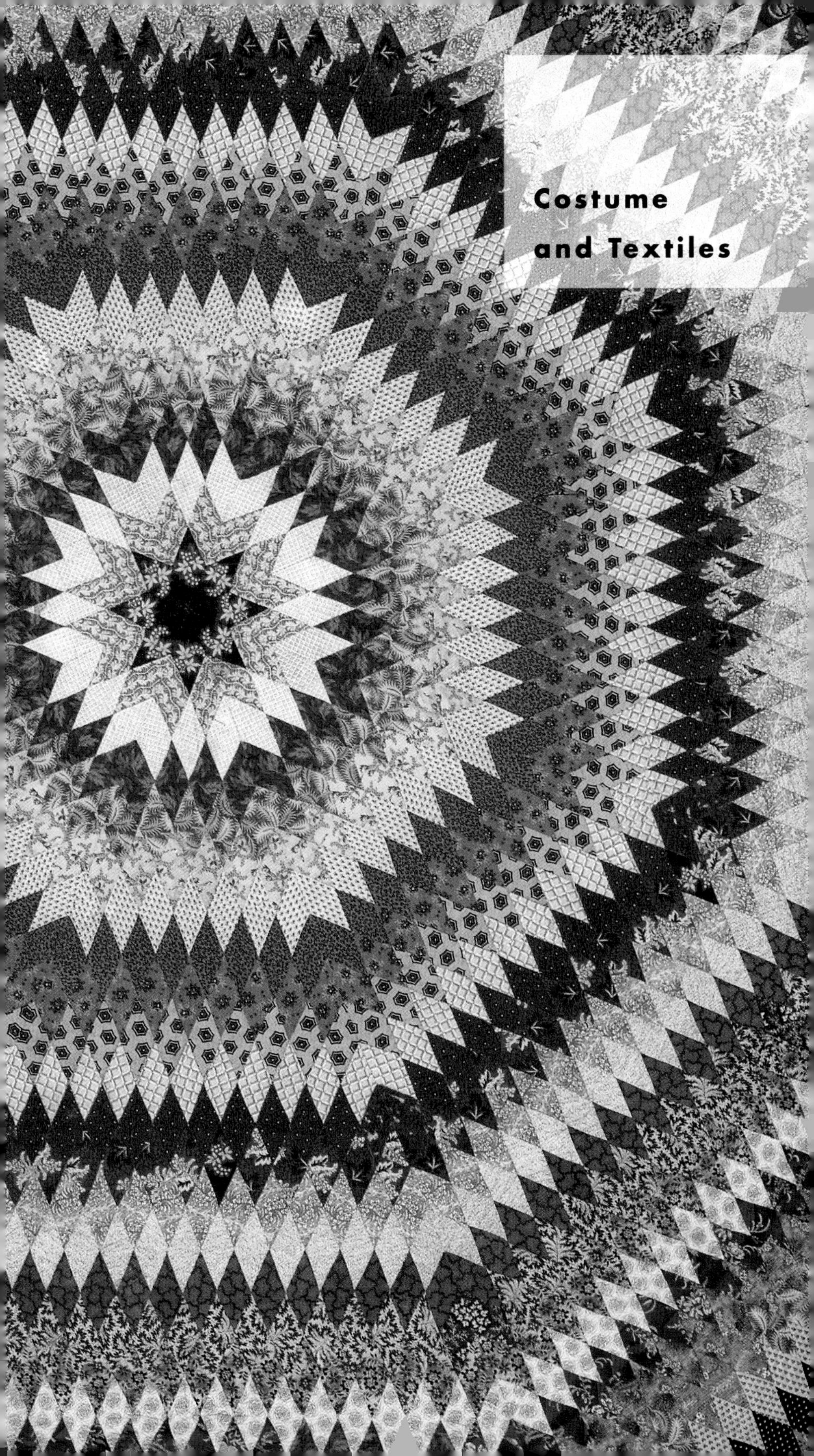

**Costume
and Textiles**

With initial acquisitions from the 1876 Philadelphia Centennial Exposition, the Museum began to establish what has become one of the nation's oldest and largest collections of costume and textiles, numbering some 20,000 objects. Gifts from the Exposition included contemporary manufactures such as Swiss embroidery and Indian textiles, while purchases that year from several of Europe's leading antique dealers included historic textiles such as Turkish velvets. The first textile collections, acquired under the guidance of the predecessor of the Victoria and Albert Museum in London, traced the development of textile design and techniques from Egypt, Greece, Persia, Turkey, and India to Europe, with an emphasis on textiles from Italy and Spain. These were supplemented by donations in 1882 and 1899 of the "industrial art" collections of the Philadelphian Mrs. Bloomfield Moore. The textile collection served as study material for both the Museum's textile school (founded in 1883) and the textile industry, thus fulfilling one of the original objectives of the Museum to further the application of art to industry.

In 1893 the collections were formally organized as the Department of Textiles, Lace, and Embroidery, one of the Museum's first three departments. Mrs. John Harrison, president of the Associate Committee of Women, was named honorary curator, serving from 1894 to 1919. Its first exhibition, in 1894, displayed the collection of the Countess de Brazza illustrating the history of lace manufacture. Acquired for the Museum by its Associate Committee of Women, it became the nucleus of the lace collection that now numbers over two thousand pieces.

Coinciding with the Museum's purchase of eighteenth-century French and English period rooms and the enrichment of the decorative arts collections, eighteenth- and nineteenth-century French printed textiles were acquired in 1929 and 1937 from the French scholar Henri Clouzot. This placed the department's holdings at the forefront of North American collections of American and European printed textiles, a specialty that now includes contemporary designs.

The acquisition of American costume and textiles began in the first years of this century with Mrs. William D. Frishmuth's gift illustrating the "home life, customs, and manufactures of colonial times." It was later expanded by major gifts of eighteenth- and nineteenth-century American material, ranging from weaving pattern books and Pennsylvania German quilts to the clothing of fashionable Philadelphians. The important collection of samplers began with the acquisition of an eighteenth-century Spanish sampler in 1877 and Mrs. Frishmuth's American samplers and needlework. Its core is the famous Whitman Sampler Collection, over five hundred American and European samplers assembled by the successful Philadelphia chocolate manufacturer and presented in 1969 by Pet Incorporated. Mrs. Frishmuth's gift in 1908 of European regional headwear formed the basis for additional folk collections, supplemented in 1941 by a gift of Eastern European costume and textiles from the art critic Christian Brinton and the bequest of Helen P. McMullan in 1966 of Italian folk costumes.

The textile collection developed in depth and breadth under the direction of Nancy Andrews Reath from 1926 to 1936. Reath's seminal work in the classification and analysis of historic fabrics by their structure established a new methodology, which is regarded as a landmark in textile studies. Significant gifts and purchases of Chinese, Japanese, Indian, Persian, and Southeast Asian costume and textiles were made from the 1920s to the early 1940s. Twenty-one Chinese Han dynasty textiles excavated in 1924–25, together with over 125 Persian examples excavated at Rayy in 1935, make the department one of the major repositories of Middle Eastern and Asian archaeological textiles in North America and Europe. Folk textiles given by the Museum's late curator of Indian art Stella Kramrisch are among the important strengths of the Indian collection.

Although Western dress had been acquired over the years it was not until 1947 that the first costume galleries were opened under the sponsorship of the Philadelphia Fashion Group. From then until 1987, the department focused on developing its collection of historic costume and contemporary fashion, under the direction of Marianna Merritt Hornor, the first curator of costume, who served until 1955, and then until 1978 under Elsie Siratz McGarvey. In 1956 the Museum received its best-known (and most popular) item of clothing, the wedding dress worn by Princess Grace of Monaco, who was, of course, Grace Kelly of Philadelphia. The most important acquisition of work by a single designer was Elsa Schiaparelli's gift of seventy-one of her costumes and accessories, including many that are icons of twentieth-century fashion.

During recent years research and review of the collections have brought attention to unexpected strengths, including American appliqué quilts, Victorian fashion dolls equipped with extensive wardrobes, and a spectacular array of twentieth-century millinery, which have each served as the basis of popular special exhibitions.

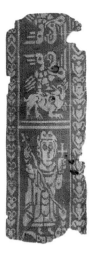

Fragment

Egypt, Akhmin
Seventh–eighth century
Silk
7 x 2½"
Gift of Howard L. Goodhart. 1933-83-1

Excavated at Akhmin in Upper Egypt, this silk fragment may originally have decorated a tunic as either a cuff band or a clavus, a type of ornament that ran vertically from the shoulders to the hemline. The highly stylized design, which dates the fragment to the seventh or eighth century, shows a warrior saint, possibly Saint George, standing with a dragon at his feet in the lower panel and a bird of prey attacking an animal above; both scenes are flanked by floral borders. In the complete textile each image was most likely repeated in each panel as a mirror of itself, which indicates that the fabric was woven on the draw-loom. The use of religious subjects to decorate clothing during the early Byzantine period was both a testament to the wearer's faith and a means of invoking divine protection. DB

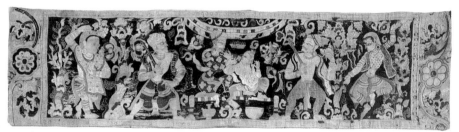

Band

Nepal
c. 1550–1650
Cotton, silk
11 x 43"
Gift of Stella Kramrisch. 1963-36-1

One of the few surviving textiles from Nepal dated earlier than 1700, this embroidery portrays two lovers feeding one another betel leaves as they are attended on either side by a male weapon-bearer and a female dancer. Although its original complete form and use are unknown, the work possibly dates to as early as the sixteenth century, and represents a later development of a style of embroidery with chiefly religious themes that can be traced back at least to the thirteenth century. This embroidery tradition appears to have parallels in Nepalese scroll painting not only in its narrative format but also in such stylistic conventions as the predominantly red background, the drapery above the seated lovers, and the stylized floral and vegetal decorative background. Both the needlework technique—brick stitch with chain-stitched outlining—and the crosses on the figures' costumes are not found in the embroidery of neighboring India, China, or Tibet, and thus appear to be unique to these early Nepalese textiles. DB

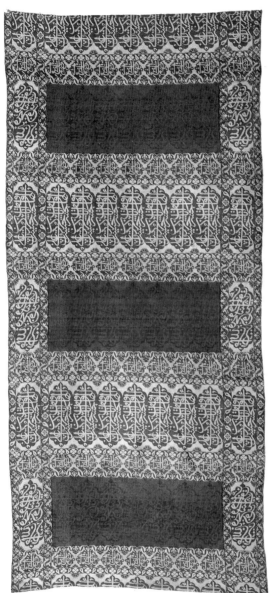

Tomb Cover
Persia
1675–1700
Silk
78¼ x 35⅛″
Purchased with the Membership Fund
1922-22-90

Calligraphy is central to the arts of Islam, with the many styles of Arabic script decorating not only handwritten manuscripts but also architecture and objects such as metalwork, ceramics, and textiles. In Persia the tombs of prominent persons were traditionally covered with lengths of costly silks, frequently woven with calligraphic passages from the Koran, the holy book of Islam. This nearly complete tomb cover combines the round, cursive Naskhi style of Arabic with foliate patterns set within a series of bands and cartouches. Three inscriptions are repeated throughout: a verse from a surah, or chapter, of the Koran; the names of the three major figures of the Shiite sect of Islam, Ali, Hussein, and Hassan; and the phrase, "Oh, the martyred Hussein." DB

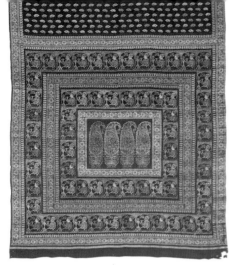

Sari (detail)
India, West Bengal, Murshidabad
district, Baluchar
c. 1800–1875
Silk
15′6¼″ x 3′8¼″
Gift of Stella Kramrisch. 1961-176-2

Silk saris such as this, which are regarded as among the finest Indian textiles, were woven in the villages around the town of Murshidabad in West Bengal during the eighteenth and nineteenth centuries, their production ending around 1900 with the death of Dubraj, the area's best known master weaver. Woven on the traditional draw-loom, their central field is usually covered with diagonal rows of small flowers or cones, from which their descriptive name, *butidar,* derives. Their end pieces are decorated with various Hindu, Muslim, and European motifs, such as the Indian courtier smoking a hookah, or water pipe, on this example. These saris most often have a ground of deep purple or dark red shot with blue, with their complex designs added through the use of multicolored supplementary weft patterning, a time-consuming process that could take the weaver and his assistant as long as six months to complete. Nine such saris were given to the Museum by Stella Kramrisch, the distinguished scholar and curator of Indian art. DB

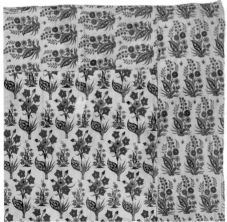

**Summer Carpet or
Floor Spread** (detail)
India
Before 1690
Cotton
41 x 85″
Bequest of Mrs. Harry Markoe
1943-51-126

This fragment of a seventeenth-century imperial Mughal summer carpet or floor spread was formerly in the collection of the Amber Palace near Jaipur, India. As was the practice with furnishing textiles in royal collections, it was inscribed upon entering the palace with its size, date, and price, and marked again during periodic inventories. The inscriptions on the reverse of this fragment indicate that the floor spread was first inventoried on April 7, 1690, when its cost was listed as 21 rupees, 12 annas; a second inscription records that it was still in use on September 6, 1701. A third of its original size, the Museum's large fragment consists of a floral-patterned field bordered on three sides with a different floral fabric. The designs on both the field and the border, like those on other high-quality Indian chintz textiles of the period, were drawn and painted by hand, and show repeats of formal flowering plants symmetrically arranged against plain backgrounds in patterns that are typical of Mughal decoration beginning in the early seventeenth century. DB

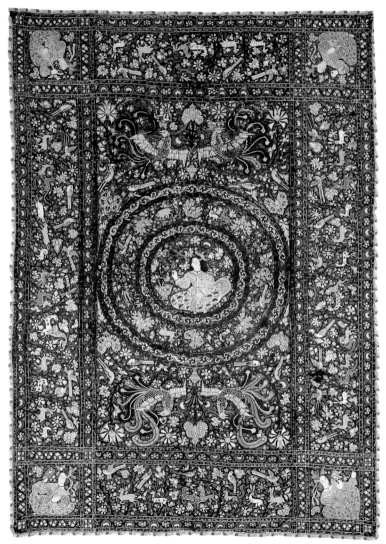

Bedcover
India or Portugal, c. 1680
Silk, 112 x 86″
Gift of the Friends of the Philadelphia Museum of Art. 1988-7-4

This indigo-dyed silk bedcover embroidered with colored silks is a charming representative of a type of bedcover, made either in Lisbon by Indian embroiderers or in India for the Portuguese market, in which the five senses was the central theme. The mixture of European, Indian, and Persian motifs found on these textiles reflects the strong cross-cultural influences on design during the sixteenth and seventeenth centuries, a period of extensive exploration, settlement, and trade. The design of this bedcover is organized around a central medallion set within a large rectangular panel surrounded by wide borders. The figure of Touch, represented as a woman petting a small animal, is shown at the center, while female figures in the corners personify the other four senses: Smell, Hearing, Sight, and Taste. Each is dressed in a combination of Indo-Persian and European costumes and hairstyles that date to about 1630–40.

The borders are populated by animals in chase and combat, a motif common to both sixteenth-century Persian carpets and seventeenth-century Mughal examples. Above and below the central medallion are pairs of the fantastic *simurgh,* the magic bird of the Persian national epic, the *Shah-nama.* DB

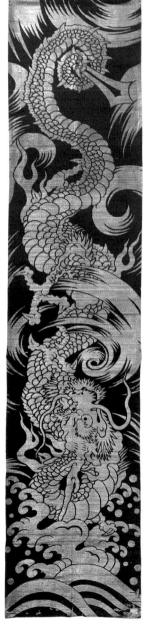

Temple Banner

Japan, Edo period (1615–1867)
1700–1800
Silk, silver foil, paper
106¾ x 24¾"
Gift of Joseph Wasserman. 1928-111-8b

The textiles decorating Buddhist temples and shrines in Japan include a set of long banners that are hung both horizontally and vertically to delineate the sacred area of the gods. Traditionally they are decorated with dragons, auspicious and benevolent creatures who act as guardians of the temple and protectors of the Buddhist faith. In this vertical banner from the Museum's set of three dating to the eighteenth century, a three-clawed dragon extends its head downward into a cloud. Of the two horizontal banners from the group, one shows a dragon carrying in its tail the sacred jewel of Buddhism, a symbol of truth and wisdom, the other, two dragons facing a flaming jewel. The banner shown here is inscribed with the names of the local timber merchant who presented the hangings to a temple in northern Japan in honor of his family in 1852 and the priest who performed the dedication ceremony. Made of *ginran,* or solid-colored silk patterned with wefts of silver foil glued to paper strips, the banners would have been used by the family for memorial services held at the temple. DB

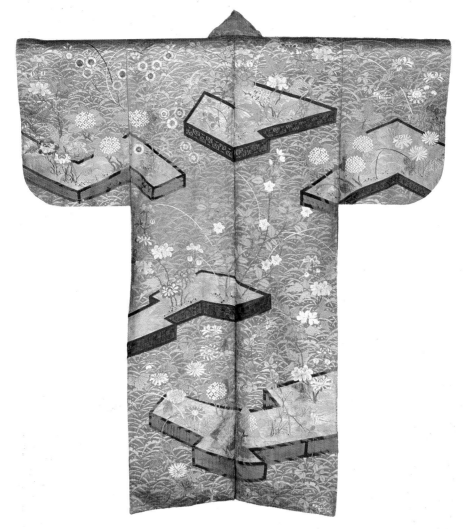

Noh Robe
Japan, Edo period (1615–1867)
c. 1750–1800
Silk, gold foil
Gift of J. C. Leff. 1953-21-2

By the fifteenth century, Japanese Noh dramas, originally performed as part of religious ceremonies, had evolved into an officially sponsored entertainment fusing poetry, music, and dance. The costumes worn by the actors were made from sumptuous fabrics, often richly detailed with gold or silver stenciling and fine embroidery, their brilliance contrasting with the austerity of the stage upon which the plays were performed. The costumes not only defined the characters' roles but also elaborated on the poetic text of the play itself. This kimono-style Noh robe was used primarily for female roles (all the actors were male), and was worn as either an outer robe or inner robe depending on the character. Its red satin fabric is decorated with both embroidery and stenciled and impressed gold foil in an asymmetrical design of flower-bed boxes, over which are scattered chrysanthemums, bellflowers, bush clover, and dewdrops. DB

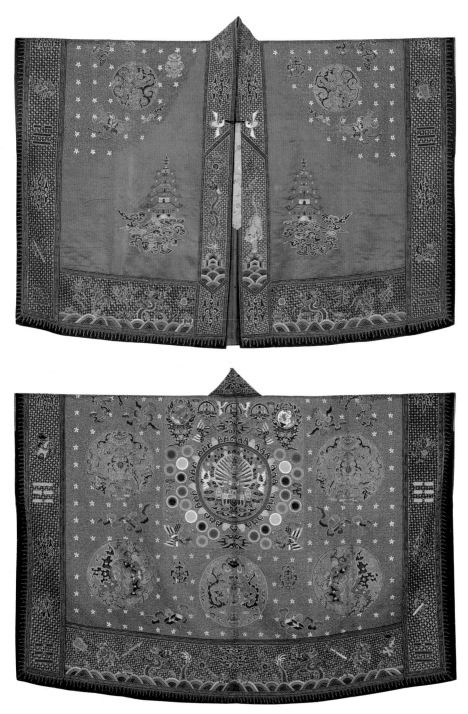

Taoist Priest's Robe
China, Ch'ing dynasty (1644–1911)
c. 1850–1900
Silk, metallic thread
Purchased with the George W. B. Taylor
Fund. 1967-144-1

This type of Chinese robe was the traditional costume worn by a Taoist high priest when officiating at rites and ceremonies such as funerals. Constructed from two lengths of fabric that were folded in half horizontally, seamed in the back, left open at the front, and sewn together at the sides, with holes left for the hands, the entire robe is embroidered with a complex iconographic scheme. By the nineteenth century, Taoism had incorporated both Buddhist and Confucian concepts into its beliefs, and although the majority of the motifs on this robe are Taoist symbols, others, such as the pagodas on the front, are purely Buddhist in origin. The back of the robe represents the Taoist cosmology and includes, at the center, the symbolic Sky Door through which the palace of the Sovereign Above is revealed. The lower border represents the sea with its monsters, while on the sleeve borders the symbols of the Eight Immortals of Taoism alternate with the Eight Triagrams, which represent the eight spatial directions. DB

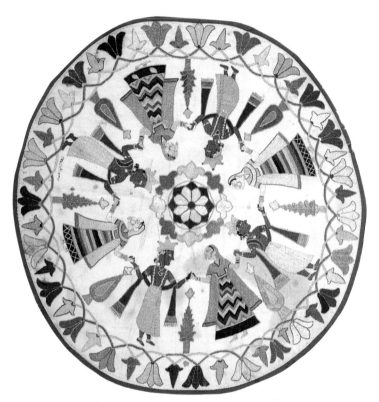

Ceremonial Cloth (Chamba Rumal)
India, Himachal Pradesh
c. 1875–1925
Cotton, silk
Diameter 27″
Purchased with funds contributed by Ann McPhail and an anonymous donor
1991-48-1

Chamba rumals, or ceremonial cloths, made between the early eighteenth century and the beginning of the twentieth in the Himachal Pradesh region are among the most charming embroideries produced in India. Their pictorial styles vary, with some designs, drawn by professional artists and embroidered by ladies at court, resembling miniature paintings, and others, worked by women in the villages, demonstrating a more "primitive," folk tradition. These cloths, which were used as wrappings for gifts exchanged between the families of a bride and groom, as offerings to deities, or as hangings placed behind religious statues or above altars, were most commonly embroidered with scenes from the life of the Hindu god Krishna. This example from the Museum's rich collection of traditional Indian textiles depicts the popular story of Krishna and the milkmaids engaged in a dance in which he assumes as many bodies as there are maidens (here four) in order to complete the circle of the dance. The entire composition is surrounded by a traditional floral border. Worked with silk thread on unbleached cotton, the embroidery is identical on both sides. DB

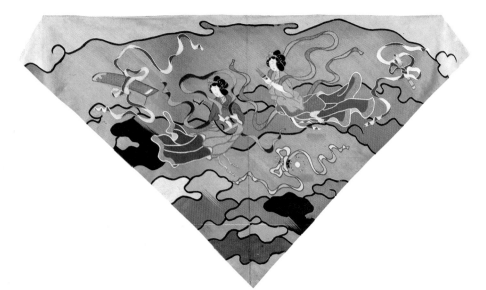

Temple Hanging
Japan, Edo period (1615–1867)
c. 1785–1850
Silk
Width 47½″
Bequest of Miss Elizabeth W. Lewis
1899-246

Textiles play a central role in Buddhist religious practice, and are used as temple banners, altar hangings, and priests' robes. This triangular hanging, woven to shape in the slit-tapestry technique, was used by the Tendai sect, an eclectic form of Buddhism of Chinese origin that was introduced into Japan in the eighth century, to cover the shelf that stands in front of the temple's main statue of the Buddha. The hanging depicts two heavenly musicians floating above the clouds; the figure on the left plays a guitar-like instrument and the one on the right, a reed organ. They are flanked by a seven-string lute and a pipe. Both the figures and their musical attributes are Chinese in origin, although they are represented here with the long faces that are characteristic of traditional Edo art. DB

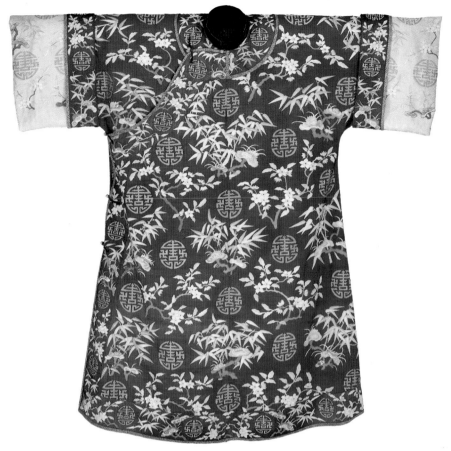

**Manchu Woman's
Informal Coat**

China, Ch'ing dynasty (1644–1911)
c. 1900–1908
Silk, metallic thread
Gift of Mrs. Bettison Bayliss. 1962-232-1

During the Ch'ing dynasty, imperial Chinese dress served as a
symbolic language that expressed the personal, political, social,
and cultural ideals of the ruling Manchu elite, which emphasized position, wealth, happiness, and long life. For example,
the bamboo stems, prunus blossoms, *ling-chih* fungus, and stylized character *shou* on this Manchu woman's informal coat
are all symbols of longevity. The principle of dualism that is
central to Chinese thought is also here represented in the use
of contrasting colors—the dark purple in the body of the coat
and the light blue and black in the wide, turned-back cuffs.
The naturalistic flowers interspersed among diagonal rows
of *shou* characters, a decorative arrangement favored by the
Dowager Empress Tz'u Hsi (1835–1908), became fashionable
on informal coats for both members of the court and others.
The small stand-up collar of black satin dates the coat, which
was woven to shape in the tapestry technique, to the late
Ch'ing dynasty. DB

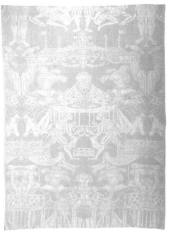

Table Napkin
Flanders
c. 1630
Linen
36½ x 27½"
Gift of Charles Edward Brinley
and Miss Katharine Faneuil Adams
1937-25-2

During the seventeenth century the weaving of fine, figured linen damask reached its artistic and technical height. In addition to the traditional floral and checked designs, such linens were often decorated with armorials or coats of arms, historical events, hunting scenes, and mythological themes as well as biblical subjects. This Flemish linen napkin is one of a set of three in the Museum's collection, each with a different scene from the Old Testament story of Judith and Holofernes. Here Judith appears both seated at a banquet table with Holofernes and again (below) with her maid, holding his head in one hand and a sword in the other while the headless body lies on a canopied bed. Large damask tablecloths and napkins, regarded as luxury items and status symbols, were often given as official gifts. One napkin in this set is embroidered with the initials *TAB;* according to family tradition, the linens were a gift from Charles I of England to Thomas Brinley (c. 1591–1661), his Auditor General of the Revenue. DB

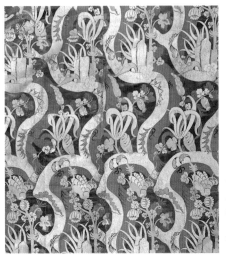

Fabric (detail)
Possibly Italy
c. 1690–1720
Silk, metallic thread
86 x 82"; repeat 30½"
Gift of Fitz Eugene Dixon, Jr.
1969-290-122

Between about 1690 and 1720, the new fashion in European silks was characterized by unconventional, abstract designs that combined influences from the Middle East and Asia with the extravagant taste of the European courts. These silks, given the name "bizarre" in the twentieth century, frequently juxtapose adaptations of the chinoiserie and indienne motifs that were popular at the time with unusual forms, resulting in particularly inventive patterns. With their exceptionally long repeats, such silks were used for furnishings, upholstery, and vestments as well as for fashionable clothing, since the length of the repeat was particularly well suited to the long, slim silhouette of the period. The silk is decorated with abstracted rocklike shapes from which sprout long, curved, spiky leaves and thick stems intertwined with branches of exotic flowers, fruits, and leaves. Its damask background, patterned with extra wefts of colored silks and gilded threads, would have reinforced the fabric's status as a highly prized luxury good. DB

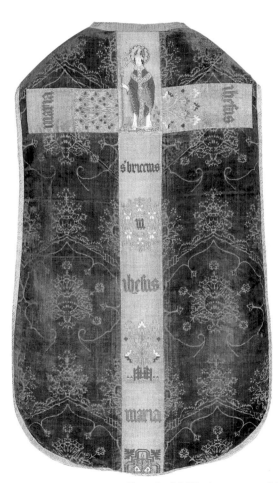

Chasuble and Orphreys

Northern Europe, probably France
c. 1475–1525
Chasuble: silk; orphreys: silk, metallic thread
Purchased with the Elizabeth Wandell Smith Fund. 1939-20-1

Since the Middle Ages some of the finest European textiles and embroideries have been created as vestments. Chasubles, overgarments worn by a priest while celebrating Mass, are traditionally made of rich silks and trimmed with decorative bands known as orphreys. The dimensions, shape, and place-ment of the orphreys of this chasuble indicate that it was used in northern Europe, probably France. Constructed from Italian cut and voided silk velvet decorated with the thin-line pomegranate pattern that was popular in the second half of the fifteenth century, it is ornamented both front and back with orphreys of a type made in Cologne, Germany, from the fourteenth to the early sixteenth century. These bands are woven with colored silks on a background of gold thread with religious inscriptions in Latin—"Jesus Mary Hail Queen [of] Sorrows" (front) and "Mary Jesus Saint Briccius" (back)—as well as the figure of Saint Brice, archbishop of Tours, which is over-embroidered in satin stitch. DB

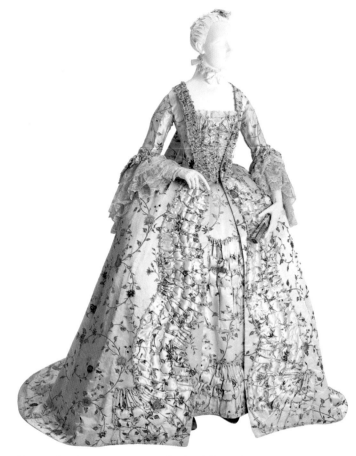

Gown, Petticoat, and Stomacher

France

c. 1755–60

Chinese export silk

Purchased with the John D. McIlhenny Fund, the John T. Morris Fund, the Elizabeth Wandell Smith Fund, and with funds contributed by Mrs. Howard H. Lewis and Marion Boulton Stroud
1988-83-1a–c

In the eighteenth century, the art—and artificiality—of dress was used in an effort to perfect the human form. Complicated processes of dressing and deportment were mastered and refined to appear natural, and included the wearing of restrictive garments with apparent ease. This seemingly fragile gown would in fact have been supported by rigid, boned stays and a hoop-petticoat. The gown's meandering floral silk, woven in China for export and made up in France, is shown off by the elegant back pleats of the fashionable sacque, or *robe à la française*. The front of the robe, the stomacher, and the petticoat are trimmed with serpentine bands of gathered and padded fabric known as ruching, which is edged with fly fringe. The luminous, delicately flowered gown, with its three-dimensional trim and fluttering fringe and sleeve ruffles, imparts a frivolous and feminine air that is the essence of Rococo taste. HKH

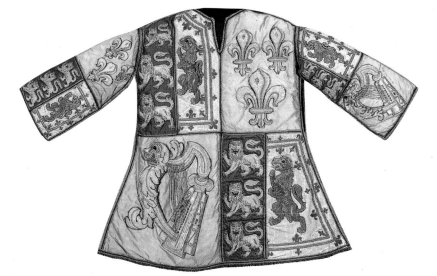

Herald's Tabard

England
1707–14
Silk, metallic thread, beads
Gift of Elizabeth Malcolm Bowman
in memory of Wendell Phillips Bowman
1930-28-1

Medieval heralds were messengers who prominently displayed their masters' insignia on their coats to be easily recognized in battle. Because they also helped to identify fallen warriors and organize tournaments, they became knowledgeable about—and gave their name to—the elaborate system of armorial symbols known as heraldry. In England, their expertise was recognized in 1483, when they were incorporated as the Heralds' College, charged with overseeing the use of coats of arms. At about the same time tabards, open-sided overgarments, went out of general use and became fossilized as the ceremonial dress of heralds, still used in Britain today. This tabard is appliquéd with embroidered motifs forming the coat of arms of Queen Anne (reigned 1702–14): the three lions of England and the lion rampant of Scotland quartered with the harp of Ireland and the fleurs-de-lis of France, then claimed by England. The Scottish symbol dates the tabard after 1707, when the parliaments of Scotland and England were combined to form the Parliament of Great Britain. HKH

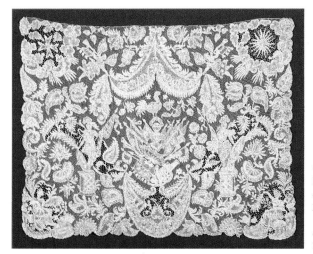

Cravat End

Flanders
c. 1700–1715
Linen
12¾ x 16½"
Gift of the Women's Committee of the
Philadelphia Museum of Art. 1990-1-2

By the third quarter of the seventeenth century lace-trimmed cravats had replaced lace collars as the fashionable form of men's neckwear at the courts of Louis XIV of France and Charles II of England. The rectangular shape of the lace trim at both ends of a fine linen cravat allowed for a wide range of designs. Brussels lace makers in particular excelled in creating delicate yet complex figurative compositions with motifs often taken from ornamental engravings. This cravat end of Brussels bobbin lace, one of the finest examples in the Museum's extensive collection of lace, contains many allusions to Louis XIV and his military victories. In the center, the cock of France perches atop trophies of war flanked by figures of Mars and Minerva, and emblems of the king—the Order of the Holy Ghost (left) and the sun (right)—fill the upper corners. Louis XIV's monogram, a double *L,* appears in the swag at the bottom center. DB

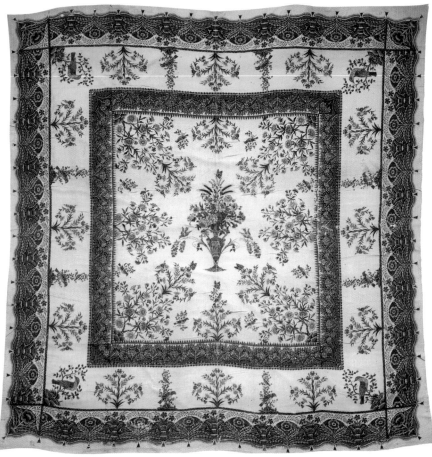

John Hewson
American, c. 1745–1821
Bedcover
Made in Philadelphia
c. 1790–1800
Cotton, linen
102¾ x 104¾"
Gift of Joseph B. Hodgson, Jr.
1930-100-1

John Hewson, the most renowned eighteenth-century American calico printer, worked in Philadelphia from 1774 to 1810 after emigrating from England, where he had been employed at Bromley Hall, one of the leading textile printworks. This bedcover, which Hewson produced at his factory in the Kensington area of Philadelphia, is considered the finest example of early American block printing. One of only three known versions of the bedcover (one is in the Henry du Pont Winterthur Museum and the other in a private collection), it belonged to Hewson himself. Elaborately patterned with drapery swags, floral borders, and a center square with a flower-filled urn flanked by butterflies and birds, the bedcover compares stylistically with the palampores printed in India during this period for the European market. The individual designs were most likely copied from pattern books and engravings. For example, the subject and arrangement of the central motifs may derive from Dutch flower-piece prints of the late sixteenth and seventeenth centuries, while the smaller images, such as the bird on a sprig, may refer to printed needlework designs. DB

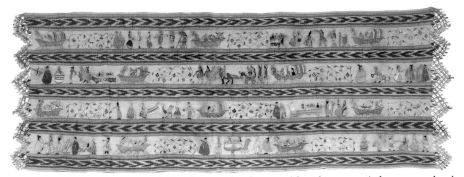

Shawl

Mexico
c. 1790
Silk, silver gilt thread
30½ x 93¾"
Gift of Mrs. George W. Childs Drexel
1939-1-19

The *rebozo,* or shawl, worn either thrown or tied over one shoulder, has held a significant place in the Mexican woman's wardrobe since the sixteenth century. The most luxurious were the embroidered shawls worn by women of the Spanish aristocracy in Mexico during the late eighteenth century, one of which is shown here. Its diagonally patterned stripes, produced with the resist-dyeing technique, are separated by plain-woven bands embroidered in colored silks and silver thread, while the ends are finished with an elaborate knotted fringe. The embroidered bands show figures engaged in a variety of pastimes, such as boating, dancing, promenading, and carriage riding. Each figure is readily identifiable by its dress as a member of one of the many social or ethnic groups within the diverse Mexican society, a theme also explored in a form of genre painting that was popular in Mexico from about 1720 until the early 1800s. DB

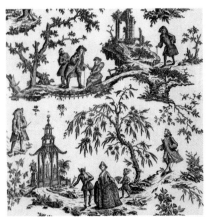

Furnishing Fabric (detail)

England
1766–74
Linen, cotton
Repeat 39 x 31½"
Gift of Miss Letitia A. Humphreys
1916-31a–k

From the mid to late eighteenth century, furnishing fabrics that were used for curtains, bed hangings, and the like were often printed with a wide range of designs, including historical, classical, and literary subjects. The fabric in this detail from a set of bed hangings is decorated with scenes from David Garrick's play *Lethe*. The textile may have been first produced at the time of the play's royal command performance in London in 1766, although the pattern could have remained in stock for as long as twenty years thereafter. Published engravings were frequently the source for fabric designs, and could be combined and then reengraved on the copperplates used in textile printing. Here, in addition to the scenes from Garrick's play, which were taken from engravings by Gabriel Smith and A. Moseley dated 1750, several of the motifs, such as the Chinese-style pavilion and the Romantic landscape in the background, refer to the latest developments in English landscape gardening. DB

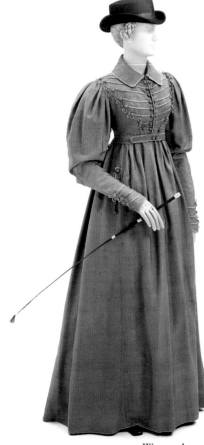

Riding Habit and Crop

United States

c. 1820

Habit: silk; crop: wood, jute, silk, ivory

Gift of Clarence Brinton in memory of Mrs. Octavia E. F. Brinton

1936-12-3a,b,e

Women began to wear specialized garments for riding in the late seventeenth century; in cut, ornamentation, and accessories these outfits were usually modeled on men's clothing, which had the advantages of being both more practical and piquantly novel to women. This early nineteenth-century riding habit makes reference to menswear through the short tail of the jacket and the shaped pocket flaps on the skirt, while the horizontal rows of cording and buttons on the bodice and cuffs echo a common feature of men's military jackets of the period. The femininity of the habit's wearer is maintained through the skirted silhouette, which corresponded to current fashion, with a fairly high waist, puffed sleeves extending beyond the wrist, and wide collar. The voluminous skirt, not yet specially cut for riding sidesaddle, is held up by shoulder straps and has an unusual concealed pocket. The habit's accessories include the crop shown here as well as earmuffs and a single stirrup. нкн

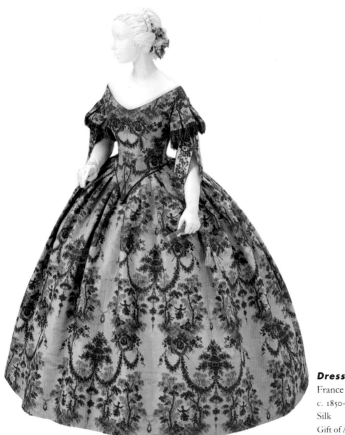

Dress
France
c. 1850–55
Silk
Gift of Alice McFadden Eyre
1926-58-1

This evening dress of about 1850, with its bodice deeply pointed at the waist, pleated sleeves trimmed with fringe and figured ribbons, and full, bell-shaped skirt, exemplifies the opulence of Second Empire France (1852–70). The fabric itself, a Jacquard-woven silk produced in Lyons, reveals the derivative nature of mid-nineteenth-century textile design, which often used elements copied directly from prints of the work of well-known artists. In this case the images were adapted from two engravings by the eighteenth-century artist Jean Antoine Watteau, who was the object of renewed interest in France during the late 1840s. The choice of the swing theme, which was used to symbolize lovemaking during the eighteenth and nineteenth centuries, was especially appropriate for an evening dress, in which the wearer would want to appear demure yet flirtatious. DB

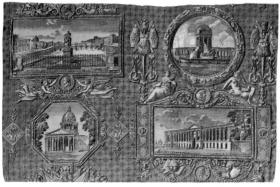

Hippolyte Le Bas
French, 1782–1867
Furnishing Fabric (detail)
c. 1816–18
Cotton
30¼ x 34½"; repeat 20¼ x 34"
Purchased with the Francis T. S. Darley
Fund. 1925-8-1

The printed cotton textiles produced at the Oberkampf factory in Jouy-en-Josas near Paris between 1760 and 1843 are among the finest ever made, noted for both their compositions and technical achievement. This furnishing fabric was designed by the prominent architect Hippolyte Le Bas, one of several well known artists who worked for the factory; his drawing was engraved onto a copper roller for printing on the cotton by Nicolas Auguste Leisnier. The composition, which is typical of the early nineteenth-century Neoclassical style, shows a repeat of four elaborately framed scenes of Parisian monuments: to the left, the statue of Henri IV and the Pont Neuf with the Pantheon; to the right, the Fontaine des Innocents with the Louvre. Each vignette is connected to a medallion portrait of the sovereign who reigned when the monuments were erected. This fabric is part of the Museum's important collection of over seven hundred English and French printed textiles from the eighteenth and nineteenth centuries. DB

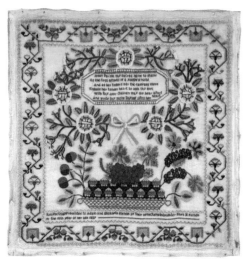

Eliza M. Kandle
American, born 1821
Sampler
Made in Philadelphia
1839
Linen, wool
22½ x 22¾"
Whitman Sampler Collection, gift of
Pet Incorporated. 1969-288-208

The eighteen-year-old "affectionate daughter" who here offers her parents "the first efforts of a youthful hand" was undoubtedly more skilled than the verse modestly acknowledges, for in the early nineteenth century girls as young as four years of age began to learn practical stitchery and would have completed a few basic samplers by about age nine. Ornamental needlework was the primary subject of middle-class girls' education, as the many "showpiece" samplers from this period, once

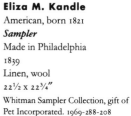

proudly displayed on parlor walls, attest. This genteel "accomplishment" was most often acquired at an academy, with the teacher dictating the sampler's composition as well as overseeing its construction. This is one of a group of at least fifteen examples known as Philadelphia presentation samplers, made at an unidentified school in the city between 1816 and 1839, whose designs usually include a basket of strawberries and grapes and a respectful dedication. The Museum's collection of over six hundred European and American samplers, which includes the famed Whitman Collection, is one of the largest of its kind. ₋HKH

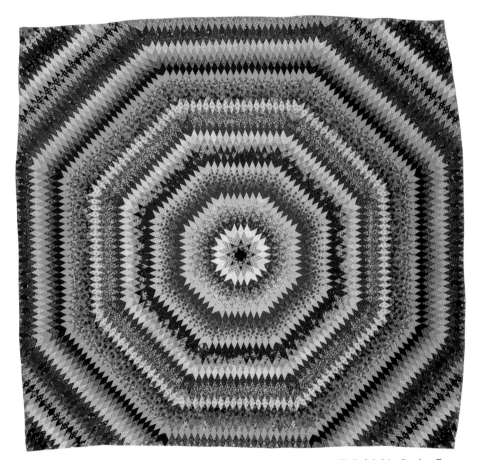

Rebecca Scattergood Savery
American, 1770–1855
Quilt
Made in Philadelphia
1839
Cotton
108½ x 117½"
Gift of Sarah Pennell Barton and Nancy Barton Barclay. 1975-5-1

In 1839, at the age of sixty-nine, the Philadelphia Quaker Rebecca Scattergood Savery made this sunburst-patterned quilt for her granddaughter Sarah Savery, who was born that year; their descendants donated the quilt to the Museum. Measuring nine feet by nearly ten feet, the quilt contains almost four thousand diamond-shaped pieces, each about four inches long, that were first basted to a paper template to ensure uniformity of size before being meticulously whip-stitched together. At least thirty-four different small-patterned, roller-printed cottons were used to form the octagonal rings that radiate from a central eight-pointed star to create a striking dark and light design. The quilting, which was stitched in a diamond pattern over very thin batting, was done by more than one hand, probably at a quilting bee where the work was combined with socializing. This quilt is the most important patchwork piece in the Museum's large quilt collection, which is especially rich in examples from the Philadelphia area. HKH

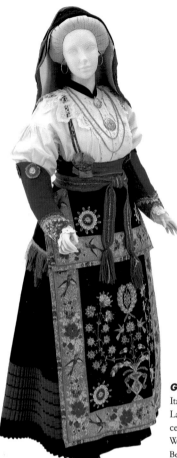

Gala Ensemble

Italy, Baranello, Molise
Late nineteenth–early twentieth
century
Wool, silk, cotton, linen, beads
Bequest of Helen P. McMullan
1966-38-6

This ensemble from the village of Baranello in central Italy would have been worn only for special occasions—Sundays, festivals, weddings, and even burial. Such regional or folk dress, outside the mainstream of Western fashion, developed in response to the dictates of custom and the desire to identify with a community. The costume itself reflected the wearer's social position: the headdress, for example, was worn only by a married woman, as were the fringed belt and lowered bodice front; the lavish jewelry and elaborate ornament, such as that on the colorful apron, were used to demonstrate wealth. The shape of the apron—a folded, flat rectangle under a brilliantly colored tie—shows off the borders of figured silk ribbon and the embroidery, which includes birds and flowers around a vase, a symbol of riches. This is one of thirty-nine costumes, collected by the Philadelphian Helen McMullan in the 1930s and bequeathed to the Museum in 1966, that form the most comprehensive collection of Italian folk dress in North America. HKH

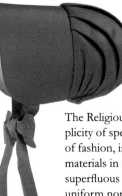

Bonnet
Made in Chester County,
Pennsylvania
c. 1860
Silk
Gift of Mrs. Harris Cooperman and
Mrs. Evertt Menelsohn. 1969-239-22

The Religious Society of Friends, or Quakers, advocated simplicity of speech, behavior, and dress. They avoided extremes of fashion, instead achieving dignity through the use of fine materials in subdued colors and skillful construction without superfluous ornament. Although Quaker clothing was neither uniform nor immune to changing fashions, certain features were retained long after they were outmoded and thus became badges of the group's separateness from the wider community. Thus bonnets such as this, which had been adapted from stylish headwear of the early nineteenth century, were by mid-century identifiably Quaker. To the initiated, subtle variations in color and form manifested doctrinal differences: the use of rigid pleating rather than soft gathers on this "plain" bonnet indicates the wearer's orthodoxy. The bonnet is covered in fine silk, while the brim is edged with wire and stiffened with cardboard, which also reinforces the buckram-lined pleats. Always worn over a fine lawn cap, the bonnet was often protected by an oilskin cover in wet weather, while a quilted silk cover would add warmth in winter. HKH

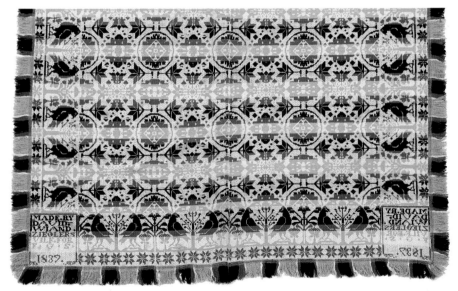

David Wiand
American, active 1837–41
Coverlet (detail)
Made in Zieglersville, Montgomery
County, Pennsylvania
1837
Wool, cotton
102 x 84″
Gift of Miss E. Kinsey. 1967-10-1

In 1805 Joseph-Marie Jacquard of Lyons, France, patented a mechanism that facilitated the weaving of intricately figured textiles. Introduced into the United States during the 1820s, the Jacquard loom attachment, which utilized commercially available perforated cards to control the elaborate pattern, not only allowed for unlimited design possibilities but also accounted for the similarity between many of the coverlets and carpets produced by professional weavers, who were usually men. The inscriptions in the bottom corners of this Jacquard-woven coverlet indicate that it was woven in 1837 by David Wiand of Zieglersville, Montgomery County, Pennsylvania, for a customer identified only as *F.G.S.* Wiand, like many other coverlet weavers in Pennsylvania, was of German background. The motifs, such as the pair of birds flanking a bush and the stylized floral field, are found in other Pennsylvania German decorative arts. This coverlet also shows the influence of Germanic weaving traditions in its tied double-weave construction. DB

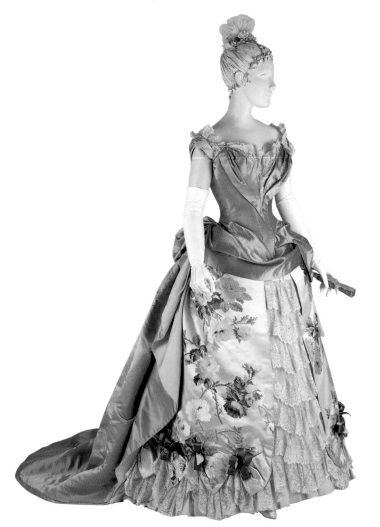

Charles Frederick Worth
English, active France, 1825–1895
Evening Dress
c. 1886–87
Silk, linen, rhinestones
Gift of Mr. and Mrs. Owen Biddle
1978-2-1

This evening dress was designed by the first great Parisian couturier, Charles Frederick Worth, an Englishman whose creative genius and promotional skills won him the credit for having elevated fashion to an art form. Worth's "compositions" featured distinctive textiles, such as the floral brocade from Lyons, here combined with satin, faille, and lace, and from the mid-1860s elicited veneration—as well as extravagant sums—from aristocratic and nouveaux-riches clients around the world. This gown, probably purchased in Paris in 1887, belonged to an American, Mrs. Ernest Fenollosa, who lived in Tokyo for twelve years and may have worn it for presentation at the Japanese imperial court. Its décolleté boned bodice, convoluted bustled and trained skirt, and myriad trimmings exemplify the late nineteenth-century concept of femininity. Strongly differentiated from the period's masculine aesthetic, this fashionable toilette—restrictive, impractical, and ornamental—was defined by Victorian society as an elegant enhancement of a woman's status and beauty. HKH

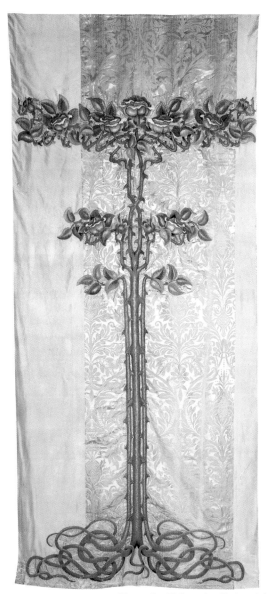

Alexander Fisher
English, 1864–1936
Curtain
1905
Silk, wool
123 x 55"
Gift of the Friends of the Philadelphia Museum of Art. 1988-7-3

Alexander Fisher, the distinguished English metalworker and enameler, designed this curtain, one of four that originally hung side by side, in 1905 for Fanhams Hall in Ware, England. It was embroidered by the Royal School of Art Needlework, which since its founding in 1872 had commissioned designs from leading artists such as Fisher, William Morris, and Sir Edward Coley Burne-Jones. Here an elongated rose tree with intertwined roots, a popular turn-of-the-century motif, is boldly embroidered in wool and silk on silk damask woven in a pattern derived from an early eighteenth-century design. By using the long-and-short stitch that the Royal School called the "English feather stitch," the embroiderers have re-created in thread the effect of Fisher's art enamels, which were distinguished by their repoussé metalwork and rich, translucent colors. DB

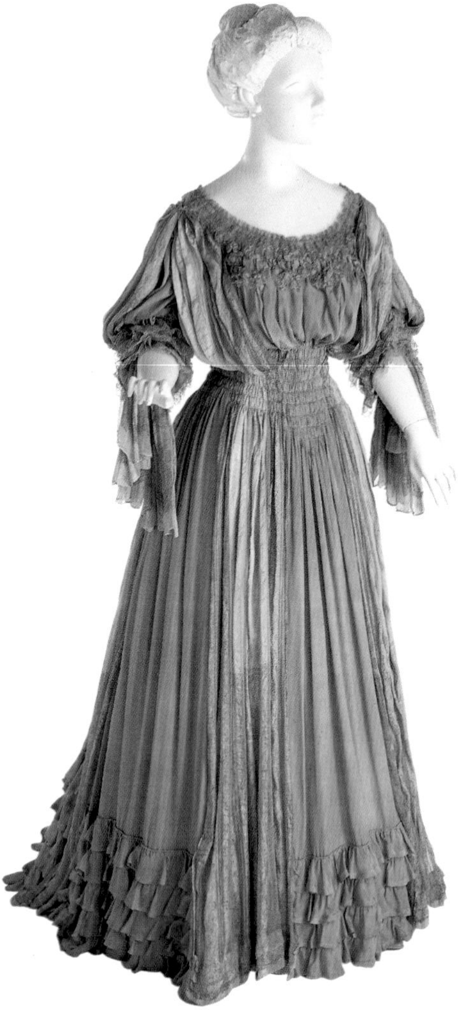

Liberty & Co.
English, London, 1875–present
Tea Gown
1906
Silk
Gift of Margaretta S. Hinchman
1951-21-20

Liberty of London, founded in 1875 by Arthur Lasenby Liberty to sell the Asian ornaments popularized by the Aesthetic movement, soon began offering fabrics, furniture, china, and other decorative arts in Eastern, European historical, and Arts and Crafts styles. In 1884 Liberty began selling dresses in the so-called artistic, or "reform," style. In contrast to the tight-waisted, heavily decorated, and boldly colored clothing that was then fashionable, the Liberty gowns featured flowing, histori-cally inspired lines and delicate pastel tints of blue, greenish yellow, gold, and coral, which became known as "Liberty col-ors." By the turn of the century, these soft colors and less constrained styles were widely adopted for the picturesque tea gowns that were worn for late afternoon "at-home" entertaining. This Liberty tea gown, lightly boned at the high waist, incorporates printed silk scarves from India to form an airy confection of drapery, ruffles, gathers, and lace that epitomizes Edwardian luxury and elegance. HKH

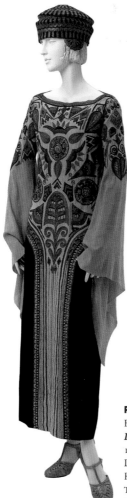

Paul Poiret
French, 1879–1944
Dress and Hat
1923
Dress: silk, metallic thread
Hat: leather, silk
The Samuel S. White 3rd and Vera White
Collection. 1951-126-3

French couturier Paul Poiret reigned as the "King of Fashion" in the decade before the outbreak of World War I in 1914. During this time he helped revolutionize feminine clothing by abolishing the artificial S-curve to emphasize the body's natural lines and introducing exotic novelties such as harem trousers and hobble skirts. While the loose, straight-line garments that he had pioneered continued to set the style after the war, he refused to modify the opulence and extravagance of his designs to suit the simpler tastes of the 1920s. In this afternoon dress and hat with Egyptian motifs, Poiret, renowned for amalgamating disparate influences to interpret the spirit of the East for a Western audience, pays homage to the rediscovery of the tomb of King Tutankhamen in 1922. The embroidery in vermilion, chestnut, and gold on the dramatically sleeved dress is set off by panels of sinuous black silk velvet and accented by a shaped cloche of fine leather appliquéd over silk. HKH

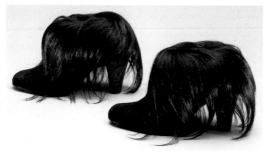

Elsa Schiaparelli
Italian, active France, 1890–1973
Boots
c. 1938
Leather, monkey fur
Gift of Mme Elsa Schiaparelli
1969-282-55

Accessories were of the greatest importance to the Italian-born fashion designer Elsa Schiaparelli, whose hats, bags, shoes, gloves, scarves, jewelry, and buttons often defied conventional expectations for such seemingly "subordinate" items in an ensemble. From gloves incongruously sporting fingernails to hats shaped as lamb chops or shoes, Schiaparelli's accessories, which she described as "witticisms" or "conceits," cried out for attention, and were responsible for much of her notoriety as fashion's great innovator before the Second World War. Schiaparelli designed these suede high-heeled boots for herself in collaboration with André Perugia, the premier shoe designer and maker in France between the wars. Here again the unexpected is the norm for Schiaparelli: the monkey fur embellishing the boots cascades onto the ground, paradoxically emancipating footwear from functionality. When paired with a black jersey top whose front and back are completely enveloped in matching fur, the boots would confer instant Surrealistic chic. They are among some seventy-five garments and accessories given to the Museum by the designer. HKH

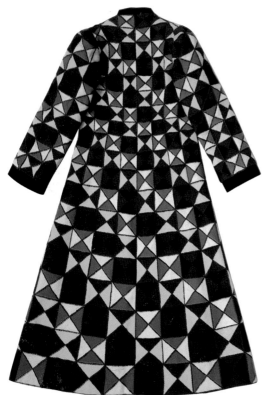

Elsa Schiaparelli
Italian, active France, 1890–1973
Evening Coat
1938–39
Wool, silk
Gift of Mme Elsa Schiaparelli
1969-232-3

This harlequin coat by Elsa Schiaparelli was described by *Harper's Bazaar* as "an utterly plain, severe coat, one straight line from neck to hem," yet characteristically for the designer the hard masculine silhouette is juxtaposed with a traditionally feminine use of ornament and brilliant color, and leavened by her eccentric wit. Schiaparelli, who collaborated with Salvador Dalí, Jean Cocteau, and other avant-garde artists, treated garments as an experimental art form, utilizing the subversive goals of Surrealism to imbue sophisticated high fashion with surprising playfulness and irreverence. This evening coat, a colorful mosaic of usually prosaic felt cleverly shaped for the torso by gradually increasing the size of the squares from neck to hem, is part of Schiaparelli's "Commedia dell'arte" collection for spring 1939. It proved to be her last great collection, presented as a mad carnival to counteract the anxious political situation in Europe, and fittingly epitomized Schiaparelli's belief that all clothing is but a masquerade. HKH

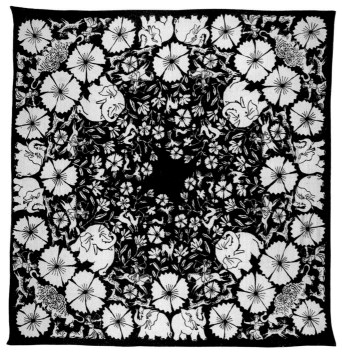

Raoul Dufy
French, 1877–1953
Shawl
c. 1928
Silk, metallic thread
53½ x 52″
Gift of Mrs. Lawrence Fuller. 1970-158-1

The painter and illustrator Raoul Dufy began his career as a textile designer by collaborating with the Paris fashion designer Paul Poiret in 1911. Dufy involved himself in all aspects of the process, from hand-carving the woodblocks to printing the fabric. In 1912 Dufy began designing for the Lyons silk manufacturer Bianchini-Férier. Although Dufy was required to supply only the drawings for the designs that were printed on the fabric, with the blocks now carved by an outside firm, Bianchini took care to ensure that the artist's deliberately naïve style was faithfully reproduced. This luxurious black and gold satin lamé shawl, printed with a design dated 1928 entitled "La Chasse à l'arc," is one of Dufy's last designs for Bianchini. Many of the

images—elephants, lions, archers, and stylized flowers—
are found frequently in Dufy's earlier textile designs of the
1910s and 1920s, and are here presented in his characteristic
"primitive" style. DB

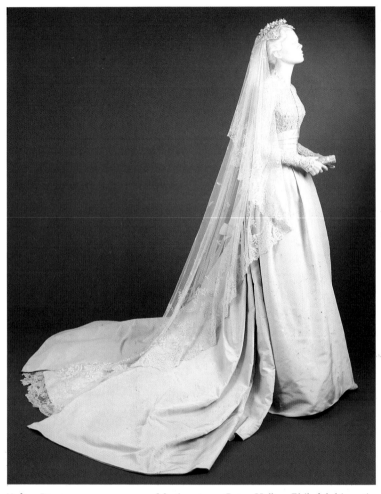

Helen Rose
American, 1904–1985
Wedding Dress
1956
Silk, linen, seed pearls
Gift of H.S.H. Princesse Grace de
Monaco. 1956-51-1-3

Movie actress Grace Kelly, a Philadelphia native, wore this wedding dress for her marriage to Prince Rainier III in the cathedral
of Monaco on April 19, 1956; Academy Award–winning designer
Helen Rose, who had created Kelly's costumes for the films
High Society and *The Swan,* was chosen to design the gown, which
was constructed by the MGM wardrobe department and later
given to the Museum by the princess. In style and detail the
dress was conceived to complement the "fairy princess" image
of the bride. Above a bell-shaped skirt of ivory peau de soie,
supported by three petticoats, a high-necked bodice of Brussels
lace was re-embroidered so the seams would be invisible and
then accented with seed pearls. Pearl-embellished lace also
covers the prayer book, shoes, and cap, which is surmounted by
an orange-blossom wreath. The circular silk net veil, especially
designed so that the bride's face could be seen, is decorated
with appliquéd lace motifs, including two tiny love birds. HKH

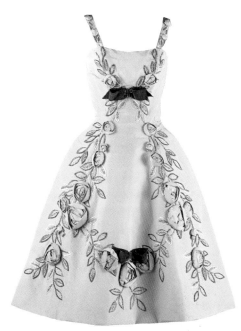

Emilio Schuberth
Italian, 1904–1972
Cocktail Dress
c. 1961
Silk, beads
Gift of Mrs. Jack M. Friedland
1972-188-2

The international debut of Italian high fashion in Florence
in 1951 unveiled an original modern style inspired by traditional
Italian culture, especially that of the Renaissance, yet perfectly
suited to the contemporary, postwar desire for uncomplicated,
wearable clothing. Renowned for its casual knit sportswear,
Italian fashion in the 1950s and 1960s also included formal
gowns created with exquisite craftsmanship, such as those by
Roman designer Emilio Schuberth. This cocktail dress, in a
fashionable shade of yellow, seems to be simply cut but in fact
is carefully shaped by darts, nylon lining, and a crinoline. The
front is decorated with self-fabric flowers surmounting leaves
of white and gold beads, some forming three-dimensional Vs
to give an illusion of shading. A favorite of Italian film stars
such as Gina Lollobrigida and Sophia Loren, Schuberth's feminine creations also appealed to Americans who appreciated
his philosophy of design—"All I do is to cover the most beautiful invention that God has placed on this earth: the body
of woman." HKH

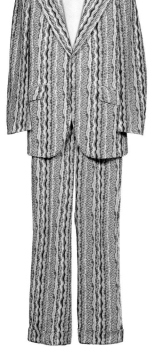

Bill Blass
American, born 1922
Man's Suit
1970
Double-knit wool and polyester
Gift of T. N. Crater. 1973-59-4a,b

Menswear, long the conservative preserve of tailors and manufacturers, became a fashion commodity in the late 1960s. Bill

Blass, known for his clothes for women that incorporated aspects of men's tailoring, was one of the first major American designers to offer a line of men's fashions, beginning in 1967; he was awarded the first Coty Menswear Award in 1968. His designs are the essence of urbane sophistication, reflecting the latest trends without slavishly aping them. Produced by the Philadelphia firm of Pincus Brothers Maxwell, this suit was given to the Museum by Tom Crater, then associated with the John Wanamaker department store, which had helped launch Blass's collection. Here the traditional form of a man's suit has been retained, albeit with modish wide lapels and trouser cuffs, but the fabric, a wildly patterned Italian double-knit, makes a refreshingly novel statement. HKH

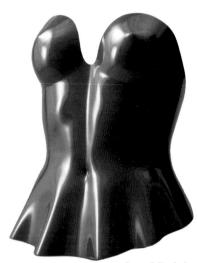

Issey Miyake
Japanese, born 1938
Bustier
1980
Plastic
Purchased with the Costume and
Textiles Revolving Fund. 1992-136-1

Issey Miyake's plastic bustier, molded on a human form and made in cooperation with a mannequin manufacturer, is a brilliant if unexpected result of the Japanese designer's ongoing exploration of the relationship between clothing and the body. Since his first Paris show in 1973, Miyake has transcended his training in Western couture to redefine the concept of wearing clothes. His designs are neither Eastern nor Western, instead uniting the traditional Japanese emphasis on materials with modern industrial technology to create original body coverings. This bustier reflects Miyake's philosophy that clothing should fuse with the personality of the wearer to become part of the body; while his draped and wrapped fashions acquire their shape when worn, the preformed bustier becomes a new layer of skin. A centerpiece of Miyake's "Bodyworks" exhibition shown internationally in 1983–85, this bold red bustier, with its reflective surface and sinuous curves, can also be appreciated as a sculpture with its own form and function. HKH

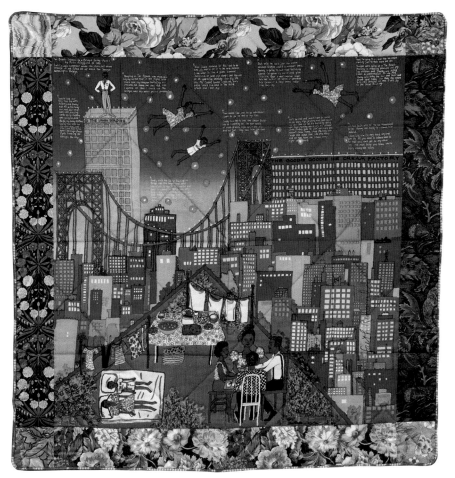

Faith Ringgold

American, born 1930

"Tar Beach 2" Quilt

1990

Silk

66 x 64½"

Purchased with funds contributed by
W. B. Dixon Stroud. 1992-100-1

In her series of narrative quilts, Faith Ringgold fuses her training in the fine arts with her familial quilt-making and story-telling traditions, incorporating African polyrhythms and geometric designs to communicate her experience as both an African American and a woman. Here, for example, the quilting pattern of eight triangles within a square derives from a traditional design of the Kuba peoples of Africa. With the quilt's central image, silkscreened at Philadelphia's Fabric Workshop as a variation on her painted and appliquéd quilts, Ringgold transforms her memories of childhood in Harlem to depict eight-year-old Cassie Louise Lightfoot's dream of freedom. One hot summer night on her apartment roof, Cassie finds she can fly among the stars; on her journey she claims the George Washington Bridge as her own and gives her father the Union Building, thus ending his employment worries. Cassie, who personifies Ringgold's vision of a heroic and creative black female, discovers, as the inscription reveals, that "anyone can fly. All you need is somewhere to go that you can't get to any other way." HKH

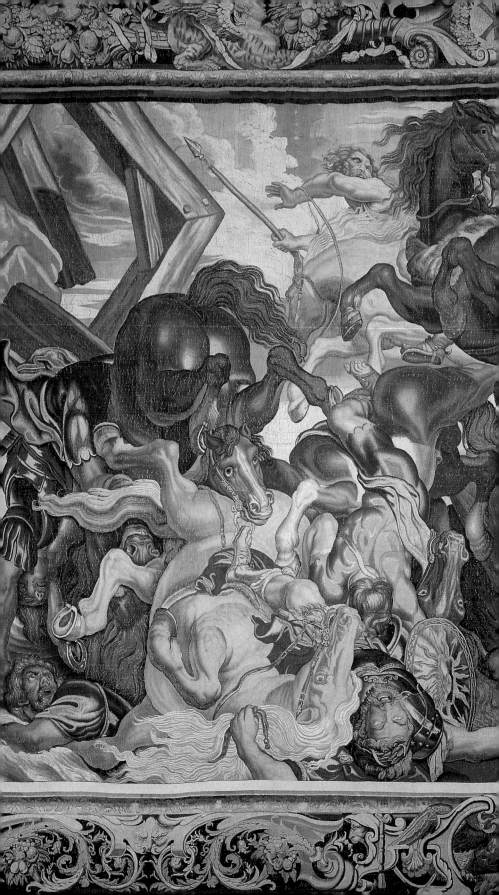

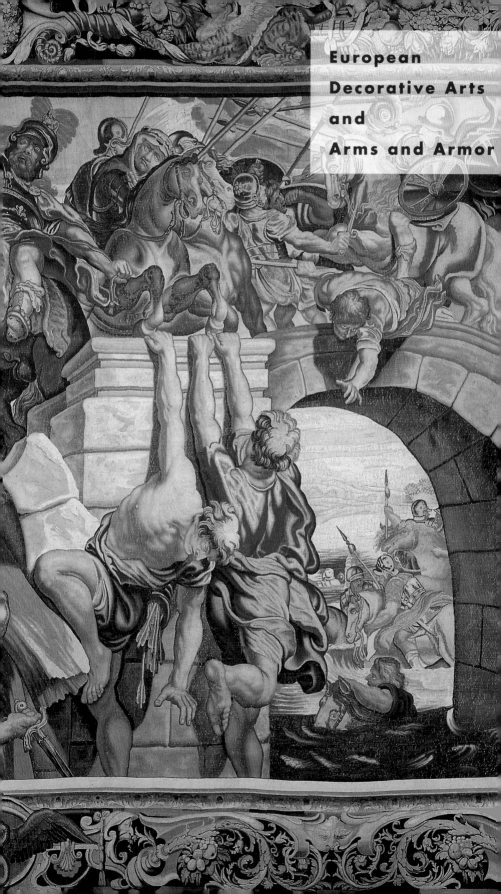

European Decorative Arts and Arms and Armor

The defining moment for the character and display of European decorative arts in the Philadelphia Museum of Art occurred in 1927, when director Fiske Kimball conceived of the second floor of the as yet unfinished new building as a "walk through time." In this plan a succession of dramatic galleries with architectural elements including entire period rooms was designed to embrace paintings, sculpture, and the applied arts in Europe from about 1100 to 1800 in order to show the unity of the arts at certain historic moments and to stimulate the imagination of visitors. American and European decorative arts were the responsibility of a single department until 1970; American rooms were included to demonstrate the cultural links between Europe and eighteenth-century America, and Philadelphia in particular, together with what Kimball called the "colonial chain" of historic houses nearby in Fairmount Park.

The creation of the architectural settings and their furnishings determined the collecting policy during Kimball's directorship, with a sequence of four major acquisitions establishing the outstanding areas of depth. In 1930 the Museum acquired the extraordinary collection of Italian and French Renaissance art formed between the 1870s and 1900 by Edmond Foulc, a French "amateur" of the old school. In 1939 the bequest of Eleanore Elkins Rice, a Philadelphian by birth, brought the Museum superb French decorative arts from the eighteenth century. From George Grey Barnard, the Pennsylvania-born sculptor and pioneering collector of medieval architecture and stone sculpture, as well as an adviser on the Museum's installations, came an impressive collection of medieval art, purchased in 1945. (Barnard's first collection was acquired by the Metropolitan Museum of Art in New York in 1925 and forms the basis for The Cloisters.) The bequest of Carl Otto von Kienbusch, whose career as a scholar, collector, and curator influenced generations of arms and armor enthusiasts, established the armory and thus brought one of this hemisphere's finest collections of such material to the Museum in 1977. Installed in galleries at the top of the Great Stair Hall, the Kienbusch Collection constitutes a popular bridge between the art of Europe before and after 1500 displayed in the wings to the north and south.

Most of the works of art in the department have come as gifts. Some reflect a pattern of collecting broad areas of applied arts that was established in the Centennial Exposition of 1876, when objects were exhibited (and some then acquired) following the model of London's Victoria and Albert Museum. The collection given in 1882, together with a purchase fund, by Mrs. Bloomfield Moore had this aim. Later collectors were often devoted to specific categories of objects, such as Francis P. Garvan to Dutch tiles and George H. Lorimer to glass. The Museum's acquisitions of European ironwork reflect a connection with the Museum's school as well as with local craftsmen; its collection was originally assembled for study purposes by Samuel Yellin, Philadelphia's celebrated artisan in iron and himself first a student and then a teacher at the school. The suite of thirteen Rubens tapestries on the life of Constantine, reunited in this century by the Samuel H. Kress Foundation, was given to the Museum in 1959 to be spectacularly installed around the balcony of the Great Stair Hall during the curatorship of David DuBon, who also compiled a catalogue for the donor. Other masterpieces now at the Museum initially came to decorate the grand houses constructed around Philadelphia in the early twentieth century, such as the pair of French eighteenth-century plaster figure groups by Clodion acquired by Mr. and Mrs. Edward T. Stotesbury for Whitemarsh Hall.

After World War II the acquisition of numerous important objects from many centuries and schools was directed by Henry P. McIlhenny, who served as head of the department from 1934 to 1964 and thereafter as Museum trustee. His own distinguished collection, bequeathed to the Museum in 1986, included one of the first groups of early nineteenth-century French furniture assembled by an American.

The collections have benefited from the particular interests of successive generations of curators. Edwin AtLee Barber's advanced taste in German, North American, and Mexican ceramics brought strength in each field at the beginning of the century, and more recently Kathryn B. Hiesinger has pursued late nineteenth-century objects and twentieth-century masterworks of design from the United States, Europe, and postwar Japan. Many of the twentieth-century acquisitions have been made possible through the generosity of COLLAB, a group of Philadelphia design professionals established in 1970 under the curatorship of Calvin S. Hathaway.

For the experience of the Museum visitor, the department's most important recent undertaking is surely the reinstallation of the galleries of European objects from 1100 to 1900. Drawing upon the rich resources of Fiske Kimball's original creation and the acquisitions assembled over a century, this project has permitted the most thorough review and reinterpretation of the vast European decorative arts collections since the galleries were first established.

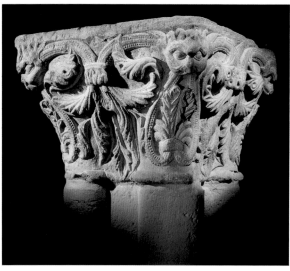

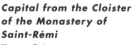

Capital from the Cloister of the Monastery of Saint-Rémi
France, Reims
c. 1140
Limestone
13 x 18½ x 18½"
Purchased from the George Grey
Barnard Collection with Museum funds
1945-25-39

Recent scholarship has determined that this capital and three others in the Museum's collection come from the cloister of the important monastery of Saint-Rémi in the city of Reims in eastern France that was commissioned by Bishop Odo around 1140. Although the cloister was destroyed in the seventeenth century, some elements remain in Reims, including a pillar fragment with four engaged columns that corresponds to the shape of the Museum's capitals. The especially skillful late Romanesque sculptor responsible for this example drew some elements of the design from ancient Roman art, such as the unusual complete symmetry and the form of the lion heads at the corners. Nevertheless, more striking is the way in which the entire surface of the capital is unified and animated by the deeply carved sinuous leaves. ED

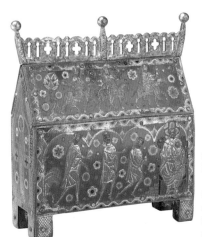

Reliquary (Chasse)
France, Limoges
1220–30
Gilded copper alloy, champlevé
enamel, painted wood, iron
8⅞ x 9½ x 3⅞"
Gift of Henry P. McIlhenny. 1950-31-1

A chasse is a church-shaped container for relics, ultimately descended from the sarcophagus used for a saint's burial. A small coffer such as this could be transported easily to an altar for veneration. The linear decoration was incised into the cold metal, and the colored areas created by pouring enamel into grooves in the surface. When heated, the enamel became glass-like and bonded with the metal; it was then polished down to the level of the surrounding metal. Finally, the three-dimensional heads were cast and attached. In the twelfth century, the production of gilded metal objects with enameled decoration became a specialty of French workshops around Limoges and developed into a flourishing international business. The visit of the Three Kings (Magi) to the newborn Christ was a popular subject for such works in the early thirteenth century. Here their journey is depicted on the roof of the chasse, while below they offer their gifts to the Virgin and Child. Given the prominence of the Magi, this chasse may have been intended to house a relic related to the kings. DW

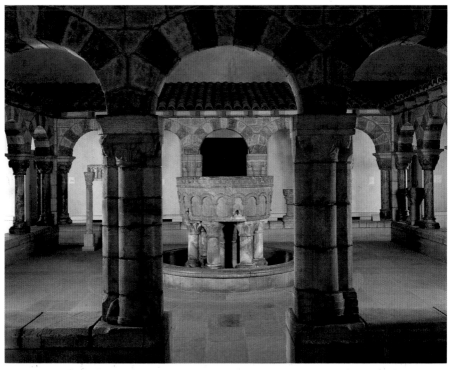

Cloister with Elements from the Abbey of Saint-Genis-des-Fontaines
France, Roussillon
1270–80s, with other medieval elements from southwestern France and twentieth-century additions
Marble
Purchased with funds contributed by Elizabeth Malcolm Bowman in memory of Wendell Phillips Bowman. 1928-57-1b

Fountain from the Monastery of Saint-Michel-de-Cuxa
France, Roussillon
1125–50
Marble, height 5′4¼″ (overall)
Gift of Mrs. William W. Fitler in memory of her husband. 1930-79-1

A medieval cloister, an arcaded walkway surrounding an open courtyard, was usually a space at the heart of a monastery where a variety of highly regulated events in the lives of members of the religious order took place, including silent prayer, meditation, or reading aloud from holy books. The design for this cloister installed in the Museum is based on that at Saint-Genis-des-Fontaines in southwestern France, the source of some of the Museum's cloister capitals. In the center of the cloister stands a rare Romanesque fountain known to have come from Saint-Michel-de-Cuxa, the largest monastery in the eastern Pyrenees. The massive basin of the fountain is decorated with a continuous design of arches on columns that echo the elements of the cloister itself. Fountains served a variety of practical purposes in monasteries, such as providing water for shaving or washing clothes. Transplanted to a museum, the fountain and its cloister setting afford late-twentieth-century visitors a space for quiet thought. ED

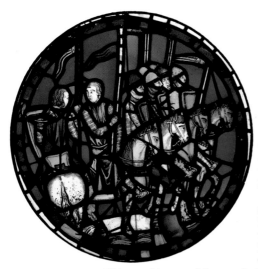

Roundel Depicting Holofernes' Army Crossing the Euphrates River
France, Paris, Sainte-Chapelle
1246–48
Stained and painted glass
Diameter 23⁵/₁₆"
Purchased with funds contributed by Mrs. Clement Biddle Wood in memory of her husband. 1930-24-3

This panel is one of three at the Museum from the Sainte-Chapelle in Paris, the spectacular Gothic church built by King Louis IX (later Saint Louis) in 1243–48 to house sacred relics. The building is illuminated by windows fifteen feet high with stained-glass scenes from the Bible. The Museum's roundel is an element from the window devoted to the Apocryphal Book of Judith. Its subject is derived from a mere phrase in the biblical text, which the unknown artist has made into a sophisticated asymmetrical composition with two conversing horsemen, one seen from the back, and a contrasting group of mounted knights. Strong lead lines and brilliant colors contribute to its easy legibility. The Museum's glass was removed in the early nineteenth century when the chapel was turned into an archive. On a trip to France, Philadelphian William Poyntell bought the three panels, one of the first important acquisitions of medieval stained glass by an American, although the Sainte-Chapelle provenance was not established until 1967. DW

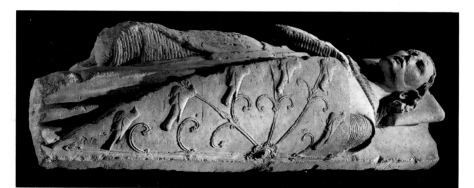

Recumbent Knight from a Tomb Sculpture
France, possibly Normandy
c. 1230–40
Stone with traces of paint
13⁹/₁₆ x 70⁵/₁₆ x 23"
Purchased from the George Grey Barnard Collection with Museum funds
1945-25-72

This tomb sculpture represents a knight wearing a long mail tunic with a hood, mail leggings, and a belted cloth surcoat, and holding a triangular shield. The birds prominently depicted in relief on the shield are *merlettes* (blackbirds), a device common in thirteenth-century heraldry in northern France. The costume is that worn by knights who joined the early Crusades to capture the Holy Land from the Muslims. The sculptor's attention to details of costume, however, does not detract from the overall strength and nobility of the form. Of exceptional quality, this figure has been related to others at Chartres Cathedral. The depiction of the dead man as an idealized youthful warrior was a convention of the period that offers eloquent testimony of the new status of knights, once merely hired soldiers, who were accepted into the ranks of the aristocracy during the thirteenth century. DW

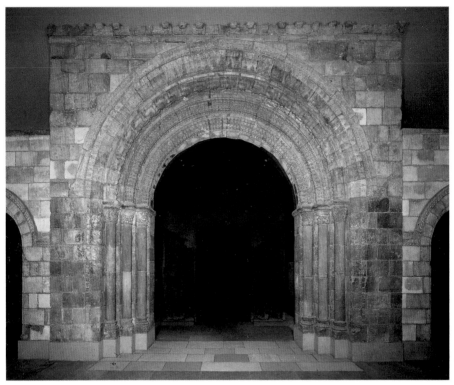

Portal from the Abbey Church of Saint-Laurent
France, near Cosne-Cours-sur-Loire
c. 1125–50
Stone
Purchased with funds contributed by Elizabeth Malcolm Bowman in memory of Wendell Phillips Bowman. 1928-57-1a

This imposing portal originally served as the main entrance to the small Augustinian abbey church of Saint-Laurent in central France, on one of the pilgrimage roads to the shrine of Santiago da Compostela in Spain. It displays bold abstract patterns on round arches and capitals with complicated intertwined branches, leaves, and birds characteristic of Romanesque architecture. The style seen here was inspired by that of the most influential Benedictine monastery in Europe, Cluny, which had founded the large church of La Charité-sur-Loire near Saint-Laurent. At the suggestion of George Grey Barnard, sculptor and collector of medieval architecture and sculpture, when the portal was installed in the Museum two smaller doorways were added on either side following a design popular in the region of Saint-Laurent, although the origin of these doors remains undetermined. In the Museum the portal faces a group of large Romanesque capitals, of which six are known to have come from the interior of the church of Saint-Laurent. DW

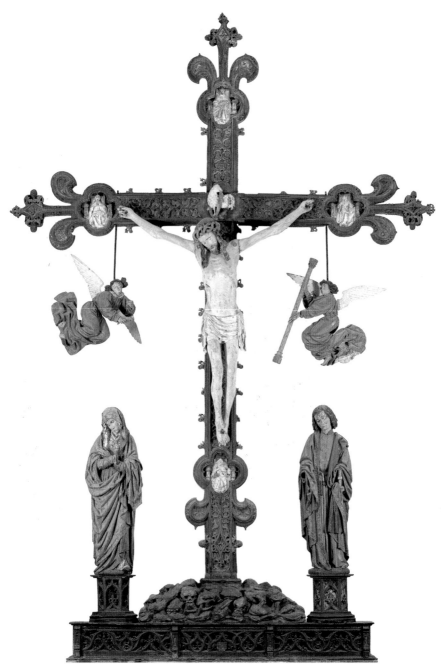

The Crucified Christ with the Virgin, Saint John the Evangelist, and Angels with Instruments of the Passion

Possibly southern Flanders
c. 1460–90
Painted oak
14' x 9'6" (cross)
Purchased from the George Grey
Barnard Collection with Museum funds
1945-25-86

When acquired by George Grey Barnard in 1925, this Crucifixion group was said to come from Oignies, a town in southern Belgium, a provenance that remains unconfirmed. Once such sculptures were common in Flemish churches, but many were destroyed in the Reformation in the sixteenth century, and this is the only example in a museum in the United States. Originally, the dramatic group would have been supported by a strong beam or screen, and stood above the entrance to a church choir with the main altar beyond. The scene of the Crucifixion of Christ is directly related to the ceremony of the Mass that would have been said below. Emphasizing the centrality of the event to church doctrine are depictions of the Latin fathers of the church at the corners of the cross (clockwise: Saints Gregory the Great, Jerome, Ambrose, and Augustine). In the Museum, the group stands at the entrance to the medieval galleries in a navelike space that echoes its original placement. DW

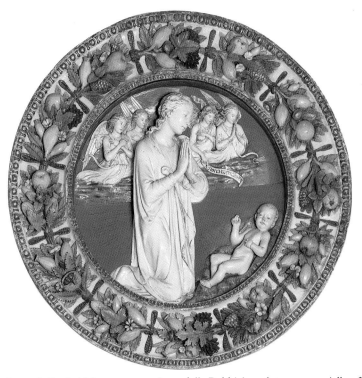

Luca della Robbia
Italian, active Florence, 1400–1482
The Virgin Adoring the Infant Jesus, usually dated c. 1472–82
Glazed terracotta with traces of gilded decoration
Diameter 65¾"
Purchased from the Edmond Foulc Collection with the W. P. Wilstach Fund
W1930-1-64a

Luca della Robbia's sculptures, especially of the Virgin and Child, are among the best-loved works of art of the Renaissance. He was especially adept at creating compositions in the circular format known as the tondo, a demanding form explored by the most ambitious artists of the time. Here the Virgin appears in front of angels, one of whom holds a scroll proclaiming *Gloria in excelsis Deo.* The subject of the relief, the incarnation of God into man, is simply and effectively conveyed by the convincing naturalism of the infant Jesus, who makes a dignified blessing gesture mature beyond his years. Primarily blue and white, this work was probably originally more brilliant, with gold rays behind the Virgin, whose hair and robe also had gilded decoration. The collector Edmond Foulc added the ceramic border of plants and fruits from the workshop of Luca's nephew Andrea. There is no early history for this important sculpture, but recent research reveals that a tondo of the Virgin and Child often decorated the bedchambers of well-to-do citizens of Florence. DW

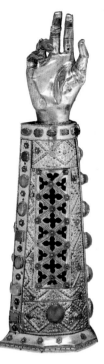

Arm Reliquary of Saint Babylas
Germany, Brunswick
1467
Silver, gilded silver, glass paste
stones, rock crystals, and one
amethyst on an oak core
Height 18⅝″
Purchased with Museum funds. 1951-12-1

According to an inventory of 1482, this life-size reliquary originally enshrined an arm bone of Saint Babylas, a bishop of Antioch martyred around A.D. 250. The object was designed for the relic to sit in the hollow chamber and be visible through the latticework door. Traditionally, vessels for relics were often made in forms appropriate to the sacred objects they contained. Here the hand, rendered in the naturalistic style of the late fifteenth century, makes a clear gesture of blessing, an activity associated with bishops that implies their benevolent communication with the faithful. This is one of a dozen arm reliquaries once part of the Guelph treasure, an important medieval sacral collection of over 140 relics and liturgical objects that was kept for centuries at the cathedral of Saint Blaise at Brunswick, Germany, until it was dispersed in the 1930s. DW

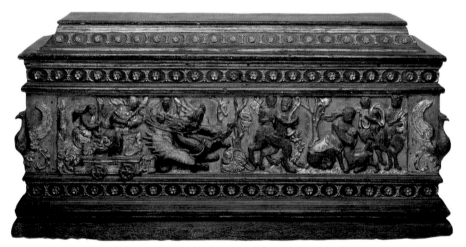

Marriage Chest Depicting Ceres Searching for Her Daughter, Proserpina
Italy, Tuscany
Late fifteenth century
Wood with painted and gilded plaster figures
36⅝ x 47⅛ x 28⅜″
Purchased with the Joseph E. Temple Fund. 1944-15-7

This marriage chest is one of a pair in the Museum depicting the abduction of Proserpina by Pluto, Roman god of the underworld. Here Proserpina's mother Ceres, goddess of agriculture, is searching for her daughter in a forest inhabited by satyrs, half-human and half-goat. Renaissance marriage chests, given to a bride by the groom's family, were frequently painted with stories from antiquity, but the Museum's pair is notable for its carved compositions derived from sculpted reliefs on ancient Roman burial containers called *sarcophagi*. The unknown designer of these narratives interpreted his ancient sources rather loosely, unlike the more classicizing approach of sixteenth-century artists. Chests as elaborate as this would have been displayed prominently and appreciated more for their decoration than their utility. The fifteenth-century Florentine reformer Girolamo Savonarola criticized the prevailing fashion for such mythological subjects for brides' chests, preferring instead more uplifting themes from the lives of saints. DW

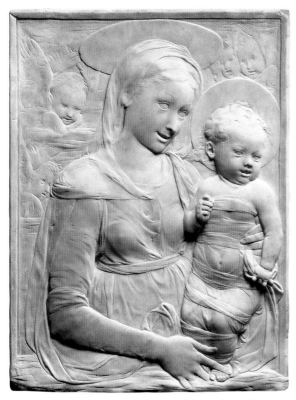

Desiderio da Settignano
Italian, active Florence,
1429/30–1464
Virgin and Child, c. 1455–60
Marble
23¾ x 18 x 2⅝"
Purchased from the Edmond Foulc
Collection with the W. P. Wilstach Fund
W1930-1-2

Among the creations of the great Renaissance sculptor Donatello was the *rilievo schiacciato,* or "flattened relief," a form of carving that depends on slight variations of a shallow surface and linear accents for its effects. Desiderio da Settignano was Donatello's most accomplished successor in this demanding technique. In Desiderio's hands the most familiar of Renaissance religious subjects has become an intimate image of almost unearthly refinement movingly evoked by the faintly smiling expressions of the Virgin and Child, both turned as if already engaging a viewer. This tour de force is achieved through the subtlest manipulation of the undulating surface of the marble. Details of the early history of the relief are unknown, but in 1877 Edmond Foulc purchased it from the hospital of Santa Maria Nuova in Florence. DW

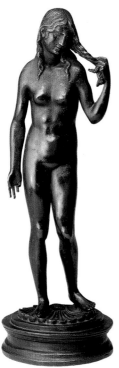

Adriano di Giovanni de' Maestri, called Adriano Fiorentino
Italian, active c. 1481–99
Venus, c. 1486–94
Bronze
Height 16⅜" (with base)
Purchased from the Edmond Foulc Collection with funds contributed by Mr. and Mrs. George D. Widener
1930-1-17

This *Venus* is a great rarity as both an early Renaissance statuette of a female nude and a work signed by the artist. Here the Latinized name of Adriano Fiorentino appears on the underside of the base. The demand for such work was related to the renewed Italian interest in ancient Greece and Rome during the second half of the 1400s, spurred by the ongoing rediscovery of antique sculpture. Adriano may well have based the pose of his figure in part on a specific Roman antiquity. Nevertheless, his goddess of love standing on a shell does not imitate ancient sculpture but rather shows the influence of Sandro Botticelli's painting *The Birth of Venus* from around 1486, now in the Uffizi in Florence. Adriano was famous for his expertise in casting bronze, amply demonstrated here in the flawless casting of the arms as part of the entire statuette and base. The sculpture's style is less unified, however, for the awkward lower legs and feet and Venus's rather mannish features are at odds with the beautiful form of her torso. DW

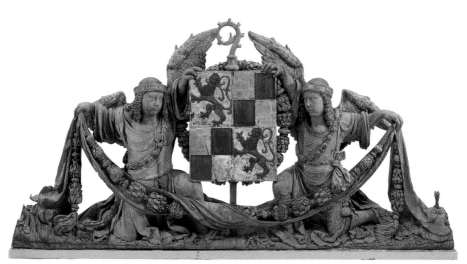

Armorial Shield Supported by Angels
France, Beauvais
Late fifteenth–early sixteenth century
Painted and gilded oak
39¾ x 43"
Purchased from the Edmond Foulc Collection with Museum funds
1930-1-166

Pairs of angels holding shields with coats of arms abound in French art and architecture from the decades around 1500. The arms on this shield have been identified as those of Antoine de Bois, abbot of Saint-Lucien in Beauvais from 1492 to 1537. Although the original location of the work is unknown, the sculpture's fine state of preservation argues for an interior placement. Throughout the early sixteenth century various stylistic currents coexisted in French art, sometimes appearing in a single work. In the Museum's sculpture, the complicated yet delicate folds of the angels' robes reveal familiarity with Italian style, while the carefully described swag and sober faces of the angels are examples of an indigenous French monumentality and naturalism. Certainly, too, the sculptor's expertise in carving the soft material of wood played an important part in this demonstration of complete mastery of the advanced styles of the time. DW

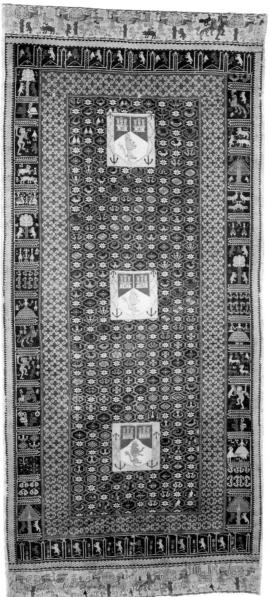

"Admiral" Heraldic Carpet
Spain
c. 1429–73
Wool
19′3/4″ x 8′91/8″
The Joseph Lees Williams Memorial Collection. 1955-65-21

It was the Muslims of North Africa who brought the craft of rug weaving to Spain, where it became an important industry in the twelfth century. This rug is one of the most distinctive early Spanish types: long narrow carpets with coats of arms woven into the design. It belongs to the famous group known as the "admiral" carpets because they bear the arms of Don Fadrique Enríquez de Mendoza (c. 1390–1473), twenty-sixth admiral of Castille. The Enríquez family donated this and other "admiral" rugs to the convent of Santa Clara in Palencia, which had been founded by Don Fadrique's father and was to be the burial place of the admirals of Castille. In this well preserved carpet the shields with the Enríquez arms stand out clearly against the shimmering patterned background. The top and bottom borders show illegible Arabic script in the angular Kufic style. Delightful secondary elements are provided by the unexplained designs in the long side borders that include birds, bears, wild-men combating animals, and women wearing enormously wide skirts. DW

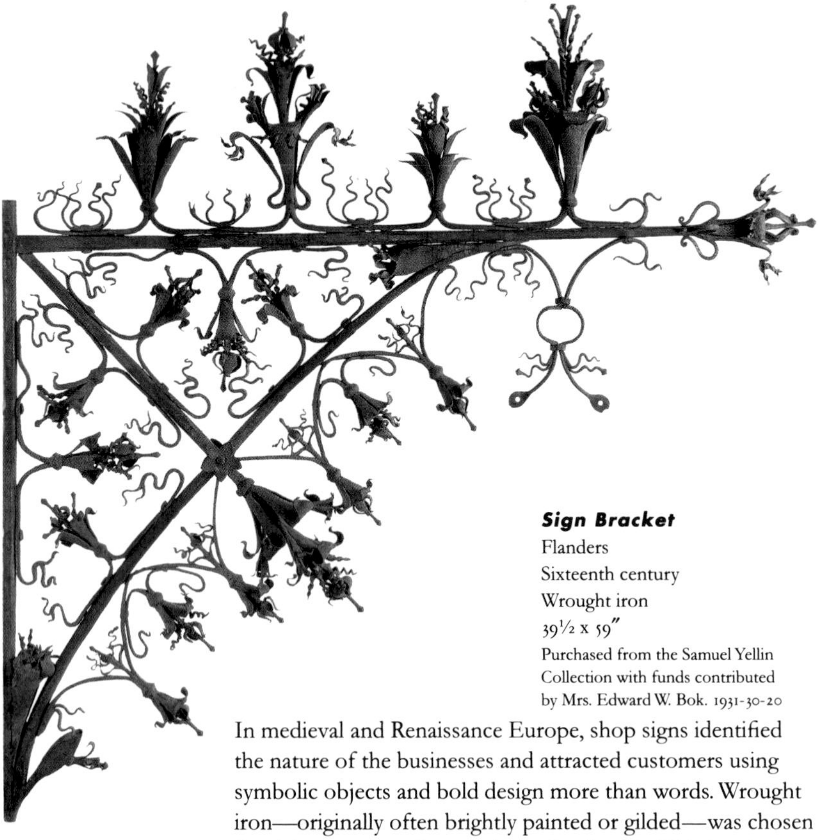

Sign Bracket
Flanders
Sixteenth century
Wrought iron
39½ x 59″
Purchased from the Samuel Yellin
Collection with funds contributed
by Mrs. Edward W. Bok. 1931-30-20

In medieval and Renaissance Europe, shop signs identified the nature of the businesses and attracted customers using symbolic objects and bold design more than words. Wrought iron—originally often brightly painted or gilded—was chosen for elaborate signs that needed to be durable. This bracket would have been attached to a building by means of the vertical bar, which allowed the sign to extend into the street over the heads of passersby. The identifying symbol providing the actual sign—now lost—would have hung free from the two eyeholes, thereby presenting a clear silhouette. This bracket is very close in design and ornamentation to one with the sign of a curry comb that was still to be seen in Bruges in Belgium at the be-ginning of this century. The Museum's piece was once in the collection of historic ironwork formed by Samuel Yellin, the brilliant Philadelphia craftsman who drew inspiration from such earlier metalwork. In several of his gates, he created variations of the conical vases with stylized bouquets seen here. DW

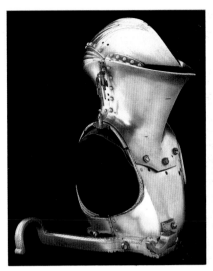

Armor for the German Joust (Stechzeug)
Made by Lorenz Helmschmid
(German, active Augsburg,
active 1467–1515)
c. 1494
Steel, brass
Height 24½″
Purchased with Museum funds
1930-63-1

Although medieval tournaments were mock combats intended to prepare knights for the rigors of battle, in effect they were almost as dangerous as warfare itself, and could involve troops of cavalry, infantry, and archers fighting with the same equipment used in actual battle. Over time the more violent aspects of tournaments were eliminated to create a pageant designed to display individual prowess. As part of this change tournament armor became increasingly specialized until it was suitable only for specific events, as exemplified by this late fifteenth-century German jousting armor known as a *Stechzeug,* used in a combat in which two horsemen armed with blunted lances scored points by breaking their own lances or unseating their opponent. Originally this *Stechzeug* included arm and hip defenses (now missing), whereas the legs, which were protected behind a large bolster placed across the horse's chest and shoulders, were left unarmored. The Museum's armor was commissioned by Archduke Maximilian of Austria from his court armorer Lorenz Helmschmid for the tournaments held in 1494 to celebrate Maximilian's wedding. DLR

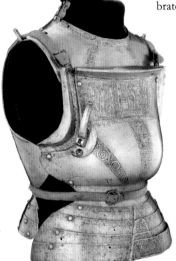

Elements of a Cavalry Armor
Italy, Milan
c. 1510
Etched and gilded steel
Height 19½″ (breastplate)
Bequest of Carl Otto von Kienbusch
1977-167-150

Despite its incomplete state, this armor is a significant example of finely made Italian cavalry armor *alla tedesca*—"in the German fashion"—that is highlighted by distinctive and delicate etched decoration. Milanese armorers had long produced armor in the style of other regions for sale abroad, but it was not until the late fifteenth century that they regularly incorporated German fashions into armors not intended for export. While in form this armor is modeled after a type introduced by German infantry and light cavalry who had campaigned in Italy during the late fifteenth and early sixteenth centuries, the etched decoration is purely Italian. The outstanding features are the classically inspired friezes of the Virgin and Child as well as saints at the top of the breastplate and backplate; beneath the breastplate frieze is a biblical quotation (in Latin)—"A bone of him shall not be broken" (John 19:36). These religious images and words not only served to ornament the armor but also offered the wearer the hope of divine protection. DLR

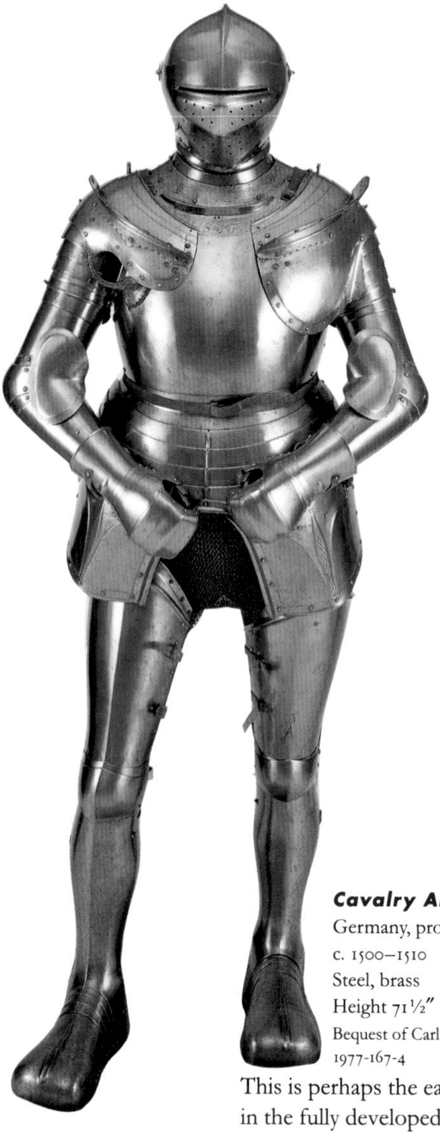

Cavalry Armor
Germany, probably Augsburg
c. 1500–1510
Steel, brass
Height 71½″
Bequest of Carl Otto von Kienbusch
1977-167-4

This is perhaps the earliest complete example of an armor in the fully developed German Renaissance style. Although it bears neither maker's mark nor date, its form, quality, and construction suggest that it was made in Augsburg, about

1500–1510. In southern Germany and Austria, this decade saw the completion of a transition in artistic trends, including armor styles, from late Gothic to early Renaissance, a movement encouraged by the close ties between Austria's ruling house of Habsburg and the courts of Burgundy and Milan. The subtle Northern Italian influence in this armor is seen in the uninterrupted smoothness and full contours of its surfaces, constituting a dramatic change from the attenuated lines and pierced ornament that distinguished the earlier German Gothic style. Certain technical features, such as the construction of the arm defenses, are also based on Italian types. The resulting armor, however, far exceeds its models and heralds a uniquely South German style, which in turn went on to influence armormaking throughout Europe. DLR

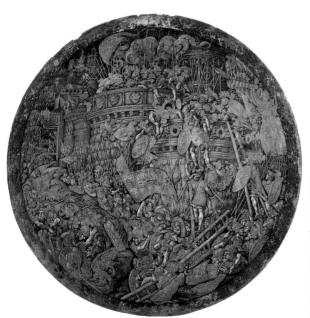

Parade Shield Depicting the Storming of New Carthage

Attributed to Girolamo di Tommaso da Treviso
(Italian, c. 1497–1544)
c. 1535
Wood, linen, gesso, gold, pigment
Diameter 24″
Bequest of Carl Otto von Kienbusch
1977-167-751

In the early sixteenth century, shields painted with biblical, mythological, or historical episodes became fashionable in Western Europe. This parade shield, one of the finest of its kind, is delicately painted with an intricate panorama of the storming of New Carthage, attributed to the North Italian artist Girolamo da Treviso after a drawing by Giulio Romano. Both the siege scene, which depicts an event that occurred in 209 B.C. during the Second Punic War, and the equestrian combat that decorates the reverse of the shield are executed in an unusual and delicate technique of applying shades of white, gray, and black over gold leaf, with details incised to reveal the gold beneath the pigments. Six similar shields that were probably made at the same time as this example can be also attributed to Girolamo da Treviso, who worked as a painter and sculptor for various noble Italian patrons. Unfortunately, neither the patron nor the reason for this commission is known, although the shield was once part of the famous armory of the Medici dukes of Florence. DLR

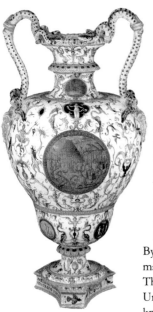

Vase
Made in the workshop of Orazio
Fontana (Italian, active Urbino,
active 1565–71)
Tin-enameled earthenware
(maiolica)
Height 21¼"
Purchased with the Bloomfield Moore
Fund and with Museum funds. 1944-15-3

By the mid-sixteenth century, Italians were unrivaled as
makers of elaborate vessels with intricate painted decoration.
This large vase is among a small number signed "made in
Urbino in the workshop of Orazio Fontana," one of the best-
known specialists in such ware. The basic materials are simple:
earthenware covered with lead glaze on which tin-enameled
colors are painted. The form, based on metalwork vases, combines a wheel-turned body with cast handles shaped as snakes.
The medallions show carefully painted biblical compositions,
including a scene of the Tower of Babel. In contrast is the
surrounding decoration with elements ranging from the non-
sensical to the outrageous, which combine to offer a lively
example of the grotesque style, the fanciful language of ornament inspired by ancient Roman wall painting first uncovered
in the 1480s. The Museum also owns a signed mate to this vase,
although the quality of their design and painting is very different. The unidentified painter of this example is notably superior, being among the most accomplished of later Renaissance
ceramic artists. DW

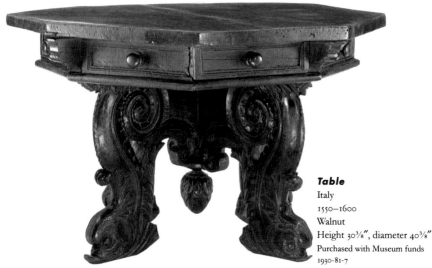

Table
Italy
1550–1600
Walnut
Height 30⅜", diameter 40⅜"
Purchased with Museum funds
1930-81-7

During the sixteenth century the octagonal table became an
established piece of domestic furniture in Italy. Renaissance

drawings and prints indicate that such tables in their grandest form were made in stone with tops ornamented with inlaid marble. A number of simpler examples in wood have survived, of which this piece—formerly in the famous Viennese collection of Albert Figdor—is one of the finest. To achieve symmetry, each side is fitted with what appears to be a drawer, although only four are functional. Most octagonal tables have supports shaped like lions' legs, which are derived from ancient precedents. Here, however, the legs are in the form of dolphins whose tails curve upward into a tight spiral; leaves and scrolls provide additional support. Dolphins are a Renaissance decorative motif that occasionally has symbolic or heraldic significance. Regardless of their possible meaning, these creatures serve as a distinctive element that contrasts with the geometric shape of the tabletop while enriching and lightening the overall design. DW

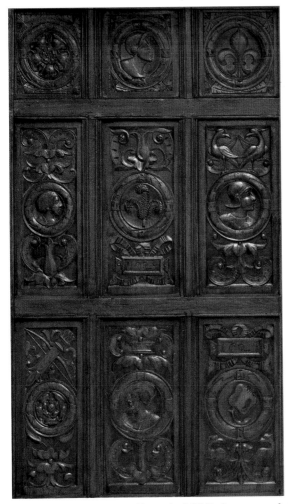

Paneling from Red Lodge
(detail)
England, Langley Park, West Wickham, Kent
1529
Oak
Purchased with funds contributed by William L. McLean. 1929-78-1

From the Middle Ages onward, domestic interiors in England were frequently clad with wood paneling that served to insulate as well as decorate. After 1500, the medieval linenfold pattern of paneling was replaced by the style seen on this example, called

"Romayne work," which incorporated profiles in roundels and Italianate motifs. Here some of the heads are distinguished by classically derived helmets, while others wear contemporary headdresses. The most telling elements are a rose, feathers, and a pomegranate, the emblems, respectively, of the royal house of Tudor, the Prince of Wales, and Catherine of Aragon, first wife of Henry VIII. The Museum's paneling is especially well carved and bears the early date of 1529, before such woodwork became common in country houses. Red Lodge, from which the paneling was taken in the 1920s, was a small structure whose early history is unknown. Although this woodwork could have been brought there from elsewhere, such elaborate decoration would have been suitable in a chamber intended for entertaining in a hunting lodge, which Red Lodge may have been originally. DW

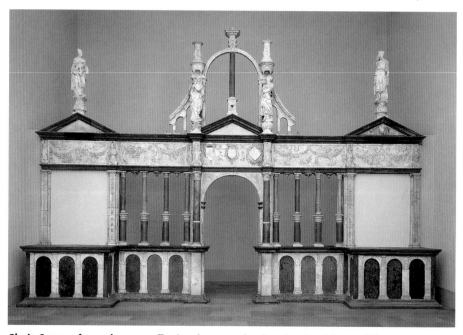

Choir Screen from the Chapel at the Château of Pagny
France, near Dijon
Dated 1536–38
Marble, alabaster
18′9″ x 28′5½″
Purchased from the Edmond Foulc Collection with funds contributed by Eli Kirk Price. 1930-1-84

During the 1530s, the chapel at the château of Pagny was embellished in successive redecoration campaigns by Philippe Chabot de Brion, admiral of France and governor of Burgundy, and his uncle by marriage, the cardinal of Givry (see opposite). One of the finest Renaissance monuments outside France, the screen originally crossed the chapel's nave in front of the main altar. The severe Italianate design of the choir screen recalls the remarkable contemporary facade of the church of Saint-Michel in Dijon, while the frieze, notably fanciful in composition and delicate in execution, demonstrates a direct knowledge of the styles of the Italian artists Rosso Fiorentino and Francesco Primaticcio, then working for Francis I of France at Fontainebleau. The frieze contains heraldic references to Chabot and the cardinal's family. The four statuettes of saints above are among the most sophisticated sculptures of their time. Appearing to move gracefully despite complicated poses and costumes, they are brilliant examples of the refined art that resulted when

French artists—here yet unidentified—melded a late Gothic Northern European heritage with the still developing Mannerist style imported from Italy. DW

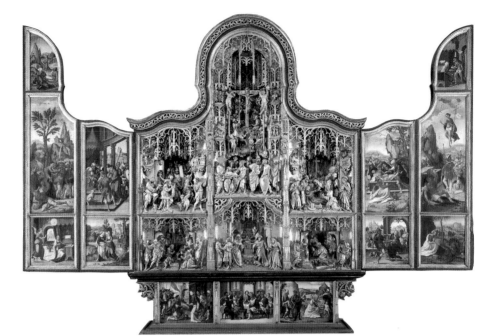

Altarpiece with Scenes of the Passion

Unknown Flemish artists, Antwerp
c. 1535
Gilded and painted wood sculptures, tempera-painted panels
Height 9'8"; width 14' (wings open), 7'6" (wings closed)
Purchased from the George Grey Barnard Collection with Museum funds
1945-25-117

This altarpiece was acquired for the high altar of the chapel at the château of Pagny during the redecoration projects of Admiral Chabot and the cardinal of Givry in the 1530s. After being removed from the chapel, its origin was forgotten until the altarpiece was reidentified in this Museum and, miraculously, rejoined with the Pagny choir screen (opposite). Such altarpieces were a specialty of Antwerp craftsmen who produced them for a widespread European market. Surprisingly, such elaborate and impressive works were not especially expensive, partly because they were made from prefabricated components and treated standardized themes such as the Passion of Christ, seen here. This example belongs to a group by an anonymous artist sometimes called the Master of the Oplinter Altar. While distinct from the Italianate and local styles found in other works at Pagny, the altarpiece, with its detailed, fully modeled, gilded figures, follows a taste for Northern art that was well established in Burgundy, which had historic links to the southern Netherlands. The paintings strike a contemporary note, echoing the then enormously influential style of Pieter Coecke (1502–1550), and would have lent a note of brilliant color to the interior of the stone chapel. DW

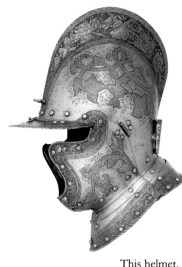

Burgonet
Attributed to Anton Peffenhauser
(German, active Augsburg,
active 1545–1603)
c. 1570
Etched and gilded steel
Height 13½″
Bequest of Carl Otto von Kienbusch
1977-167-119

This helmet, known as a burgonet, was part of a large and costly garniture, an armor ensemble that included a variety of extra pieces designed for specific types of field and tournament use. In this case the garniture consisted of a complete, heavy cavalry armor for man and horse, which, with the removal of some parts and the addition of others, could have been worn either for light cavalry duty or for different kinds of tournaments fought on horseback and on foot. The burgonet was part of the light cavalry equipment. Its open-faced design is derived from a helmet widely used by the Ottoman Turks, who controlled much of eastern Europe at the time. The burgonet is attributed to the long-lived and highly regarded Augsburg armorer Anton Peffenhauser. Its etched and gilded decoration, featuring gracefully entwined foliage and a vivid array of martial emblems, is a particularly fine example of the type of ornament found on Peffenhauser's best works. DLR

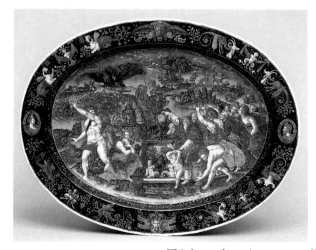

Platter Depicting the Sacrifice of Iphigenia
Made by Jean de Court (French,
active Limoges, active 1555–85)
c. 1575–85
Painted enamel on copper
16⅛ x 21⅝ x 2⅝″
Gift of the Women's Committee of the
Philadelphia Museum of Art. 1979-90-1

This large platter is an outstanding example of the enamel work produced by Jean de Court, the last of a family of enamelers working for the French court, who inscribed the piece *IC*. Originally, an object like this was made not for use but for display with many others in elaborate symmetrical arrangements. While enameled platters with similar borders exist, the narrative scene is apparently unique in Jean de Court's oeuvre. For the composition, he relied on a design from a print by Nicolas Béatrizet, a Frenchman active in Rome, who had labeled the subject as the ancient myth of Iphigenia, thus misunderstanding a now lost drawing by the Italian artist Francesco Salviati. In adapting the engraving to the oval format of the platter, Jean de Court interpolated a background landscape in the French style. While the colors on the front are mysterious and rich, the back is painted in grisaille, with subtle variations of black, white, and gray. ED

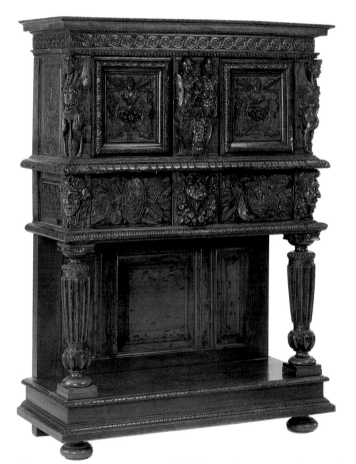

Dresser
Central France, region of Lyons and Burgundy
c. 1560–90, with later restorations
Walnut, oak
56¼ x 42⅛ x 18½"
Purchased from the Edmond Foulc Collection with Museum funds
1930-1-184

This dresser demonstrates the transformation of a late medieval form of furniture through the use of late Renaissance ornament. Providing areas on top and at bottom for the display of objects, it also has compartments that can be secured by lock and key. There is considerable variation in the carving. The side panels have simplified designs in flat relief. More elaborate is the carving on the lower doors, which are embellished with military trophies. The upper doors, still finer and even more expertly carved, could be the product of another, superior workshop. In highest relief are heads and chimeras in the corners, and the central pair of male and female warriors behind ancient arms. We can only speculate about the meaning of the decoration. Are the trophies a symbol for an assemblage of valuable objects that the cupboard was designed to contain? Could the warriors, who engage glances and link their arms, represent protagonists of an epic romance of the type so popular in the late Renaissance in France? DW

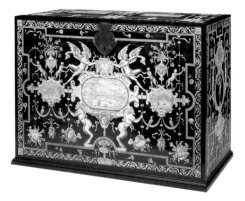

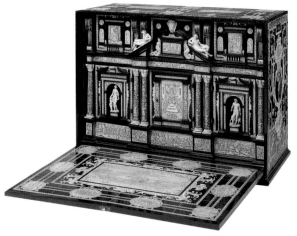

Writing Cabinet

Made in the workshop of Iacobus Fiamengo (Netherlandish, recorded in Naples, 1594–1602)
Scenes based on engravings by Dirck Coornhert (Netherlandish, 1519–1590), after designs by Maarten van Heemskerck (Netherlandish, 1498–1574)
c. 1600
Ebony with ivory inlay
24⅞ x 34⅝ x 16⅛"
Purchased from the Edmond Foulc Collection with Museum funds
1930-1-188

This writing cabinet, which was probably ordered as an official state gift, is decorated on the interior and exterior with scenes of military victories of Charles V, king of Spain and Holy Roman Emperor (1500–1558). The worldwide importance of Spain and its empire is celebrated by maps on the front of the cabinet that represent areas under Spanish rule or influence. This panel opens to reveal an interior, containing functional drawers, that imitates a building facade with a central image showing Charles V enthroned. The cabinet belongs to a luxurious furniture type produced by craftsmen who worked in collaboration using images from various sources. Its primary artisan was Iacobus Fiamengo, a Northern European active in Naples, which was then under Spanish control. Fiamengo must have been both well recognized and prolific: twenty-three cabinets are now known from his workshop. For the decorations on this piece he drew on compositions by Maarten van Heemskerck, which were available in the form of prints by a third Northern artist, Dirck Coornhert. DW

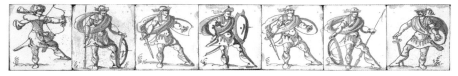

Tiles

The Netherlands, Rotterdam
1590–1625
Tin-enameled earthenware
Approximately 5⅛ x 5⅛" (each)
Gift of Anthony N. B. Garvan
1983-101-104–7, 109–12

Soldiers were a common sight in the Netherlands during the first half of the seventeenth century, and swaggering warriors such as those seen here became a favorite decoration on Dutch tiles. These exceptional tiles are masterfully painted in blue with black outlines and forceful details of orange and green; the Saracen archers wear turbans, billowing scarves, and caftans, while the Roman warriors sport plumed helmets, flowing sashes, and cuirasses. The figures are simplified variations of those conceived by the Netherlandish artist Hendrick Goltzius for his series of engravings entitled "The Roman Heroes" (c. 1586). However, although the warriors' costumes closely follow this model, the exotic dress of the archers is a departure from Goltzius's original. Many of the tiles produced between 1580 and 1625 were decorated with a repeat pattern composed of sixteen tiles that formed wall panels, but the absence of corner motifs on these examples indicate that they were made for use as baseboards. ES

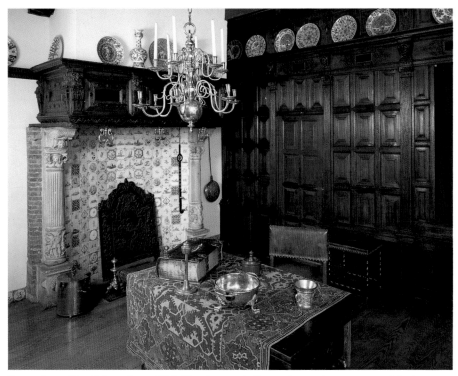

Room from Het Scheepje (The Little Ship)

The Netherlands, Haarlem
Early seventeenth century
Gift of Edward W. Bok. 1928-66-1

This Dutch room is from a house that was part of the brewery complex in Haarlem known as Het Scheepje (The Little Ship). In the early seventeenth century the house was owned by Dirk Dirick, a former skipper who became a successful brewer and burgomaster. Located on the first floor, this room was used for both daytime activities and sleeping, for a bed is built into the wall facing the windows, a typical arrangement even in prosperous Dutch households. Tiles depicting children, boats, birds, and flowers line the imposing fireplace, while the oak mantelpiece and paneling are carved with ornaments, such as pilasters and masks inlaid with ebony, adapted from pattern books of the period. The table is from the original room, whereas the cabinet, linen press, and chairs, although not from the room, are of the same period and style as the woodwork. Ceramic, brass, pewter, glass, and iron objects contribute to making this fine example of a domestic interior from the Golden Age of Holland one of the most appealing and complete period rooms in the Museum. ED

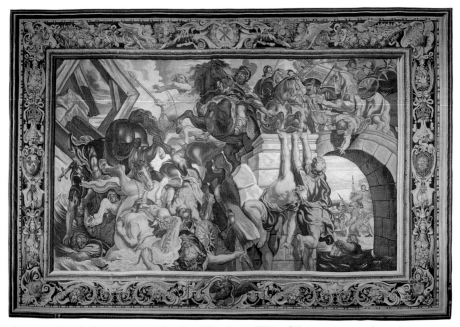

Tapestry Depicting the Battle of the Milvian Bridge
Designed by Peter Paul Rubens
(Flemish, 1577–1640)
Woven at the Comans–La Planche manufactory in the workshop of Hans Taye and Filippe Maëcht, Faubourg Saint-Marcel, Paris
1623–25
Wool, silk, gold and silver thread
15′ 11″ x 24′ 5″
Gift of the Samuel H. Kress Foundation. 1959-78-3

In 1625, King Louis XIII of France presented papal envoy Cardinal Francesco Barberini with a series of seven tapestries, designed by Peter Paul Rubens and woven in Paris, on the life of Constantine, the first Roman emperor to convert to Christianity. This tumultuous scene from the series represents the battle of the Milvian Bridge near Rome in A.D. 312, when Constantine defeated Maxentius to become sole emperor in the West. Upon returning to Rome, Cardinal Barberini established his own tapestry works and commissioned Pietro da Cortona to design additional tapestries for the Constantine series. Both Rubens and Cortona were great masters of the Baroque, a dynamic art ideally suited for just such large-scale, complicated narratives as the Constantine story. The Museum's thirteen Constantine tapestries from the Barberini collection, reunited by the Kress Foundation in the 1950s, permit a rare comprehensive demonstration of the Baroque style and form an appropriately sumptuous decoration for the second-floor balcony of the Museum's Great Stair Hall. DW

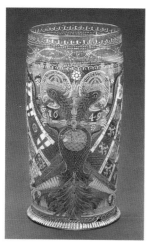

Imperial Eagle Beaker

South Germany, probably
Franconia
1649
Soda-lime glass with enamel
decoration
Height 8⅞″
The George H. Lorimer Collection
1938-23-69

The imperial eagle beaker *(Reichsadlerhumpen),* a type of tall,
cylindrical glass that generally had a cover and was decorated
with the double eagle of the Holy Roman Empire, was produced with little change in form or ornament for over 150 years
from the mid-sixteenth century onward; in the seventeenth
century the ability to paint a *Reichsadlerhumpen* in one-and-a-half
days was one of the skills necessary to become a master glassmaker. Used for important ceremonial occasions and often
the result of specific commissions, these glasses were probably
displayed on the cornice of the paneling of a room. Most of
these glasses, including this example, are dated; the earliest,
dated 1571, is in the British Museum in London. Here the
double eagle, with an orb on its chest, bears on its wings fifty-
six shields representing an idealized version of the constituent
parts of the Holy Roman Empire, to which its inscription
refers: "The Holy Roman Empire with all its members. The
year of our Lord 1649." DC

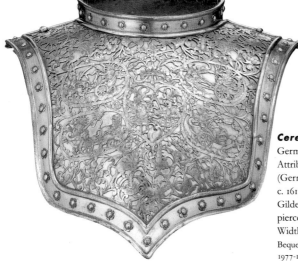

Ceremonial Gorget

Germany, Dresden
Attributed to Michael Botta
(German, c. 1592–1633)
c. 1617
Gilded copper, engraved and
pierced silver
Width 13¼″
Bequest of Carl Otto von Kienbusch
1977-167-218

In the sixteenth century plate armor for the neck, known as
a gorget, was worn beneath the breastplate and backplate to
support their weight while protecting a vulnerable part of the
body. During the seventeenth century gorgets were frequently
worn alone or over a sturdy leather garment called a buff coat.
Highly decorative gorgets, also worn without armor, functioned

as symbols of rank on ceremonial occasions. One of the earliest and most sumptuous examples of the latter type is this gorget made for the Prince Elector of Saxony Johann Georg I. The silver sheet overlaying the gorget's gilded copper base is delicately pierced and engraved with medallions depicting mythological personifications of the seven known planets, surrounded by lush foliage and armored figures. Engraved near the front neck rim are the imperial eagle and Bohemian lion, heraldic insignia of Emperor Matthias, suggesting that Johann Georg may have worn this gorget in honor of the emperor's state visit to Dresden in 1617. DLR

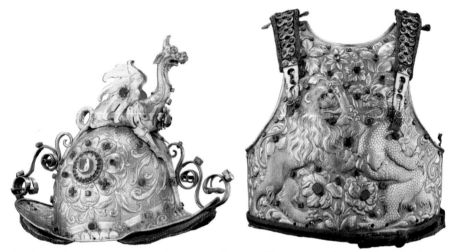

Costume Armor
Germany, Saxony
c. 1650–60
Embossed and gilded copper,
paste jewels, silk, gold
Height 13¼″ (helmet), 14″ (cuirass)
Bequest of Carl Otto von Kienbusch
1977-167-44

The prince electors of Saxony were famous throughout seventeenth- and eighteenth-century Europe for the splendor of their courts. State visits, religious festivals, and weddings were marked by celebrations that at times lasted weeks or even months, and included banquets, massive fireworks displays, theatrical performances, hunting parties, and tournaments. Rather than the bone-jarring melees of the past, however, these tournaments were lavishly costumed theatrical events, usually with a specific historical or mythological theme. The leading participants in these equestrian dramas frequently wore magnificent outfits that were a unique hybrid of court costume and pageant armor. Few such costume armors survive, but one of the most splendid is this helmet and cuirass (breastplate and backplate), originally owned by Johann Georg II, prince elector of Saxony from 1656 to 1681. This armor is made of embossed and gilded copper and set with paste jewels; the helmet is lined with embroidered red silk. Louis XIV of France and Carl XI of Sweden were among the few other rulers able to indulge in this rarefied and expensive form of noble theater. DLR

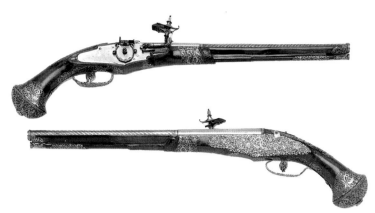

Pair of Wheellock Pistols

Italy, Brescia
c. 1650
Steel, walnut
Length 22½″ (each)
Bequest of Carl Otto von Kienbusch
1977-167-808

The wheellock, a relatively complex but versatile firing mechanism, was developed early in the sixteenth century. Well suited to hunting as well as warfare, wheellock firearms quickly found favor with the nobility, who created a demand for both functional and highly decorated weapons. In Italy much of this demand was satisfied by Brescia, the leading arms-making center. Foremost among the town's many famous gunmakers was the Cominazzo family of barrelsmiths, who flourished from the mid-sixteenth to the early nineteenth century. This fine pair of wheellock pistols, with barrels signed *Lazarino Cominazo,* was made about 1650, Brescia's peak period for the production of luxury arms. The name *Lazarino* actually belonged to one of the sixteenth-century founders of the dynasty, but continued to be used like a brand name by his successors for several generations. The gun locks were made and signed by the Brescian locksmith Jacopo Colombo. The pistols' intricately pierced mounts and slender gun stocks, by anonymous craftsmen, combine with the ornate Cominazzo barrels to create the light and elegant style that was the hallmark of Brescian firearms. DLR

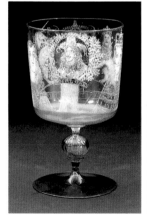

Royal Oak *Goblet*

England
1663
Colored soda-lime glass with
diamond-point engraved
decoration
Height 5⅝″
The George H. Lorimer Collection
1938-23-1

Celebrated as a rare example of seventeenth-century English glassmaking, an industry then in its infancy, this goblet is dated 1663 and engraved with portraits of Charles II of England and Catherine of Braganza, his queen consort. Set between their likenesses is a bust of the king wreathed in the branches of a tree inscribed *Royal Oak*. This alludes to an incident of 1651 in which Charles, defeated by Oliver Cromwell's anti-Royalist forces, hid in a large oak tree before escaping to France, returning to England only when the monarchy was restored in 1660. The goblet has an unbroken history of ownership from the seventeenth century, beginning with John Grenville, a close member of Charles's court. Its origin early in the king's reign coincides with the founding of a glasshouse at Greenwich near London by another of his loyal supporters, George Villiers, to whom the goblet has frequently been attributed. This was the trophy among the more than five hundred pieces of largely British and American glass that George Horace Lorimer bequeathed to the Museum in 1938. KBH

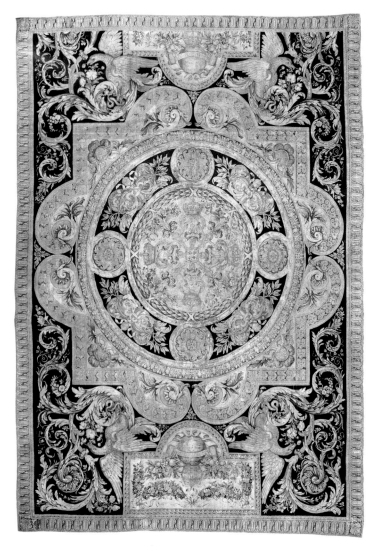

Carpet
Woven at the royal Savonnerie manufactory (Paris, established 1627)
1670–77
Wool, linen
26′3″ x 18′6″
Bequest of Eleanore Elkins Rice
1939-41-27

This is one of ninety-three carpets commissioned by Louis XIV for the long gallery that joined the Louvre and Tuileries palaces in Paris. Among the grandest weaving projects in European history, the scheme required carpets of the unprecedented length of over 29 feet each to be laid in two rows along the 1,450-foot gallery. Using specially built large looms housed in newly constructed buildings, two rival workshops in the royal Savonnerie carpet manufactory worked simultaneously on the project from 1668 to 1685. In scale and splendor the suite of carpets is comparable to the king's other celebrated achievements, such as the gardens at Versailles. The center of the present carpet, twenty-sixth in the series, is filled with four of the king's double-*L* monograms intertwined beneath crowns; a crowned globe inscribed with the royal motto and flanked by eagles appears at each end. This carpet, which has been shortened at one end with the border reattached, was one of a pair of the same design. KBH

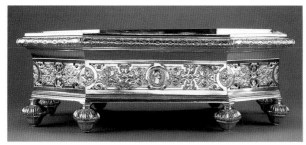

Stand
Made by Elie Pacot (French, 1657–1721)
1709–10
Silver
Length 15⁷⁄₁₆″
Gift of Henry P. McIlhenny. 1961-196-1

This silver stand formed part of a nineteen-piece ensemble of table decorations known as a *surtout de table*. Similarly decorated with portrait medallions, strapwork, laurel husks, and rosettes, the *surtout* comprised a centerpiece, four oval stands, a triangular pair, and four octagonal and eight hexagonal stands (including this example), now divided among various collections. The elements of such a grand *surtout* would have been artfully arranged in calculated patterns on a very large table, each stand filled with flowers, brioche, fruits, or tablewares, according to the occasion. The fashion set in Paris by Louis XIV for such elaborate and ritualistic dining was followed by aristocrats and the newly prosperous elsewhere in Europe. This stand, like the rest of the service, bears the mark of the Lille silversmith Elie Pacot and letters for the years 1709–10, when Lille was occupied by English, Dutch, and Austrian troops, who are known to have placed large orders for silver. The complete *surtout* belonged to the English Lord Gwydir, and it was to such clients that Pacot owed his financial success. KBH

Ceremonial Partisan
France
c. 1670–80
Blued gilded and damascened iron
Length 87¼″
Bequest of Carl Otto von Kienbusch
1977-167-406

This elegant polearm, of a type known as a partisan, was probably carried by an officer in the Guards of the Sleeve, one of the elite bodyguard units of Louis XIV of France. Such polearms, which were made in a series with matching, elaborately decorated heads, were traditionally carried by the ceremonial guards of European monarchs, the upper echelon of the nobility, and the highest-ranking churchmen. This example is decorated with personal symbols of Louis XIV rather than the heraldic insignia usually found on these weapons. A prominent feature is the radiant head of Apollo, god of the sun, a favorite emblem of Louis XIV, the Sun King; it is surrounded by his motto. Below is the figure of Hercules—long associated with the French monarchy—before a column, representing the king's military power. The design of the partisan has been attributed to the influential court ornament designer Jean Berain, who was also responsible for the decoration of royal firearms. DLR

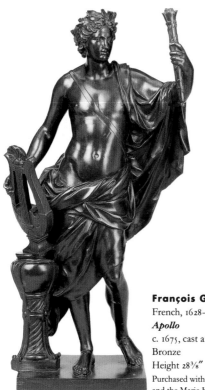

François Girardon
French, 1628–1715
Apollo
c. 1675, cast after 1715
Bronze
Height 28⅜″
Purchased with the Fiske Kimball Fund
and the Marie Kimball Fund. 1976-39-1

This statuette is rare in being a well-documented French bronze. A terracotta model of the subject by François Girardon appears in a print depicting objects in his possession and was mentioned in an inventory of the sculptor's studio drawn up after his death. One version of Girardon's *Apollo* in bronze—perhaps this very piece—was at the palace of Schleissheim in Germany by 1722, evidence that bronze casts of the terracotta were made soon after the sculptor's death in 1715. The subject represents the sun god, symbol of Louis XIV of France, who provided most of Girardon's commissions. The sculptor almost certainly began with a compositional sketch by Charles Le Brun, first painter to the king. The size and detail of this work are those of a finished model to be shown to a patron for approval. The *Apollo* seems not to have been carried out on a large scale, but the dignified style of this bronze exemplifies the courtly art created for Louis XIV's palace at Versailles. DW

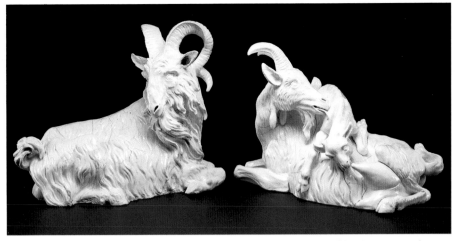

Pair of Goats
Modeled by Johann Joachim
Kaendler (German, 1706–1775)
Made at the royal porcelain
factory, Meissen, Germany
(established 1710)
c. 1732–33
Porcelain
21 x 28 x 13" (he-goat)
18 x 27¼ x 14" (she-goat)
Bequest of John T. Dorrance, Jr.
1989-22-1, 2

Among the largest porcelains produced by the Meissen factory
near Dresden, these life-size goats display numerous fire cracks
that attest to the enormous technical challenge they presented
to an industry still in its infancy. In 1710, under the sponsorship
of Augustus the Strong of Saxony, Meissen was the first European factory to produce hard-paste porcelain successfully. To
house the factory's best products as well as his celebrated collection of Chinese and Japanese porcelains that had inspired
the Meissen experiments in porcelain-making, Augustus
planned a palace-museum in Dresden, for which he commissioned hundreds of life-size white porcelain animals and birds,
including these goats. The furnishing of the palace was left
unfinished at Augustus's death in 1733, but the factory continued to supply porcelain animals to his son and successor Augustus III. Most of the figures delivered to the palace remained
there, save for those sent abroad as gifts by the Saxon heads
of state and those sold from the Saxon state collection in 1919,
which may include the present she-goat. KBH

Cup-Hilted Rapier
Made by Francesco Maria Rivolta
(Italian, active Milan, documented
1678), c. 1670–80
Steel
Length 46¾"
Bequest of Carl Otto von Kienbusch
1977-167-616

By the early sixteenth century a European nobleman customarily wore a sword while in civilian dress. To defend his unarmored hand, more protective sword hilts were developed,
which, when fitted with a narrow blade intended for thrusting
more than cutting, became known as a rapier. This lethal
weapon was also the most prominent accessory to a nobleman's

costume and therefore was fashionably decorated. By the seventeenth century the use of rapiers was being taught in several styles, or schools, of fencing. The Spanish school favored a characteristic type of cup-hilted rapier used with a left-handed dagger. It was practiced not only in Spain but also in areas under Spanish rule, such as the Kingdom of Naples and the Duchy of Milan. This ornate example was made in Milan and signed by the Milanese swordmaker Francesco Maria Rivolta. Its sturdy steel cup is chiseled with a swirling floral design that shows the strong influence of contemporary metalwork from Brescia. Cup-hilted rapiers remained popular in Spanish territories until the late eighteenth century, long after the use of rapiers had gone out of fashion elsewhere. DLR

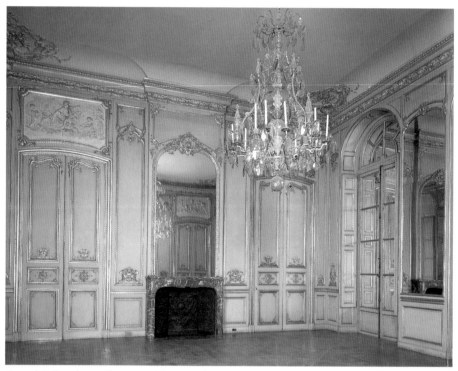

Grand Salon from the Château de Draveil
France
c. 1735
Purchased with Museum funds
1928-58-1

This grand salon was the centerpiece of the magnificent château that Marin de la Haye built at Draveil, about twelve miles south of Paris. De la Haye purchased the property in 1720, only two years after he had obtained the lucrative office of royal tax collector. Provided with sufficient means to establish himself in society, De la Haye transformed the simple house he found at Draveil into a large château with spacious and varied gardens. At the axial center of the house was the grand salon, which he used as the state room for formal receptions. Decorated to demonstrate his wealth and status with immense mirrors, carved and gilded paneling, and sculpted reliefs, the salon opened through three round-headed doors onto a balcony that overlooked the celebrated park. When De la Haye died without direct heirs, Draveil passed to various private owners, the last of whom sold the woodwork of the grand salon to the Parisian art dealer from whom the Museum purchased it in 1928. KBH

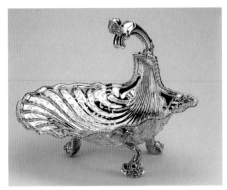

Basket
Made by Paul de Lamerie (English,
born Holland, 1688–1751)
1743–44
Silver
10½ x 14 x 10¾"
Gift of Mrs. Widener Dixon and
George D. Widener. 1959-151-6

Silver baskets such as this for holding cake or bread were first
made in the sixteenth century. They were given their most
imaginative treatment in the eighteenth century by silversmiths
such as Paul de Lamerie, head of one of the most celebrated
English silver workshops of the day, which produced numerous
baskets of various shapes between 1724 and 1751. This example
belongs to a group of silver objects, bearing Lamerie's mark and
dating from about 1737 to about 1745, that are boldly sculptural
in style and that may be the work of an unidentified modeler
working for Lamerie, perhaps continental in origin. Several of
the decorative elements on this basket, including the scallop-
shell shape, mermaid handle, and dolphin supports, were derived from sixteenth- and seventeenth-century silver. The form
of this basket proved very popular, and was copied by other
English silversmiths both before and after Lamerie's death. DC

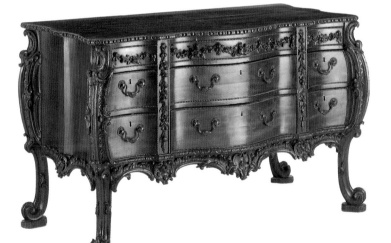

Commode
Attributed to Thomas Chippendale
(English, 1718–1779)
c. 1755–60
Mahogany, oak, pine, ormolu
33 x 55 x 25½"
Purchased with the John D. McIlhenny
Fund. 1941-73-1

This commode from Raynham Hall in Norfolk, England, has
long been considered one of the great masterpieces of English
eighteenth-century furniture because of its innovative design
and fine craftsmanship. It is attributed to Thomas Chippendale
on the basis of its close similarity to an engraving of a "French
Commode Table" in his *Gentleman and Cabinet-Maker's Director*
of 1754, the high quality of its carving and workmanship, and a
construction method that is typical of his work. The attribution

is further strengthened by the fact that Chippendale is known to have made furniture for relatives of the Townshends of Raynham Hall and that his son worked for the Townshends themselves. However, because Chippendale did not label his furniture and no bill or other evidence survives, the attribution cannot be definitively confirmed. Sold at auction by the Townshends in the 1920s, the commode was owned successively by two great twentieth-century collectors, the Englishman H. H. Mulliner and the American William Randolph Hearst, who sold it to the Museum in 1941. JHMS

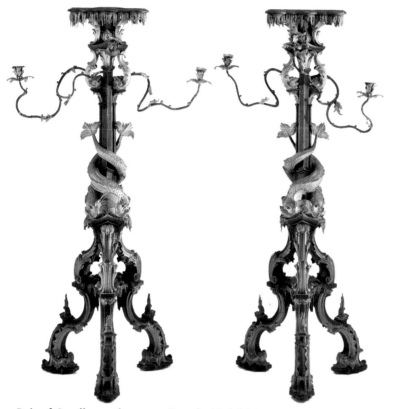

Pair of Candlestands

Attributed to Thomas Johnson
(English, 1714–1778)

c. 1757

Limewood, glazed and painted over gilding, with iron and composition candle arms fitted with gilded brass cups and drip pans

62½ x 37 x 22"

Purchased with Museum funds
1950-83-3, 4

Carved with dolphins, grottoes, stalactites, and stalagmites, and with twisting, branchlike arms ending in candle cups shaped like oak leaves, these elaborate candlestands embody the imaginative naturalism of the eighteenth-century Rococo style in England. They are from a set of four designed to flank a pier table in the Long Gallery of Hagley Hall, Worcestershire, the English country house of George, 1st Baron Lyttelton. These candlestands are most closely related to two designs published in the London carver Thomas Johnson's collections of designs of 1758, and were probably designed by him and carved in his Soho workshop. Johnson most likely also designed the four wall sconces in the same rustic style from Hagley Hall's Long Gallery that are in the Museum's collection. JHMS

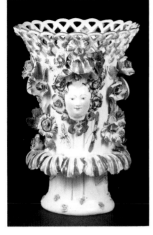

Vase

Made at the Derby porcelain
factory (Derby, England,
1756–1848)
c. 1765
Porcelain with overglaze enamel
decoration
Height 6¹¹⁄₁₆"
Gift of Sarah McLean Williams
in memory of Mrs. William L. McLean
1942-101-70

Although porcelain may have been produced in the English
town of Derby as early as 1750, the date of the formation of the
Derby porcelain factory has been established as 1756, the year
that the output of the royal porcelain factory at Meissen, outside Dresden, Germany, began to diminish because of the
Seven Years' War (1756–63). Determined to take advantage of
the gap left by Meissen, William Duesbury, part-proprietor and
manager of the Derby factory, advertised Derby as a "second
Dresden." Much of the decoration of this charming vase, including the applied masks and flowers, painted butterflies and
other insects, and open basketwork rim, shows the Meissen
influence. These beaker-like vases, popularly known as "frill"
vases because of the frill-like ornament above the foot, were often sold in sets that were used as chimneypiece garnitures. DC

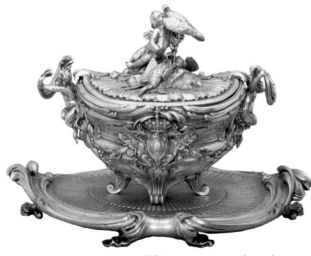

Soup Tureen and Stand

Made by François-Thomas
Germain (French, 1726–1791)
1759
Gilded silver
15⁷⁄₈ x 24 x 17³⁄₄"
Purchased with Museum funds
1954-81-1a–c

This soup tureen and stand are part of the so-called Paris
table service of some three hundred pieces commissioned by
Empress Elizabeth of Russia from the Parisian silversmith
François-Thomas Germain around 1756. Finished in 1761, the
complete service was finally delivered after Elizabeth's death
to her successor, Catherine the Great, who added Russian-made
pieces to the set later in the century. With their curvaceous lines
and asymmetrical composition, the tureen and stand reflect
the popular Rococo style, while the richness of their sculptural
decoration and the scale of their form befit a royal patron.

Germain counted among his clients other members of Europe's nobility, including King Joseph of Portugal, to whom he had delivered a similarly decorated service in 1756–57. In the nineteenth century the "Paris service" began to be dispersed, and in 1930–31 some of the remaining pieces, including this tureen, were sold by the Soviet government. DC

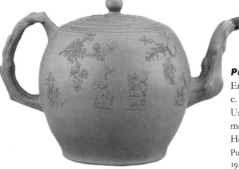

Punch or Tea Pot
England, Staffordshire
c. 1765
Unglazed red stoneware with mold-applied decoration
Height 7½"
Purchased with the Baugh-Barber Fund
1922-24-12a,b

The mid-eighteenth-century English taste for the arts of Asia is strongly apparent in this capacious punch pot made of unglazed red stoneware, which was produced in England after about 1684 in imitation of the Chinese ceramic. The naturalistic treatment of its handle and spout and the figures that ornament its body likewise reflect the English fashion for things Chinese. Like much of the red stoneware produced in England at the time, it also bears a pseudo-Chinese seal mark, which has not been identified as belonging to a particular factory. Red stoneware was especially popular for objects associated with the drinking of tea, which the English had been importing from Asia since the seventeenth century. Although this particular pot was primarily intended for punch, which in the eighteenth century was served hot from pots as well as bowls, pots of such a size were also used for serving large quantities of tea. DC

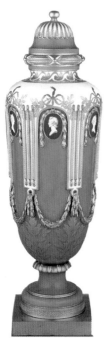

Vase
Made at the royal porcelain factory, Sèvres, France (established Vincennes, 1740)
c. 1768–69
Porcelain with enamel and gilt decoration
Height 23¾"
Bequest of Eleanore Elkins Rice
1939-41-36Aa,b

This vase and its mate are among the forty-one pieces of eighteenth-century Sèvres porcelain that decorated the drawing room of Eleanore Elkins Rice's town house on Fifth Avenue in New York, which in 1939 was bequeathed to the Museum, where it is installed in its entirety. The vase is divided vertically in six panels, each containing a classically inspired grisaille portrait medallion. This type of simulated cameo ornament was introduced at Sèvres in 1768 and has been attributed to Jean-

Baptiste-Etienne Genest, head of the painters' workshop, who was responsible for the design and decoration of some of the factory's most important pieces, including a famous dinner service with similar portrait medallions that was commissioned in 1776 by Catherine the Great of Russia. DC

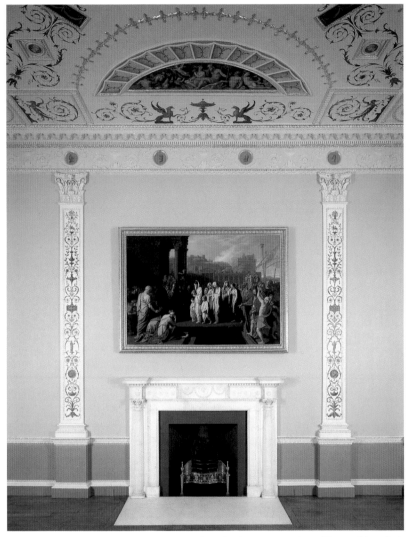

Drawing Room from Lansdowne House

England, London
c. 1766–75
Designed by Robert Adam
(Scottish, 1728–1792)
Painted on canvas by Giovanni
Battista Cipriani (Italian,
1727–1785); on paper by Antonio
Zucchi (Italian, 1726–1795)
Gilded by Joseph Perfetti (Italian,
active London, active 1760–78)
Gift of Graeme Lorimer and Sarah
Moss Lorimer in memory of George
Horace Lorimer. 1931-104-1

With its fanciful decoration of scrolling and interlacing figures and foliage in the antique style, the drawing room from Lansdowne House in London is an archetypal example of the work of the architect Robert Adam, who so popularized this type of Neoclassical ornament that it has since been identified with his name. Adam provided his client, the Earl of Shelburne, with the designs for the room, and a team of artists and craftsmen executed Adam's plans in Shelburne's grand and fashionable house over a period of years. Yet when the house was first occupied in 1767, the drawing room was still unfinished. In fact, the room's most expensive decorations, the gilding and paintings, were completed only some four years later. Lord

Shelburne used the drawing room to display his important collection of paintings and antique sculpture as well as to entertain many of the most brilliant men of the age. Britain's prime minister in 1782–83, he helped negotiate the treaty that ended the American Revolution and was created 1st Marquis of Lansdowne for his services. KBH

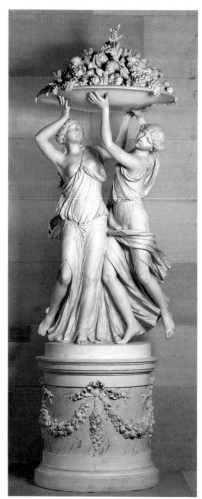

Claude Michel, called Clodion
French, 1738–1814
Nymphs Holding Aloft a Platter Charged with Fruit
c. 1785–93
Plaster
Height 7′5½″ (without base)
Gift of Eva Roberts Stotesbury in memory of Edward T. Stotesbury
1938-24-7

Until the mid-eighteenth century, French houses did not often have a room specifically designated for dining. After the 1770s, however, fashionable clients commissioned dining rooms with lavish decoration that sometimes included large sculptures. This group of nymphs, along with a pendant group in the Museum and an identical pair in the Musée des Arts Décoratifs in Paris, was made for four corner niches in the dining room of the Parisian town house of the count of Botterel-Quintin at number 44, rue des Petites-Ecuries. The dining room was a masterpiece of its time. The painted ceiling was devoted to the four seasons, a theme loosely related to the fruits borne by these plaster nymphs. The details throughout the room were in the popular Neoclassical style. Clodion was the great master of creating sculptures that combined an antique flavor with a sense of movement and lightly erotic charm. The nymphs' dancing poses and apparently weightless burden make the viewer forget Clodion's sculptural prowess in realizing these graceful figures at nearly the scale of life. DW

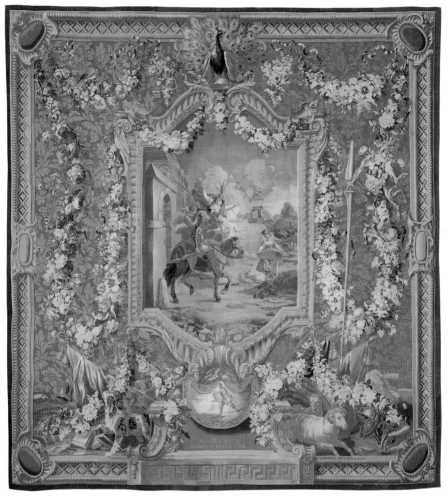

Tapestry Depicting Don Quixote Guided by Folly

Central composition after a painting of c. 1716 by Charles Coypel (French, 1694–1752)
Woven at the Gobelins manufactory, Paris, in the workshop of Jacques Neilson (French, 1714–1788)
1780–83 (from the seventh series, woven 1762–87)
Wool, silk
12′2″ x 11′8″
Gift of Mrs. Widener Dixon. 1945-90-1

This tapestry depicts the famous passage from Miguel de Cervantes's novel *Don Quixote* in which the knightly hero sets off to attack a windmill, which he sees as an armed giant. In the painting on which this composition is based, Charles Coypel took liberties with the text by adding the peasant woman Dulcinea (Don Quixote's Empress of La Mancha) and an airborne figure of Folly brandishing a jester's head. This personification is a clever play on the convention of including a figure of Victory in scenes of departing warriors. This witty approach extends to the border, where a monkey brandishes a lance and military trophies are overturned by fleeing sheep and obscured by luxuriant swags of flowers. Light-hearted and sumptuous, the Don Quixote tapestries produced by the Gobelins manufactory in Paris were among the most popular weavings of the eighteenth century. Coypel created twenty-eight compositions based on the novel, and nine series were ordered from 1720 to 1794. During the French Revolution, even the censors approved the series as representing the follies of the deposed aristocracy. DW

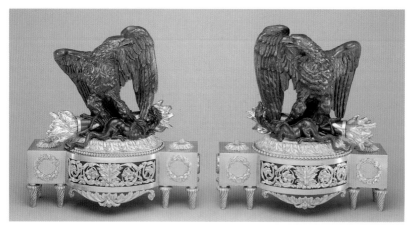

Pair of Andirons

Made by Pierre Gouthière
(French, 1732–1813)
c. 1781
Patinated bronze with gilt
decoration
17½ x 16½ x 8½" (each)
Bequest of Eleanore Elkins Rice
1939-41-25a,b

These andirons, decorated with an eagle and salamander, were
among the gilded bronze objects made by Pierre Gouthière for
the duchess of Mazarin, whose Paris town house was sumptu-
ously redecorated at vast expense in the 1760s and 1770s. The
andirons were created for the fireplace of the grand salon, for
which Gouthière had already supplied ornamental sculpture
as well as fittings for a console table and a pair of pedestals.
Celebrated for his skill in finishing cast bronze and for creating
varied surface textures with mat and highly burnished gilding,
Gouthière defended his high price for the andirons by describ-
ing each element that required chasing, mounting, soldering,
and repairing as well as the especially requested mat gold with
overgilding, which amounted to half the total cost. Like other
artisans who worked for the duchess, Gouthière probably remained unpaid: she died covered with debts, and he, who had
to advance the costly materials he used, had to declare bank-
ruptcy and close his workshop in 1787. Other versions of the
andirons include a pair in the Mobilier National, Paris. KBH

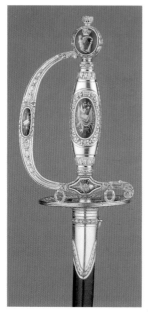

Presentation Sword

Made by James Morisset
(English, active London, active
c. 1766–c. 1800)
Hallmarked 1798–99
Gilded silver, enamel, steel, leather
Length 40"
Bequest of Carl Otto von Kienbusch
1977-167-648

For centuries the sword was both the primary weapon and the
universal symbol of Europe's noble classes. But as firearms
became more efficient, the sword's importance on the battle-
field gradually diminished, although its symbolic value remained
and even increased. Swords had long been bestowed as gifts,
and by the third quarter of the eighteenth century governments
and civic groups began presenting specially decorated swords
to individuals to commemorate acts of heroism. Of typically
high quality is this example, given to Major General Henry
Johnson for valor at the battle of Ross, fought on June 5, 1798,

during the Irish wars. The focal point of such a sword is usually the hilt, which was frequently made by a goldsmith rather than a cutler. Here the hilt, made by the noted London goldsmith and jeweler James Morisset, is of gilded silver in the latest Neoclassical style, set with vibrantly blue enamel plaques that prominently display the arms of Ireland. A dedicatory inscription is engraved on the shell guard, which separates the blade from the grip. DLR

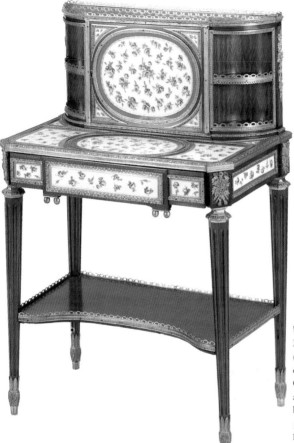

Writing Table
Made by Martin Carlin
(French, c. 1730–1785)
c. 1777–80
Oak with satinwood, tulipwood, and mahogany veneers; gilded bronze mounts; porcelain plaques
39 x 27⁹⁄₁₆ x 16¹⁄₈″
Bequest of Eleanore Elkins Rice
1939-41-6

This writing table, or bonheur-du-jour (literally, "happiness of the day"), was made by Martin Carlin, a leading Parisian cabinetmaker of the second half of the eighteenth century. Working primarily on commissions from dealers rather than for individual clients, he made high-quality furniture such as this table, ornamented with exotic veneers and porcelain or lacquer plaques. The fourteen porcelain plaques seen here were made at Sèvres in 1776, and most are dated and signed by the factory's flower painters Jean-Baptiste Tandart and Vincent Taillandier. Bonheurs-du-jour are typically small scale, portable, and dual purpose, often serving as both writing and toiletry tables, with numerous drawers and compartments to hold the necessary tools. This table is fitted out as a desk with a hinged writing panel and compartments for ink and pens in the drawer. JHMS

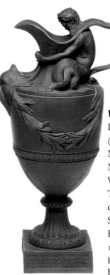

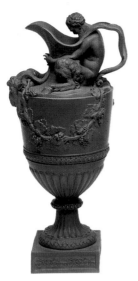

Wine and Water Ewers
Designed by John Flaxman, Sr.
(English, 1726–1795), after Sigisbert
Michel (French, 1728–1811)
Made at the factory of Josiah
Wedgwood (Etruria, Stoke-on-
Trent, England, established 1759)
c. 1785
Stoneware
Height 15¼″ (wine ewer),
15″ (water ewer)
Purchased with the Bloomfield Moore
Fund. 1912-226, 227

On March 25, 1775, the plastermaker John Flaxman, Sr., billed
the Wedgwood pottery firm for the models for this pair of
ewers, which are among the most elaborately sculpted pieces
ever produced by the factory. One, ornamented with satyr, goat,
and grapevine, was to be used for wine; the other, decorated
with triton, dolphin, and kelp, was to hold water. Flaxman had
been providing Wedgwood with models and casts since 1771,
usually copied from classical, French, and Italian sources. These
ewers, for example, were copied from a pair of plaster vases
that the French sculptor Sigisbert Michel had exhibited in Paris
in 1774. Their design proved to be popular from the eighteenth
to the twentieth century, and was produced in various materials,
including silver, bronze, and the fine-grained black stoneware
(known as basalt) seen here. KBH

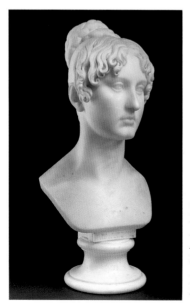

Bertel Thorvaldsen
Danish, 1770–1844
*Portrait Bust of the Honorable
Mrs. Pellew,* 1817
Marble
Height 22⅛″ (with base)
Purchased with funds bequeathed by
Walter E. Stait. 1994-1-1

Bertel Thorvaldsen, a Dane active in Rome for much of his
career, was the most sought-after portrait sculptor in Europe

in the early nineteenth century. This bust was carved when the sitter, a celebrated English beauty, was in Italy on her wedding trip. Thorvaldsen derived the design from ancient Roman portraits, but in this mature work all specific ancient references have been transcended, achieving a natural likeness in contemporary style. The lower contour of the bust corresponds to the neckline of an early nineteenth-century dress, and the coiffure is also in a fashion of the day. The grasp of likeness, linear elegance, and fine granular marble surface are hallmarks of Thorvaldsen's art. But this bust belongs to a rarer category of his work in which the sculptor, inspired by the sitter, attains an image of ineffable ideal beauty. Such timelessness and affecting refinement were among the highest aims of the Neoclassical style of which Thorvaldsen was a leading figure. DW

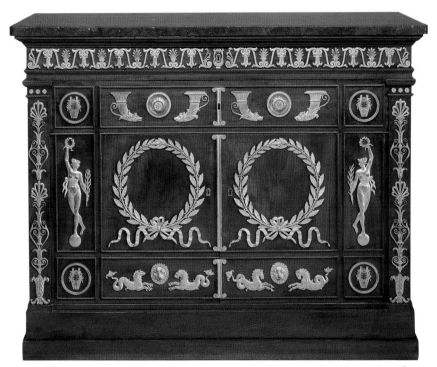

Writing Cabinet
Made by Georges Jacob
(French, 1739–1814) and
François-Honoré-Georges Jacob,
called Jacob-Desmalter (French,
1770–1841)
1810–13
Mahogany, oak, marble, gilded
bronze mounts
46¼ x 60 x 25″
The Henry P. McIlhenny Collection
in memory of Frances P. McIlhenny
1986-26-86

Georges Jacob, a prominent French cabinetmaker whose career spanned the rules of Louis XV, Louis XVI, and Napoleon I, was the founder of a dynasty of French cabinetmakers, foremost among whom was his son Jacob-Desmalter, with whom he worked in partnership between 1803 and 1813. This writing cabinet, fitted with shelves and a drop-front drawer that served as a desk, was made by their firm sometime after 1810. A massive cabinet with rich mahogany veneers, a thick marble top, and gilded bronze mounts, the commode is typical of the large mahogany case furniture with classically inspired ornament, such as the laurel wreaths and lyres seen here, that was fashionable during the Napoleonic Empire (1804–14). Napoleon, eager for his empire to be compared to those of Greece and Rome, adopted classical motifs as his symbols and encouraged their use in furniture. JHMS

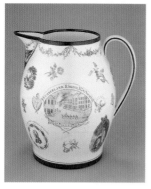

Jug

Probably made at the Herculaneum
Pottery (Liverpool, England,
1796–1841)
c. 1814
Creamware with transfer-printed
decoration
Height 15½"
Bequest of R. Wistar Harvey. 1940-16-113

The relatively inexpensive technique of transfer printing, in
which a print from a copper or steel plate is applied to an
enamel or ceramic object while the ink is wet and then fixed
by firing, was introduced in England in the mid-eighteenth
century. Although transfer-printed objects were often decorated
with more than one scene, this large barrel-shaped jug, one of
nearly four hundred pieces of such ceramics given to the Museum by R. Wistar Harvey in 1940, is remarkable for its twenty-
one designs. It was probably made in Liverpool, a major center
for the production of transfer-printed ceramics. Because the
city was a port of call for American vessels, its enterprising
potters began to decorate their wares with American themes
(George Washington and James Madison are shown here).
Although the original client for this jug is not known, the central scene and inscription suggest that it was made to honor
the fire company of Cumberland, Maryland, for its role in
fighting fires during the British invasion of Washington, D.C.,
in the War of 1812. DC

Armchair

France
c. 1825–35
Elm, purpleheart
31⅓ x 21 x 21¼"
The Henry P. McIlhenny Collection
in memory of Frances P. McIlhenny
1986-26-124

Made around 1830, this armchair is an adaptation of a style that
had been popular since the reign of Napoleon (1799–1815),
when chairs *en gondole,* so named for their backs curved like the
prows of gondolas, were made for both of his wives, Josephine

and Marie Louise. Swans, seen on the arms of this chair, had been adopted by Josephine as her emblem and continued to ornament furniture long after her divorce from Napoleon in 1809. Similarly, classical motifs like the Greek key design on the seat rail and the anthemia on the swans' breasts, which were common on furniture of the Napoleonic era, remained popular well into the 1830s. This armchair is made of elm, a wood widely used in French furniture during the Napoleonic wars, when British blockades of French ports necessitated the choice of domestic rather than imported woods. Domestic woods remained fashionable even after Napoleon's defeat in 1815, with imported woods, like the purpleheart inlay seen here, generally used only for decorative details. The chair is one of a large group of French elmwood furniture of this period assembled by the Philadelphia collector Henry P. McIlhenny and bequeathed to the Museum in 1986. JHMS

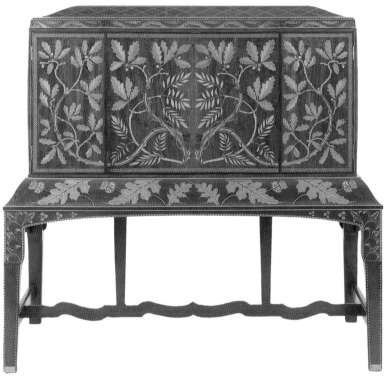

"Secretaire Cabinet"

Designed by George Washington Jack (American, active England, 1855–1932)

Made by Morris and Company (London, 1861–1940)

c. 1889

Mahogany with hardwood inlays 51½ x 55½ x 27"

Purchased with funds contributed by the Friends of the Philadelphia Museum of Art and with the gift (by exchange) of Julia G. Fahnestock in memory of her husband, William Fahnestock. 1986-128-1

This "secretaire cabinet," a desk with drawers and pigeonholes behind two doors and a fall-front writing surface, demonstrates the sophisticated cabinetmaking skills that Morris and Company could offer its most affluent clients. It was praised by contemporaries for the perfection of its decoration: the design, skill, and freedom of its marquetry; the choice of woods; the cutting; and the coloring. Credit was given to its designer, George Jack, an architect and skilled woodcarver who was responsible for most of the outstanding inlaid furniture produced by Morris in the 1880s and 1890s. A student of historic furniture that he used as models for his decorative techniques, Jack applied the richly inlaid scrolls of thistle, oak, and ash foliage (repeated mirror fashion like a Morris textile pattern), cross-banding, and checkered border to an overall conception based on a stately eighteenth-century English cabinet-on-stand. KBH

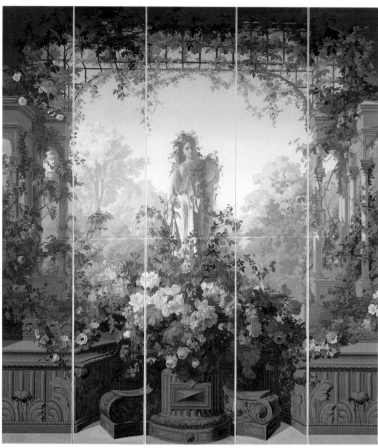

Wallpaper Depicting the Garden of Armida
Designed by Edouard Muller
(French, 1823–1876)
Made by Jules Desfossé
(French, died 1889)
c. 1855
Block-printed wallpaper
12'8" x 11'
Gift (by exchange) of Julia G. Fahnestock in memory of her husband, William Fahnestock. 1988-57-1a–e

This panoramic wallpaper was the centerpiece of Jules Desfossé's exhibit at the Paris Exposition Universelle of 1855, where his display was awarded a first-class medal. An ensemble of three tableaux, of which this was the central panel, the wallpaper depicts the magical garden of the enchantress Armida, described by the Renaissance poet Torquato Tasso in his masterwork, *Jerusalem Delivered* (1575). This learned reference was interpreted for the wallpaper with great originality by the flower painter Edouard Muller, whose lush and botanically accurate vegetation overruns the imaginary garden architecture. At the center of the scene is an ornamental statue, which Muller copied with similar exactitude from a sculpture of Pandora by James Pradier. Seeking both inspiration and instruction in these literary and visual sources, Desfossé was determined to raise the industrial production of wallpaper to the level of fine art, employing in his factory such recognized artists as Muller to spread the art of decoration to even "the most modest interiors," as a critic noted in 1855. KBH

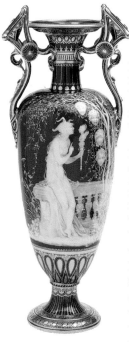

Jester Vase

Designed and painted by Marc-Louis-Emmanuel Solon
(French, 1835–1913)
Made by Mintons, Ltd. (Stoke-on-Trent, England, established 1793)
1894
Parian ware with *pâte-sur-pâte* and gilt decoration
Height 23⅞"
Purchased with the Joseph E. Temple Fund. 1898-95

The *Jester* vase, so named for the main character in its design, belongs to an important series of porcelain wares painted with the *pâte-sur-pâte* decoration for which the English firm of Mintons became famous after the French designer Marc-Louis Solon brought the technique to the factory in 1870. This time-consuming and expensive method of painting cameolike images with thin layers of transparent porcelain slip and finishing them with steel tools was invented at the Sèvres manufactory in France, where Solon had worked. He was acknowledged as the master of the technique for both his originality of design and his decorative skill. For this vase, which shows the influence of sources ranging from Renaissance engravings to contemporary ephemera, Solon adopts the antic manner of Victorian greeting cards for the jester and winged cherubs. KBH

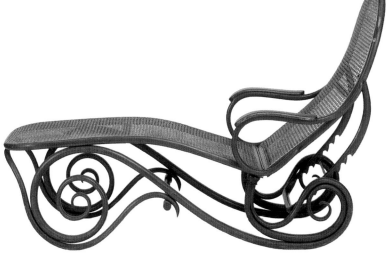

Chaise Longue, Model No. 2

Made by Gebrüder Thonet
(Vienna, established 1853)
Designed before 1887
Bent beechwood, caning
45 x 56½ x 26"
Purchased with the Director's Discretionary Fund. 1970-237-1

With its series of sinuous curves and countercurves, this chaise longue is one of the most elegant forms produced by the firm of Gebrüder Thonet. First exhibited in London in July 1887, the piece exemplifies the successful realization of the goal of the firm's founder, Michael Thonet, to make furniture that was at once functional, inexpensive, and beautiful. Thonet had begun experimenting around 1830 with producing furniture made of veneered wood that had been bent into curved shapes, and later invented a process by which solid lengths of beechwood could be bent to form long, curved rods for chair frames. By 1859, six years after he had established Gebrüder Thonet, he was using a largely mechanized process to make bentwood chairs from which he had eliminated ornament and traditional joinery. It is this lack of ornament, which was part of Thonet's functionalist aesthetic, that places these chairs at the forefront of the modern design movement and that made them popular with early twentieth-century architects such as Le Corbusier. DC

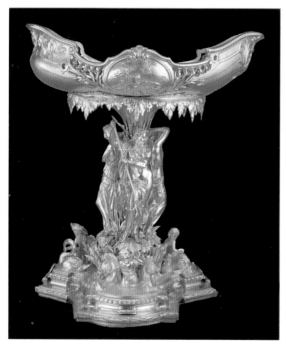

Centerpiece
Designed by Jean-Jacques Feuchère
(French, 1807–1852)
Made by P.-H.-Emile Froment-
Meurice (French, 1837–1913)
1860
Silver
Height 27⁹/₁₆"
Gift of Dr. and Mrs. Joseph Sataloff
1980-41-1

The Parisian firm of Emile Froment-Meurice produced this monumental centerpiece for a spectacular ensemble of silver table decorations, all ornamented with mythological figures and other motifs culled from an eclectic combination of Italian High Renaissance sources. The centerpiece was conceived by the sculptor Jean-Jacques Feuchère as a table fountain decorated with such aquatic images as figures of Neptune, Venus, and a sea nymph, and topped with a boat-shaped dish that would have contained an elaborate arrangement of fruit and sweets. One of the most fashionable silversmiths of mid-nineteenth-century Paris, Froment-Meurice played a significant role in the revival of the Italian Renaissance style in France, largely through its collaboration with Feuchère. This style offered a luxuriant choice of motifs and materials to the members of the French court and aristocracy who were among the clients of Froment-Meurice, and was the favored decoration for their Parisian dining rooms, where they entertained with the opulence and authority of Renaissance princes. KBH

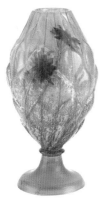

Vase
Designed and made by Emile Gallé
(French, 1846–1904)
c. 1900
Mold-blown glass with "marquetry"
and carved decoration
Height 8⅛″
Gift of John T. Morris. 1900-219

Embodying both a Romantic floral naturalism and the poetic feeling of the Symbolists, the work of Emile Gallé was hailed by his contemporaries for liberating French decorative art from historicism through its innovative and modern applications of stylized plant forms. Much of his glass is inscribed with lines of Symbolist poetry or verses by Victor Hugo, with whom he shared a love of nature. In this vase Gallé has translated into glass the inscribed quotation from Hugo: "The bluets found it beautiful." Superimposed on an artichoke form, this wildflower has transformed the homely vegetable into a thing of beauty, with flamelike streaks and metal particles inlaid in the glass itself. An inventor of dazzling decorative techniques, Gallé realized the bluets by his patented process of glass "marquetry," and it was for such technical innovation as well as for his remarkable naturalistic aesthetic that his works were collected by the Museum in its early years. KBH

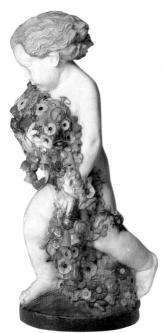

Figure of Spring
Designed by Michael Powolny
(Austrian, 1871–1954)
Made by Wiener Keramik
(Vienna, established 1906)
1912
Glazed earthenware
Height 31″
Purchased with the John D. McIlhenny
Fund. 1990-47-1

Michael Powolny was one of the chief ceramic artists of the Secession movement in Vienna, which sought to improve the quality and craftsmanship of decorative and utilitarian objects at the turn of the century. He revived the traditional practice of modeling freestanding figures in ceramic and encouraged the use of his work as architectural or interior ornament. Wiener Keramik, the manufacturing firm that Powolny co-founded and directed, collaborated with the craft workshops of the Wiener Werkstätte (Vienna Workshop) in important architectural projects, which included the production of some seven thousand colored tiles for the walls of the bar room of the Fledermaus cabaret in Vienna and Powolny's own figure of Pallas Athenae for the entrance porch of the Stoclet family house in Brussels. This life-size statue of *Spring* is one of Powolny's largest figures, and is typical of his boldly decorative style in its classicizing subject of a cherub with stylized garlands treated with simplified surfaces, strong colors, and monumental effect. KBH

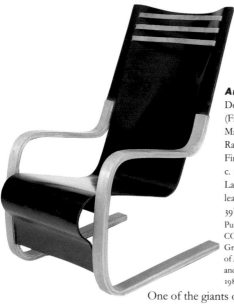

Armchair

Designed by Alvar Aalto
(Finnish, 1898–1976)
Made by O.Y. Huonekalu-ja
Rakennustyötehdas A.B. (Turku,
Finland, established 1910)
c. 1932
Laminated birch, birch plywood,
leather
39¼ x 22 x 36¼"

Purchased with funds contributed by
COLLAB: The Contemporary Design
Group for the Philadelphia Museum
of Art, in honor of Cynthia W. Drayton,
and with the Fiske Kimball Fund
1985-67-1

One of the giants of twentieth-century architecture and design, Alvar Aalto created a new vocabulary of furniture forms as well as the technology necessary to produce it. Dedicated to creating high-quality household products at reasonable cost by industrial methods, Aalto used Finnish birch plywood and laminated wood for his furniture because these materials were local, inexpensive, comfortable, and, he said, more "human" than the tubular steel being introduced in furniture elsewhere in Europe during the 1930s. Aalto tried to make wood elastic, creating for this armchair a resilient seat and back formed from one long, elegantly curving panel of springy molded plywood, suspended in a bent, laminated-wood frame. One of only a few made-to-order high-back variants of Aalto's commercially manufactured "standard" chair, this version is only slightly more elaborate than the mass-produced model, which reflects his social commitment to mass production. KBH

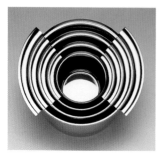

Center Line *Cookware*

Designed by Roberto Sambonet
(Italian, born 1924)
Made by Sambonet (Vercelli, Italy,
established 1856)
1963–65
Stainless steel
Height 7⅟₁₆" (largest pot, covered)

Gift of Sambonet. 1983-141-1–8

Stainless steel was introduced to the domestic kitchen during the 1920s largely for cutlery, but its use became widespread after World War II, when its low cost, highly polished silvery surface, and durability made it popular for both cooking and informal dining. No designer has used this metal with greater originality or elegance than Roberto Sambonet, who here explores the possibilities of standardizing cookwares in mathematically derived modular elements that form different configurations in several combinations. Four deep pots and four shallow ones of corresponding diameters that can be used either as lids, pans, or trays, the *Center Line* pieces nest compactly in a convenient arrangement of great formal beauty and decorative effect provided by the flaring segmental flanges used to lift and move the pots, the contrast of sizes, and the brilliant finish of the steel. Like other Italian designers, Sambonet has turned the efficient into the beautiful, adding artistic creativity to the refining process of calculation. KBH

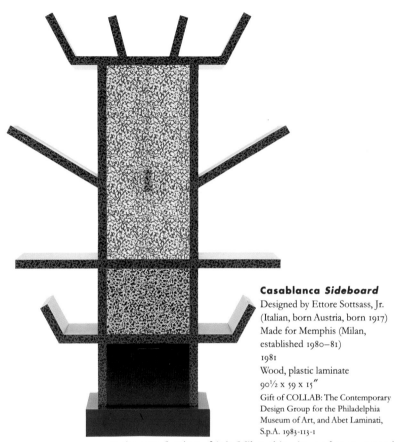

Casablanca *Sideboard*
Designed by Ettore Sottsass, Jr.
(Italian, born Austria, born 1917)
Made for Memphis (Milan, established 1980–81)
1981
Wood, plastic laminate
90½ x 59 x 15″
Gift of COLLAB: The Contemporary Design Group for the Philadelphia Museum of Art, and Abet Laminati, S.p.A. 1983-113-1

At the 1981 furniture fair in Milan, this witty and monumental sideboard was the centerpiece of a disparate exhibition of objects that came to define "postmodern" design. It was the signature piece of Ettore Sottsass, Jr., who had commissioned the works from an international group of architects and designers, and founded the enterprise to produce them known as "Memphis." Like the name itself, which refers to both the ancient capital of Egypt and the center of American popular music in Tennessee, the objects endorsed eclecticism, appropriation, metaphor, ambiguity, and humor. With its irregular, arm-waving silhouette and brightly colored, close-patterned surface decoration, the *Casablanca* sideboard announced a radically new aesthetic that defied the spare forms and functional values of traditional modernism. Relying largely on industrial materials such as the 1950s-style plastic laminate used here, Memphis adopted color, ornament, and novel shapes to restore the sense of individuality, freedom, and humanity that Sottsass believed modern design had lost. KBH

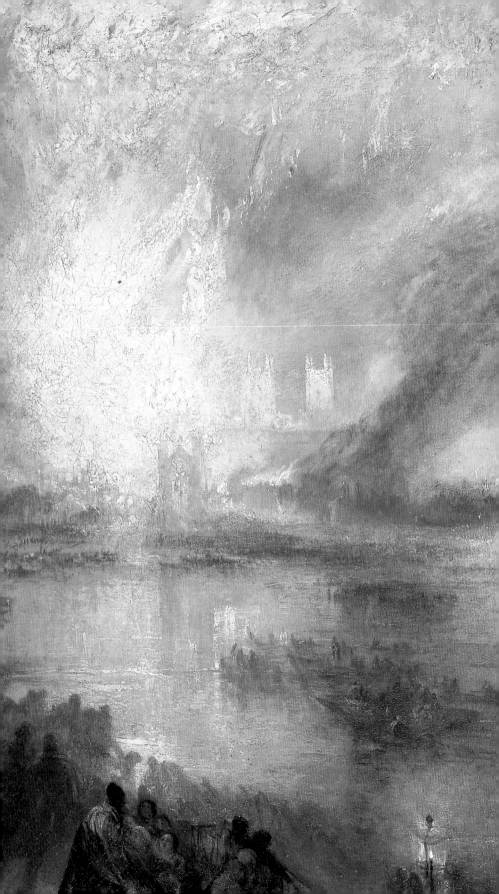

European Painting and Sculpture before 1900, Including the John G. Johnson Collection

The bequest in 1893 of some 150 paintings from Mrs. William P. Wilstach, along with a handsome fund for acquisitions, set an ambitious standard for the Museum's collection, which had already received about half a dozen paintings in 1882 from Mrs. Bloomfield Moore. This fund was administered by the renowned lawyer and collector John G. Johnson, who was director of the Wilstach Committee by 1901. Purchases made under his direction as well as the collection itself displayed a remarkable mix of old and new, European and American.

Johnson died in 1917, leaving to the citizens of Philadelphia a celebrated group of 1,271 paintings in his house on South Broad Street, which were later moved to the Museum. Over a long period, their status and permanent residence here were clarified by a series of court orders in the 1950s and 1960s and, more recently, by a 1989 decision that settled their long-range life in the building and permitted their juxtaposition with paintings from other collections and with decorative arts and architectural ensembles. The John G. Johnson Collection contains most of the Museum's Italian and Northern European Renaissance paintings, a very large number of seventeenth-century Dutch pictures, including eight by Jan Steen, as well as some of the most important nineteenth-century works by Johnson's contemporaries, such as Claude Monet and Edgar Degas. Since Johnson's death the collection has been in the charge of a series of industrious curators, namely Horace Bell (who faced the difficult task of dealing with the collection in Johnson's house) and Henri Marceau, whose task it was to organize the move to Fairmount at the time he was serving as the Museum's assistant director. From 1931 Barbara Sweeney watched over the collection and its records with a remarkably loyal stewardship; she served as curator from 1954 until 1974, during which time she published the critical two-volume catalogue of Johnson's Italian and Northern Renaissance pictures.

In 1921, through the purchase of a choice group of Impressionist works from the family of Alexander Cassatt, Mary Cassatt's brother, a pattern of interest in this field emerged that celebrated the enthusiasm of Philadelphia's many collectors for Impressionism, and culminated in 1936 and 1937 with the purchase of Paul Cézanne's late *Mont Sainte-Victoire* and his *Large Bathers*. The Philadelphia painter Carroll S. Tyson was passionate in his advocacy of the great Cézanne acquisitions, and the superb painting collection he and his wife formed came to the Museum in 1963. A group of additional bequests made the nineteenth-century French collections among the most important in the country: Lisa Norris Elkins in 1950, Louis E. Stern in 1963, Samuel S. and Vera White in 1967, and, most recently, the superb gift from Henry P. McIlhenny in 1986.

Another great strength of the collections, English painting, depends almost entirely on the donations of William L. and George W. Elkins in 1924 (which included distinguished Dutch pictures as well) and of John Howard McFadden in 1928. McFadden's forty-three paintings, the first to be shown in the new building on Fairmount, include Turner's *Burning of the Houses of Lords and Commons* and Constable's *Sketch for "A Boat Passing a Lock."*

Like most other large museum holdings of old master paintings in the United States, Philadelphia's is very much composed of other collections, each donated as a whole and reflecting the taste and values of individual patrons rather than the professional staff, although Philadelphia has been particularly fortunate in having some of its major donors directly connected with the daily working of the institution, figures such as Henry Clifford, Louis C. Madeira, and Henry P. McIlhenny, all of whom served as curators. Relatively few truly major European paintings have come to the Museum through purchase, but the handful that have are of great note, each adding a pivotal moment in the history of art and a memorable masterpiece to the collections: Poussin's *Birth of Venus* in 1932, Rubens's *Prometheus Bound* in 1950, Degas's *After the Bath* in 1980, and Goltzius's *Sine Cerere et Libero friget Venus* in 1990.

The responsibility for European sculpture has been variously shared by the painting and decorative arts departments. Beyond the distinguished medieval and Renaissance pieces acquired *en bloc* from the Foulc and Barnard collections, later sculpture came through smaller gifts and selective purchases. A large and representative group of *animalier* bronzes were given by the Elkins family in 1951, but the other nineteenth-century works of note—the *Sibyl* by Marcello and a portrait bust by Gemito—were acquired by purchase. Far and away the most important cache of nineteenth-century sculpture is the Jules Mastbaum bequest of works by Auguste Rodin, which he assembled between 1922 and 1926. Second only to the collections at the Hotel Biron in Paris, it consists of 127 bronzes, marbles, and plasters representing all aspects of the artist's career and all his major projects, and includes the first bronze cast of *The Gates of Hell*.

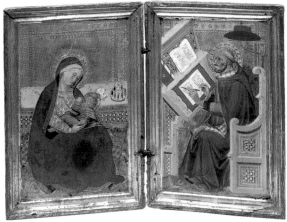

Attributed to
Benedetto di Bindo
Italian, active Siena and Perugia,
first securely documented 1410,
died 1417
The Virgin of Humility, and Saint
Jerome Translating the Gospel of
John, c. 1400–1405
Tempera and tooled gold on poplar
panel
11⅞ x 16⅝″
John G. Johnson Collection. Cat. 153

The hinged panels of this little diptych contain an unusual
juxtaposition of two subjects in which books play a distinguishing role. On the right Saint Jerome translates into Latin the
opening lines of the Gospel of John. (The artist has rendered
the Latin correctly, but not the unfamiliar Greek original.) On
the left, the nursing Virgin is seated on the floor as a sign of her
humility, while a small manuscript, known as a book of hours,
rests on the bench behind her. This text, which contained
prayers to be recited at regular hourly intervals, is open to an
invocation intoned at 3 p.m., a symbol of the time of Christ's
death that cultured fifteenth-century viewers would have understood as prophesying the fate of the baby. Jerome's scholarly
pursuit likewise suggests the respect accorded to book learning
for its ability to elucidate the hidden meanings of seemingly
common images like a nursing mother. CBS

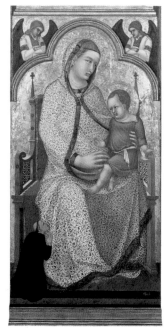

Pietro Lorenzetti
Italian, active Siena, Assisi, Arezzo,
and Florence, first securely docu-
mented 1320, last documented 1344
Enthroned Virgin and Child, with
a Donor and Two Angels, 1320s
Tempera and tooled gold on poplar
panel
51¾ x 27½″ (overall)
John G. Johnson Collection. Cat. 91
(main panel)
Purchased with the George W. Elkins
Fund, the W. P. Wilstach Fund, and the
J. Stogdell Stokes Fund
EW1985-21-1, 2 (spandrels)

Even though a regularized system of perspective had not yet
been developed, early fourteenth-century Italian artists like

Pietro Lorenzetti searched for ways to suggest that a painting was a window onto another visible world in which the artist tried to control the perception of forms in space. These panels, which formed the center of a large altarpiece (whose other elements are now dispersed and lost), represent one of Lorenzetti's most successful and carefully calculated illusions of three-dimensionality. The angels in the spandrels rest their folded arms on the frame as if to mark a limit between their world and that of the viewer, while the Virgin and Child twist in opposite directions to draw attention to their positions within the painting's space. Subtle details, such as the fringe from the Virgin's mantle that falls over the front step, add to our awareness of depth. The kneeling figure is a monk or friar. As was then traditional, his diminutive dimensions identify him as a donor and underscore his devotion to the holy figures. It was probably he who commissioned the altarpiece for his church. CBS

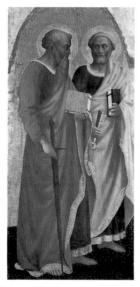

Masaccio
Italian, active Florence, Pisa, and Rome, 1401–1428, and
Masolino
Italian, active Florence, Hungary, Rome, Todi, and Castiglione d'Olona, documented 1423–44
Saints Paul and Peter, c. 1428
Tempera, oil, and tooled gold on poplar panel
45 x 21 3/8″
John G. Johnson Collection. Inv. 408

Martin V, who reigned from 1417 to 1431 as the first pope of the Roman Catholic church newly reunited after a long schism, set about rebuilding and ornamenting the degraded city of Rome. As a consequence, many artists, including Masaccio and Masolino from Florence, were attracted by commissions to Rome. The two worked on an altarpiece for the basilica of Santa Maria Maggiore. This image of Saints Paul and Peter is one of two panels in the Museum that were originally opposite sides of a single section of the altarpiece. They were begun by Masaccio and finished by Masolino after the former's untimely death at age twenty-seven. Masolino's task was not an easy one, because he was asked to reverse the saints' positions. Masolino made the requested modifications, but did so by incorporating what work Masaccio had finished. In *Saints Paul and Peter,* for example, he carefully painted around the already executed hands, feet, and blue drapery to adapt Masaccio's design to the new iconography. CBS

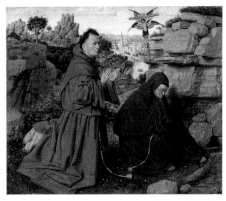

Jan van Eyck
Netherlandish, active Bruges,
first documented 1422, died 1441
*Saint Francis of Assisi Receiving
the Stigmata,* c. 1438–40
Oil on vellum on oak panel
5 x 5¾"
John G. Johnson Collection. Cat. 314

Jan van Eyck was the most celebrated painter in northern
Europe during the fifteenth century, widely hailed for his
nearly miraculous ability to depict observed reality with a refinement verging on the microscopic. The effect of such intense
realism was to create pictures that seemed at once very sharp
yet very far away. Here Saint Francis is receiving on the palms
of his hands and the soles of his feet the same wounds suffered
by the crucified Christ, who appears as an image held aloft by
an angel. The saint's stigmata would never heal and became
for many the living proof of his holiness. Although Van Eyck's
representation of this legend follows the original Franciscan
text quite literally, his one departure from earlier, chiefly Italian
depictions is the inclusion of a great, panoramic landscape with
a distant view of a bustling city. The scene is thus presented
as a miracle being witnessed within the context of the whole
sweep of nature and human life, which may seem magically
beautiful but is in fact quite oblivious to the sacred action in
the foreground. JJR

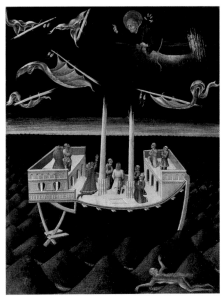

Giovanni di Paolo
Italian, active Siena, first securely
documented 1411, died 1482
*Saint Nicholas of Tolentino Saving
a Ship,* 1457
Tempera and tooled gold on poplar
panel
20½ x 16⅝"
John G. Johnson Collection. Inv. 723

One of many examples of fifteenth-century Italian narrative
painting in the John G. Johnson Collection, this panel was
originally part of an altarpiece depicting Saint Nicholas of
Tolentino and his miracles that was commissioned for a church

in Montepulciano in southern Tuscany. Giovanni di Paolo may have had access to first-hand accounts of the miracles because the government of his hometown of Siena owned a copy of the testimony of witnesses to the events. The shipwreck episode offered fodder for the artist's bizarre imagination, as survivors vividly described the terror of the rolling waves, broken mast, flying sails, and radiant light emanating from the saint who came to save them. However, it was Giovanni di Paolo who added the naked siren swimming in the foreground, enticing sailors to steer off course. The picture's fantastic quality made it an appropriate selection for a group of "forerunners" in the exhibition *Fantastic Art, Dada, Surrealism,* held at the Museum of Modern Art in New York in 1936. CBS

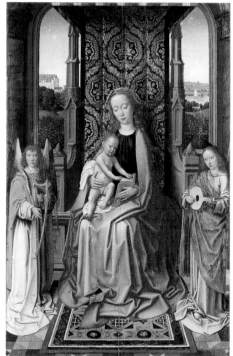

Gerard David
Netherlandish, active Bruges, first documented 1484, died 1523
Enthroned Virgin and Child, with Angels, c. 1490–95
Oil on oak panel
39¹/₁₆ x 25¹¹/₁₆″
John G. Johnson Collection. Cat. 329

In one of the most enchanting early Flemish paintings in the Johnson Collection, Gerard David presents the Virgin enthroned as the Queen of Heaven, and uses simple, monumental forms to underscore the majestic solemnity of her presence. As queen, the Virgin is seated upon an ornately carved throne that is shaded by an embroidered canopy and backed by a shimmering, brocaded cloth of honor; at her feet lies a luxurious carpet with an orientalizing design. The angels wear robes made of shot, or *changeant,* silk, so called because its color differs depending on the angle from which it is viewed. The celebratory nature of the moment is emphasized by the harp and the lute held by the angels, which allude to the celestial music surrounding the Virgin and Child. All of these severe and formal regal adornments are counterbalanced by the intimacy of the scene, which focuses on the interaction of the mother and child, and his playful attention to the leaves of her prayer book. KCL

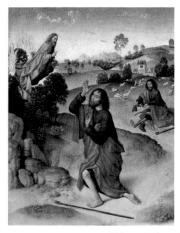

Attributed to
Dierick Bouts
Netherlandish, active Louvain,
first securely documented 1447,
died 1475
Moses and the Burning Bush,
with Moses Removing His Shoes
c. 1465–70
Oil on panel
17⅝ x 14″
John G. Johnson Collection. Cat. 339

Although there is no obvious division in the picture's space,
Dierick Bouts has in fact depicted two sequential events from
Moses' life within the verdant countryside in this compressed
narrative. In the middle right, Moses, a shepherd, sits on the
ground. He had been tending his flock when he noticed a burning bush that was miraculously not consumed by the fire. As he
was approaching the bush, God told him to remove his shoes,
which he is doing, before walking on the holy ground. In the
foreground, Moses has approached the burning bush, in which
God appears to instruct him to lead his people into the Prom-
ised Land. The inclusion of Moses' shepherd's staff in the two
scenes, as well as the focus on the removal of his shoes, accen-
tuates both his role as a protector of his people and his humility
before God. KCL

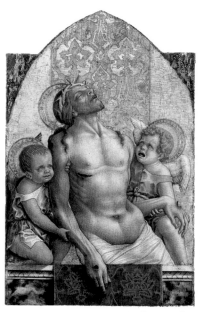

Carlo Crivelli
Italian, active Venice and Marches,
first documented 1457,
died 1495–1500
Dead Christ Supported by Two
Angels, c. 1472
Tempera and tooled gold on poplar
panel
28 x 18⅝″
John G. Johnson Collection. Cat. 158

Carlo Crivelli, originally from Venice, led the life of a successful
itinerant painter working along the Italian Adriatic coast. Although his isolation from major artistic centers resulted in a
strange style marked by a caricatured realism, Crivelli's training
in figure drawing underpinned his permutations of the norm,
evident in the precise observation of Christ's anatomy. The

nude body racked by the stiffening aftermath of death afforded the artist ample opportunity to demonstrate his taut draftsmanship, and in his detailed depiction of Christ's wounds and graying skin, the angels' tears, and their anguished expressions, Crivelli displayed his fine brushwork. The artist accentuated the realism of sorrow and death for dramatic effect and because of the painting's original position as the crowning element of an altarpiece. He compensated for the height at which the painting would have been seen by emphasizing the curve and weight of the dead body, which the angels can barely support. CBS

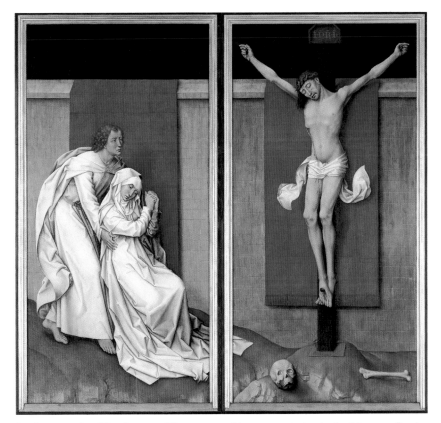

Rogier van der Weyden

Netherlandish, active Tournai and Brussels, 1399/1400–1464
The Crucifixion, with the Virgin and Saint John the Evangelist Mourning, c. 1460–64
Oil on oak panel
71 x 36⅝″ (left panel), 71 x 36⅞″ (right panel)
John G. Johnson Collection
Cats. 335, 334

The greatest old master painting in the Museum, Rogier van der Weyden's diptych presents the Crucifixion as a timeless dramatic narrative. To convey overwhelming depths of human emotion, Rogier located monumental forms in a shallow, austere, nocturnal space accented only by brilliant red hangings. He focused on the experience of the Virgin, her unbearable grief expressed by her swooning into the arms of John the Evangelist. The intensity of her anguish is echoed in the agitated, fluttering loincloth that moves around Christ's motionless body as if the air itself were astir with sorrow. Rogier's use of two panels in a diptych, rather than the more usual three found in a triptych, is rare in paintings of this period, and allowed the artist to balance the human despair at the darkest hour of the Christian faith against the promise of redemption. KCL

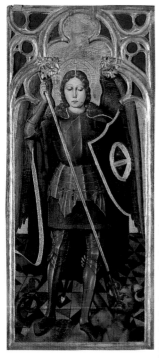

Juan Ximénez

Spanish, active Aragon, first
documented 1500, died 1505
The Archangel Michael, 1500–1503
Oil and tooled gold on panel
50½ x 22¹¹/₁₆"
John G. Johnson Collection. Inv. 183

This panel was removed sometime before 1917 from an elaborate altarpiece, or *retablo,* that dominated the east end of the church of Tamarite de Litera near Huesca in eastern Spain, forming a wall of images that included over twenty-three scenes. The rest of the altarpiece was destroyed in the 1930s during the Spanish Civil War. Part of the projecting outer edge of the altarpiece, commonly known as the dustguard, was composed of individual standing figures of saints, including this panel of *The Archangel Michael,* an image that in early sixteenth-century Spain commemorated the recent reconquest of Muslim-held territories and the expulsion of the Jews. More than one artist was required to paint all the panels and carve the frame of the immense *retablo,* a uniquely Iberian type of altarpiece. Documents indicate that Juan Ximénez collaborated with his father Miguel on the *retablo* for Tamarite de Litera, with Miguel working on the principal scenes and Juan on the dustguard. Other artists were also called in to work on this enormous project, which had to be completed in three years. CBS

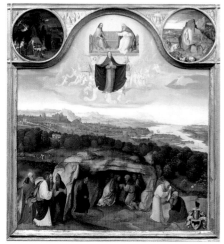

Joachim Patinir

Netherlandish, active Antwerp,
c. 1485–1524
The Assumption of the Virgin,
with the Nativity, the Resurrection,
the Adoration of the Magi, the
Ascension of Christ, Saint Mark
and an Angel, and Saint Luke and
an Ox, c. 1510–20
Oil on oak panel
24½ x 23⅛"
John G. Johnson Collection. Cat. 378

The unusual format of this painting, which consists of a large central panel surmounted by two roundels, was perhaps specified by Lucas Rem, a wealthy Augsburg merchant whose coat of arms appears at the lower right. Rem probably requested the subject as well, since the Assumption of the Virgin was rarely depicted in Flemish painting of the period. Joachim Patinir has illustrated the moment after the Apostles have discovered the Virgin's empty tomb, unaware that she has risen to heaven. Only Thomas, the dark-bearded Apostle to the left, knew of her Assumption, since she had dropped her belt to him as she rose. In Patinir's painting, Thomas rushes up to the other Apostles, Mary's belt and rosary in hand, to share the good news. The vast and beautifully painted panoramic countryside within which the events occur was the hallmark of Patinir's fame, and also heralded the shift toward Mannerist inversion of subject matter in sixteenth-century Antwerp, as narrative events were reduced in scale in relation to the surrounding landscape. KCL

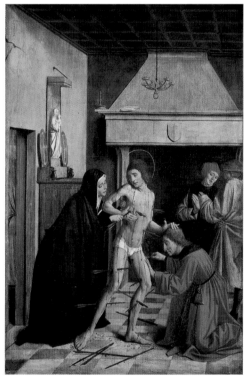

Josse Lieferinxe
French, documented 1493–1505/8
Saint Sebastian Cured by Irene
c. 1497
Oil on walnut panel
32 x 21⁹⁄₁₆″
John G. Johnson Collection. Cat. 767

This panel is one of four in the John G. Johnson Collection that come from Josse Lieferinxe's altarpiece for the chapel of a lay religious club in the church of Notre-Dame-des-Accoules in Marseilles. They all show scenes from the life of the Roman soldier Sebastian, who, soon after he converted to Christianity around 283, was tortured for his faith by being shot with arrows. Here the wounded Sebastian is being nursed back to health by a Roman woman named Irene in a room that is depicted as a typical wood-paneled interior of the late 1400s. The furnishings, including a canopied statue of the Virgin on the cabinet, resemble those found in the homes of the Marseilles merchants who belonged to the club that commissioned the altarpiece. Such anachronistic details would have made the ancient story seem more immediate and familiar to its contemporary audience. CBS

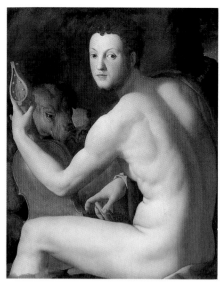

Agnolo Bronzino
Italian, active Florence, 1503–1572
Portrait of Cosimo I de' Medici as Orpheus, c. 1538–40
Oil on poplar panel
36⅞ x 30 1/16"
Gift of Mrs. John Wintersteen
1950-86-1

Cosimo I de' Medici, sixteenth-century ruler of Florence, is here personified as the mythological poet and musician Orpheus at the mouth of Hades, where he had gone to reclaim his dead wife Eurydice. The felicitous circumstances of this allegorical portrait, which was painted at the time of Cosimo's marriage to Eleanor of Toledo in 1539, may have warranted several changes during the picture's execution. For example, technical evidence shows that the three-headed dog Cerberus, guardian of the underworld, originally growled at Orpheus's attempts to gain admittance, but here has been calmed by soothing music. The newly married couple would have appreciated the romantic overtones achieved in the revised version. In addition, many contemporary viewers would have noticed that the seductive turn of Cosimo's muscular body was based on the much admired ancient sculpture known as the *Torso Belvedere,* then as now on display in the Vatican in Rome. CBS

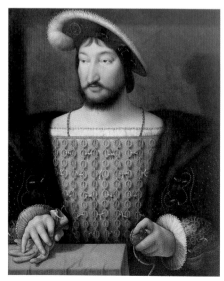

Joos van Cleve
Netherlandish, active Antwerp and France, first documented 1511, died 1540/41
Portrait of Francis I, King of France, c. 1525
Oil on oak panel
28⅜ x 23 5/16"
John G. Johnson Collection. Cat. 769

Francis I, king of France from 1515 to 1547, summoned Joos van Cleve to his Parisian court to paint his portrait around 1525, when the monarch was about thirty years old. In this royal portrait Joos, who was acclaimed for his painterly and coloristic abilities, emphasized the play between the three-dimensionality of the king's face and hands and the flat, decorative patterning of his costume. Francis is strongly illuminated from the right so that his body casts a strong shadow behind him, securely locating his form in space. Similarly, his hands are modeled with exquisite attention to the way that light falls across them and to their location in front of Francis's body. This heightened spatial illusionism is challenged by the ornate elements of the king's richly decorated and bejeweled costume, which is painted almost like a flat enameled surface. Unlike Francis's elaborate costume of state, Joos did not idealize his face and even emphasized its more homely aspects. Indeed, his large, coarse features and sly expression contrast with the formality of his dress and betray the man behind the head of state. Francis was a great patron of the arts, and the Museum is particularly rich in architectural elements and decorative arts created during his reign. KCL

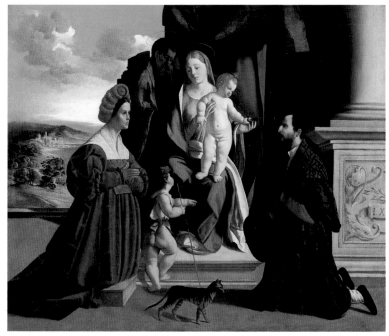

Dosso Dossi
Italian, active Ferrara, first recorded 1512, died 1542
The Holy Family, with the Young Saint John the Baptist and Two Donors, c. 1512–13
Oil on canvas
38 1/16 x 45 3/4″
John G. Johnson Collection. Cat. 197

Nothing is documented about why this altarpiece was commissioned, but the composition provides clues about the man and woman in contemporary dress. On the right a man in black kneels on the ground, his cast shadow intersecting that of the young John the Baptist, who presents him to the Holy Family. The woman, undoubtedly the man's wife, kneels on a low wooden stool on the right side of the Virgin, a place of greater honor than that of her husband, which implies that she had died before the picture was painted. The couple's relative positions suggest that the man had commissioned Dosso Dossi to make this painting as a memorial to his deceased wife. The cat's theological meaning may be lost on a modern viewer, but for

Dosso it would have symbolized the bestial nature of human-kind that is capable of damning the soul, represented here by the bird held by the Christ Child. CBS

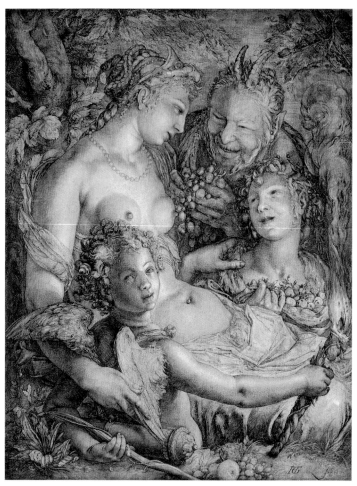

Hendrick Goltzius
Dutch, active Haarlem, 1558–1617
Sine Cerere et Libero friget Venus
(Without Ceres and Bacchus,
Venus Would Freeze), c. 1600–1603
Ink and oil on canvas
41 3/8 x 31 1/2″

Purchased with the Mr. and Mrs. Walter H. Annenberg Fund for Major Acquisitions, the Henry P. McIlhenny Fund in memory of Frances P. McIlhenny, bequest (by exchange) of Mr. and Mrs. Herbert C. Morris, and gift (by exchange) of Frank and Alice Osborn
1990-100-1

Cupid's flaming torch is the source of illumination in Hendrick Goltzius's acclaimed "pen work"; it is also a focal point of the narrative and the locus of Goltzius's own great technical innovation in this painting. Venus, the goddess of love, awakens from a deep slumber, roused by the flaming torch held by Cupid. Two satyrs offer her grapes and other fruits of the harvest, illustrative of the theme that without food and wine, love cannot flourish. Goltzius's large painting on canvas was meant to imitate a pen drawing made gigantic, yet it is a drawing transfigured by touches of rosy paint in the areas of the illumination cast by Cupid's torch. The importance of this masterpiece of northern Mannerism is reflected in its exalted pedigree. It was in several royal collections, including those of Rudolf II, the Holy Roman Emperor, who had his court at Prague in the early seventeenth century; Queen Christina of Sweden, whose troops looted Prague in 1636 and absconded with innumerable art treasures; and Charles II of England, where it remained until at least 1720. KCL

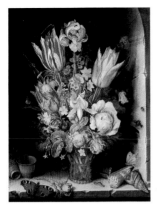

Christoffel van den Berghe

Dutch, active Middelburg,
active c. 1617–c. 1642
Still Life with Flowers in a Vase
1617
Oil on copper
14 13/16 x 11 5/8″
John G. Johnson Collection. Cat. 648

Christoffel van den Berghe was a flower painter active in the
Dutch town of Middelburg, which was known for its horticul-
tural collections. Here he depicts a bouquet that includes both
large, cultivated flowers, such as tulips, roses, irises, and lilies,
as well as smaller wild flowers, such as snowflakes and nastur-
tiums. The larger cultivated flowers are rather stiffly arranged in
a type of Dutch glass known as a roemer, while the wild specimens are haphazardly inserted between them. This combination
of order and disorder, like the contrast between cultivated and
wild specimens, suggests that the bouquet functions as a *me-
mento mori,* or reminder of the transience of life and physical
beauty. Other elements of the composition are equally evocative
references to the fleeting nature of life. The caterpillar, for example, will become a glorious butterfly, but will live only moments in its splendor. Likewise, the stone niche in which the
bouquet is placed is reminiscent of a tomb, and the chips
around its edges are a testament to the permanence of death
and decay. KCL

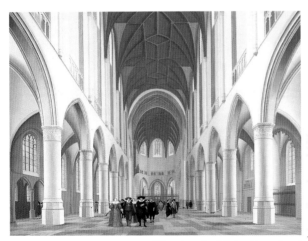

Pieter Jansz. Saenredam

Dutch, active Haarlem and Utrecht,
1597–1665
Interior of Saint Bavo, Haarlem
1631
Oil on oak panel
32 5/8 x 43 1/2″
John G. Johnson Collection. Cat. 599

The church of Saint Bavo dominated the Dutch city of Haarlem
in the seventeenth century; its tower was the highest in the
city, and prominent local burghers were interred under its floor.
Pieter Jansz. Saenredam, the foremost architectural painter in
Holland, had studied the mathematical science of perspective,
and utilized the actual measurements of the church in composing this painting, the earliest and one of the most celebrated

of his many images of Saint Bavo. Because of its technical diffi-
culty, architectural painting appealed to patrician patrons such
as the wealthy burghers here taking a tour of the church. At
middle right, a man points to a painting of Saint Bavo that in
Saenredam's day was thought to have been the work of Haarlem's greatest fifteenth-century artist, Geertgen tot Sint Jans.
By including Geertgen's view of the church in his own painting,
Saenredam attests to both his own exalted lineage as a painter
of architectural images as well as his ability to surpass the
achievements of his forebears. KCL

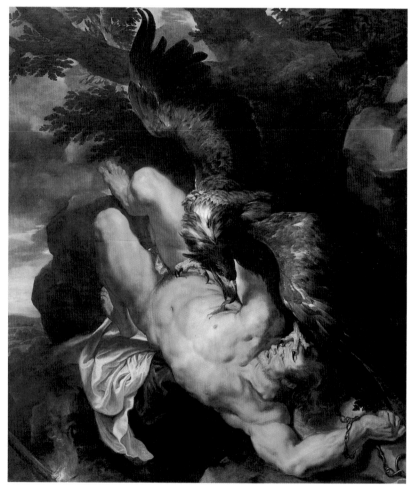

Peter Paul Rubens
Flemish, active Italy, Antwerp,
and England, 1577–1640, and
Frans Snyders
Flemish, active Antwerp,
1579–1657
Prometheus Bound, begun
c. 1611–12, completed by 1618
Oil on canvas
95½ x 82½″
Purchased with the W. P. Wilstach Fund
W1950-3-1

Peter Paul Rubens kept this enormous painting of *Prometheus
Bound* in his personal collection for several years and in a letter
of 1618 described it as one of his most important creations.
Known to have collaborated with other artists, Rubens noted
in the same letter that Frans Snyders, who was distinguished
for his depictions of flowers and animals, had painted the eagle.
This enormous bird, whose wings span the width of the canvas, tears the hero's powerfully muscled body with its sharp
talons, rips open his side, and devours his liver. Part of Prometheus's punishment for having dared to steal fire from the gods
was that his liver regenerated daily, only to be eaten again by

the eagle. Interpretations of this Greek myth of an epic struggle between the eagle and Prometheus had acquired many allegorical resonances by the early seventeenth century, which Rubens, one of the most cultivated and literate figures of his time, would have surely known. This complex painting could be regarded as the artist's commentary on either the struggles of creativity or the ideal of heroic spiritual suffering. KCL

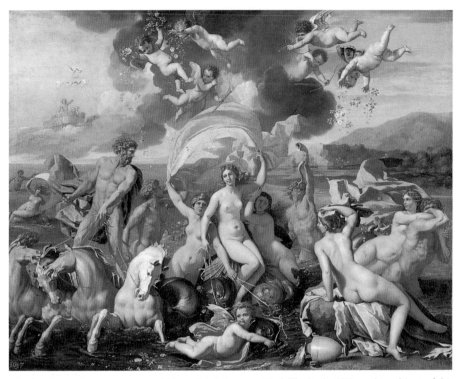

Nicolas Poussin
French, 1594–1665
The Birth of Venus, 1635 or 1636
Oil on canvas
38¼ x 42½″
The George W. Elkins Collection
E1932-1-1

Although it is here entitled *The Birth of Venus,* the subject of this painting remains the focus of lively scholarly debate. Is it in fact the birth of Venus or her triumph? Or is it the triumph of Neptune—or of the sea nymph Galatea? The very uncertainty suggests, however, that Nicolas Poussin was not restricted by strict textual precedent but felt free to invent and to introduce multiple meanings and allusive ambiguities into his paintings on classical themes. One of the artist's most scintillating and luminous masterpieces, it shows him audaciously combining the lively interplay of magnificent nude protagonists and a friezelike compositional grandeur. Here, elegant gesture and windswept movement are frozen in time. Sold to Catherine the Great of Russia in 1771, the painting was sold again from the Hermitage Museum in Leningrad (now Saint Petersburg) by a Soviet government desperate for Western currency in 1930, shortly before it was acquired by the Philadelphia Museum of Art. CR

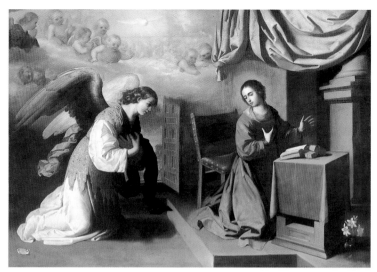

Francisco de Zurbarán
Spanish, 1598–1664
The Annunciation, 1650
Oil on canvas
85⅝ x 124½"
Purchased with the W. P. Wilstach Fund
W1900-1-16

Francisco de Zurbarán was the first painter in the Iberian Peninsula to realize fully the magnitude of the revolution in painting that had occurred in Italy in the early seventeenth century, as the decorative sophistication, attenuated figures, and oblique narratives of the previous generation were abandoned in favor of blunt realism. This new style was perfectly suited to the church's attempts to popularize holy images for a broader audience in danger of being lost to the Protestant Reformation. In Spain in particular these changes created some of the most immediate and profoundly moving religious paintings in the history of art. This *Annunciation* falls quite late in Zurbarán's career, when his simple and abrupt modeling, dark to light, begins to soften and blur. His palette becomes less strident and more blended, while the nearly militaristic urgency of his earlier work is replaced by an intimacy and tenderness. The walls of the Virgin Mary's room literally dissolve in a flood of cherubs bathed in light, as the angel Gabriel with great gallantry and discretion announces that she is with child. JJR

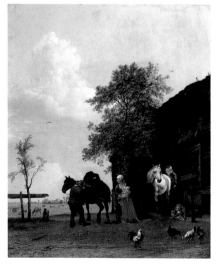

Paulus Potter
Dutch, active The Hague, Delft, and Amsterdam, 1625–1654
Figures with Horses by a Stable
1647
Oil on oak panel
17¾ x 14¾"
The William L. Elkins Collection
E1924-3-17

Paulus Potter died young, but during his short lifetime he was acclaimed for his skillful and detailed painting technique and his acute observation of peasant life. In this scene, which is typical of Potter's mature works, a farmer grooms his horse in a barn, while in the yard a mother suckles her infant as one peasant helps another mount a horse. Chickens and a dog also populate the barnyard, and grazing cattle are visible in the meadow beyond. The lighting of the painting is unusual; the distant meadow is suffused with sunlight, as is the horse in the stable, yet the barnyard is blanketed in shadow. Potter's patrons would have understood this painting as a celebration of the prosperous Dutch countryside. The simple, rustic lives of the peasants, living in productive harmony with nature, was idealized by his contemporaries as virtuous and noble, and urban intellectuals viewed life in the country as happier, healthier, and more peaceful than life in the city. KCL

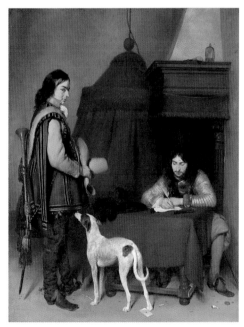

Gerard ter Borch
Dutch, active Deventer after 1654, 1617–1681
Officer Writing a Letter, with a Trumpeter, c. 1658–59
Oil on canvas
22⅜ x 17¼"
The William L. Elkins Collection
E1924-3-21

Letter writing and reading—together with guard room scenes—were among Gerard ter Borch's favorite subjects. Here the artist has combined the two, locating the quiet, reflective moment of letter writing within the traditionally boisterous environment of the guard room. He contrasts the intense absorption of the letter writer with the standing messenger, who waits patiently for the seated soldier to complete his missive. Ter Borch's technical prowess in the representation of luxurious materials, textures, and light in paint heightens the immediacy of the moment. The contents of the officer's letter are suggested by the ace of hearts, a traditional emblem of love, that lies on the floor; card playing itself was also a favorite activity of lovers. The broken shards of clay pipe scattered on the floor attest to the merry-making activities usual in such a room, as well as to the frustrations and difficulties the writer has had in expressing his amorous feelings in a letter. KCL

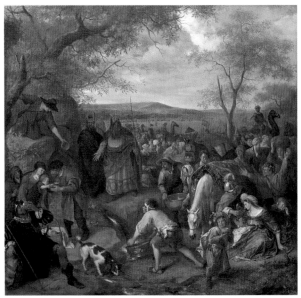

Jan Steen
Dutch, active Leiden, Haarlem, and
The Hague, 1625/26–1679
Moses Striking the Rock
c. 1660–61
Oil on canvas
37⅜ x 38¾″
John G. Johnson Collection. Cat. 509

Jan Steen, beloved painter of earthy and comic domestic scenes, also painted a few subjects with serious moralizing messages drawn from the Bible. Yet even when addressing such elevated themes, Steen used his keen observation of human nature and foibles to enliven his rather untraditional renditions. For instance, in this representation of Moses striking water from the rock, as told in the Book of Exodus, Steen draws attention away from Moses and the miracle itself to the moment after the water has come forth. Reminding us that thirst afflicts rich and poor alike, he shows an elegantly attired woman on the right drinking out of an exotic cup made from a shell, while the humble couple at the left offer water to their child before partaking of it themselves. In this painting, one of ten by Steen in the Museum, he has utilized his skills at depicting a rich variety of characters to enliven the moral message of the Old Testament event. KCL

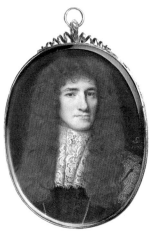

Samuel Cooper
English, 1609–1672
*Portrait of Anthony Ashley
Cooper, First Earl of Shaftesbury*
1670
Watercolor on vellum
3³⁄₁₆ x 2½″
Gift of Mrs. Daniel J. McCarthy
1953-142-10

Small in scale, jewel-like, and coloristically brilliant, miniature portrait paintings were once offered as tokens of love or friendship, and worn by the recipients like precious gems. They were also exchanged among monarchs, noblemen, and politicians as statements of political favor. Samuel Cooper (unrelated to his sitter) was the leading miniature portraitist in the England of his day, and perhaps the last great practitioner of the art in an innovative tradition that reached back two centuries. He painted the great and famous of the age, investing his sitters with both nobility and wit, and was described at his death as "the most famous limner of the world for a face." The first earl of Shaftesbury was an ambitious and complex politician who briefly served as Chancellor of the Exchequer soon after this portrait was painted. The identification of the sitter is based only on its resemblance to a known portrait and has been called into question, but the work itself is one of the finest examples in the Museum's extensive collection of miniatures. CR

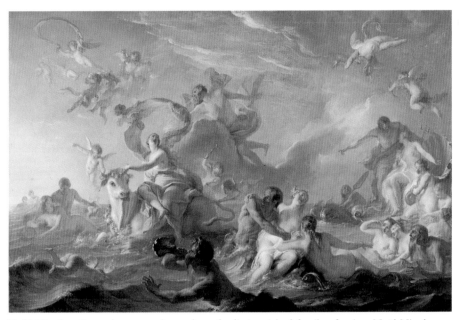

Noël-Nicolas Coypel
French, 1690–1734
The Rape of Europa, 1726–27
Oil on canvas
50¼ x 76⅜"
Gift of John Cadwalader. 1978-160-1

A member of a distinguished family of artists, Noël-Nicolas Coypel entered this work in a now-famous competition among twelve leading French painters that King Louis XV called in 1727. His submission did not win, but numerous visitors to the exhibition of contest paintings commented that Coypel's was by far the finest. Coypel chose a traditional mythological subject, based on Ovid's *Metamorphoses:* in love with the beautiful Europa, the god Jupiter transforms himself into a bull and abducts the nymph. What surely attracted critical attention was the new tone that Coypel's painting introduced into French art, for the palette, ranging from brilliant yellow to palest pinks and blues, the dance of sunlight across the picture plane, the refined, subtle gestures of the figures, and the delicate emotions that play across their features all anticipate the Rococo movement. This painting has been in Philadelphia since 1815, when it came with the art collection of the exiled Joseph Bonaparte, brother of the fallen Emperor Napoleon, and was given by Bonaparte to the Cadwalader family, in which it descended. CR

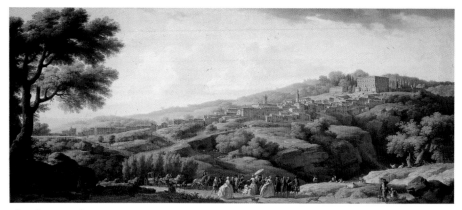

Claude-Joseph Vernet
French, 1714–1789
Villa at Caprarola, 1746
Oil on canvas
52³⁄₁₆ x 121¹³⁄₁₆″
Purchased with the Edith H. Bell Fund
1977-79-1

The most famous French landscape painter of the eighteenth century, Claude-Joseph Vernet worked in Italy between 1734 and 1751, executing sweeping, light-filled, yet meticulously observed views of Rome, Naples, and the surrounding countrysides. In 1745 Cardinal Acquaviva, Spanish ambassador to Rome, commissioned this painting to commemorate the visit of the Italian-born queen of Spain, Elizabeth Farnese, to one of her ancestral homes, the Villa Farnese at Caprarola near Rome. Here Elizabeth, the cardinal, and their elegant entourage have descended from their carriages to take the air. Simple shepherds stare at the grandees in amazement, while at the left Vernet himself sketches the colorful scene. Beyond them the humble village climbs the hillside toward the pentagonal palace-villa, a stately monument to the power of the Farnese family. It was for his ability to combine minute topographical specificity with grandly sweeping landscape in panoramic paintings such as this that Vernet was most appreciated. This picture has been in Philadelphia since 1815, when it was brought by Joseph Bonaparte, who lived here in exile after the fall of his brother Napoleon. CR

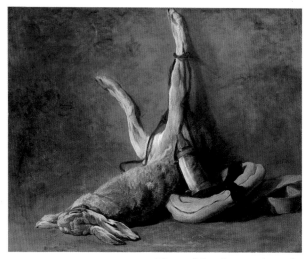

Jean-Baptiste-Siméon Chardin
French, 1699–1779
Still Life with a Hare, c. 1730
Oil on canvas
25⅝ x 32″
Gift of Henry P. McIlhenny. 1958-144-1

The traditional game piece of seventeenth-century Dutch and Flemish painting is a highly colored, elaborately detailed, and often gory trophy of the hunt, where mounds of slaughter, slippery with blood and viscera, spill from laden tabletops. Jean-

Baptiste-Siméon Chardin had no interest in the hunt itself but adapted the genre to his own quiet contemplation of natural phenomena. Bringing to bear close visual scrutiny and a brilliant ability to evoke tactile sensations, he created some of the greatest still-life paintings of the eighteenth century. In a series of game pieces painted around 1730 he depicted dead hares placed among a few simple hunting implements, such as the horn powder flask and hunting bag seen here, studio props that also appear in other paintings. Chardin explored the properties of materials and textures as well as the play of light on objects. Marked by audacious simplicity and directness, this composition is almost monochromatic, the artist's subtle visual discriminations richly evoking tactile experiences and demanding of the viewer equal precision in the act of looking. CR

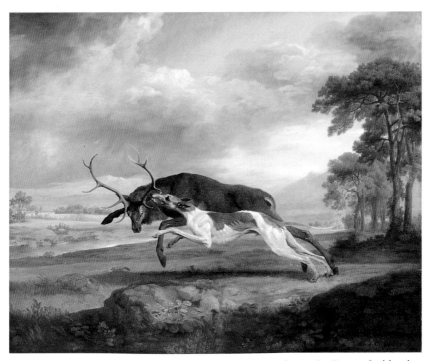

George Stubbs
English, 1724–1806
Hound Coursing a Stag, c. 1762
Oil on canvas
39⅜ x 49½"
Purchased with the W. P. Wilstach Fund, the John D. McIlhenny Fund, and gifts (by exchange) of Samuel S. White 3rd and Vera White, Mrs. R. Barclay Scull, and Edna M. Welsh. W1984-57-1

The preeminent painter of animals, George Stubbs elevated what had been the mundane recording of the sports and amusements of the English aristocracy and country gentry to a new artistic and expressive level. The subject of this canvas derives from the grand seventeenth-century hunt paintings of Peter Paul Rubens and Frans Snyders, and prefigures the more emotional themes explored in the nineteenth century by Sir Edwin Landseer. The image itself is horrific: the dog, after a long and exhausting pursuit, has finally succeeded in attaching himself to the stag; the beast, eyes bulging in terror, flings his stately antlers toward his pursuer. Yet what in the nineteenth century would become a dark and moralistic drama is here played out with balletic elegance and complete detachment, the principals placed against a panoramic landscape bathed in a gentle, blond light. Man seems far distant, and something more cosmic and eternal than mere sport is afoot. JJR

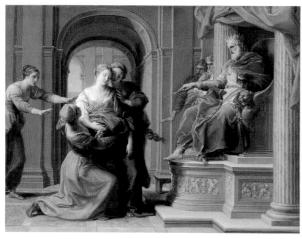

Pompeo Batoni was the dean of painting in eighteenth-century Rome, the most serious link in that city, then still the artistic center of Europe, with the ancients, the masters of the High Renaissance, and the more classical side of the Baroque. Although his reputation today depends on his grand and stylish portraits, it was his ability as a narrative painter within the Roman classical tradition that drew young artists to Batoni's studio. *Esther Before Ahasuerus* is a splendid example of Batoni's use of discretion and restraint in both color and expression to describe an event. According to the Old Testament, it was forbidden by penalty of death to enter unsummoned the presence of Ahasuerus, king of the Medes and Persians. But his wife Esther, seeking his aid in thwarting the plot to destroy her own people, the Jews, defies the royal order and enters the throne room dressed in her finest robes. First stunned, and then overwhelmed by her beauty and heroism, the king forgives her by lowering his scepter and later will join her in destroying her enemy Haman. JJR

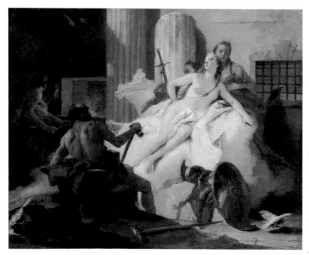

This painting by Giovanni Battista Tiepolo illustrates the episode in Virgil's *Aeneid* in which the goddess Venus visits her estranged husband, Vulcan, at his forge on the island of Lemnos. Reclining haughtily on a cloud, she persuades him to make weapons for her son, Aeneas, and, still moved by his desire for her, Vulcan cannot refuse. Traditionally, the painting has been identified as a sketch for part of the ceiling decoration of the guard room in the Palacio Real, Madrid, where such a pseudo-martial theme would have been elegantly appropriate. More recently, however, scholars have identified it as the pendant to a painting of *Apollo and Daphne,* now in the National Gallery of Art, Washington, D.C. Likely painted as overdoors, both paintings turn on themes of seduction and desire among the deities of classical mythology. CR

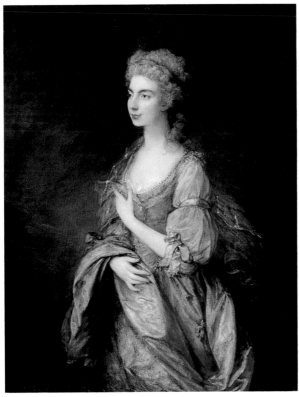

Thomas Gainsborough
English, 1727–1788
Portrait of Lady Rodney, c. 1781
Oil on canvas
50¼ x 39⅞"
The John Howard McFadden
Collection. M1928-1-8

Along with Sir Joshua Reynolds, Thomas Gainsborough was the leading portraitist of eighteenth-century English society. His handling of thin paint brilliantly applied, his ravishingly elegant costumes, and the wit and sophistication with which he endowed his sitters ensured him a steady stream of clients. His subject here is Anne Harley, a daughter of a former lord mayor of London. In April 1781 she married the eldest son of the naval hero Lord Rodney, who would succeed to his father's title in 1793. It has been suggested that the portrait was painted some months after the marriage, and that Anne's delicate gesture of lifting her train to her stomach and her sensual smile signal pregnancy and deep contentment at approaching motherhood. Gainsborough painted a pendant portrait (private collection) of Anne's sister Martha, Lady George Drummond, wearing a similar elegant, low-cut gown of blue silk that is trimmed with pearls. CR

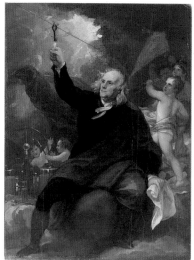

Benjamin West
English, born America, 1738–1820
*Benjamin Franklin Drawing
Electricity from the Sky,* c. 1816
Oil on slate
13⅜ x 10¹/₁₆″
Gift of Mr. and Mrs. Wharton Sinkler
1958-132-1

The painting is a sketch for a large-scale portrait, never executed, that Benjamin West planned for the Pennsylvania Hospital in Philadelphia. It shows Benjamin Franklin engaged in the
famous experiment of June 1752 that proved that lightning was
electricity. West depicts the moment when a spark of electricity,
passing through a key attached to a kite flying in a stormy sky,
jumps to Franklin's raised knuckle. The scene rises to the level
of allegory, however, with Franklin perched on clouds and
surrounded by angelic assistants. Although West and Franklin
were friends in London between 1765 and 1775, and the states-
man/scientist was godfather to the artist's second son, the
portrait was not done from life. Rather, West seems to have
relied on an engraving or a copy after a miniature portrait by
the French artist Jean-Baptiste Weyler of about 1782. CR

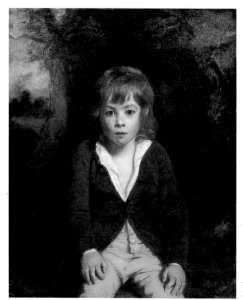

Sir Joshua Reynolds
English, 1723–1792
Portrait of Master Bunbury
1780 or 1781
Oil on canvas
30⅛ x 25⅛″
The John Howard McFadden
Collection. M1928-1-29

The most honored British painter of his time, and founder
and first president of the Royal Academy of Arts in 1768, Joshua

Reynolds stood at the vital center of the social and intellectual life of late eighteenth-century London. A renowned portraitist, faithful in descriptive detail but endowing his sitters with rare grace and elevation, he painted the most august and elegant figures of his day. A more tender note entered his art when his subjects were children, whose vulnerable, trusting natures he captured with exquisite sympathy. Here, the result is particularly intimate as the three-year-old boy is the artist's own godson, Henry Edward Bunbury, the second son of dear friends, whose enthralled attention Reynolds captured during their sittings by telling fairy tales. The artist kept the painting by his side all his life. CR

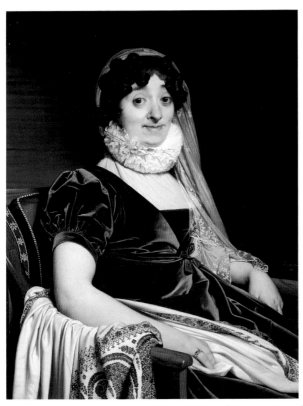

Jean-Auguste-Dominique Ingres
French, 1780–1867
Portrait of the Countess of Tournon, 1812
Oil on canvas
36³⁄₈ x 28¹³⁄₁₆″
The Henry P. McIlhenny Collection in memory of Frances P. McIlhenny
1986-26-22

This painting of the countess of Tournon is one of Jean-Auguste-Dominique Ingres's liveliest and most accomplished early portraits. The countess was a member of the French expatriate colony in Rome, where her son held high office during the Napoleonic occupation. Long past her youth—she was Ingres's only elderly female sitter—and far from beautiful, she was nevertheless witty and wise, and, as with all his most beguiling sitters, Ingres responded with wit and sympathy of his own as he shows her confronting the viewer with a direct, assured gaze full of natural vivacity. The artist pays particular attention to the full, rounded volumes of her arms and her luxurious costume, brilliantly differentiating among the velvet, challis, cashmere, and tulle. Such splendid accouterments in no way swamp the countess's vivid personality. CR

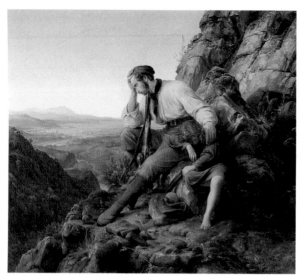

Karl Friedrich Lessing
German, 1808–1880
The Robber and His Child, 1832
Oil on canvas
16⅝ x 19⅛"
The W. P. Wilstach Collection, bequest
of Anna H. Wilstach. W1893-1-65

The noble victim—the man, or surprisingly often, the woman, forced by cruel circumstance to lead a life of crime—was a popular and potent theme in Romantic literature and art. In Germany in particular the saga of the robber was common in both novels and paintings after the late eighteenth century. Karl Friedrich Lessing's depiction of a defeated (and remorseful) man accompanied by his child, who rests on his flight to his mountain lair, takes this genre to a new level of narrative subtlety and human insight. The dramatic effect depends to a large degree on the panoramic landscape that falls away below the exhausted pair. Having been trained in Berlin by a generation of artists steeped in the Germanic landscape tradition (which ironically had developed in Rome at the beginning of the century), Lessing then moved to Düsseldorf, where he is credited with having invented historical landscape painting. JJR

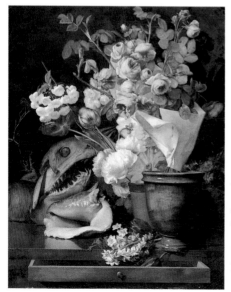

Antoine Berjon
French, 1754–1843
*Still Life with Flowers, Shells,
a Shark's Head, and Petrifications*
1819
Oil on canvas
42½ x 34⁹/₁₆"
Purchased with the Edith H. Bell Fund
1981-62-1

In 1810, Antoine Berjon left Paris for his native Lyons to take up the post of professor of flower painting at the newly founded Ecole des Beaux-Arts. The school had been established by the Napoleonic government in large part to revitalize the city's once-lucrative production of luxury textiles, for which the design of floral patterns and motifs was critical. However, Berjon did not simply transport to Lyons the charming and extremely refined still-life painting style he had practiced in Paris, a style couched in seventeenth-century Dutch painting that was much favored in the court of Empress Josephine. Instead, after his return, his pictures—while still exquisitely observed and rendered—take on a darker and more complex mood, as sensual and expressive conflicts—dry to moist, sharp to soft, sensuous to sinister—are brought nearly to the brink. This work, shown in the Paris Salon of 1819, is perhaps Berjon's masterpiece, standing as it does just between the fresh pleasures of the Neoclassical eighteenth century and the disquieting troubles of the Romantic age. JJR

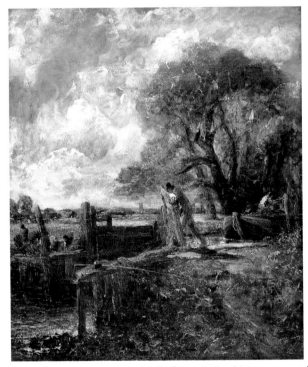

John Constable
English, 1776–1837
Sketch for "A Boat Passing a Lock," 1822–24
Oil on canvas
55½ x 48″
The John Howard McFadden Collection. M1928-1-2

Before painting his monumental, highly finished submissions to the annual exhibitions of the Royal Academy in London, John Constable painted preliminary sketches at the same large scale but with far freer execution. In this sketch for a painting shown at the 1824 exhibition and now in the Thyssen-Bornemisza Collection, Constable worked out the massing of principal forms and, with vivid patches of impasto, the dominant tonalities of the composition. The picture shows a worker opening a sluice gate on a lock while a barge awaits; the setting is Flatford on the River Stour, which was for Constable a constant source of motifs. As the artist himself said of the painting, "It is a lovely subject, of the canal kind, lively—& soothing—calm and exhilarating, fresh—& blowing." CR

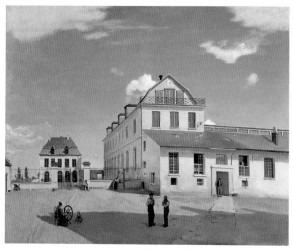

Jean-Baptiste-Camille Corot
French, 1796–1875
House and Factory of Monsieur Henry, 1833
Oil on canvas
32¹/₁₆ x 39½"
Purchased with the W. P. Wilstach Fund
W1950-1-1

Early in his career, Jean-Baptiste-Camille Corot sought to capture the appearance of the physical world with an unblinking directness that seems to anticipate the photograph. During the 1830s he traveled in northern France, painting detailed architectural studies that in their simple volumetric clarity also recall the cityscapes and architectural views of seventeenth-century Dutch painters. Monsieur Henry was a cloth manufacturer, proud of his provincial prosperity, whose house and factory in Soissons, a suburb of Reims, he commissioned the artist to paint in 1833. A pendant showing another view of his property and, across the fields, the spires of Soissons Cathedral, is in the Rijksmuseum Kröller-Müller, Otterlo. Regarding Corot as an amateur who required no compensation, Henry neglected to pay him for the works, now considered to be among the finest of the artist's early career. Corot himself repainted parts of this picture in 1871, when he came to fear it looked too much like the kind of picture postcard that, ironically, did not exist when he first worked on the canvas. CR

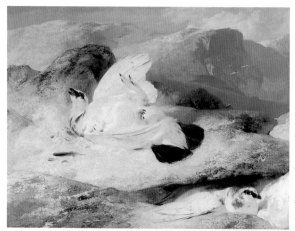

Sir Edwin Landseer
English, 1802–1873
Ptarmigan in a Landscape, by 1833
Oil on panel
19½ x 25¾"
The Henry P. McIlhenny Collection
in memory of Frances P. McIlhenny
1986-26-280

Sir Edwin Landseer drew few distinctions between traditional narrative painting and the depiction of animals. The characters in his pictures are rarely human, yet they play out the drama with the same weight and conviction. Here the protagonists are ptarmigans, the favorite bird of sport in Scotland, which famously mate for life. The male bird has been fatally wounded, his neck turned in mute appeal. The female apparently has also been hit, yet still guards the nest. Four luckier birds escape the slaughter and fly down a huge, empty valley. Such a scene has nobility and tragedy enough for any pair of ill-fated classical lovers. Landseer's great genius is his ability to charm us into abandoning our fear of sentimentality and to engage us in these "pathetic fallacies," which for so much of this century were dismissed as Victorian triviality. Perhaps we need the horrible distance from nature of the post-industrial age to understand again the truth of his observations and sentiments. JJR

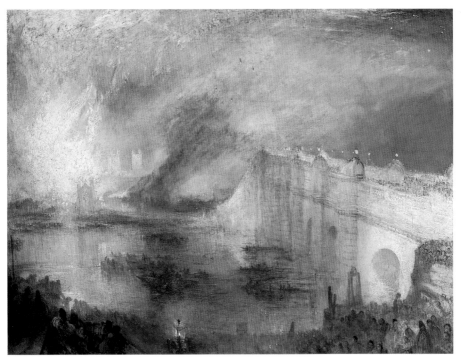

Joseph Mallord William Turner
English, 1775–1851
The Burning of the Houses of Lords and Commons, October 16, 1834, 1834 or 1835
Oil on canvas
36¼ x 48½"
The John Howard McFadden Collection. M1928-1-41

The Houses of Parliament in London burned on the night of October 16, 1834. Along with tens of thousands of spectators, Joseph Mallord William Turner viewed the conflagration from directly opposite the Palace of Westminster, on the south bank of the Thames. Here he exaggerates the scale of Westminster Bridge, which rises like a massive iceberg at right and then on the opposite bank seems to plunge down and dissolve in the blaze. At the dazzling heart of the flames is Saint Stephen's Hall, the House of Commons, while beyond the towers of Westminster Abbey, which would be spared, are eerily illuminated. Turner was drawn to depictions of nature in cataclysmic eruption, and here in the middle of London he confronted a scene of terrifying force and drama that he recorded in several water-color sketches and two paintings, now both in American public collections. The second, painted from further down the river near Waterloo Bridge, is in the Cleveland Museum of Art. CR

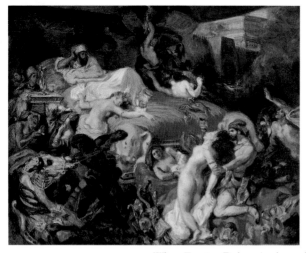

Ferdinand-Victor-Eugène Delacroix
French, 1798–1863
The Death of Sardanapalus, 1846
Oil on canvas
29 x 32⁷⁄₁₆″
The Henry P. McIlhenny Collection
in memory of Frances P. McIlhenny
1986-26-17

When Eugène Delacroix showed his huge painting inspired by Lord Byron's play *Sardanapalus* in the Paris Salon of 1827–28, he changed the history of art completely. With its appearance the splendor and opulence of Baroque painting returned full force, putting to question all the restraint and clarity that had been revered as classical truths. It marked the coming of age of Romanticism and launched the thirty-year-old Parisian's meteoric career. Yet for all its notoriety, Delacroix's painting, now in the Louvre in Paris, was not sold until 1846, when, it is thought, the Museum's quickly worked picture was done as a reprise (in much reduced proportions). The artist's obvious pleasure in mixing color and relaying drama remains undiminished in the copy, as Delacroix records the last moments of the Assyrian king. As his palace is besieged, Sardanapalus reclines on a sumptuous bed atop an immense pyre that will soon be set aflame, and orders the slaughter of all his women, his attendants, and even his horses and dogs, so that no objects of his pleasure would outlive him. JJR

Jean-Baptiste Carpeaux
French, 1827–1875
Princess Mathilde, 1862
Plaster
Height 37″
Purchased with the Fiske Kimball Fund
and funds contributed by the Friends of
the Philadelphia Museum of Art
1978-113-2

Princess Mathilde was the cousin of Louis-Napoleon Bonaparte, who declared himself Emperor Napoleon III of France in 1852. As his official hostess until his marriage and through her alliance with the Superintendent of Fine Arts, Count Alfred Nieuwerkerke, she became the second most powerful woman in France and, by virtue of her interest in the visual arts, a great force in the making of taste and artists' reputations. Mathilde's request that Jean-Baptiste Carpeaux sculpt her portrait in 1861 was therefore a critical step in his official ascendancy, and laid the foundation for him to receive a series of commissions from the imperial family and the state. Her faith in this artist steeped in the traditions of Hellenistic sculpture and Michelangelo's Rome would prove to be well founded, for Carpeaux broke completely with the conservative classicism of sculptural portraiture of the time, returning instead to the full-blown representationalism of seventeenth-century French sculpture— aloof and splendid and tremendously alive. JJR

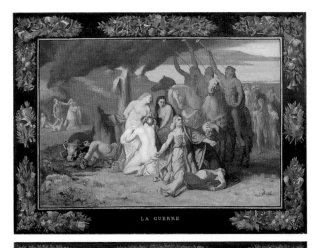

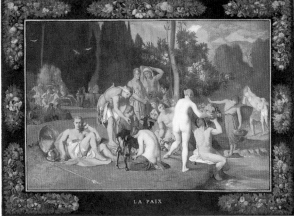

Pierre Puvis de Chavannes
French, 1824–1898
War (top) and **Peace** (bottom)
1867
Oil on canvas
43⅛ x 58¾" (*War*)
42⅞ x 58½" (*Peace*)
John G. Johnson Collection
Cats. 1062, 1063

By the end of the nineteenth century, Pierre Puvis de Chavannes was among the best known and most praised French artists. The fame of his murals made him a great public figure, with all the association with convention that this implies. Over time this "official" persona obscured Puvis's truly innovative contributions. With Jean-Baptiste-Camille Corot he was at the foundation of French progressive painting, distancing himself from his subjects through poetic homogenization in a way that would attract Paul Cézanne, and introducing the harmonious and blurred pictorial effect that would profoundly influence Paul Gauguin and the Symbolists. These two paintings are reduced versions of Puvis's large murals shown first in 1861. The historical vagueness of the subjects is intentional: *War* takes place in some general Northern Druidic/Gallic time, while *Peace* seems to move closer to the Mediterranean and a golden age of eternal youth. Through his tremendously subtle and understated use of color and ability to retain a graceful unity within a complex design, Puvis lifted decorative painting to a new level. JJR

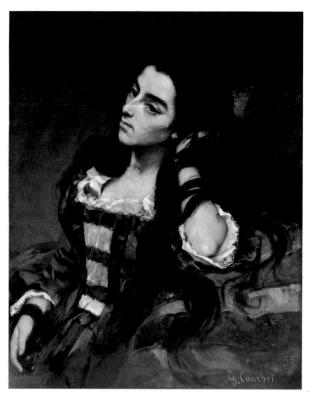

Gustave Courbet
French, 1819–1877
Spanish Woman, 1855
Oil on canvas
31 ⅝ x 25 ½″
John G. Johnson Collection. Inv. 2265

Gustave Courbet showed eleven paintings, including some of his largest and most ambitious works, at the enormous art exhibition associated with the Exposition Universelle in Paris in 1855. It was this relatively small, straightforward depiction of a Spanish woman, however, that attracted the most scathing criticism. One critic declared the sitter a victim of Parisian dissipation, while another wondered why she was so swarthy and haggard. In fact, her meditative and sensual pose, fingers entwined in cascading hair, derives from an impeccable Renaissance prototype, and such depictions of national "types" were by no means novel in Courbet's time. Rather, the directness of paint handling and vivid contrasts of bright and somber colors, with their anticipation of Edouard Manet's art a decade later, may have struck an uneasy note with the critics who sensed that traditional modes of painting and canons of beauty would henceforth be under siege. The sitter may have been a Spanish woman whom the artist had met in Lyons in 1854. Visible by X ray underneath is a completed half-length portrait of another, quite different woman. CR

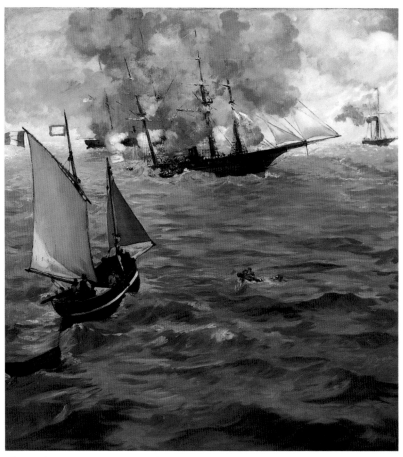

Edouard Manet
French, 1832–1883
The Battle of the "Kearsarge" and the "Alabama," 1864
Oil on canvas
54¼ x 50¾"
John G. Johnson Collection. Cat. 1027

On the morning of June 19, 1864, one of the most important naval battles of the American Civil War took place on the high seas beyond the harbor of Cherbourg, France, as the Confederate warship the *Alabama* engaged the Union ship the *Kearsarge;* at the battle's end, the *Alabama* was sunk. This long-anticipated combat attracted huge crowds of sightseers, including perhaps Edouard Manet, who is reported to have witnessed the scene from a pilot boat. Less than a month later this painting was on display in the window of a Paris picture dealer's shop, where it attracted praise for its verisimilitude. Manet's first attempt at depicting a contemporary event, the painting shows the influence of Japanese prints in its audacious spatial organization and use of vivid colors, and represents a startling break with the conventions of marine painting. CR

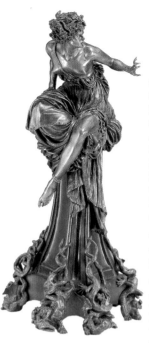

Marcello (Duchesse de Castiglione-Colonna, born Adèle d'Affry)
Swiss, 1836–1879
Pythian Sibyl, after 1869–70
Bronze
Height 31½″
Purchased with the Fiske Kimball Fund
and the Marie Kimball Fund. 1973-251-1

Like the contemporary writer George Sand, Adèle d'Affry, widow of the duke of Castiglione-Colonna, gave her name a sexual shift when she exhibited and signed her work "Marcello." She was one of the most celebrated women artists of her day, receiving several commissions from the French state during the Second Empire (1852–70) and exhibiting regularly at the Paris Salon. Her artistic biases were very much those of her close friend Jean-Baptiste Carpeaux, with sixteenth-century Italian sculpture, particularly that of Michelangelo, as their standard. Marcello often did figures of heroic women, and in the 1870 Salon showed a *Pythian Sibyl,* one of the mythical seers of antiquity. Charles Garnier commissioned it in bronze, at twice the size of life, for his new opera house in Paris, where it is placed as if in a grotto, the snakes and lizards rising up from a pool of water that casts an eerie up-light on the twisting figure. This bronze is a reduction of the one in the Paris Opéra. JJR

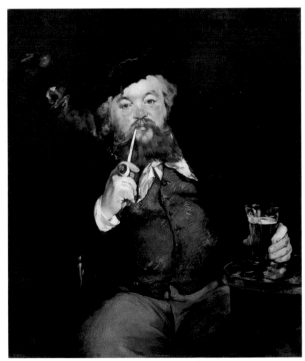

Edouard Manet
French, 1832–1883
Le Bon Bock, 1873
Oil on canvas
37¼ x 32¹³⁄₁₆″
The Mr. and Mrs. Carroll S. Tyson, Jr.,
Collection. 1963-116-9

In 1872 Edouard Manet traveled to Holland, and the trip reinvigorated his long-standing appreciation of seventeenth-century

Dutch genre painting. At the Paris Salon the following year he showed this lively picture of a man enjoying his *bock,* or springtime beer, that is directly influenced by such images. The warm tonalities and lively handling of paint particularly recall the work of Frans Hals. The painting was well received at the Salon, where the evocation of old master painting styles was much appreciated. This work also presented few of those surprising disjunctions of color to which conventional critics of Manet often reacted violently. Manet's model, who endured more than sixty sittings, was a neighbor of the artist named Bellot. CR

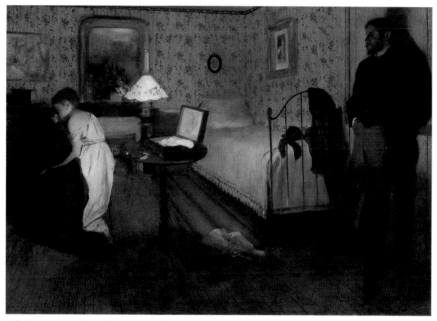

Hilaire-Germain-Edgar Degas
French, 1834–1917
Interior, 1868 or 1869
Oil on canvas
32 x 45"
The Henry P. McIlhenny Collection in memory of Frances P. McIlhenny
1986-26-10

After years of ambitious if equivocal attempts at monumental paintings on grand historical themes, by the late 1860s Edgar Degas increasingly turned to depictions of modern subjects. The dramatic play of artificial light and evening shadow in this painting, and the palpable sense of anxiety it transmits, are unique in Degas's scenes of private life. Although it is not without discrepancies in detail, the most convincing identification of the subject, proposed by the Degas scholar Theodore Reff, is that it illustrates a scene from Emile Zola's novel *Thérèse Raquin* (1867). Reunited on their wedding night, one year after they have killed Thérèse's husband, the lovers are overwhelmed by the enormity of their crime and retreat from one another into bitter isolation. Degas himself referred to it as "my genre picture," and it may have been intended for British collectors who appreciated the psychological tension in narratives painted by artists such as Sir John Everett Millais and Degas's friend James Tissot. The alternate title, *The Rape,* by which the picture also has long been known, does not seem to derive from Degas himself. CR

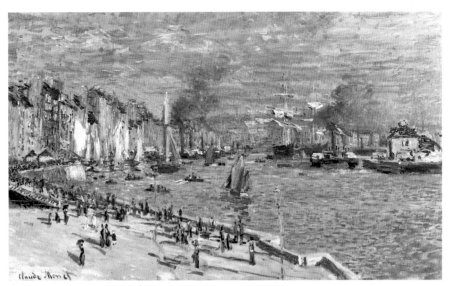

Claude Monet
French, 1840–1926
Port of Le Havre, 1874
Oil on canvas
23¾ x 40⅛"
Bequest of Mrs. Frank Graham
Thomson. 1961-48-3

In 1874, the year in which he painted this canvas, Claude Monet was staying with his family at the Hôtel l'Amirauté in Le Havre, which gave him a good view down into the busy port. It was nearly the same vista that he painted in the fog in *Impression: Fog* (1872), whose title gave rise to the name that was to be applied to Monet and his fellow independent artists when they exhibited together. Works such as *Port of Le Havre* have the quality of coming from the dawn of a movement. All of Monet's ideas and gestures expressed in the painting seem completely fresh, uncalculated, and direct, very much in keeping with the animated view out his hotel window that he was recording. Among the nineteen paintings by Monet in the Museum, this is perhaps the most firmly aligned to all of the revolutionary energy and change that marked the early years of Impressionism. JJR

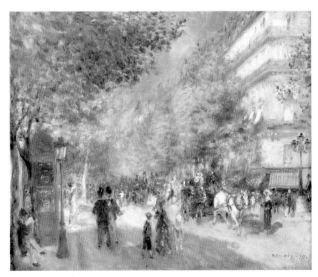

Pierre-Auguste Renoir
French, 1841–1919
The Grand Boulevards, 1875
Oil on canvas
20½ x 25"
The Henry P. McIlhenny Collection
in memory of Frances P. McIlhenny
1986-26-29

While many of the greatest Impressionist paintings of the 1870s by Pierre-Auguste Renoir and his contemporaries are festive scenes of suburban or rural sociability, the city, particularly Paris, also provided a constant source of vibrant motifs. In this painting, executed the year after the first Impressionist exhibition was held in Paris, Renoir depicts one of the so-called *grands boulevards* cutting through the heart of the city. These broad new avenues lined with uniform—some thought monotonous—stone facades had been built in the 1850s and 1860s by the town-planner Baron Georges Eugène Haussmann, and they transformed Paris into a modern metropolis. Renoir clearly relishes the contemporary bustle, filling his canvas with traffic and commerce and lively, hurried sociability, all unified by the shimmering play of light filtering through the treetops. CR

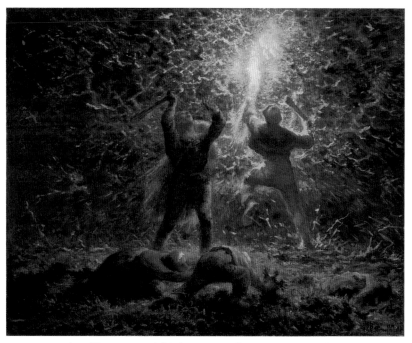

Jean-François Millet
French, 1814–1875
Bird's-Nesters, 1874
Oil on canvas
29 x 36½"
The William L. Elkins Collection
E1924-3-14

This haunting and strange picture—brutishly literal yet terrifyingly generic—is the final painting by Jean-François Millet, a remarkable last testament by one of the most profound artists of the nineteenth century. He drew on his own boyhood experiences in depicting the subject of bird's-nesters, who would hunt flocks of pigeons at night by blinding them with torchlight and then clubbing them to death. By the 1870s Millet's paintings of rural life were among the most famous in France. His subjects are nearly all drawn from the peasantry, done just as the countryside was being depopulated by immigration to the new industrial centers. But unlike many other artists who worked in the very popular specialty of "peasant painting," Millet's great genius was his ability to bond his subjects to their native place while simultaneously elevating them to a level of universal humanity. Much of his success was based on his evocation of a communal memory of a lost rural world that was either arcadian or pathetic or a combination of both. JJR

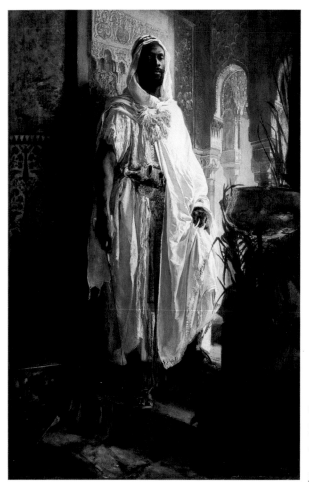

Eduard Charlemont
Austrian, 1848–1906
The Moorish Chief, 1878
Oil on panel
59⅛ x 38½″
John G. Johnson Collection. Cat. 951

The exotically elusive yet strongly suggestive effect of this
picture is demonstrated by the migration of its title. Shown at
the Paris Salon in 1878 as *The Guardian of the Seraglio,* it was purchased by John G. Johnson in 1892 as *The Alhambra Guard* and
published by him in 1914 as *The Moorish Chief,* the name that has
stuck. Thus from its earliest days something about this image
of a commanding black man, sword bared, who stands before
a space modeled on the Alhambra in Spain, impelled both a
clarification of his role and an elevation of his rank. Only part
of Eduard Charlemont's career was given over to the popular
genre of "Orientalist" painting, which represented subjects
drawn from North Africa and the Middle East. Perhaps it was
his Austrian background that spawned a kind of overripe, hot-
house style in his work that saved him from falling into the
all-too-conventional drawing-room titillation that plagued
Orientalism as a genre. Here his sense of staging is perfect,
and his leading man a star. JJR

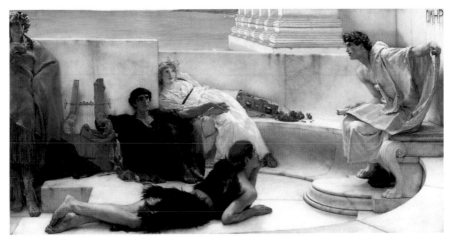

**Sir Lawrence
Alma-Tadema**

English, born Netherlands,
1836–1912
A Reading from Homer, 1885
Oil on canvas
36⅛ x 72¼"
The George W. Elkins Collection
E1924-4-1

When this picture was bought by one of the Museum's most generous donors, George W. Elkins, in 1903, it was one of the most expensive works of art ever sold. A taste for this type of "Victorians in Toga" painting did not last into the next generation, however, and by the 1920s Sir Lawrence Alma-Tadema's reputation, and market, had plummeted. But those things that had so pleased Elkins as well as Henry Marquand, who had commissioned this painting for his New York recital room, are now again a little more within our reach. The story told in the painting is a wonder of simplicity, just as the execution is a marvel in the rendering of materials and textures. In a marble palace far above the sea a handsome man, crowned with laurels, reads from a long scroll to a rapt if varied audience. As depicted by Alma-Tadema, himself a completely guileless and genuine storyteller and craftsman, such a far-off time does not seem so very inaccessible, and such seemingly noble people do not seem so very different from us. JJR

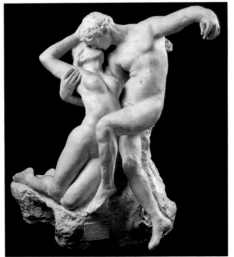

Auguste Rodin

French, 1840–1917
Eternal Springtime, 1884
Painted plaster
Height 26"
Gift of Paul Rosenberg. 1953-26-1

Like many of Auguste Rodin's most innovative works, this sculpture is a compilation of separately conceived elements. The female nude was made in 1882 as an independent work, and two years later the artist combined it with the male nude figure to create a deeply human, intensely erotic celebration of physical love. Here, Rodin explores the bodily expression of extreme emotional states, the audaciously outstretched arm of the man investing the sculpture with a sense that the force of emotion has propelled the lovers into a precarious, free-floating vortex of love and longing, beyond the constraints of the physical world. At this time the artist was frequently sketching live models as they moved around him, and the spirit of youth and freedom in those drawings informs such daring sculptures as well. In 1885 Rodin gave this plaster to the writer Robert Louis Stevenson, inscribing it, at the bottom, "to the sympathetic Artist, to the great and dear poet." The Philadelphia collection also contains a bronze cast of the work. CR

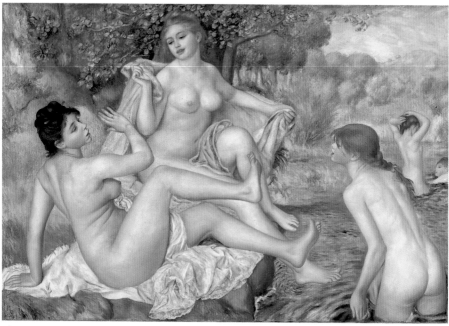

Pierre-Auguste Renoir
French, 1841–1919
The Great Bathers, 1884–87
Oil on canvas
46⅜ x 67¼″
The Mr. and Mrs. Carroll S. Tyson, Jr.,
Collection. 1963-116-13

In the 1880s Pierre-Auguste Renoir sought to move his art beyond Impressionism and to forge a link between modern art and the classical tradition of French painting, represented for him by such great painters and sculptors of the past as Jean Goujon, François Girardon, and Nicolas Poussin. The result was this large-scale composition of nude bathers, which occupied much of his attention for some three years and was preceded by numerous preparatory studies. Using as his source a bas-relief by the seventeenth-century sculptor Girardon in the garden of Versailles, he executed a perfectly still, carefully composed grouping of monumental figures. Although the theme of nude bathers would stay with Renoir throughout his career, some of his Impressionist colleagues thought that with this work he had betrayed the cause of modernist painting by retreating to classicism. CR

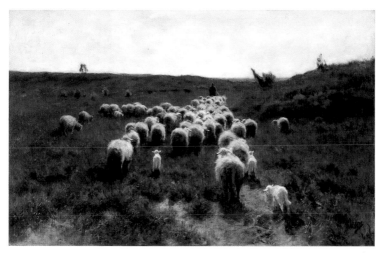

Anton Mauve
Dutch, active Haarlem, Amsterdam, The Hague, and Laren,
1838–1888
The Return of the Flock, Laren
c. 1886–87
Oil on canvas
39⁷⁄₁₆ x 63½″
The George W. Elkins Collection
E1924-4-21

Despite the high regard that Vincent van Gogh had for his cousin Anton Mauve (and the strong influence that the elder Mauve had on Vincent's early style), it was only recently that some of the very great reputation that Mauve and his fellow painters of the so-called Hague School enjoyed in their own day has been partly regained. Luckily this Museum owns an important and representative collection of the works of these artists, of whom Mauve is one of the most affecting. Mauve was a master of depicting moist, low places populated by domestic animals and their anonymous keepers. As *The Return of the Flock, Laren,* so convincingly demonstrates, his ability to control gentle, nearly monochromatic tones, while not losing a sense of either the place or the moment, puts him in direct and happy comparison with the two French artists he most admired: Jean-Baptiste-Camille Corot and Jean-François Millet. JJR

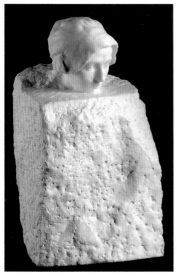

Auguste Rodin
French, 1840–1917
Thought, 1886–89
Marble
Height 29⅛″
John G. Johnson Collection. Cat. 1148

For Auguste Rodin, sculptural meaning always resided in the human form, and with *Thought* he explores the power of intellection, resident in the mind, to animate and transmute blind nature. This work was an experiment, as he once explained, an attempt to see if he could sculpt a head that seemed so alive as to give vitality to the stone from which it was made. Here a beautiful and subtly carved female head emerges from a jagged block of raw marble. Her chin still embedded in rock, the transformation is incomplete, and the dichotomy between inert matter and pulsing flesh remains tensely unresolved. Poignantly, the model for *Thought* was the talented sculptor Camille Claudel, who was Rodin's mistress at the time and his collaborator before their definitive rupture in the early 1890s. CR

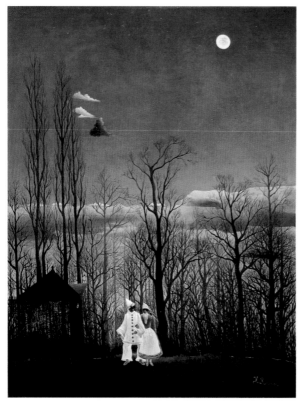

Henri-Julien-Félix Rousseau
French, 1844–1910
Carnival Evening, 1886
Oil on canvas
46 3/16 x 35 1/4"
The Louis E. Stern Collection
1963-181-64

First shown in the second Salon des Indépendants in Paris in 1886, this painting is an early demonstration of Henri Rousseau's unique chromatic imagination, his proto-Surrealist ability to juggle unexpected pictorial elements, and his untutored but brilliant skill in the stylization of forms. An officer in the French customs service, Rousseau scoured picture books of adventures in exotic locales in search of pictorial motifs. He combined these disparate elements in compelling images that early in the twentieth century attracted the devotion of vanguard artists such as Pablo Picasso. Here Rousseau locates mute, unmoving figures in carnival costume against a calligraphic backdrop of bare black tree trunks and branches. The dwindling light of dusk that filters down through the trees and the crisp winter chill, vividly evoked, both carry a hint of menace. Isolated and vulnerable in their fantasy clothing, the two figures confront the viewer bravely and with naïve conviction, like characters waiting for Samuel Beckett to write them a play. CR

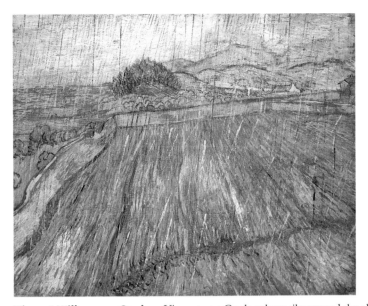

Vincent Willem van Gogh
Dutch, 1853–1890
Rain, 1889
Oil on canvas
28⅞ x 36⅜"
The Henry P. McIlhenny Collection
in memory of Frances P. McIlhenny
1986-26-36

Vincent van Gogh voluntarily entered the clinic of Saint-Paul-de-Mausolée in southern France on May 8, 1889. The sanatorium sits just over the mountains from Arles, where Vincent had spent the previous winter producing some of his more energetic and moving canvases. It was also where he had suffered his most severe mental breakdowns, which eventually prompted his hospitalization. From his workroom at the clinic Van Gogh looked down on an enclosed field of wheat. During his eleven-month stay he drew or painted this view some twelve times. This picture of the wheat field during a rainstorm is the only work of its kind he did in the South, and while the idea of representing rainfall by diagonal slashes of paint clearly relates to Van Gogh's interest in Japanese prints, the final effect is completely personal and well beyond any borrowed source. There is truly nothing quite like it in his considerable output— truly nothing so gently and objectively observed, nothing so completely revealing his own state of mind. JJR

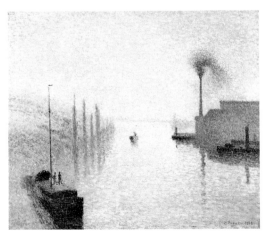

Camille Pissarro
Danish, active France, 1830–1903
L'Ile Lacroix, Rouen (The Effect of Fog), 1888
Oil on canvas
18⅜ x 22"
John G. Johnson Collection. Cat. 1060

During the late 1880s, Camille Pissarro was drawn to the brilliant young artist Georges Seurat's pointillist painting technique, which consisted of composing images by using countless tiny dots of color. Not only did Pissarro champion Seurat's works to skeptical friends but also, for a few years, himself adopted the pointillist style. With its subtle palette of pink, white, and rose, this simple, atmospheric view of a docked boat seen through the fog achieves a stillness and serenity comparable to the almost hypnotic slowness of Seurat's own seacoast landscapes. Pissarro's composition precisely follows an etching of 1883 and was probably done entirely in his studio rather than before the actual scene. Painting in this manner was excruciatingly slow, however, and Pissarro, an especially prolific artist, executed relatively few works in the pointillist style. Indeed, he would soon move on to a revised Impressionist style and abandon pointillism, not only because it hampered his naturally spontaneous temperament, but also perhaps because he found it difficult to produce a sufficient body of work to support a large and demanding family. CR

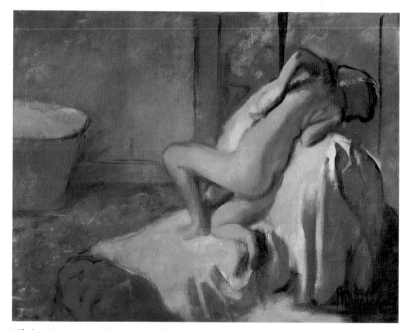

Hilaire-Germain-Edgar Degas

French, 1834–1917
After the Bath (Woman Drying Herself), c. 1896
Oil on canvas
35¼ x 46″
Purchased with funds from the estate of George D. Widener. 1980-6-1

This is one of three paintings that Edgar Degas executed around 1896 of a woman seen from the rear as she reclines awkwardly on the back of a chaise longue. Anticipated by both a photograph (The J. Paul Getty Museum, Malibu) and a drawing (private collection), the paintings have elicited wide-ranging interpretations from critics attempting to understand the woman's contorted pose and the strange fusion of eroticism and anguish it suggests. Of the three paintings, this is the simplest, the most thinly painted, and the most monochromatic, characteristics that have indicated to some that the work is unfinished. More likely, the fiery red canvas is evidence of Degas's increasing interest in pictorial abstraction in his later years, and his daring play with viewers' expectations of compositional completeness. Even in its simplicity and spareness, this is a fully resolved composition, and brilliant evidence of Degas's ability to innovate throughout his long career. CR

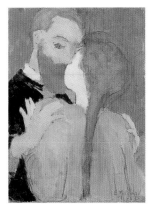

Edouard Vuillard
French, 1868–1940
Self-Portrait with Sister, c. 1892
Oil on paper on cardboard
9 x 6½"
The Louis E. Stern Collection
1963-181-76

During the 1890s, when he was part of the group of experimental young artists who called themselves the Nabis, Edouard Vuillard developed a painting style that incorporated broad areas of flat color, simple, stylized forms, and the decorative play of elegant line. His works of the period bear often-unsettling intimations of psychological, moral, and spiritual complexity. Even small paintings like this, jewel-like in the brilliance of its matte colors, suggest depths of emotional intensity. Here, Vuillard, bearded, depicts himself embracing his sister Marie (Mimi). In reality she was seven years his senior, but, with her long pigtail, she appears far younger than the artist. The strange melding of the two forms and the intense and febrile intimacy of the embrace hint at a troubling ambiguity in the dynamics of family life. In later years, Vuillard's family and friends, observed at moments of domestic intimacy, provided constant subjects for his art. Rarely, however, are the images as haunting and ambivalent. CR

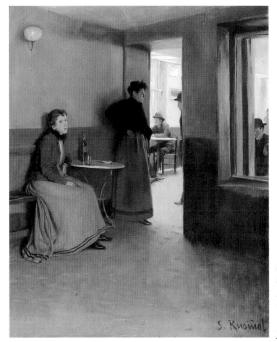

Santiago Rusiñol
Spanish (Catalan), 1861–1931
Interior of a Café, 1892
Oil on canvas
39½ x 32"
John G. Johnson Collection. Cat. 1078

A painter, writer, and collector active in the *modernista* movement in Spain, Santiago Rusiñol from 1889 divided his time between Paris and Barcelona, where he was a founder of the avant-garde art group El Quatre Gats, and a friend and confidant of the young Pablo Picasso. In 1892 Rusiñol exhibited this picture in Paris as *The Aquarium,* the name referring to a Barcelona café whose walls were painted a vivid aquamarine. The dark realism of the image and the isolation of the principal figure, most likely a prostitute far gone in drink, recall the Parisian café scenes of Edgar Degas, while the high-keyed coloration and poetic stylization of forms anticipate Picasso's own works of his so-called Blue Period a decade later. The painting was bought in Paris in 1892 on behalf of the great Philadelphia collector John G. Johnson. Best known for his early Italian and seventeenth-century Dutch paintings, Johnson was also an important patron of the art of his own time, including the latest currents emerging in Europe. CR

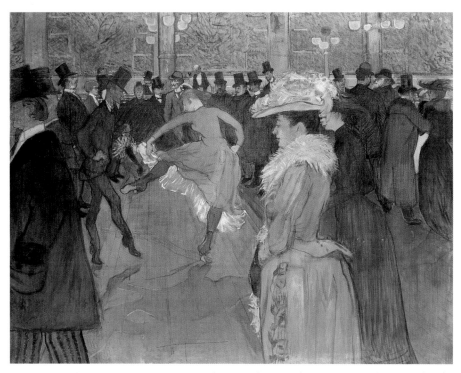

Henri de Toulouse-Lautrec
French, 1864–1901
At the Moulin Rouge: The Dance
1890
Oil on canvas
45½ x 59″
The Henry P. McIlhenny Collection
in memory of Frances P. McIlhenny
1986-26-32

A recently discovered penciled inscription, in the artist's hand, on the back of this famous painting reads: "The instruction of the new ones by Valentine the Boneless." Henri de Toulouse-Lautrec was thus not depicting an ordinary evening at the Moulin Rouge, the fashionable Parisian nightclub, but rather a specific moment when a man now known only by his nickname (which certainly describes his nimbleness as a dancer) appears to be teaching the "can-can." Many of the inhabitants of the scene are well-known members of Lautrec's demimonde of prostitutes and artists and people seen only at night, including the white-bearded Irish poet William Butler Yeats, who leans on the bar. One of the mysteries, however, is the dominant woman in the foreground, the beauty of her profile made all the more so in comparison with that of her chinless companion. It is the latter who expresses better than nearly any other character in this full stage of people Lautrec's profoundly touching ability to be brutally truthful but also truly kind in his observations. JJR

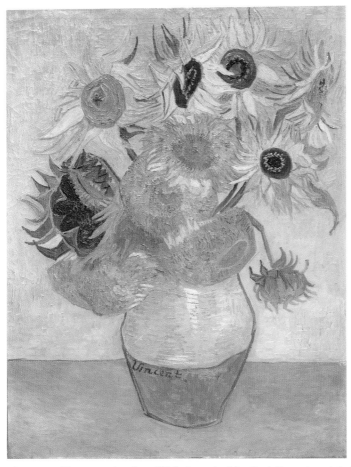

Vincent Willem van Gogh
Dutch, 1853–1890
Sunflowers, 1888 or 1889
Oil on canvas
36⅜ x 28″
The Mr. and Mrs. Carroll S. Tyson, Jr.,
Collection. 1963-116-19

While he waited for Paul Gauguin to join him in the Provençal city of Arles in 1888, Vincent van Gogh painted five audaciously decorative still lifes of sunflowers in simple earthenware jugs. At least two of these canvases decorated Gauguin's bedroom when he reached the city late in October, and the French painter came to admire them greatly. Always defensive about the tragic outcome of his stay—it ended with Van Gogh's self-mutilation and madness—Gauguin later claimed that the sunflower paintings directly reflected his own good advice, generously offered in Arles, that his Dutch friend avoid monotony by adding "bugle notes" of brilliant color to his paintings. Whether the Philadelphia *Sunflowers* precedes Gauguin's visit or is one of two replicas Van Gogh painted the following year, it is an explosion of brilliant color and agitated outlines, the twelve flowers as full of angular energy and as vital and vivid in personality as the artist who painted them. CR

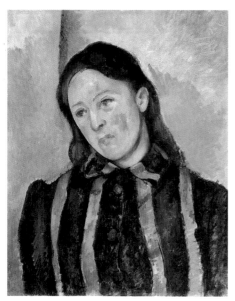

Paul Cézanne
French, 1839–1906
Portrait of Madame Cézanne
1890–92
Oil on canvas
24⅜ x 20⅛″
The Henry P. McIlhenny Collection
in memory of Frances P. McIlhenny
1986-26-1

Paul Cézanne met Hortense Fiquet in Paris in 1869, when she was a nineteen-year-old artist's model. Their only child, Paul, Jr., was born in 1872; the couple married, perhaps as much to please Cézanne's dying father as for any other reason, in 1886. From what little is known of their lives, their relationship was difficult, and she certainly never comprehended the importance of her husband's art, although she did sit for him for some forty-four portraits. For all the formal power of these images, which often, as seen here, have a sense of volume in space that is nearly sculptural, they are also among the most moving portraits of the nineteenth century, a quality that is never more evident than in this melancholy and haunting picture. JJR

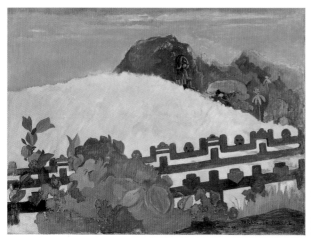

Paul Gauguin
French, 1848–1903
*The Sacred Mountain
(Parahi Te Marae),* 1892
Oil on canvas
26 x 35″
Gift of Mr. and Mrs. Rodolphe
Meyer de Schauensee. 1980-1-1

Paul Gauguin was a cheat and a liar and an all-around cad. He was also a very great genius who took, or forced, French progressive painting to a new level of experimental invention, all the while creating a mythology about himself—the savage rebel—and a place—Tahiti and the South Seas—that has withstood debunking for over a century. Gauguin made his first trip to Tahiti in 1891, but soon retreated, sick and broke, back to

Paris, where he showed this and other Tahitian works with little success. With time, however, came public awareness of the great imaginative power of these paintings, which arises from the magical world Gauguin invented after his encounter with a truly exotic (and slightly scary) civilization. Here, although the fence with its decoration of skulls, the idol on the hill, and the evocation of sacrifice in a thread of smoke ascending before the demanding god have no basis in Tahitian culture, Gauguin has created another kind of paradise in the opulence of his color and the splendid sensuality of his images. JJR

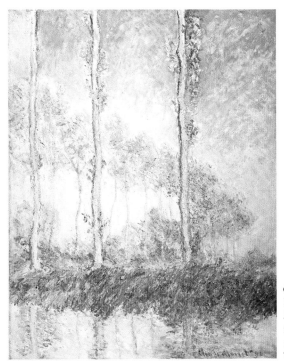

Claude Monet
French, 1840–1926
Poplars, 1891
Oil on canvas
36⅝ x 29⁹⁄₁₆″
The Chester Dale Collection. 1951-109-1

During much of 1891 Claude Monet worked on a series of paintings depicting the tall, thin poplar trees that lined the River Epte near his home at Giverny, France. Painting from a small boat, he worked on several pictures at once, exchanging one canvas for another as light and weather conditions changed during the day. When he learned that the poplars were in danger of destruction, he and a wood seller bought the trees, his partner agreeing to spare them until Monet had completed his work. Moving up and down the river, the artist chose certain groups of trees, capturing them and their shimmering reflections in the water under changing intensities of sunlight and shadow; this painting is one of several, full of the golden light of autumn, that focus on three poplars in the foreground and a great arc of trees curving away beyond. Monet's second great series exploring motifs in the French countryside—his "Grainstacks" had come a year before—some fifteen "Poplars," including this canvas, were first exhibited to rapturous acclaim at the Galerie Durand-Ruel in Paris in February 1892. CR

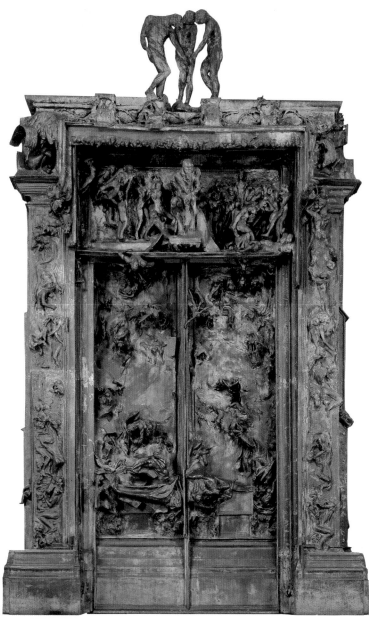

Auguste Rodin
French, 1840–1917
The Gates of Hell, 1880–1917
Bronze
250¾ x 158 x 33⅜″
Bequest of Jules E. Mastbaum
F1929-7-128

From the moment the work was commissioned in 1880 until his death thirty-seven years later, *The Gates of Hell* dominated much of Auguste Rodin's life, thought, and labor. Inspired by Dante's *Inferno* and permeated by the sense of anguish expressed in the numerous writhing, nude figures, *The Gates* conveys Rodin's own deeply felt sense of the tragic fate of humanity. Over the years, the artist constantly reworked the doors, adding, subtracting, and altering figures and their relationships. Many of his most memorable individual sculptures, including *The Thinker,* began as figures for *The Gates.* The planned museum in Paris for which the doors had been commissioned remained unbuilt, however, and Rodin's great project existed only in plaster when he died. It was the Philadelphia theater entrepreneur Jules Mastbaum who commissioned the first two bronze casts of the doors, one for his native city and the other for the Musée Rodin in Paris. Today the Philadelphia cast still stands at the entrance to the Rodin Museum that Mastbaum gave to the City of Philadelphia. CR

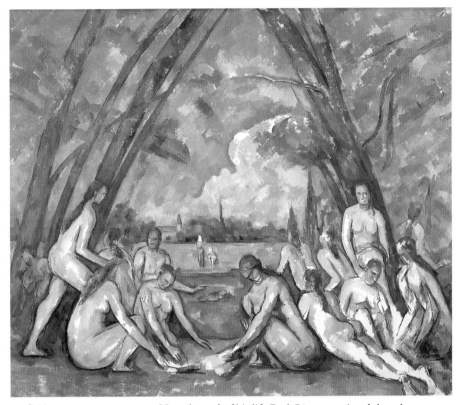

Paul Cézanne
French, 1839–1906
The Large Bathers, 1906
Oil on canvas
82⅞ x 98¾"
Purchased with the W. P. Wilstach Fund
W1937-1-1

Near the end of his life Paul Cézanne painted three large canvases of female nudes disporting in a landscape. They derive in part from pastoral images of female bathers, such as the goddess Diana and her maidens, long favored in French art. These works seem to have been, for Cézanne, the culmination of a lifetime of exploration on the nude, his final testament within the grand tradition of French narrative painting on the nature of the human condition. They differ greatly from one another, these three paintings (the others are in the Barnes Foundation, Merion, Pennsylvania, and the National Gallery, London). The Philadelphia version, perhaps because of its unfinished state, is both the most exalted and the most serene. The women command a great stage, very much like goddesses in some grand opera production, with the arched trees acting as the proscenium. They are completely at ease, and for all the motion and activity there is a profound sense of eternal calm and resolution, as well as a quality of monumentality achieved through the most lucid and unlabored means. JJR

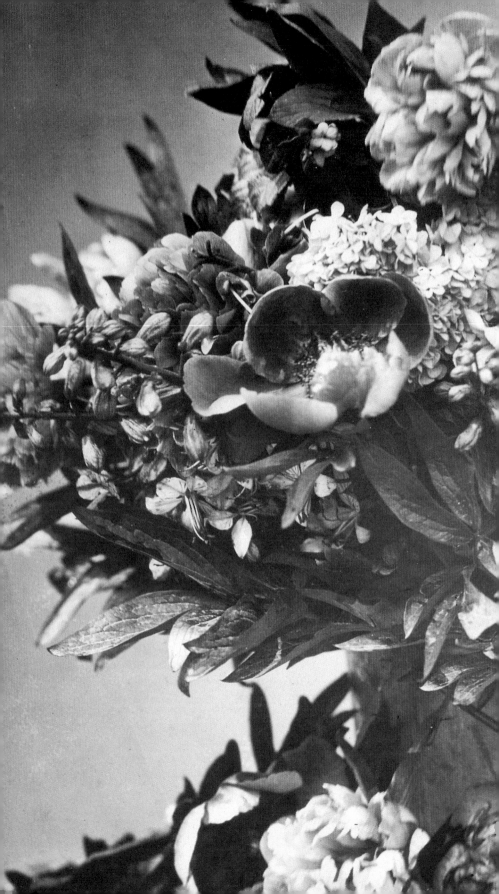

Prints, Drawings, and Photographs

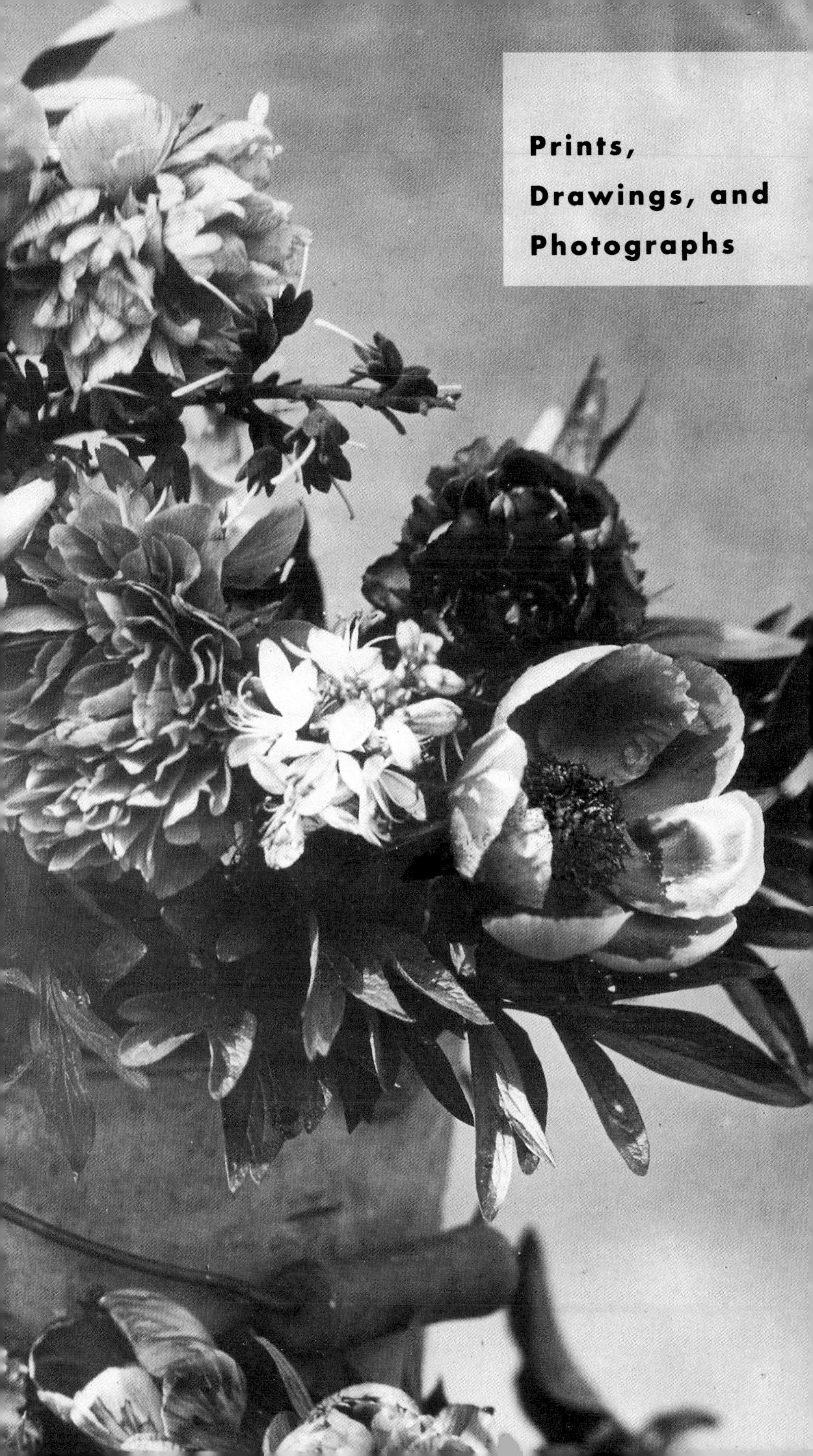

Prints, Drawings, and Photographs

With the appointment of Carl Zigrosser as curator of prints in 1940, the department began to assume its present shape as a comprehensive collection of works of art on paper, formed chiefly with the gifts of collectors and artists. A prolific author and zealous collector, Zigrosser came to the Museum from the Weyhe Gallery in New York. With meager purchase funds at his disposal, he made use of his personal contacts with artists and dealers to build a collection that concentrated on what were still affordable areas: nineteenth- and twentieth-century American and European prints. He formed master collections of the prints of Sloan, Hopper, and Marin, which were joined by large groups of prints and drawings by artists he had shown at the Weyhe Gallery, such as Howard Cook, Wanda Gág, and Rockwell Kent. Important color prints by Toulouse-Lautrec, Bonnard, and Vuillard were added through purchase as well as gift, along with German Expressionist prints and twentieth-century Mexican prints and drawings by Rivera, Orozco, and Siqueiros. The drawings collection, already distinguished by numerous sheets by Rodin, Sargent, and Eakins, was enriched during the 1950s and 1960s by the gifts of the Arensberg, Gallatin, Stern, and White collections, which included great modern drawings by Cézanne, Seurat, Klee, Picasso, Braque, Duchamp, and the Americans Marin, Sheeler, and Demuth (all three of whom had studied in Philadelphia). The Arensberg collection also created the basis for the large and unconventional holdings of ephemeral material by and related to Marcel Duchamp.

In 1949 two new areas of collecting were introduced. The Philadelphia pharmaceutical firm Smith, Kline and French gave the first of a continuing series of grants to form the Ars Medica Collection of art with medical subject matter, which now numbers more than two thousand prints, drawings, and photographs of all periods, and includes an important group of medical and pharmaceutical prints, posters, and ephemera given by William H. Helfand. Also in 1949, sixty-nine photographs by Alfred Stieglitz were received from the artist's own collection, which Zigrosser had been the first to show in its entirety in 1944. Stemming from this bequest, the Alfred Stieglitz Center for Photography was established in 1968 with generous support from Stieglitz's friend and pupil Dorothy Norman. With the appointment of Michael E. Hoffman as adviser to the center, the exhibiting, publishing, and collecting of large groups of works by major photographers, including

Ansel Adams, Frederick Evans, Robert Frank, Paul Strand, Josef Sudek, and Minor White, have been pursued.

Zigrosser was succeeded in 1964 by his assistant Kneeland McNulty, through whose interests significant holdings of Japanese prints were acquired, notably groups of Osaka theatrical prints, Russo-Japanese War reportage, and the largest collection outside of Japan of the works of Tsukioka Yoshitoshi. The department's longstanding tradition of publishing was distinguished by important exhibition catalogues of the work of such diverse artists as the Master E. S., Giovanni Benedetto Castiglione, and Jasper Johns. Between 1966 and 1982 the department's strengths were reinforced with the purchase of American and European prints and drawings of the 1930s and 1940s, including a group of important Mexican works from the collection of Carl and Laura Zigrosser.

The foundations of the Museum's old master print collections were the gifts of the collections of Charles M. Lea in 1928 and William S. Pilling in 1933. In 1978 the bequest of the art historian Anthony M. Clark enriched the old master drawings collection, particularly with eighteenth-century Roman works. Happily, the collections nearly doubled in size and new areas of strength were established in 1984–85, when, through the generosity of Muriel and Philip Berman, some 2,500 drawings and 42,000 prints by European masters of the sixteenth through the nineteenth centuries were acquired from the Pennsylvania Academy of the Fine Arts. By this acquisition, the John S. Phillips Collection, the largest and most comprehensive in late nineteenth-century America, was preserved in the city in which it was formed.

A group of major French drawings bequeathed by Henry P. McIlhenny in 1986 and the gift of two of Paul Cézanne's sketchbooks from Mr. and Mrs. Walter H. Annenberg in 1987 have added further depth and distinction to the nineteenth-century collections. Since 1979 a series of grants from the Hunt Manufacturing Co. has enabled the Museum to make adventuresome acquisitions of contemporary works of art on paper. The entire collection of the Department of Prints, Drawings, and Photographs currently numbers some 139,000 objects, which rotate on public view in the Museum's Berman and Stieglitz galleries, and are available for study by appointment.

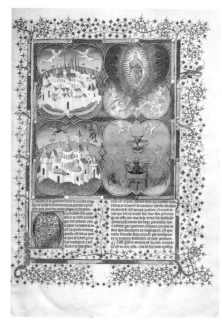

The Orosius Master and assistants

French, active Paris, c. 1400–1418

The City of God, God the Father, Pagan City, and the Fall of the Rebel Angels, from Saint Augustine, **La Cité de Dieu,** 1408–10

Tempera, gold, and pen and ink on parchment

17⅛ x 12⅜″ (page)

The Philip S. Collins Collection, gift of Mrs. Philip S. Collins in memory of her husband. 1945-65-1

Saint Augustine's fifth-century Latin treatise *De Civitate Dei* (The City of God) was translated into French in 1375 to satisfy the courtly taste for ancient history during the reign of Charles V. Romantically embellishing the saint's theological arguments, the translation, known as *La Cité de Dieu,* was spiced with commentaries in courtly dialect and illustrated for its noble French audience. The Museum's manuscript is among the most richly illustrated of the translations, with miniatures and border decorations by one of the numerous manuscript workshops active in Paris in the early fifteenth century. This is the largest of the manuscript's sixty-one miniatures and serves as an emblem of its title, for within the four quatrefoil frames the walled Gothic City of God (upper left), blessed by God the Father, is juxtaposed with an onion-domed pagan city, flanked by the Fall of the Rebel Angels. The artist enlivens this contrast with minute descriptive details, such as the darkened hands of the plummeting rebel angels that have taken on the color of the devils. IHS

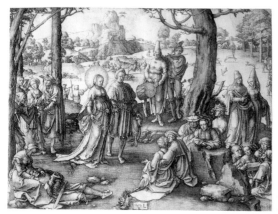

Lucas van Leyden

Dutch, 1489/94–1553

The Dance of Saint Mary Magdalene, 1519

Engraving

11¹¹⁄₁₆ x 15⅞″

Purchased with the Alice Newton Osborn Fund, the Lola Downin Peck Fund, the Print Revolving Fund, and with funds contributed by various donors. 1979-65-1

Early writers and artists elaborated the legend of Mary Magdalene's progress from sin to sanctity in songs, religious pageants, fresco cycles, and illuminated manuscripts, making her the most popular female saint of the waning Middle Ages. In a single picture full of captivating detail Lucas van Leyden, a printmaking prodigy of the early sixteenth century, compresses three episodes of her exemplary life, in each of which she wears a halo to mark her future sainthood: in the foreground she promenades at dawn after a night of revelry; in the middle she rides out stag hunting in the midday sun; while in the far distance, outside the mountain cave where she fasted in solitary penitence for the last thirty years of her life, she is lifted heavenward by angels for a celestial feast. The masterpiece of his maturity, Lucas's *Dance of Saint Mary Magdalene* is a marvel of subtle atmospheric effects of light and shadow that can only be appreciated in early proofs such as this, before the artist's silvery burin lines quickly wore down under the repeated pressure of the printing press. JI

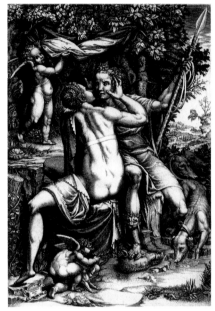

Giorgio Ghisi
Italian, 1520–1582
Venus and Adonis, c. 1570
Engraving, after a painting by
Teodoro Ghisi (Italian, 1536–1601)
12 ¹³⁄₁₆ x 9″
Purchased with the Lola Downin Peck
Fund. 1975-28-2

As a way of making otherwise inaccessible images available to the public, sixteenth-century Italian engravers frequently based their compositions upon other works of art. Giorgio Ghisi, for example, engraved *Venus and Adonis* after a painting by his brother Teodoro, whose name appears in the plaque at the lower left; Giorgio's initials are on the ground to the right. This is the only known impression of the print before the publisher's name was added to the plate. Giorgio Ghisi's training as a copperplate engraver and ornamental metalworker is reflected in the fine, decorative details that fill this engraving, yet the large, brightly lit figures have been made to stand out clearly from the dense surroundings. The print illustrates the story, told by the ancient author Ovid, of how the amorous Venus warned the young hunter Adonis of the dangers of hunting wild animals. Here, the boar's head beneath Adonis's foot indicates his recent victory over prey, but a small scene in the distant background foretells his death in a boar hunt, thus confirming the wisdom of Venus's admonition. IHS

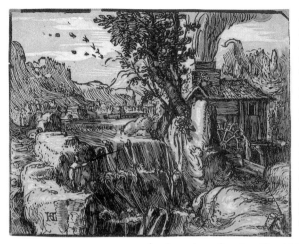

Hendrick Goltzius

Dutch, active Haarlem, 1558–1617
Landscape with a Waterfall
c. 1597–1600
Color woodcut
4¾ x 5¾"

The Muriel and Philip Berman Gift, acquired from the John S. Phillips bequest of 1876 to the Pennsylvania Academy of the Fine Arts, with funds contributed by Muriel and Philip Berman, gifts (by exchange) of Lisa Norris Elkins, Bryant W. Langston, and Samuel S. White 3rd and Vera White, with additional funds contributed by John Howard McFadden, Jr., Thomas Skelton Harrison, and the Philip H. and A.S.W. Rosenbach Foundation
1985-52-1498

A printmaker of genius, Hendrick Goltzius won his reputation for the elegance of the burin work he used in hundreds of engravings to envelop the human figure in a supple interlace of curving lines. His rare woodblock prints possess the sturdy grace of this little woodcut, with its jaunty fisherman casting a line into the furious torrent below. *Landscape with a Waterfall* is one of a set of four compact views, each of which echoes on a small scale the sweeping grandeur of Titian's large woodcut designs published in Venice in the early decades of the sixteenth century. Goltzius first issued each of the four miniature landscapes as nocturnes, printing the outline block by itself in black on blue paper, then adding white highlights by hand with a brush to suggest moonlight. Later, in imitation of Italian chiaroscuro woodcuts, he added color blocks for the background, printing them in warm tones of ocher and green on creamy paper to obtain the sunnier effect seen here. JI

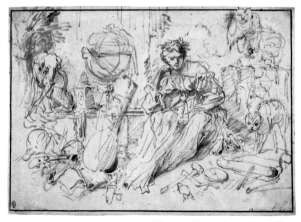

Giovanni Benedetto Castiglione

Italian, 1609–1664
Melancholia, c. 1660
Brush and paint with touches of pigment on laid paper
11⅛ x 16⅛"

The Muriel and Philip Berman Gift, acquired from the Matthew Carey Lea bequest of 1898 to the Pennsylvania Academy of the Fine Arts, with funds contributed by Muriel and Philip Berman and the Edgar Viguers Seeler Fund (by exchange). 1984-56-39

Giovanni Benedetto Castiglione was one of the most versatile and inventive artists of his time. A noted printmaker, he introduced the influence of Rembrandt into Italian etching and produced the first known monotypes. His paintings range from biblical, pastoral, and mythological scenes—frequently filled with the animal and still-life details in which he was something of a specialist—to altarpieces in the Baroque grand manner. He is most admired, however, for his marvelous "brush drawings," executed in a technique he invented in emulation of oil sketches by Peter Paul Rubens and Anthony van Dyck, in which he combined linseed oil with rather coarsely ground reddish-brown or brown pigment. These compositions are highly finished works, almost like small paintings, often enriched with colorful accents. This sheet represents Melancholy as a woman immobilized by dejection amid attributes of artistic and scientific achievement. The fragility of human life, the futility of human endeavor, and the passage of time that reduces all earthly accomplishments to ruin were subjects that had occupied Castiglione since the 1640s and continued to concern him in this work that can be dated toward the end of his career. AP

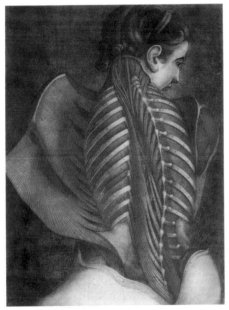

Jacques-Fabien Gautier-Dagoty
French, 1716–1785
Muscles of the Back, from Joseph Guichard Duverney, *Essai d'anatomie,* 1746
Color mezzotint
23¹⁵⁄₁₆ x 18⅛"
Purchased with the SmithKline Beckman (now SmithKline Beecham) Fund for the Ars Medica Collection
1968-25-79m

Opportunely, Jacques-Fabien Gautier-Dagoty began publishing "printed paintings" as colorplates in anatomical texts just when Paris had become the European center for teaching surgical dissection and when surgery was itself the most progressive branch of medical science. Claiming as his own a method of four-color printing developed earlier by an old German lately come to Paris, Gautier-Dagoty exploited this system, derived from Sir Isaac Newton's three primary colors, of printing three plates in succession, each separately inked in red, yellow, and blue, followed by a final plate inked in black. Although his images were based on the anatomical demonstrations of a prominent surgeon, fault has been found with the accuracy of some of Gautier-Dagoty's prints. What has never been in doubt, however, is the arresting character of his imagery, as here, where living flesh appears to have been unzipped and folded out to reveal the muscles and rib cage of a naked nymph with a modest sideways glance, a figure seemingly lifted from a painting by Titian. The Museum's extensive collection of Ars Medica encompasses prints, drawings, photographs, and illustrated books, selected as much for artistic merit as for historical documentation. JI

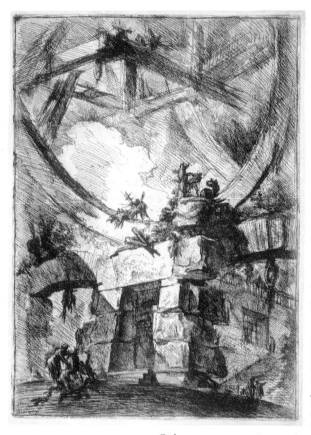

Giovanni Battista Piranesi
Italian, 1720–1778
An Entrance to an Imaginary Prison, from *Invenzioni capric di carceri,* c. 1749–50
Etching
22⅛ x 16⅛"
The Muriel and Philip Berman Gift, acquired from the John S. Phillips bequest of 1876 to the Pennsylvania Academy of the Fine Arts, with funds contributed by Muriel and Philip Berman, gifts (by exchange) of Lisa Norris Elkins, Bryant W. Langston, and Samuel S. White 3rd and Vera White, with additional funds contributed by John Howard McFadden, Jr., Thomas Skelton Harrison, and the Philip H. and A.S.W. Rosenbach Foundation
1985-52-1306

Only a master mason's son schooled in Venetian theatrical set design could have conjured up this giant oculus set at an angle above a monolithic doorway seen from below, as if from the audience. Shortly after settling in Rome in 1747, Giovanni Battista Piranesi etched fourteen copperplates of imaginary prisons filled with just such stagecraft effects of smoke and shadow. He went on to win international acclaim with antiquarian and architect alike by etching a series of hefty tomes, interleaving prints of ancient ruins with images of Baroque churches and palazzos. Piranesi later made a second edition of the prison etchings, drastically darkening them to conform to his archaeologist's eye, grown accustomed to the gloom of subterranean excavations pierced by shafts of sunlight. The Museum's complete first edition of the prison images is one of the exceedingly rare early printings, issued before Piranesi had time to make corrections on the title plate to his Roman publisher's name, Bouchard, which he had given a Venetian twist, spelling it by ear as *Buzard.* JI

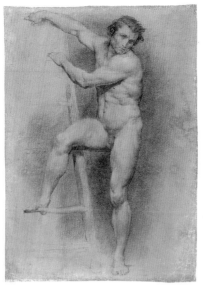

Pompeo Girolamo Batoni
Italian, 1708–1787
Male Nude Leaning on a Ladder
c. 1765
Chalks on prepared paper
21⅛ x 15⅜″
Bequest of Anthony Morris Clark
1978-70-170

From the Renaissance onward the drawing of the nude human figure from life was a basic element of artistic training as well as an essential part of the preparatory process for paintings or sculptures. This traditional approach was Pompeo Batoni's method of working, and he was one of its masters. At the time this drawing was made Batoni was among the best known painters in Italy and indeed probably in Europe, and his private academy for drawing from life was the most celebrated in Rome. Born in the Tuscan town of Lucca, he had worked in Rome since 1727, producing highly accomplished religious and history paintings and stunningly elegant portraits. For Batoni "academies," as these nude drawings from life were known, were not mere student exercises but virtuoso performances of his maturity, often signed and dated and executed on carefully prepared toned paper. Meticulously rendered with great accuracy and naturalism, they were highly valued demonstrations of his mastery of the primary element of a history painter's vocabulary, the human body. AP

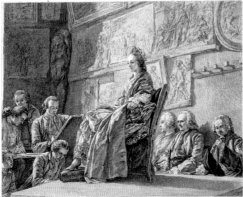

CONCOURS pour le PRIX de l'Etude des TÊTES et de l'EXPRESSION.
Fondé à l'Académie Royale de Peinture et Sculpture par M.r le Comte de CAYLUS, Honoraire Amateur, en 1760.

Charles-Nicolas Cochin
French, 1715–1790
Contest for the Prize for the Study of Expression, 1763
Etching with engraving by Jean-Jacques Flipart (French, 1719–1782), after a drawing by Cochin
9⅛ x 11″
Purchased with the W. P. Wilstach Fund
W1958-1-575

To improve neglected skills, in 1759 the French Royal Academy of Painting and Sculpture funded a yearly prize for the student's work that most convincingly conveyed a suitably lofty emotion as expressed on a model's countenance. Here, amid the casts of antique sculpture lining the classroom walls, Charles-Nicolas Cochin sets aside his own high rank in the Academy to join the drawing students around the posing platform to record the contest held in 1761. A telling draftsman himself, Cochin seems less interested in the model's becalmed features (*douceur,* or gentleness, was the emotion assigned) than in catching unawares the students diligently absorbed in the task at hand, as well as his own bored colleagues who patiently monitor the three-hour session. The core of the Museum's collection of more than one thousand works by Cochin is an annotated portfolio of 69 drawings and 758 prints, including 525 rare proofs. Assembled in chronological order by a contemporary of Cochin, the portfolio is a unique document of the graphic oeuvre of this prominent figure in French art circles during the reign of Louis XV. JI

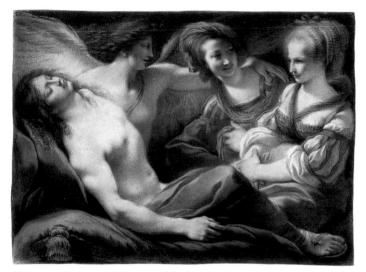

Giuseppe Cades
Italian, 1750–1799
A Woman Gazing at a Sleeping Man, Attended by a Winged Youth and a Young Woman, 1775–84
Pastel on laid paper
12⅜ x 17⅜"
Purchased with the Henry P. McIlhenny Fund in memory of Frances P. McIlhenny, funds contributed by George Cheston, and Museum funds. 1990-49-1

A brilliant if erratic artistic personality of great originality and chameleon-like contradictions, Giuseppe Cades was one of the best history painters in Rome during the last quarter of the eighteenth century. He was a precocious beginner whose mature style continued the late Roman classical Baroque manner at the same time that it adopted an avant-garde neo-Mannerism and extravagant, fantastic, romantic Neoclassicism. Today Cades seems years ahead of his time, almost a nineteenth-century painter, in his romantic depiction of themes from Italy's medieval and Renaissance past and his attempts to achieve verisimilitude in period costumes and architecture. Although its subject is not clear, this drawing was undoubtedly created as a finished work in itself, the equivalent of a small painting. With its layering of fine, parallel shading lines, its subtle use of color, and its atmospheric contrast of light and dark, the sheet is a masterpiece of Cades's fluent and imaginative drawn oeuvre as well as a keystone of the Museum's splendid holding of eighteenth-century Roman drawings. AP

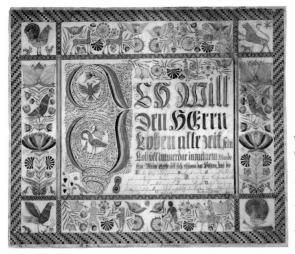

The Reverend Georg Geistweit
American, active c. 1790–1820
Religious Text, 1801
Ink with transparent and opaque watercolor on laid paper
12½ x 15¼"
The Titus C. Geesey Collection
1954-85-7

This elaborately decorated quotation from Psalm 34, which begins, "I will bless the Lord at all times," was created by the Reverend Georg Geistweit, a traveling minister of the German Reformed Church in rural Pennsylvania, who served various frontier congregations in the Upper Susquehanna Valley between about 1794 and 1804. In addition to their religious function, such illuminated biblical texts of the period were also used as writing examples for the instruction of children and were usually produced by itinerant ministers, schoolmasters, or craftsmen. Known as *Fraktur,* after an old German manner of lettering, these colorfully stylized images in watercolor and ink also embellished birth and baptismal certificates, bookplates, house blessings, and other domestic records for the early German-speaking settlers of Pennsylvania, Virginia, and Ohio. Similar flower, bird, and animal motifs appear on plates, glasses, tinware, painted furniture, and textiles in the Museum's notable collection of art produced between about 1750 and 1840 by this group, who clung tenaciously to their European language and culture until well into the latter nineteenth century. AP

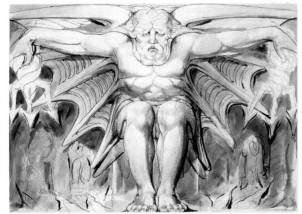

William Blake
English, 1757–1827
A Destroying Deity, c. 1820–25
Pen, brush, and ink; watercolor washes; and graphite on wove paper
8⅛ x 11¾"
Gift of Mrs. William T. Tonner
1964-110-7

Among the English artists of the late eighteenth and early nineteenth centuries, only William Blake was gifted so equally in poetry and in painting. His output of drawings, temperas, watercolors, and prints was as prodigious as it was visually and technically inventive, and the books of verse that he wrote, illustrated, printed, and bound rank him among the finest English Romantic poets. Yet Blake's art was so poorly received during his lifetime that he was virtually unknown except to a limited circle of friends and patrons. He was notably opposed to the contemporary academic art establishment, and instead promoted an international style of Romantic Neoclassicism that eschewed the copying of nature and illusionistic representation, celebrating the pure linear outline and flowing contours of Greek vase painting and the heroic, muscular nudity of the human body. Thus in Blake's work backgrounds are abstracted and naturalistic space is flattened or suppressed, often to the point of disappearance, as in his *Destroying Deity,* the subject of which has never been exactly identified. AP

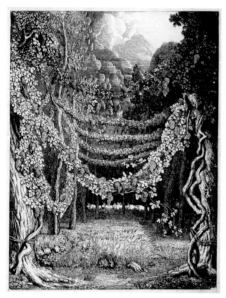

Wilhelm Tischbein
German, 1751–1829
A Vineyard Along the Way to the Cave of Polyphemus, from *Homer nach Antiken gezeichnet,* 1796
Etching
17¹³⁄₁₆ x 14″
The Muriel and Philip Berman Gift, acquired from the John S. Phillips bequest of 1876 to the Pennsylvania Academy of the Fine Arts, with funds contributed by Muriel and Philip Berman, gifts (by exchange) of Lisa Norris Elkins, Bryant W. Langston, and Samuel S. White 3rd and Vera White, with additional funds contributed by John Howard McFadden, Jr., Thomas Skelton Harrison, and the Philip H. and A.S.W. Rosenbach Foundation
1985-52-14217

Wilhelm Tischbein is best known today for his memorable portrait of the great German writer Johann von Goethe wearing a broad-brimmed hat, reclining among the ruins of Roman Campagna—a head and hat given wider currency in the 1980s in a series of paintings by Andy Warhol. Tischbein acted as Goethe's guide in Rome in 1786, and the next spring they traveled together to southern Italy. Like Goethe, Tischbein was enthralled by the lush terrain around Naples, seemingly unchanged since Homer's time. This etching of tended trees and festooned vines served to introduce the section of the *Odyssey* devoted to Ulysses' encounter with the one-eyed giant Polyphemus in an illustrated edition of Homer begun in Naples by Tischbein around 1796. For the other pictures, rather than inventing settings, as he did here, for a text he knew by heart in German, the artist brought the epic to life by recording the features of Homer's heroes from ancient sculpture in local Italian collections and by copying scenes of Ulysses' adventures from antique pots recently excavated in the nearby countryside. The Museum's collection of German prints from around the turn of the nineteenth century, of which this is an example, is the richest in the United States. JI

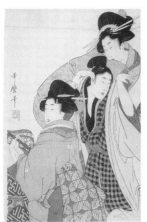

Kitagawa Utamaro
Japanese, 1753–1806
Two Geishas and a Tipsy Client
c. 1805
Color woodcut
15⅛ x 10¼″
The Samuel S. White 3rd and Vera White
Collection. 1967-30-215

In the teeming Japanese capital of Edo (now Tokyo), a city of strict rank and privilege, the Yoshiwara pleasure district was set aside to cater to every class and pocketbook, from swagger merchant to impoverished samurai, providing access to an enchanted realm known as *ukiyo,* or the "floating world," that centered on rowdy Kabuki theaters, crowded teahouses, and perfumed brothels. Popular woodcuts celebrated the aristocrats of this demimonde in best-selling pinups: fearsome actors in their starring roles and glamorous geishas in the latest fashions. A habitué of the Yoshiwara himself, Kitagawa Utamaro specialized in brothel subjects. By the 1790s he had become the most popular print designer in Japan, with a forceful flowing line that coordinated quirky patterns with graceful gestures, as in this playful depiction of a tipsy young samurai giving a mincing imitation of a geisha's elegant dance steps. JI

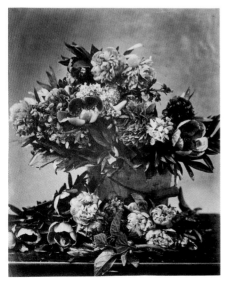

Charles Aubry
French, 1811–1877
Still Life with Peonies, 1864
Albumen silver print
17³⁄₁₆ x 14³⁄₁₆″
Purchased with funds contributed by
the American Museum of Photography
1971-4-123

Before his brief foray into photography in the 1860s, Charles Aubry had worked for over thirty years in Paris as a designer of patterns for carpets, fabrics, and wallpapers. His photography was a natural outgrowth of his profession, as he intended to sell his photographic still-life studies as models for architectural draftsmen and students of the industrial arts. In 1864 an elaborate presentation album of his large-scale albumen silver prints, including this still life, received a medal from Emperor Napoleon III, yet Aubry's photographs were not a commercial success, for French schools were not accustomed to using photographs as instructional tools and the prevailing fashion was for stylized rather than naturalistic ornamentation. *Still Life with Peonies,* which is typical of his work in both its naturalistic detail of flowers and leaves and lavish arrangement of forms, is one of three large-scale still lifes by Aubry in the Museum's collection, representative of the best of a small but select group of nineteenth-century French photographs acquired in 1971 at the time of the groundbreaking exhibition *French Primitive Photography.* MC

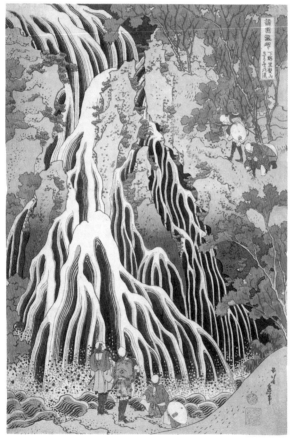

Katsushika Hokusai
Japanese, 1760–1849
Pilgrims at Kirifuri Waterfall on Mount Kurokami in Shimotsuke Province, from ***Going Round the Waterfalls in Various Provinces***
c. 1831–32
Color woodcut
14⅞ x 10⅛″
The Samuel S. White 3rd and Vera White Collection. 1958-151-26

In later years Katsushika Hokusai liked to sign himself "The Old Man Mad for Drawing," an apt nickname for an artist who made more than thirty thousand drawings in his lifetime, many of them sketches for a series of fifteen "how-to" manuals for aspiring artists, first published in 1814. When the final volume appeared in 1878, twenty-nine years after his death, Hokusai's earlier designs had already been carried to artists such as

Edouard Manet and Edgar Degas in Paris on the great wave of exports from Japan after its harbors were first opened to European and American traders in the 1850s. At the age of seventy, Hokusai began issuing sets of large landscape prints of cool, countryside vistas, far removed from the urbane pleasures of Kabuki theater or geisha houses, the customary subjects for Japanese popular color prints. No Japanese artist ever strayed so far from classical Chinese landscape models as Hokusai in this close-up view of tumbling waterfall and rugged rock face, shutting out both the sky and any far-off mountain peak. JI

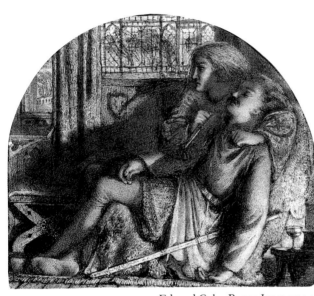

Sir Edward Coley Burne-Jones
English, 1833–1898
"I rose up in the silent night; I made my dagger sharp and bright," c. 1859–60
Pen and ink over pencil with touches of heightening on wove paper
5 x 5¾"
Purchased with the Alice Newton Osborn Fund. 1991-50-1

Edward Coley Burne-Jones was a second-generation member of the Pre-Raphaelite Brotherhood, which had been founded by English painters and poets in 1848 to promote a return to the innocence and honesty that they found in Italian art before the time of Raphael (1483–1520). Pre-Raphaelite artists favored Romantic literary and poetic themes, which they rendered with graphic clarity and in minute detail. Often they made small finished drawings like this one for presentation to their friends. Burne-Jones's drawing is based on a quotation from Alfred Lord Tennyson's "The Sisters," a romantic ballad about a young woman's vengeful murder of her sister's lover. Treating the tragic tale as a somber meditation on the act of murder rather than as a narrative, Burne-Jones evokes the style of early Renaissance drawings through his precise penwork and his compressed, planar arrangement of figures and setting, as well as through his use of period costumes and furnishings. IHS

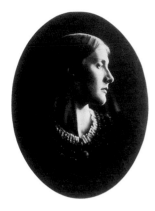

Julia Margaret Cameron
English, 1815–1879
Mrs. Herbert Duckworth, 1867
Albumen silver print
13½ x 10¼″
Purchased with the Alice Newton
Osborn Fund. 1980-4-1

One of the great portraitists of the Victorian era, Julia Margaret
Cameron photographed her niece Julia Jackson (Mrs. Herbert)
Duckworth in 1867. Nearly sixty years later, Duckworth's
daughter from a later marriage, the novelist Virginia Woolf,
published a collection of her great-aunt's photographs in
Victorian Photographs of Famous Men and Fair Women, for which
she wrote a fascinating biographical sketch about Cameron's
exuberant and inexhaustible energy in the pursuit of art and the
society of creative people. Taking up the camera for the first
time at age forty-eight, Cameron set out to revolutionize the
photography of her day by wresting it into the realm of high art.
She thought photography perfectly suitable for traditional
religious and allegorical subjects as well as for illustrations for
romance literature. Her deliberately out-of-focus style brought
waves of critical reaction, but it was for her the means toward
the highest expression of purity of form, ideal beauty, and
truth of feeling. MC

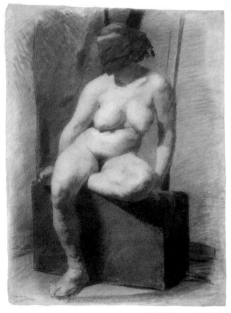

Thomas Eakins
American, 1844–1916
*Study of a Seated Nude Woman
Wearing a Mask,* 1863–76
Charcoal and crayon with stumping
on laid paper
24¼ x 18¼″
Gift of Mrs. Thomas Eakins and
Miss Mary Adeline Williams. 1929-184-49

This masked female nude is the best known of the few surviving figure studies drawn from life by Thomas Eakins, the premier Realist painter of the United States, who spent virtually
his entire career in Philadelphia, where his primary subjects
were the life and people around him. A gifted teacher, Eakins

stressed that the study of art should be based on the figure as drawn—or better yet, painted—from life, not from casts of antique sculptures, which was then the standard practice; his disregard of taboos against use of the nude model in mixed-sex classes (which explains the concealed identity of this sitter) led to repeated conflicts with the schools where he taught. Eakins combined in his work his profound artistic and scientific interests, insisting on developing compositions through calculated measurements and perspective studies and on becoming familiar with the human body through intense anatomical study, dissection, and modeling. In this nude study, the rough, blocky massing of solid, lit, and shadowed forms reflects his emphasis on the essential construction of the human figure rather than details of pose or anatomy. AP

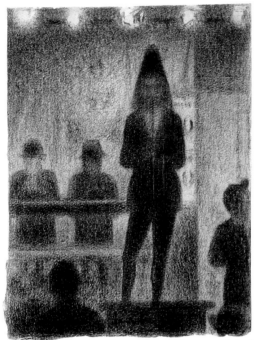

Georges Seurat
French, 1859–1891
Trombonist (Study for "Circus Side Show"), 1887–88
Conté crayon and chalk on laid paper
12¼ x 9⅜"
The Henry P. McIlhenny Collection in memory of Frances P. McIlhenny
1986-26-31

The towering silhouette of the lone trombonist and the strong horizontal and vertical definition of shallow space mark Georges Seurat's first nocturnal painting, *Circus Side Show* (The Metropolitan Museum of Art, New York), as mysterious and complex, qualities that it shares with this preparatory drawing for the center third of the final composition. The immobile, self-contained figures paradoxically suggest silence rather than gay circus music, while the emphatic placement of every element in the composition gives a strange weight and timelessness to a fleeting moment of entertainment. Seurat's method of drawing without lines formed an empirical equivalent to his scientifically based pointillist paintings, in which he juxtaposed dots of pure colors that blended optically to produce another color. In this and his other drawings Seurat used black conté crayon on a textured paper to create a luminous ambience against which dark figures and objects were silhouetted. The white of the paper generally creates the highlights, but occasionally Seurat points up significant elements with white chalk, as he does with the long loop of the trombone that stands out against the musician's dark costume. IHS

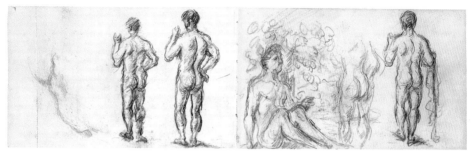

Paul Cézanne
French, 1839–1906
Male Bathers (right) and *Standing Male Bather, Atlas* (left), from Sketchbook II, 1885–1900
Graphite pencil on wove paper
5 x 8½" (each)
Gift of Mr. and Mrs. Walter H. Annenberg. 1987-53-78b, 79a

Paul Cézanne habitually carried small, unbleached linen sketchbooks in his pockets, which he would fill in no particular order, often using them over many years. His sketchbooks functioned rather like diaries—the ever-present recipients of his thoughts and interests, whether fleeting or resolved. Few of the sketches are directly related to his paintings, and most are of stationary subjects: works of art by other artists, his son sleeping, household objects, landscape details. The adjacent sheets shown here come from one of two sketchbooks in the Museum's collection. Cézanne's informal and unsystematic approach to his sketchbooks, his habit of jotting notes on the pages, and his tendency to include unrelated subjects on a single page combine to give a remarkably immediate view of his thoughts and working methods. He never tired of returning to certain favorite figures and compositions, such as the standing male bather seen from the back, which reappears in a number of his paintings between the mid-1870s and the mid-1890s. IHS

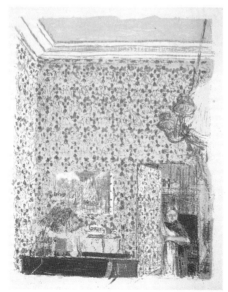

Edouard Vuillard
French, 1868–1940
Interior with Pink Wallpaper I,
from *Paysages et intérieurs*
c. 1899
Color lithograph
13¾ x 11"
Purchased with the John D. McIlhenny Fund. 1941-8-152

Throughout the 1890s Edouard Vuillard trained his eye on various rooms in the succession of Paris apartments he shared with his widowed mother. At the end of the decade he enumerated the accouterments of their domesticity in a series of entrancing color lithographs, often portraying the dining room seen here, always the heart of their cozy flats, whether used for family meals or as his mother's workroom for her corset-making trade. In paintings and prints alike Vuillard discarded conventional academic notions that aimed at accurate representation of outward appearances for an inner vision, studiously summarizing the details of his surroundings as decorative patterns of shape and color—note the hanging lamp silhouetted against the pink wallpaper in this image—while seeming to capture the setting casually, as in a candid photograph. JI

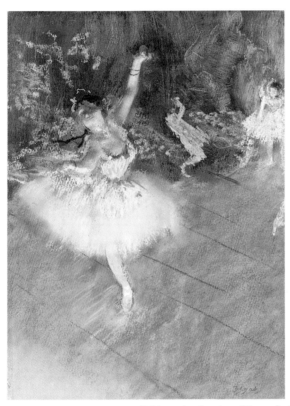

Hilaire-Germain-Edgar Degas
French, 1834–1917
The Star, c. 1876–78
Pastel over ink monotype
on laid paper
17⅜ x 13½″
Bequest of Charlotte Dorrance Wright
1978-1-50

Cultivated, witty, irascible, and obsessed with perfecting his art, Edgar Degas was arguably—along with Paul Cézanne—the greatest French artist of his generation. He worked in Paris most of his life, and his favorite subjects were drawn from that city's high life and demimonde alike: racecourses, ballet, opera, café concerts, brothels, and nudes at their baths. Degas's technical inventiveness was endless, as he worked in a wide range of mediums that he frequently combined in deft and experimental ways. In *The Star,* one of the earliest of Degas's over three hundred monotypes and another of his theatrical subjects, the base image was created on a metal plate with printer's ink worked with brushes, rags, and perhaps the artist's fingers; the plate was then run through a printing press to offset the image onto a dampened sheet of paper. Degas worked up the resultant impression with layers of pastel, altering the monochromatic inky image through the addition of rich veils and accents of brilliant chalky color. AP

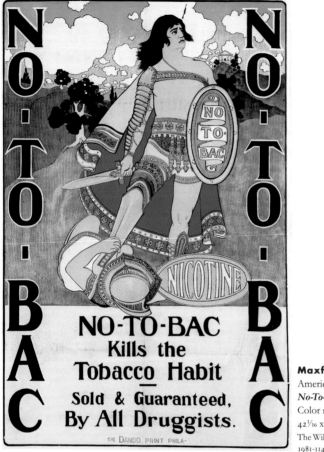

Maxfield Parrish
American, 1870–1966
No-To-Bac, 1896
Color relief print
42¹⁄₁₆ x 29⅛″
The William H. Helfand Collection
1981-114-36

By 1913, when he turned down an invitation to head Yale University's art department, Maxfield Parrish was already famous for his whimsical murals in hotels across the country: *Old King Cole* in New York, *Sing a Song of Sixpence* in Chicago, and *The Pied Piper* in San Francisco. The master of make-believe, he proceeded to make a fortune in the 1920s with fairyland dreamscapes commissioned as candy-box decorations and later sold as prints, suitably framed, in dime stores for ten dollars apiece. Parrish began his career as a commercial artist, designing prize-winning posters while still a student at the Pennsylvania Academy of the Fine Arts in Philadelphia in the mid-1890s, a decade of poster mania in Europe and the United States that heralded the advertising age. Using the age-old signboard techniques of bright colors and bold outlines, Parrish here delineated the stalwart figure of a victorious gladiator to sell No-To-Bac, a cure promising to vanquish the smoking habit. JI

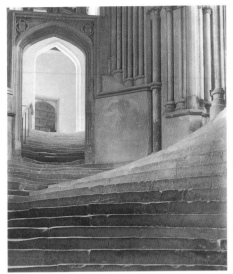

Frederick H. Evans
English, 1853–1943
"A Sea of Steps"—Wells Cathedral: Stairs to the Chapter House and Bridge to Vicar's Close, 1903
Gelatin bromide print
8⅞ x 7⁹⁄₁₆″
Purchased with the Director's Discretionary Fund. 1970-31-24

A prolific writer with strong literary interests, Frederick Evans ran a successful London bookstore with clients like Aubrey Beardsley and George Bernard Shaw before leaving the business at age forty-seven to concentrate full-time on photography, for which he had already established a reputation. Evans said that he took up photography because of his love of beauty, and his approach to his subjects, whether great cathedrals, groves of trees, or intimate interiors, originated from a deep emotion. Profoundly dedicated to pure photography, he never altered the printing of negatives for aesthetic effects; rather, the eloquence of his images comes from his ability to capture the supremely expressive viewpoint at the most telling moment of light and shadow. In *A Sea of Steps,* a key image among the Museum's 195 photographs by Evans, the composition is filled with the converging cascades of ancient steps of Wells Cathedral, taken at the precise moment when the light made their worn, undulating edges appear as thin, wavering lines. IHS

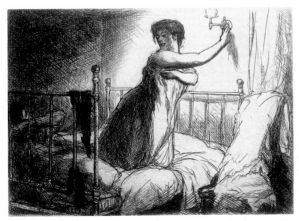

John Sloan
American, 1871–1951
Turning Out the Light, from "New York City Life," 1905
Etching
4¹³⁄₁₆ x 6⅞″
Gift of Alice Newton Osborn
1959-35-59

In *Turning Out the Light* John Sloan offers a glimpse through his New York studio window at a woman reaching to extinguish the gas light while exchanging a suggestive glance with her waiting bed partner. At the time of its creation, this work, like Sloan's other prints and paintings of the period, was considered extraordinary in its realism. In fact, this unblushing illustration was rejected as indecent when it was submitted to an exhibition at the National Academy of Design in New York. Sloan would instead come to exhibit with the group of artists known as The Eight (five of whom, including Sloan, had trained in Philadelphia), who sought independence from the traditional art establishment mainly by taking their subjects from the daily life of the urban working class. *Turning Out the Light* is one of over nine hundred prints and drawings by Sloan in the Museum, which owns the world's most comprehensive collection of the graphic work of this illustrious printmaker. JG

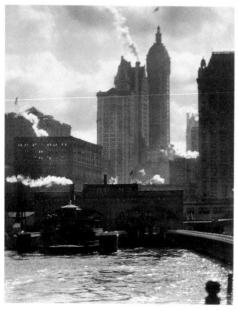

Alfred Stieglitz
American, 1864–1946
The City of Ambition, 1910
Gelatin silver print
4¼ x 3⅜"
The Alfred Stieglitz Collection
1949-18-47

In *The City of Ambition,* the newly built skyscrapers of New York rise above the harbor like the topmost sails of the clipper ships with which they were compared. For Alfred Stieglitz, skyscrapers were symbols of both the physical magnificence of the city and what he disparaged as the immoderate human ambition responsible for their creation. Yet while others focused their cameras downward into the shadowy chasms of New York's streets, he invariably focused upward toward the sky as a reminder of the transcendence of art over mundane life and human shortcomings. Stieglitz, who is known as the most influential champion of photography as fine art, was also a tireless supporter of American artists, such as John Marin and Georgia O'Keeffe, his wife, and one of the first advocates in the United States for modern European art. His personal collection of modern American and European art was exhibited at this Museum in 1944. After his death, the Museum was one of the five recipients of the Alfred Stieglitz Collection, which included an important group of his own remarkable photographs, such as the image shown here. MC

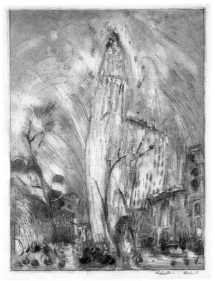

John Marin
American, 1870–1953
Woolworth Building, No. 1, 1913
Etching with wiped plate tone
11¹³⁄₁₆ x 9⅞"
The J. Wolfe Golden and Celeste
Golden Collection of Marin Etchings
1969-81-86

After five years of study in Europe, John Marin returned to
New York in 1910 in time to witness work begin on the Woolworth Building, which would be the world's tallest skyscraper
and Manhattan's most visible landmark when completed in
1913. Its shimmering tower surges skyward in four dazzling
watercolors that Marin showed at the legendary international
exhibition of modern art at the Armory in New York in 1913.
In this etching, the first of four prints of the subject that Marin
created the same year, the Woolworth Building seems to glisten
in the rainy night. Marin evoked this singular effect by first
enveloping the jagged etched lines of skyscraper and leafless
trees with a lush brown wash of ink—known as plate tone—
and then impulsively wiping highlights on the inky plate with
fingertip and dauber before printing. This rare print, one of six
recorded, is part of the J. Wolfe Golden and Celeste Golden
Collection of Marin Etchings, the master set of 181 prints purchased for the Museum from the artist's estate. JI

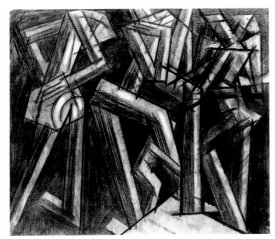

David Bomberg
English, 1890–1957
Acrobats, 1913–14
Charcoal and crayon on laid paper
18½ x 22⁷⁄₁₆"
Purchased with the Lola Downin Peck
Fund and the Fiske Kimball Fund
1981-21-1

Although he received a diploma in traditional life drawing
from London's Slade School in 1912, David Bomberg was at this

point already working independently in a simplified and extra-ordinarily dynamic abstract style, in part inspired by Cubism and Italian Futurism. By the following year Bomberg's abstract compositions of figures, derived from the steel forms of the modern city and from the heightened gestures that he saw in Jewish theatrical performances in London, had established his reputation as a leader of the English avant-garde. *Acrobats* is a daring and forceful example of Bomberg's early drawing style. The huge cubed figures, resembling angular metal robots, are packed to bursting from the top to the bottom of the sheet. Over the gyrating bodies heavy charcoal lines form a dynamic web, lending their movements greater emphasis and direction. This major example of early British modernism has broader significance when viewed alongside the Museum's distinguished collection of early twentieth-century French drawings. IHS

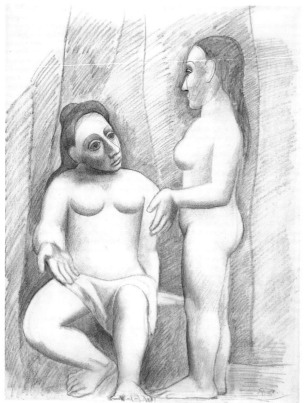

Pablo Ruiz y Picasso
Spanish, 1881–1973
Seated Nude and Standing Nude
1907
Charcoal on laid paper
25 x 18¾″
The Louise and Walter Arensberg
Collection. 1950-134-162

During the early months of 1907, just before he created the groundbreaking painting *Les Demoiselles d'Avignon* (The Museum of Modern Art, New York), Pablo Picasso's art entered a phase of austere and monumental classicism, stripped of sentiment or narrative expression. This large, highly finished charcoal draw-ing epitomizes that moment, during which Picasso was inspired by two powerful, ancient sculptural styles: the masklike faces of the squat yet statuesque women, with their heavy eyelids and stylized, arched brows, find their origin in the Iberian sculptures that Picasso had seen in an exhibition at the Louvre in Paris in 1906, while their severe planar poses and hieratic gestures recall archaic and classical Greek sculptures, which the artist would also have seen in the Louvre, particularly the mourners in Greek grave reliefs who similarly stand or sit in shallow, curtained spaces. IHS

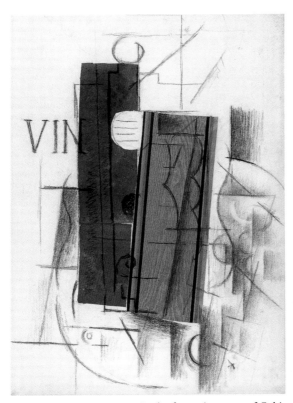

Georges Braque
French, 1882–1963
Still Life (with the word *Vin*)
1912
Collage of charcoal, cut printed paper, and cut wove paper on laid paper, adhered to cardboard
24⅜ x 18¹⁵/₁₆″
The Louise and Walter Arensberg Collection. 1950-134-24

In the formative years of Cubism, Georges Braque and Pablo Picasso strove to make paintings that would not be perceived as illusionistic renditions of reality. Accordingly forms became shifting planes and color was all but eliminated, because colored forms would have suggested traditional illusionism. Finally, in late 1912, when Braque made the first Cubist collage, or *papier collé* (literally "pasted paper"), by pasting strips of wallpaper on to a charcoal drawing, he had found a solution for allowing form and color to exist as independent elements in a composition; the strips of paper served as the color, while the forms were drawn in charcoal. In this early *papier collé* the charcoal forms of a guitar hover above and around three pasted paper planes that, because of their subtly angled juxtaposition, also suggest a slight shifting. Certain calculated ambiguities, such as the arc cut out of the blue paper, seemingly to reveal an opening below, and the placement of the word *Vin* (wine), whose last letter is partly written on the blue paper, likewise create the sense of overlapping planes perpetually shifting in space. IHS

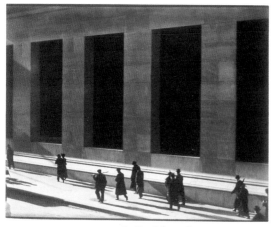

Paul Strand
American, 1890–1976
Wall Street, 1915
Platinum print
9¹⁵/₁₆ x 12⅝"
The Paul Strand Retrospective
Collection, 1915–1975, gift of the
estate of Paul Strand. 1980-21-2

In Paul Strand's 1915 photograph of Wall Street workers passing in front of the monolithic Morgan Trust Company can be seen the quintessential representation of the uneasy relationship between early twentieth-century Americans and their new cities. Here the people are seen not as individuals but as abstract silhouettes trailing long shadows down the chasms of commerce. The intuitive empathy that Strand demonstrates for these workers of New York's financial district would be evident throughout the wide and varied career of this seminal American photographer and filmmaker, who increasingly became involved with the hardships of working people around the world. In this and his other early photographs of New York, Strand helped set a trend toward pure photography of subject and away from the "pictorialist" imitation of painting. *Wall Street* is one of only two known vintage platinum prints of this image and one of the treasures of the some five hundred photographs in the Museum's Paul Strand Retrospective Collection. MC

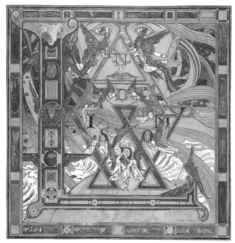

Violet Oakley
American, 1874–1961
Study for "Divine Law," c. 1917
Graphite, ink, bole and gold leaf,
opaque watercolor, and oil on
cardboard
20½ x 20½"
Purchased with the Director's
Discretionary Fund. 1976-211-1

By the end of the first decade of this century Violet Oakley had become the first American woman to achieve success as a mural painter, in a traditionally male field. In 1905 she won a medal for the first room that she decorated in the new Pennsylvania State Capitol in Harrisburg, and in 1911 she was commissioned to paint murals for two other chambers in the building. This drawing is a study for *Divine Law*, the first of sixteen large canvases painted for the Supreme Court Room in the Capitol between 1917 and 1927. Designed as an enlarged version of an illuminated manuscript on the historical development of law, the series represents the culmination of Oakley's social and political ideology with its celebration of the triumph of law over force. In *Divine Law*, behind the monumental letters spelling *Law* looms the face of Truth, half-concealed, half-revealed. A committed antimodernist academic painter, Oakley spent her entire career in Philadelphia. A renewed appreciation of academic art has recently revived interest in her work, which is preserved in depth in this Museum and in the National Museum of American Art in Washington, D.C. AP

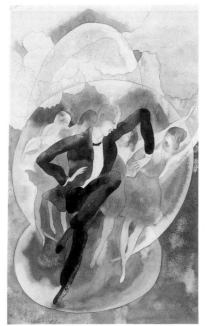

Charles Demuth
American, 1883–1935
In Vaudeville (Dancer with Chorus), 1918
Transparent and opaque watercolor with graphite on laid paper
13 x 8⅛"
A. E. Gallatin Collection. 1952-61-18

As both a personality and an artist Charles Demuth was multifaceted, an adventurous American modernist who was part of the artistic and literary avant-garde in New York and Paris in the teens and twenties while remaining a lifelong resident of the small town of Lancaster, Pennsylvania, where his family had been solidly established since 1770. After studying art in Philadelphia for some years, Demuth lived in Paris in 1912–14, when Cubism became a major influence on his slowly maturing style. He was at his most creative between 1915 and 1919, during which time he produced this and a number of other watercolors inspired by his beloved circus and vaudeville performances. In these works Demuth uses a watercolor technique that combines intense yet subtle coloring with supple pencil lines overlaid with transparent washes to achieve a Cubist flattening and segmenting of space. European in his stylistic inspirations, the artist nonetheless strove for a genuinely American vernacular expression that is summarized in these vaudeville watercolors as well as his architectural abstractions done primarily in Lancaster. AP

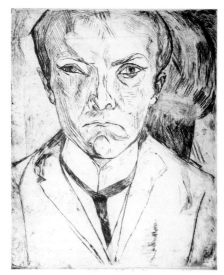

Max Beckmann
German, 1884–1950
Self-Portrait with House Gable in Background, 1918
Drypoint
12 x 10¹⁄₁₆″
Print Club of Philadelphia Permanent Collection. 1951-59-8

From 1900 to 1950, during a half-century of war, chaos, and exile, Max Beckmann made more than eighty self-portraits. None is more revealing than this unflinching attempt by Beckmann to confront the anguish he had endured as a volunteer in the field hospitals at the front in World War I. Here he underscored his discomfort with ink-clogged, rough-edged strokes of a drypoint needle cut impulsively into the surface of the copperplate. Beckmann must have printed this unique proof to review the changes he had made as he progressively developed his image. At left, above his shoulder, are traces of drypoint lines that in an earlier stage of the composition had extended a form on the right—perhaps the back of a chair with a triangular top—now half-obscured by curving dark lines. In a final transformation Beckmann reworked these sweeping curves to suggest a curtain billowing in front of a window with a view of the house gable that is designated in the title. JI

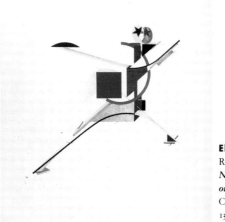

El Lissitzky
Russian, 1890–1941
New Man, from *Victory over the Sun,* 1923
Color lithograph
13 x 12⅛″
Gift of Dr. George Roth. 1953-23-10

The Futurist opera *Victory over the Sun,* first staged in Moscow in 1913, tells the tale of modern man's technological triumph over the sun's energy, a revolutionary theme carried out in avant-garde sets and costumes designed by the Russian artist Kasimir Malevich. By painting a solid black square on the curtain, it was here that Malevich introduced the stark emblem of Suprematism, a new art purged of subject matter and reduced to flat geometric forms executed in solid colors. El Lissitzky articulated some of his own provocative theories a decade later in Germany, where he played an activist's role in promoting Russian reformist art movements, with his portfolio of nine lithographs of emblematic characters for a new production of *Victory over the Sun*. Based on ideas that he had formulated back in Russia about 1920, Lissitzky's production was to be enacted by electronically driven mechanical figures, manlike machines that were geometric abstractions in themselves. Lissitzky designed this figure of *New Man* as a striding hero sporting a red square as the badge of his conquest. JI

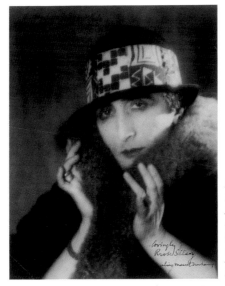

Man Ray
American, 1890–1976
Marcel Duchamp as Rrose Sélavy
c. 1920–21
Gelatin silver print
8¼ x 6¹³⁄₁₆″
The Samuel S. White 3rd and Vera White Collection. 1957-49-1

Rrose Sélavy, the feminine alter ego created by Marcel Duchamp, is one of the most complex and pervasive pieces in the enigmatic puzzle of the artist's oeuvre. She first emerged in portraits made by the photographer Man Ray in New York in the early 1920s, when Duchamp and Man Ray were collaborating on a number of conceptual photographic works. Rrose Sélavy lived on as the person to whom Duchamp attributed specific works of art, Readymades, puns, and writings throughout his career. By creating for himself this female persona whose attributes are beauty and eroticism, he deliberately and characteristically complicated the understanding of his ideas and motives. Only a few prints of this photograph are known. This version, inscribed in 1924 by Duchamp to the Philadelphian Samuel S. White 3rd, came to the Museum with White's collection of paintings and drawings. It forms part of the Museum's world-famous holdings of works by Duchamp and is central to a group of Man Ray photographs related to the life and work of Duchamp also owned by the Museum. MC

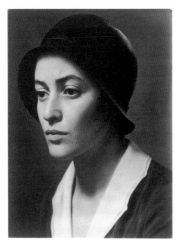

Alfred Stieglitz
American, 1864–1946
Portrait of Dorothy Norman IX
1930
Gelatin silver print
4⁹⁄₁₆ x 3⁷⁄₁₆″
From the Collection of Dorothy
Norman. 1972-23-5

From 1930 to 1937, Alfred Stieglitz created a series of portraits of his intimate friend, supporter, and biographer, Dorothy Norman. Norman was born in Philadelphia, but in 1925, after studying art at the Barnes Foundation in suburban Merion, she moved to New York. It was there that she met Stieglitz, whose charismatic personality and total commitment to art would engage her profound interest and change her life. As equally involved with social causes as with art, she founded and edited *Twice a Year,* a journal of literature, the arts, and civil liberties. She was primarily responsible for Stieglitz's last gallery, An American Place, where he held an exhibition of his photographs of her in 1932. As a whole, these portraits, such as this example, draw a close circle around this active woman and look deep into the innocent, caring, and spiritual soul within. In 1968, Norman helped·to found the Alfred Stieglitz Center at the Philadelphia Museum of Art to which she donated her remarkable collection of his photographs, including the entire series of her portraits. MC

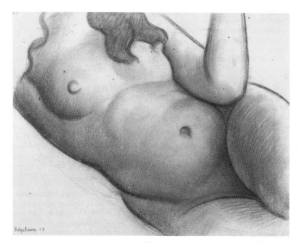

José Diego Maria Rivera
Mexican, 1886–1957
Torso of a Woman, 1925
Charcoal on laid paper
18⁷⁄₈ x 24³⁄₄″
Purchased from the Carl and Laura
Zigrosser Collection with the Lola
Downin Peck Fund. 1976-97-96

Diego Rivera was something of a prodigy, having established many of his passionate lifelong interests—Mexican folk art, history, landscape, and popular customs—by the age of twelve. Academically trained, he spent most of the time from 1907 to

1921 painting in Europe, slowly evolving through a remarkable Cubist phase to arrive at his mature "classical" style, with which he began in 1922 a thirty-year career in Mexico and the United States as one of the most important muralists of the twentieth century. Rivera was determined to put his art at the service of his revolutionary ideals. The fresco for which this robust and powerful torso is a study was executed in 1926–27 at the national agricultural school near Mexico City. The enormous nude female figure in the fresco, reclining on bare brown earth with one hand upraised in a gesture of benediction and the other holding a budding plant, represents the liberated Earth with its natural forces controlled by man, part of a complex decorative program that parallels gestation and growth in nature with social revolution in human history. AP

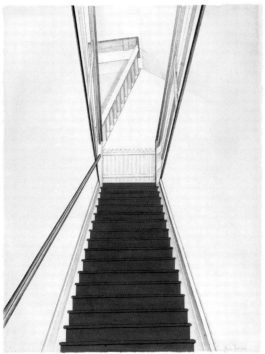

Charles Sheeler
American, 1883–1965
Stairway to the Studio, 1924
Chalk, crayon, and opaque watercolor on laid paper
25⅜ x 19¾″
Bequest of Mrs. Earl Horter in memory of her husband. 1985-59-1

In the course of his fifty-year career as a painter and photographer, which spanned the 1910s through the 1950s, Philadelphia-born and -trained Charles Sheeler became widely known as an important American modernist. He was among those artists who developed a style known as Precisionism, which was characterized by sharp, clear pictorial definitions and contrasts, the pursuit of either extreme realism or Cubist-derived abstraction, and a focus on American regional landscapes or cityscapes. Sheeler was particularly interested in applying the cool rigor of Precisionism to his numerous views of staircases, which he depicted in various mediums, including oil, crayon, gouache, and photography. Extracted from any context, compositionally isolated, reduced to geometric essentials, and abstracted into textureless patterns of line and plane, Sheeler's staircases are typical of his mature architectural subjects in their strict simplification. This drawing of 1924, which represents the stairs to Sheeler's studio at 10 West Eighth Street in New York, is the most abstract and austere of all his staircase works. AP

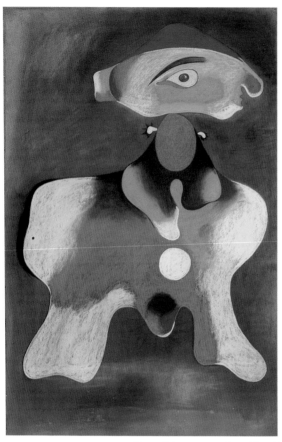

Joan Miró
Spanish, 1893–1983
Woman, 1934
Pastel, graphite, and scoring or scratching on wove artist's sandpaper with a prepared surface
42⅛ x 28⅛″
The Louise and Walter Arensberg Collection. 1950-134-146

One of the greatest Spanish painters of the twentieth century, Joan Miró had established by the mid-1920s the visual idiom that he was to develop throughout his long and international career. An enigmatic fusion of Abstraction and Surrealism, yet somewhat distanced from each movement, his style is distinguished by thin-washed, monochromatic, often horizonless backgrounds and playful, imaginative, flat, and usually linear motifs worked in counterpoint to rich, lush areas of color. At first glance spontaneous and almost childlike in nature, his works are in fact the result of intense, systematic, painstaking thought and great technical mastery, with their intuitive and emotional qualities always ultimately rooted in literal reality. *Woman* is one of fifteen monumental pastels done in 1934 in which Miró was experimenting with mediums and paper types. He vigorously worked the pigment into the fibrous, sandlike top layer of the paper, scratching or abrading it throughout to reveal its dark gray coating beneath. The brilliant colors of the image contrast oddly with the figure's grotesque distortions. AP

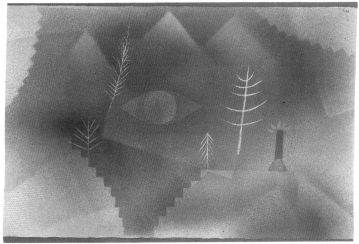

Paul Klee
Swiss, 1879–1940
Glance of a Landscape, 1926
Transparent and opaque watercolor
sprayed over stencils and brush
applied on laid paper mounted on
Bristol board
11⁵/₁₆ x 18⅛″
The Louise and Walter Arensberg
Collection. 1950-134-120

In the 1920s, while the Swiss painter and graphic artist Paul
Klee was teaching at the Bauhaus, the innovative German art
school, he began to push his painstaking watercolor glazing
methods in new directions by using a spraying or spattering
technique. *Glance of a Landscape,* which dates from the middle
of this period, exemplifies Klee's experimental approach to
materials, as well as the inherent tension in his work between
abstraction and representation, and between narrative linear
elements and overlapping transparent planes of color. The large
eye somewhat startlingly planted in the center of the landscape
bears witness to a certain mystical or otherworldly quality often
apparent in Klee's art. The hint of childlike naïveté is likewise
typically found in his images and reflects his attraction to the
work of untrained "outsiders" such as children or mental pa-
tients. Klee was a talented musician, and many properties of his
visual style—such as thematic development, rhythm, and harmony—were consciously inspired by musical composition. AP

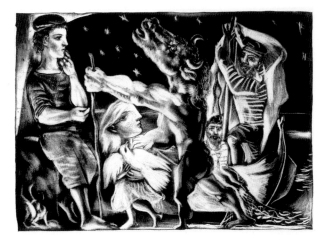

Pablo Ruiz y Picasso
Spanish, 1881–1973
*Blind Minotaur Led Through the
Night by a Girl with a Fluttering
Dove,* 1934
Aquatint, scraper, and drypoint
9⅞ x 13¹¹/₁₆″
Purchased with the Lisa Norris Elkins
Fund. 1950-129-110

Between 1930 and 1937 Pablo Picasso made one hundred
prints for the dealer/publisher Ambroise Vollard that formed a
loosely knit series of subjects revealing nuances of his personal

life and his reflections on being an artist, couched in the elegiac vocabulary of Greek mythology. One thread in this timeless tale is that of the ancient minotaur, half-man, half-bull, whose paradoxical nature became Picasso's metaphor for the artist. This print from the Museum's complete Vollard Suite shows the blind man-beast's unbridled anguish at his powerlessness as he submits to the guidance of a young girl; the transfixed stares of two sailors and the absorbed musings of a young man allude to the unspeakable tragedy of blindness for an artist. Most of the prints in the Vollard Suite are composed of spare black outlines on a white ground, but for this night scene Picasso added aquatint, a tone process creating a textured surface to hold ink on the plate. His aim was to emulate the deep blacks in the etchings of Rembrandt, one of the metaphoric figures appearing in several of the Vollard prints. IHS

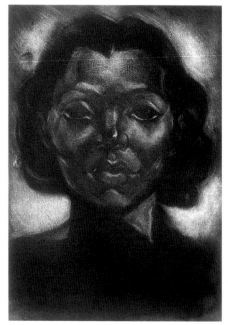

Dox Thrash
American, 1892–1965
Mary Lou, 1936–39
Carbograph
9⅞ x 7″ (plate)
Gift of E. M. Benson. 1942-86-3

Georgia-born painter and sculptor Dox Thrash was one of a number of African American artists who thrived in the Philadelphia print workshop established in 1936 under the government-sponsored Works Progress Administration (WPA), which provided artists throughout the country with materials, studio space, and a modest stipend during the Depression. Outstanding among the prints created in the Philadelphia workshop is Thrash's forthright portrait of a woman, identified only as Mary Lou, in which he masterfully exploits the sculptural effects attainable by the carbograph process, a technique that he invented during his WPA tenure and that would become his preferred medium for recording scenes of his adopted community. Thrash first scraped the image into the surface of a metal plate roughened with Carborundum crystals. After inking, the rough areas of the plate printed as rich skin tones, while the scraped areas produced the highlights on Mary Lou's face and the patches of light in the background. JG

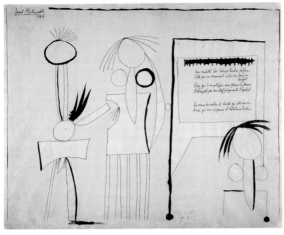

The youngest of the Abstract Expressionist artists who
emerged in New York in the 1940s and the only one whose
training was not grounded in the figurative tradition, Robert
Motherwell relied upon a body of forms and ideas that usually
occurred first in his spontaneously produced drawings. This
example of 1944 is an unusually clear summary of Motherwell's
interests as he began to form his artistic vocabulary. The picto-
graphic figures inspired by Pablo Picasso, the frontal disposi-
tion of forms, and the rough gestural handling of pen and
brush would recur again and again in his work. The inscribed
lines from Stéphane Mallarmé's poem "La Chevelure" are
in no way illustrated by the figures in the drawing, however;
instead they seem to act as poetic equivalents to the charged
significance those forms held for Motherwell. The inscription
also openly acknowledges Mallarmé's influence on Motherwell
in the early 1940s, for the French poet's exploration of the
symbolic essence of feeling in form coincided with the artist's
desire to charge simple forms and colors with maximum
meaning and emotion. IHS

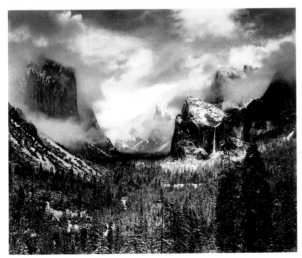

Ansel Adams first saw Yosemite National Park in California at
age fourteen in 1916, the same year he received his first camera,

and his lifelong relationship with both Yosemite and photography is apparent in his 1944 masterpiece *Clearing Winter Storm, Yosemite Valley.* He knew every vantage point of Yosemite intimately, and knew how to wait with great patience and deliberation until the light brought out the utmost grandeur and majesty of the mountain ranges, rushing waterfalls, and clouds clearing over the valley. Adams is widely recognized as the most eloquent American photographic poet of the Western wilderness landscape. His passionate feeling for the land as mountaineer, photographer, and preservationist, and his consummate craftsmanship with camera and light were celebrated through the inspired gift of one hundred Adams photographs from Robert and Lorna Hauslohner on the occasion of the Museum's centennial in 1976. MC

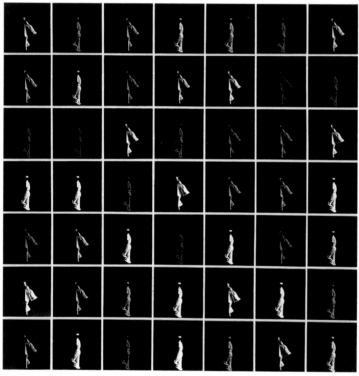

Ray K. Metzker
American, born 1931
Composites: Philadelphia, 1964
Gelatin silver prints
12⁷/₈ x 12⁷/₈"

Purchased with the Contemporary Photography Exhibition Fund, the Alfred Stieglitz Center Restricted Fund, and the Alice Newton Osborn Fund
1977-73-3

Ray K. Metzker, a Philadelphian since 1962, is one of the great contemporary experimenters with form and aesthetics in photography. *Composites: Philadelphia,* of 1964, is the first of a series in which he explores the synthesis of multiple visual elements expanded beyond the single-frame photograph. This work is made from forty-nine two-by-two-inch prints of sailors, printed to different densities, that have been mounted in a square grid to form a graphic pattern of receding and advancing darks and lights, like a coded message of signal flags. The composition resonates with references to the photographic studies of sequential motion that were carried out in the late nineteenth century in Philadelphia by Eadweard Muybridge and Thomas Eakins, a legacy that has provided a rich vein of inspiration for Metzker. Many other photographers have in turn been inspired by Metzker's translation of these scientific experiments into works of art. MC

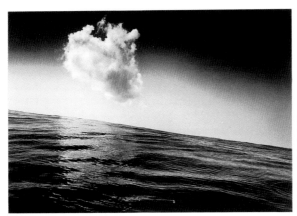

Shomei Tomatsu
Japanese, born 1930
Hateruma Island, Okinawa, 1971
Gelatin silver print
8½ x 12⁷⁄₁₆″
Purchased with funds contributed by the E. Rhodes and Leona B. Carpenter Foundation. 1990-51-104

Although the central theme of Shomei Tomatsu's work is the physical and psychological ruin of Japan at the end of the Second World War and the traumatic consequences of the country's rapid postwar social and economic change, there could be no more compelling and universal metaphor for respite from care than this serene image of a single cloud hovering above the tilted ocean, its reflection appearing as an island of pure and transparent simplicity. Tomatsu made this photograph at the fishing and farming community on the small island of Hateruma to which he often retreated, a place that he considered his spiritual and cultural home. The Museum acquired a representative group of Tomatsu's photographs along with those of three other contemporary Japanese photographers who had been included in the Museum's 1986 exhibition *Black Sun: The Eyes of Four.* MC

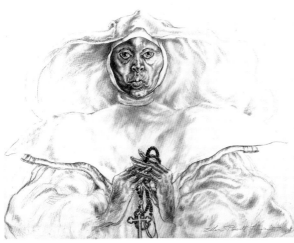

Ellen Powell Tiberino
American, 1937–1992
Sister Jennieva, c. 1980
Graphite with stumping and erasing on wove paper
19 x 24″
Purchased with the Julius Bloch Memorial Fund. 1990-117-1

Ellen Powell Tiberino was a painter, draftsman, and printmaker who lived and worked in Philadelphia nearly all her life. A representational, figurative artist, her subjects were drawn from everyday life, and particularly the experiences of African American culture. A swinging, rollicking line dense with energy characterizes her style, which is reminiscent of that of American Social Realists of the 1930s and 1940s such as Thomas Hart Benton and Reginald Marsh. Her images are rendered with a great deal of emotional and psychological impact, humor, and sympathy, which are matched by the vigor of her draftsmanship. Greatly affecting Tiberino's work and her approach to life was her fourteen-year battle with cancer, which influenced her choice of subjects and intensified her attachment to the world around her. The subject of this drawing is her cousin Sister Jennieva Lassiter, who served as a missionary in Tanzania. A virtuoso display of Tiberino's skill with a pencil, the work is not a literal portrait but rather the artist's "mental impression" of Sister Jennieva and the spiritual forces that motivated her. AP

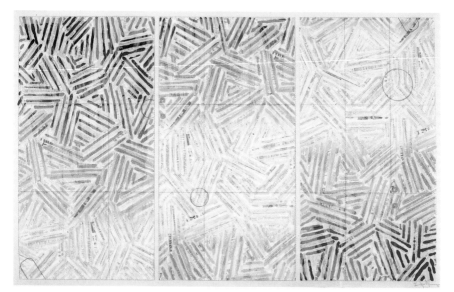

Jasper Johns
American, born 1930
Usuyuki, 1979–81
Silkscreen
29½ x 47¼"
Purchased with the Lola Downin Peck Fund. 1983-67-1

Printmaking has always been an integral part of Jasper Johns's art, and he has expanded the possibilities of each of the print techniques he has used. Because Johns is more interested in exploring the printmaking medium than in creating new imagery, he has usually based his prints upon his paintings. In the silkscreen *Usuyuki,* one of a number of works by this title, Johns gave the traditionally flat, unmodulated silkscreen surface the appearance of layered brushstrokes by working on the screens freely with a brush and using additional screens to reinforce the painted shapes. The title *Usuyuki,* the Japanese word for "light snow," only hints at the meaning of this lyrical three-part composition of crosshatchings hovering lightly above printed newspaper fragments. Almost imperceptibly, the pattern adheres to a predetermined system of repetition that shifts slightly in each panel. Thin grids and mysterious shapes, also systematically arranged, offer small clues to the pattern's changing direction, as do the photographically screen-printed newspaper clippings whose images and text recur in different locations on each of the three panels. IHS

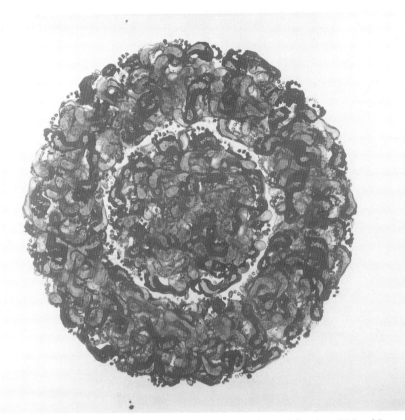

Richard Long
English, born 1945
Mud Foot Circles, 1985
River Avon mud on wove paper,
mounted on board
76⅜ x 87½"
Purchased for the Hunt Manufacturing
Co. Arts Collection Program. 1987-14-1

In his sculptures, photographs, and drawings Richard Long combines austere intellectual or conceptual premises with a highly romantic and English "rootedness" in nature, landscape, and sense of place. Since he began to work in the late 1960s his pieces have been executed primarily out-of-doors throughout the world, from Ireland to Nepal, during the walks he takes from one place to another, often displacing stones, earth, or grass along the way to create elementary linear or circular configurations. These conceptual pieces assume a more enduring physical form through Long's production of site photographs and drawings made with his hands or feet from mud or muddy water on walls or paper. Here the use of mud from the River Avon in England reflects the artist's profound interest in the surface of the earth, as the passage of footprints around and around the sheet of paper evokes his long walks outdoors. Within the simple geometric shape of the circle the dense, opaque brown mud, with its tendency to pool and splatter, creates an impression of sensuous emotional turbulence. AP

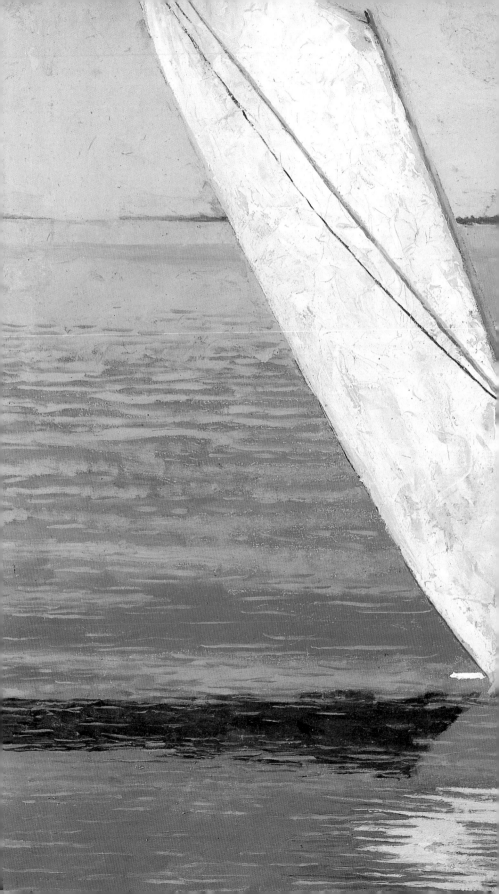

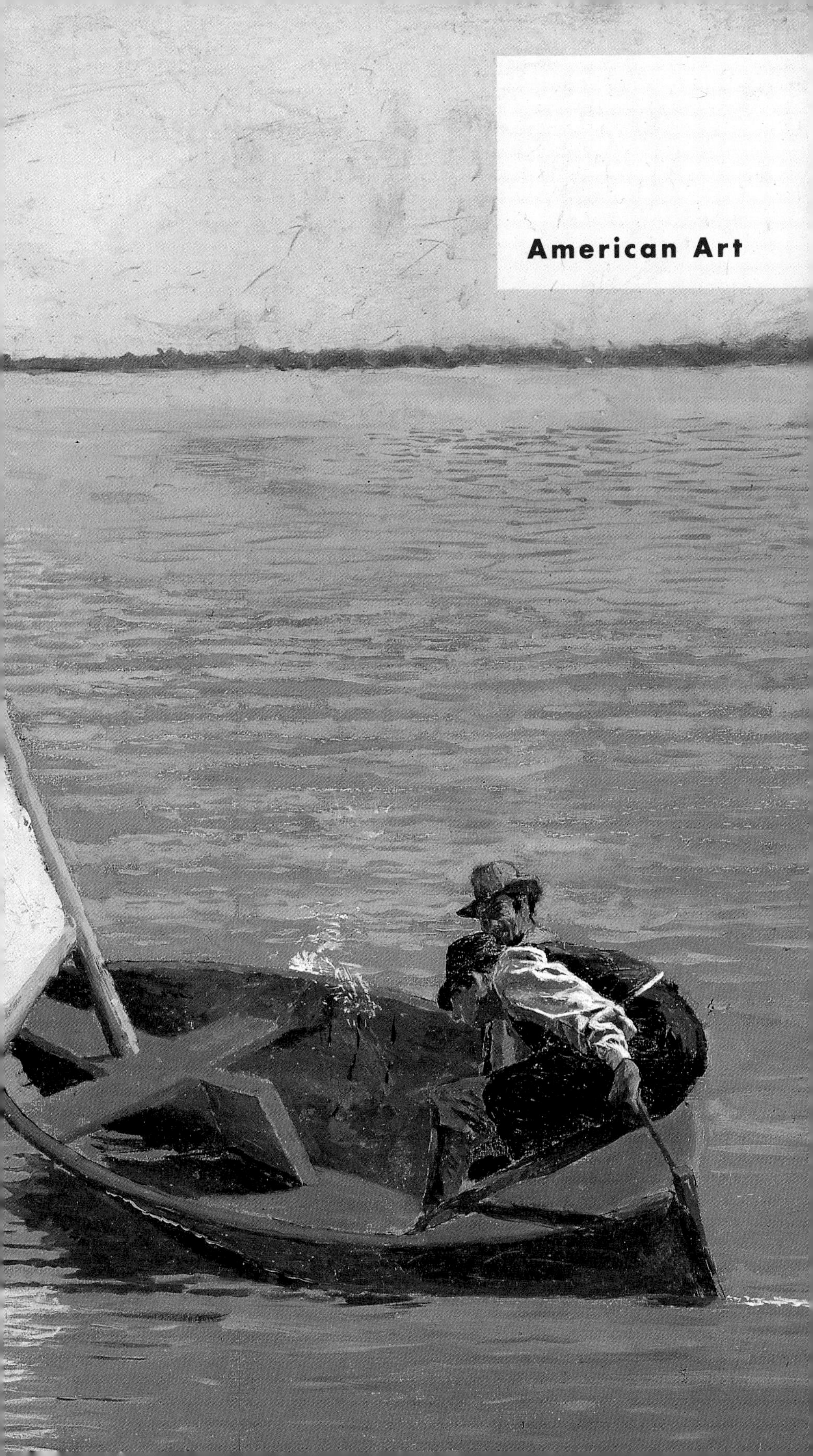

American Art

American Art

The importance of the Philadelphia region as a center for artistic production and the strength of history and tradition in the city assured the Museum's strong commitment to American arts. Major examples of decorative arts, painting, and sculpture have been acquired steadily since its founding in 1876. Today the collection, which continues to grow rapidly, is recognized as one of the finest public holdings of American art in existence.

Outstanding areas of the collections are eighteenth- and nineteenth-century Philadelphia furniture and silver, assembled primarily by gifts from R. Wistar Harvey, Mr. and Mrs. Walter Jeffords, H. Richard Dietrich, Jr., Robert L. McNeil, Jr., and members of many other Philadelphia families. The rural Pennsylvania collection, which began at the turn of the century with the enthusiasms of curator and director Edwin AtLee Barber and patrons John T. Morris and Mrs. William Frishmuth, grew dramatically with large gifts from J. Stogdell Stokes, Titus C. Geesey, and most recently the heirs of Ralph Beaver Strassburger and May Bourne Strassburger. Other decorative arts of note are the unmatched collection of porcelain objects, design books, papers, and tools relating to the short-lived manufacturing venture of William and Thomas Tucker in Philadelphia in the 1820s and 1830s, given by their descendant Anne Tucker Earp in 1951; the five hundred examples of American glass and their European prototypes given by George Horace Lorimer in 1938; and the Shaker furniture and objects given by Mr. and Mrs. Julius Zieget.

Mrs. William P. Wilstach's bequest of paintings in 1893 included works that constituted the beginning of the American paintings collection. Among the first purchases with the fund she established were pictures by J.A.M. Whistler and George Inness in 1895, and, in 1899, *The Annunciation* by Henry Ossawa Tanner, the first painting by the young African American artist to enter a public collection in the United States. The Museum is fortunate to house a remarkable group of portraits by the Philadelphia artist and scientist Charles Willson Peale, including *Rachel Weeping* and his *Staircase Group,* and the five family portraits in the Cadwalader Collection, which, together with their related furniture, represent a unique commission in eighteenth-century America. The work of the pioneering early nineteenth-century Philadelphia sculptor William Rush has its most extensive representation in the Museum as a result of his public commissions to decorate buildings in the city. By far the most notable component of the nineteenth-century painting holdings, which also include four splendid works by Winslow Homer, is the

Thomas Eakins Collection, given by the artist's widow, Susan Macdowell Eakins, and their friend Mary Adeline Williams in 1929 and 1930. Encompassing paintings, sculpture, sketches, and archival material, this formed the nucleus for the largest collection of the artist's work in existence.

In 1981 the Women's Committee of the Museum began to contribute funds from the proceeds of its annual craft show for the purchase of contemporary crafts, which would bring the historically strong collection of decorative arts up to the present day. These objects provide a focus for the growing collection of contemporary craft art, which includes the Museum's most recent acquisition of period architectural elements, the library fireplace and doorway, acquired together with a wood-paneled music room, designed and carved in 1936 and 1937 by Wharton Esherick for the Curtis Bok house in Gulph Mills, Pennsylvania.

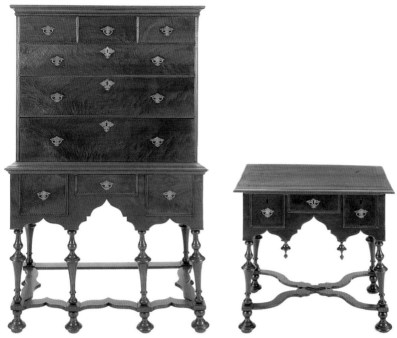

High Chest of Drawers and Dressing Table

Made in Philadelphia
c. 1720–26
American black walnut, yellow pine, cedar, brass
66¹⁵⁄₁₆ x 42⅛ x 23¼″ (chest)
30¹¹⁄₁₆ x 33¹⁵⁄₁₆ x 23⅝″ (table)
Gift of Lydia Thompson Morris
1928-7-12, 13

While a high chest of drawers with a matching dressing table had become unfashionable in Great Britain by the end of the seventeenth century, such furniture remained popular in stylish American households for most of the eighteenth century, and this Museum's collections include several spectacular pairs. Although such items regularly appear in early Philadelphia inventories, these examples, made for Catherine Johnson and Caspar Wistar shortly before their marriage in 1726, are the only known surviving pair made in the city during this early period. Wistar, a prominent merchant, furnished his home according to the latest tastes, and this chest and table are typical of the earliest case furniture fashioned by Philadelphia's best craftsmen using local materials. While London examples of these forms are most often embellished with figured grained veneers, here the case, drawer fronts, legs, and stretchers are constructed of solid black walnut, with highly figured grains carefully selected to give the effect of veneer. The refined skills of Philadelphia's early cabinetmakers are further evident in the crisp profiles of the turned legs, the curves of the arched skirts and stretchers, and the solidity of the drawer cases. JLL

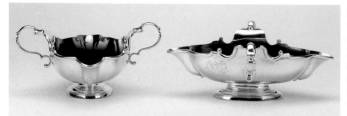

Pair of Sauceboats

Made by Charles Le Roux
(American, 1689–1745)
Made in New York
c. 1725–35
Silver
Length 8⅞″ (each)
Gift of Daniel Blain, Jr.
1991-158-1, 2

Although the form of these low, double-lipped, footed sauceboats was relatively common in late seventeenth- and early eighteenth-century English ceramics and silver, it is virtually unknown in colonial American silver. This pair was produced by the New York silversmith Charles Le Roux for Patrick Gordon, governor of Pennsylvania from 1726 to 1736. The Gordon coat of arms, skillfully engraved within an ornate cartouche, provides the only surface ornament to these impressive Baroque forms. The sauceboats' central bodies, as well as the applied spouts, handles, and feet, were cast as separate components and then joined to create their refined, undulating curves. Charles Le Roux had apprenticed to his father, Bartholomew, and greatly benefited from his father's experiences in Amsterdam and London as well as from his reputation in New York. The younger Le Roux was also apprenticed to the New York Board of Aldermen, through which he made the connections that led to such prestigious private and official commissions as these sauceboats for Governor Gordon. JLL

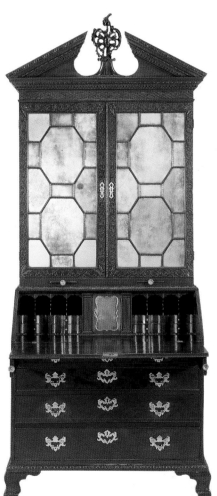

Secretary Bookcase
Made in Philadelphia
c. 1755–60
Mahogany, red cedar, pine, poplar, with gilt decoration and mirror
102 x 42 x 24″
Purchased with the Walter H. Annenberg Fund for Major Acquisitions, with supporting funds from the Henry P. McIlhenny Fund in memory of Frances P. McIlhenny, funds contributed by H. Richard Dietrich, Jr., and other private donors by contribution and exchange
1990-46-1

This fine and rare secretary bookcase exhibits one of the earliest stages in the transformation from Georgian conservatism to the "modern" Rococo taste in the decorative arts of Philadelphia. Believed to have been made for Ann Shippen Willing, who married Tench Francis, Jr., in 1758, the desk descended in the family in a remarkable state of preservation. The mirrored glazing in the doors has survived virtually intact, as have the carved and gilded ornaments in the interior compartments. The pitched pediment, with its intricately carved and molded cornice, relates most closely in form and proportion to the ornate doorframes and entablatures in the grandest contemporary Philadelphia townhouses. The regularity of the extensive carved fret work, together with the scroll-and-leaf motifs on the corners of the doors, presents a stylistic contrast to the less rigid, asymmetrical decoration on later, Rococo-inspired Philadelphia furniture of the late 1760s and 1770s. Only the central cartouche of the pediment, with its swirling counterbalance of scrolls and acanthus leaves, hints at the rocaille design that would prove so popular in only five to ten years. JLL

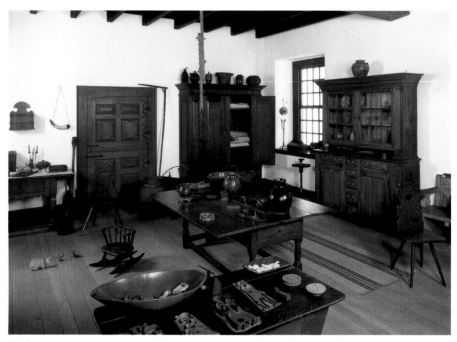

Kitchen
Made in Millbach, Lebanon County, Pennsylvania
c. 1752
Gift of Mr. and Mrs. Pierre S. du Pont and Mr. and Mrs. Lammot du Pont
1926-74-1

The two-story stone house that originally contained this kitchen was the home of Jerg Muler, a prosperous mill owner of Millbach, a small community in Lebanon County, Pennsylvania. Muler was one of the large number of German immigrants who had arrived in Pennsylvania during the second quarter of the eighteenth century and built their houses with rooms such as this kitchen based on European models. The carved panels of the door with its shaped wrought iron hinges (along with the ten-foot-wide mantel carved from a solid piece of oak and the square newel post and balusters of the stair) have their design origins in the German-speaking areas of late seventeenth-century northern Europe. The room's furnishings of paneled chairs, glazed earthenware on sturdy tables, and wrought iron kitchen wares are typical of the Pennsylvania Germans' meticulous workmanship and attention to decorative detail, and express the love of beauty in everyday objects that these early immigrants brought from Europe. MCH

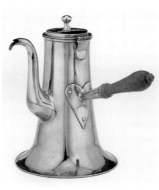

Coffeepot
Made by Benjamin Harbeson
(American, 1728–1809)
Made in Philadelphia
c. 1765–75
Copper, brass, wood
Height 9½″
Purchased with the Joseph E. Temple
Fund, the J. Stogdell Stokes Fund, and
the John T. Morris Fund. 1977-113-1

This form of coffeepot, which derived from earlier Middle Eastern examples, was common in late seventeenth- and early eighteenth-century Dutch and English households, and was most often made of brass, copper, or a similar metal alloy. Its wide, flaring base provided the broadest possible contact with the fire, while the extended wooden handle protected the user from the heat that radiated up its tapered sides. Bearing the mark of the Philadelphia metalsmith Benjamin Harbeson under its handle, this coffeepot is the only known American example of the form. In comparison to its English prototypes, Harbeson's version exhibits more refined proportions and superior workmanship. Harbeson became one of the city's most successful metal craftsmen, and a trade card promoting his shop includes an image of an identical coffeepot among a wide range of other domestic copper and brass goods. JLL

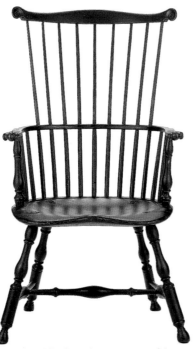

Armchair
Made in Philadelphia
c. 1750–60
Painted hardwoods
43¾ x 25³⁄₁₆ x 18⅞″
Gift of Lydia Thompson Morris
1928-7-111

The broad stance, graceful proportions, and crisp turnings of this armchair, made for a member of the Morris family of

Philadelphia, are typical of the fully developed Windsor style produced during the mid-eighteenth century by Philadelphia craftsmen, whose continual experimentation and refinement insured the city's leadership in the evolution of this furniture form in colonial America. Windsor chairs of this type were first popular in Great Britain during the reign of George I (1714–27), most often as fashionable furnishings in formal gardens. Their mixed woods were painted (usually green), which united the various structural elements aesthetically and protected them from the weather. This pattern of usage seems to have been transferred to the colonies, specifically to Philadelphia, where inventories document the use of imported Windsor chairs (so called from their use at Windsor Castle) in both interior and exterior domestic spaces. The earliest advertisement for a Philadelphia-made Windsor was placed in 1748 by David Chambers, whose chairs probably had the high spindle back, turned legs and arm supports, and wide saddle seat seen here. JLL

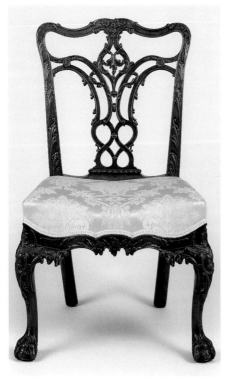

Side Chair
Attributed to the shop of
Thomas Affleck (American,
born Scotland, 1740–1795)
Made in Philadelphia
c. 1770–72
Mahogany, white cedar
36⁷/₈ x 21⁷/₈ x 18³/₈"
Gift of Robert L. McNeil, Jr. 1991-74-1

This elaborately carved side chair in the French-inspired Rococo taste is part of an extensive and important suite of ornate furnishings commissioned in 1770–71 by John Cadwalader for his new town house on Second Street in Philadelphia. Cadwalader and his wife, Elizabeth Lloyd, patronized a number of the city's leading artisans and craftsmen, who produced stylistically sophisticated forms in response to the demands of such discerning, well informed clients (see opposite). Surviving invoices document that the Cadwalader suite consisted of at least thirteen chairs, a pair of *"commode sophias"* (serpentine-front sofas), a pair of card tables (one of which is now owned by the Museum), an easy chair, and four fire screens. Their sweeping, serpentine forms, richly embellished with carved rocaille ornament, represent the zenith of Philadelphia cabinetmaking during the late eighteenth century. JLL

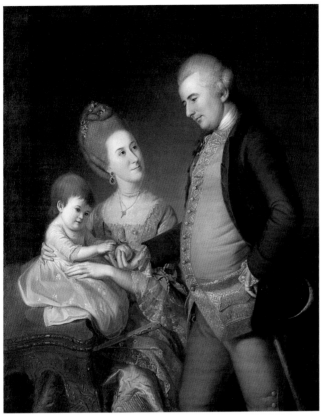

Charles Willson Peale
American, 1741–1827
Portrait of John and Elizabeth Lloyd Cadwalader and Their Daughter Anne, 1772
Oil on canvas
51½ x 41¼″
Purchased for the Cadwalader Collection with funds contributed by the Mabel Pew Myrin Trust and the gift of an anonymous donor. 1983-90-3

Like Thomas Eakins, Charles Willson Peale is inextricably linked with Philadelphia, yet the young artist was living in his native Maryland in 1770 when John Cadwalader's commission for family portraits allowed him to test the market for his talents in the city. Cadwalader's order for five large portraits in elaborately carved and gilded frames, to be hung in the house on Second Street that he was renovating and furnishing in grand style, was unique in colonial America, and Peale rose to the occasion, applying all he had learned about stylish portraiture from Benjamin West in London. This portrait of the Cadwalader family is clearly the centerpiece of the group, and the artist has detailed the gold embroidery on Cadwalader's waistcoat, Elizabeth Cadwalader's large jeweled earring, and the serpentine-front card table—part of an outstanding suite of American Rococo furniture (see opposite)—to express the young couple's affluence and taste. The affection and pleasure of family life that animate the scene are unique to Peale in eighteenth-century American painting, and reflect the artist's profoundest feelings about his own growing family. DS

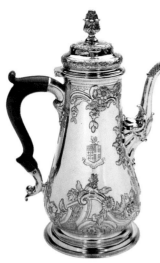

Coffeepot
Made by Philip Syng, Jr.
(American, 1703–1789)
Made in Philadelphia
c. 1753
Silver, wood
Height 11⅞″
Purchased with the John D. McIlhenny
Fund. 1966-20-1

While closely related in form and design to silver made in London in the 1740s and 1750s, through the exuberance and individualized character of its decorations this coffeepot ranks among the most sophisticated examples of Rococo-inspired American silver from the third quarter of the eighteenth century. Its robust, single-bellied body recalls an earlier Baroque style, but its elaborate scroll and floral patterns are typical of the ornament produced by the London-trained chasers and engravers who were collaborating with master silversmiths in Philadelphia during the 1750s and 1760s. Because of the presence of these specially skilled artisans, this type of ornate silver decoration was more highly developed in Philadelphia than in any other colonial American city. One such craftsman was Laurence Hubert, a French Huguenot silver engraver, trained in London, who in 1748 arrived in the Philadelphia shop of Philip Syng, Jr., where this coffeepot was produced for the prominent lawyer Joseph Galloway. Its sophisticated design and abundant ornamentation attest to both the craftsman's ability and the wealth and confident taste of his patron. JLL

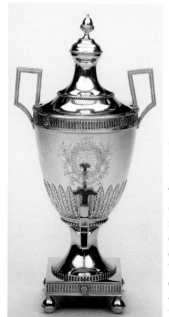

Hot Water Urn
Made by Richard Humphreys
(American, born West Indies,
1749–1832)
Made in Philadelphia
1774
Silver, iron, ivory; height 21½″
Purchased with funds contributed by
the Dietrich American Foundation
1977-88-1

This hot water urn is one of the earliest known pieces of American silver in the Neoclassical style. Its impressive scale and innovative design are characteristic of the type of American silver commissioned as presentation gifts in the late eighteenth and early nineteenth centuries. In 1774 this example was presented by the First Continental Congress, sitting in Philadelphia, to Charles Thomson, its first secretary, in recognition of his service to the governmental body. While well versed in the popular Rococo style, Richard Humphreys, one of Philadelphia's leading silversmiths, used this important commission to experiment with the latest fashion for Neoclassical designs. Based on contemporary English prototypes, its classical urn shape, acanthus leaf and rosette decorations, and squared base with ball feet embody this new style, which would dominate domestic tastes some ten years later, during the Federal period. JLL

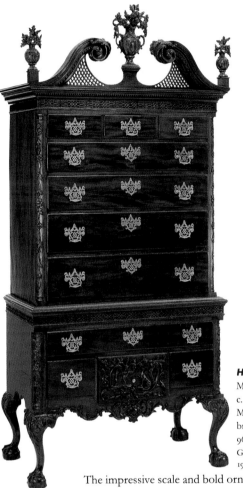

High Chest
Made in Philadelphia
c. 1770–75
Mahogany, pine, poplar, cedar, brass
96¾ x 45½ x 24½"
Gift of Mrs. Henry V. Greenough
1957-129-1

The impressive scale and bold ornament of this Philadelphia high chest, produced during the height of the taste for the Rococo, demonstrate the sophistication and talent of American cabinetmakers working in this style during the last half of the eighteenth century. Its ornately carved pediment is balanced by the light rocaille trails of flowers and vines along the sides, the relief-carved vignette at the bottom, and the boldly scrolled decorations along the undulating skirt and the S-curved cabriole legs. The production of such an elaborate piece of furniture was a collaborative process, with joiners constructing the case that carvers then ornamented. Here the strong architectonic proportions of the case have determined the placement of its decorative carving. The scene of the fox and grapes depicted on both the bottom drawer of this chest and its matching dressing table was probably based on motifs derived from folk tales published in the eighteenth century. JLL

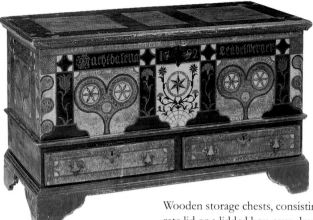

Chest
Attributed to John Bieber
(American, 1768–1825)
Made in Lehigh or Berks County,
Pennsylvania
1792
Painted poplar and white pine
30½ x 53 x 24"
Purchased with the Thomas Skelton
Harrison Fund, the Fiske Kimball Fund,
and the Joseph E. Temple Fund
1982-68-1

Wooden storage chests, consisting of an open box with a separate lid or a lidded box-over-drawers, are among the earliest forms of Germanic household furniture found in North America, and could be adapted for additional use as seating or a table. As part of the continuation of this tradition, rural Pennsylvania German craftsmen combined earlier joinery techniques with the ornamental painting styles of central Europe to produce a wide range of decorative and utilitarian chests throughout the late eighteenth and early nineteenth century. These chests were often presented to a bride as part of her dowry, and this example, one of twenty-one in the Museum's rich Pennsylvania German collection, was made in 1792 for the marriage of Magdelena Leabelsperger of Berks County, Pennsylvania. The entire surface of this chest, which is the most ornate of a group of chests attributed to John Bieber, is decorated with traditional Germanic motifs executed in various painting techniques, including faux graining, sponge decoration, and compass-inscribed geometric designs, upon architecturally derived panels reminiscent of European models. JLL

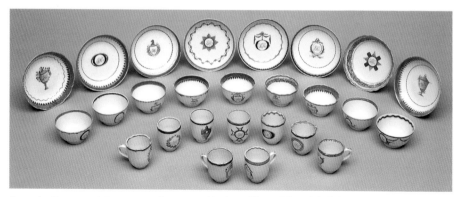

Sample Cups and Saucers
China, for the American market
c. 1790–95
Porcelain with underglaze, overglaze enamel, and gilt decoration
Height 2½" (handled cup),
2" (evening cup), 1⅜" (saucer)
Gift of Mrs. George G. Chandler
1986-81-7–24

In 1784, with the sailing of the Philadelphia-financed *Empress of China,* the new republic of the United States began to trade directly with Asia, as enterprising mariners and merchants looked to the promise of rich rewards from importing silk, porcelain, tea, and other fine goods for an eager clientele. This sample assortment of twenty-six cups and saucers that belonged to Samuel Howell, Jr., a successful Philadelphia merchant in the China trade, is unique for its completeness and presents the variety of porcelain patterns that his customers could order from China by referring to the numbers within each monogram. Almost limitless individualized designs were possible by combining the various motifs and decorative borders. The gilded initials in the monograms are those of Howell's wife Margaret Emlen and their fifteen children. MCH

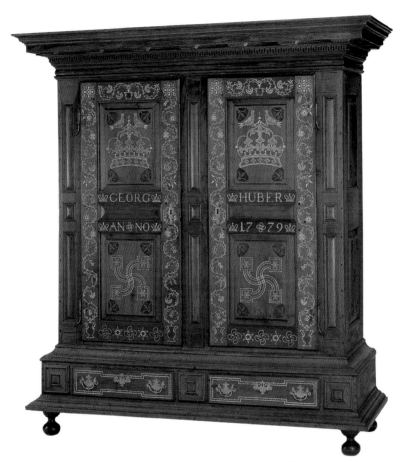

Wardrobe

Attributed to Peter Holl III
(American, died 1825) and
Christian Huber (American, n.d.)
Made in Manheim and Warwick
townships, Lancaster County,
Pennsylvania
1779
Black walnut with sulfur inlay,
poplar, pine, oak, iron
83⅛ x 78 x 27½"
Purchased with Museum funds
1957-30-1

The robust character of the form and ornament of this majestic wardrobe, or *Schrank* (storage chest), is characteristic of the traditional decorative folk style brought to southeastern Pennsylvania by Swiss craftsmen during the mid-eighteenth century. The large, extended cornice moldings, convex-molded carved panels, and symmetrically conceived designs of sulfur inlay firmly place this piece among the most artistically ambitious examples of the Baroque style as interpreted by Germanic immigrants in the third quarter of the eighteenth century. The technique of sulfur inlay, in which the molten material is poured into incised areas of decoration, has been documented among a small group of eighteenth-century Delaware Valley furniture. Peter Holl III possibly experimented with sulfur's decorative potential in conjunction with his work as a joiner and pump maker, a craft in which the material was often used to repair metal components. JLL

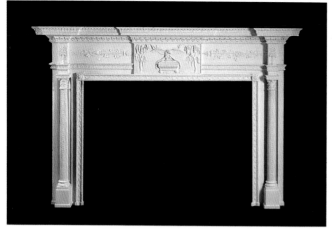

Mantel
Made by Robert Wellford
(American, active c. 1798–1839)
Made in Philadelphia
c. 1801–10
Painted pine with composition
decoration
57 x 88″
Purchased with the Joseph E. Temple
Fund. 1920-76-1

Elaborately ornamented mantels such as this served as the central element in the refined schemes of decorative wood-work prescribed for many Neoclassical interiors in Philadelphia during the Federal era. Its ornamental surfaces show a combination of various carved and applied motifs made of "composition," a plaster-like material, that were inspired by the recently rediscovered archaeological styles of ancient Greece and Rome that were celebrated during the late eighteenth and early nineteenth centuries. Robert Wellford of Philadelphia perfected the manufacture of "ornamental composition," and supplied a wide range of molded decorative elements to carpenters and house builders along with instructions facilitating their proper "tempering and fixing" to interior woodwork. This mantel, which is one of thirteen in the Museum's extensive collection of architectural woodwork, is signed by Wellford on the central sarcophagus and thus is one of the few examples firmly documented to this influential craftsman/inventor. JLL

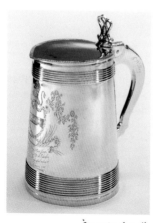

Tankard
Made by Joseph Anthony, Jr.
(American, 1762–1814)
Made in Philadelphia
1788
Silver
Height 6⅞″
Purchased with Museum funds
1950-53-1

In 1782 the silversmith Joseph Anthony, Jr., moved from Newport, Rhode Island, to Philadelphia, where post-Revolutionary trade was brisk and the newest Neoclassical styles from abroad were in vogue. This tankard is a grand expression of the new style, which featured straight, plain surfaces fashioned from rolled sheet silver and often, as here, embellished with applied decorative bandings. The engraved arms of the Penn family, enframed with fluttering floral garlands, and the elegant script are also characteristic of the latest fashion. The tankard was presented to the lawyer Charles Jarvis, who in 1787 had represented the cousins John Penn and John Penn, Jr., in petitions to the state of Pennsylvania regarding land inherited from William Penn's original grant from Charles II. Anthony also made an identical tankard, now in the Wadsworth Atheneum in Hartford, which the Penns gave to the surveyor who had worked on their behalf. The Penns' petitions were unsuccessful, however, and both men returned to England in 1788, thus signaling the end of the family's proprietary interests in Pennsylvania. BBG

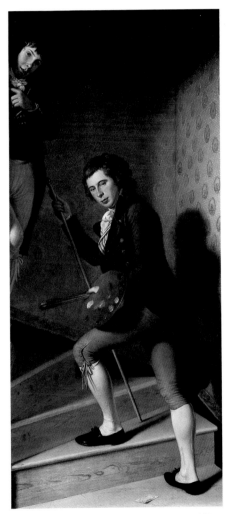

Charles Willson Peale
American, 1741–1827
Staircase Group (Portrait of Raphaelle Peale and Titian Ramsey Peale), 1795
Oil on canvas
89½ x 39⅜"
The George W. Elkins Collection
E1945-1-1

By the time that Charles Willson Peale painted the *Staircase Group,* he had abandoned commercial portraiture to devote himself to natural science and to his museum and zoo at Philosophical Hall. To help foster the arts in Philadelphia, however, he was instrumental in founding the Columbianum, an artists' association modeled on the Royal Academy in London. For its first and only exhibition, Peale executed this painting to demonstrate that he remained one of the city's preeminent artists. On an unusually large canvas, he made one of his rare full-length portraits, showing two of his sons on an enclosed spiral staircase. Its high degree of detail and finish shows that the painting was clearly intended to be a trompe l'oeil "deception," an effect that Peale never attempted elsewhere. To enhance the illusion, he installed the painting within a doorframe in his studio, with a real step in front. Rembrandt Peale, another son, recalled that his father's friend George Washington, misled by Peale's artifice, tipped his hat and greeted the two young men as he walked by. DS

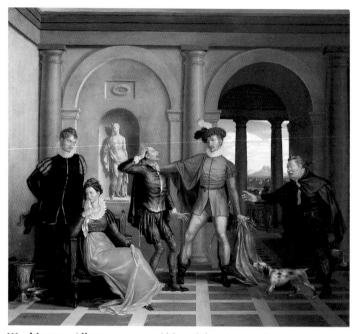

Washington Allston
American, 1779–1843
Scene from "The Taming of the Shrew," 1809
Oil on canvas
27³/₄ x 30⁷/₈"
Purchased with the Edith H. Bell Fund and the J. Stogdell Stokes Fund. 1987-8-1

Although best known for his romantic landscapes and monumental history paintings, Washington Allston also made small narrative paintings, including nine subjects from Shakespearean plays. This scene from *The Taming of the Shrew,* once owned by Philadelphian Edwin Forrest, one of the most renowned actors of the mid-nineteenth century, shows the predicament of Catherine, whose husband Petruchio is trying to "tame" her tempestuous spirit by denying her the luxuries she finds so .appealing. Here he is about to destroy a gown that he has ordered for her with the excuse that it is not good enough, much to the tailor's consternation. Certainly the most animated of Allston's theatrical pictures, this work is also the best preserved. Allston painted by applying transparent layers of color, a technique that he developed by studying the work of Venetian artists of the Renaissance. In many of his paintings, these delicate layers have been removed or marred by harsh cleanings, leaving monochromatic, generalized underpainting. Fortunately here the varied, glowing colors and meticulous details have remained remarkably intact, evidence of the talent that brought Allston acclaim as the foremost American artist in the first half of the nineteenth century. DS

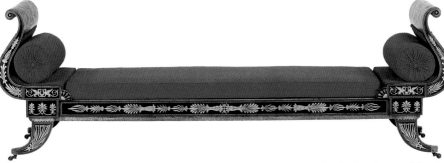

Sofa

Designed by Benjamin Henry
Latrobe (American, born England,
1764–1820)
Made in Philadelphia
c. 1808
Gessoed and painted tulipwood
and maple with gilt decoration;
caning
33½ x 103 x 23½"

Gift (by exchange) of Mrs. Alex Simpson, Jr., and A. Carson Simpson, and
purchased with funds contributed by
Mr. and Mrs. Robert L. Raley and
various donors. 1986-126-2

Benjamin Henry Latrobe's designs for the interiors and furnishings of the town house of the Philadelphia merchant William
Waln, begun in 1805, were among the architect's most comprehensive domestic projects. Inspired by French and English
designers working in the Neoclassical idiom, Latrobe's preference for a correct archaeological style drawn from Greek antiquities is clearly demonstrated in this double-scroll-armed sofa
with saber-shaped legs from a suite of drawing room furniture
for the Waln house. The other surviving components of the
group include seventeen side chairs, two card tables, two window benches, and a pier table. The Museum's group has remained in remarkable condition, retaining its original ornate
painting and gilding, caned seat platforms, and traces of the
silk upholstery. JLL

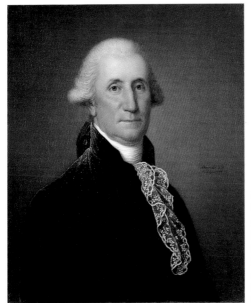

Adolph Ulrich Wertmüller

Swedish, active United States,
1751–1811
Portrait of George Washington
c. 1794
Oil on canvas
25⅜ x 21⅛"
Gift of Mr. and Mrs. John Wagner
1986-100-1

Adolph Ulrich Wertmüller had a successful career in his native
Sweden and in France before he came to Philadelphia, the
capital of the new United States, in the 1790s. He, like scores
of other artists, was hoping for commissions for portraits of
statesmen and government officials, of whom George Washington was certainly the most desired. Washington, aware of his
symbolic importance, complied with many requests for por-

traits, and posed for Wertmüller in Independence Hall in 1794. This painting, which is strikingly different from Gilbert Stuart's iconic image, familiar from the dollar bill, was given to the Museum by descendants of the family that had purchased it from the artist's estate. Wertmüller's emphasis on the texture of Washington's velvet suit, the dusting on his shoulders from his freshly powdered hair, and his frilly lace jabot characterizes the president as something of a dandy, just as his representation of a long, thin face and close-set eyes gives Washington an aristocratic appearance, which must have appealed to the sizable faction who wanted the new government to have the splendor of a court with a kingly chief executive. DS

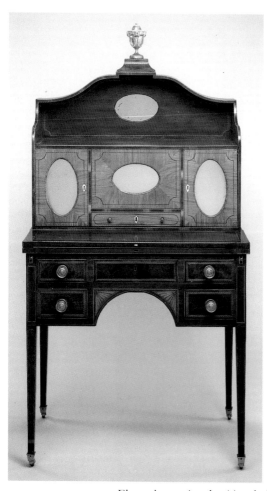

Writing Desk

Attributed to William Sinclair
(American, active 1798–1826)
Made in Philadelphia
c. 1801–5
Mahogany and satinwood
with ivory, wood inlay, and mirrors
59½ x 30½ x 19¾"
Bequest of Miss Fanny Norris in
memory of Louis Marie Clapier
1940-46-2

Elegantly appointed writing desks with rich veneers and ornamental surfaces became essential furnishings for the stylish American woman's boudoir or drawing room during the Federal era. In addition to supplying a writing surface, these desks provided secure storage space for fragile possessions, jewelry, and other keepsakes. Contemporary periodicals prescribed the forms and patterns of the fashionable writing desks, or bonheurs-du-jour (literally, "happiness of the day"), and their style and decorative flourishes show the marked influence of French prototypes. This desk descended in the family of Louis

Clapier, a successful Philadelphia merchant of French ancestry who invested extensively in the city's trade with Paris. It was probably among the furnishings he acquired upon his marriage to Maria Heyle in 1801 for their elegant town house at Sixth and Lombard streets. JLL

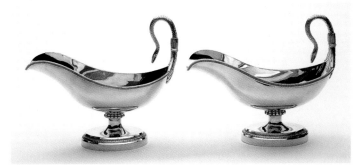

Pair of Sauceboats

Made by Simon Chaudron
(American, born France,
1758–1846)
Made in Philadelphia
1800–1805
Silver
Height 8¾″ (each)
Purchased with the Richardson Fund
and funds from the bequest of Mrs.
James Alan Montgomery. 1991-1-1, 2

Famous since its founding in the late seventeenth century as a city of religious and political tolerance, Philadelphia gained further renown in the early years of the newly independent United States as a haven for the French who were seeking peace and prosperity in the wake of the French Revolution of 1789. One of these émigrés was Simon Chaudron, a jeweler trained in Paris and Switzerland, who moved to Philadelphia in 1794. With their snake-shaped handles socketed into bold, flaring leaf-and-anthemion motifs and the classical banding that delineated their upper edges and bases, this pair of silver sauceboats by Chaudron are early manifestations of the newest neo-Grec fashion in the United States. Capacious sauceboats such as these were usually made in pairs and sometimes in fours, and are elegant renditions of a form deemed essential to a well-set table in the early nineteenth century. BBG

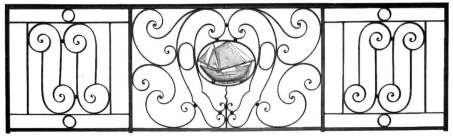

Railing

Made in Philadelphia
c. 1796–1800
Wrought and cast iron,
copper alloy, modern gilding
38½ x 60¹³⁄₁₆″
Purchased with the Joseph E. Temple
Fund. 1921-24-1

Ornately scrolled iron grilles, balconies, and railings became popular ornaments on Neoclassical houses and commercial buildings erected in Philadelphia in the late eighteenth and early nineteenth centuries. This railing is one of the surviving examples that once embellished Stephen Girard's home and offices on Water Street in Philadelphia. Girard, a wealthy merchant and philanthropist who was intimately familiar with the latest French vogue for Neoclassicism, may have commissioned these railings from the French-trained ironworker John Fairpoux, who is known to have produced work in this style for a number of Philadelphia clients. His skillful manipulation of raw materials transformed into an elegant series of repeating curves is characteristic of the best ironwork produced in Federal Philadelphia. JLL

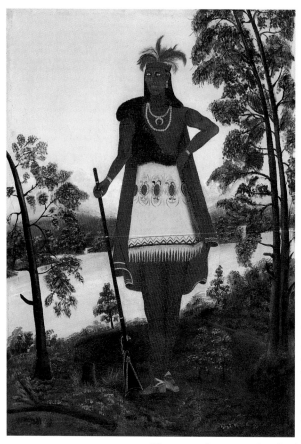

Unknown Artist
American, nineteenth century
Portrait of a Native American
Man of the Northeast Woodlands
c. 1820
Oil on canvas
45⅛ x 31⅞"
The Collection of Edgar William and
Bernice Chrysler Garbisch. 1966-219-3

The strong features and authoritative presence of the blue-eyed Native American who dominates the foreground and the many tributaries flowing into the river in the background suggest that this is a portrait of a specific person in a specific place. In fact, the subject had been identified as Shikellamy, an important Oneida leader. However, no lifetime portraits of Shikellamy, who died in 1748, are known, and its style and color scheme suggest that the painting dates to the early nineteenth century. The full-length pose holding a matchlock, with the left arm akimbo, derives from the English artist John Verelst's portrait of an Iroquois chief. This man, clearly a person of status, wears a garb that appears to be a composite of elements worn by Northeast Woodlands peoples that the artist has boldly and freely abstracted. The decorative band of ovals on the apron, for example, more resembles designs on the painted toleware produced by white New England artists than the Iroquois quill- and beadwork that was its starting point. This picture is one of over seventy paintings given to the Museum by the pioneering collectors of American naïve art Edgar William and Bernice Chrysler Garbisch. DS

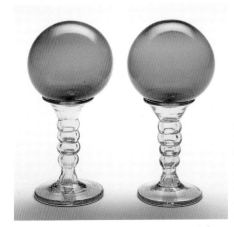

Mantel Ornaments
Probably made in southern
New Jersey
1820–45
Blown glass
Height 9¼" (each)
The George H. Lorimer Collection
1953-29-110a,b, 111a,b

These blown-glass mantel decorations are composed of stands, similar in form to candlesticks, that serve as supports for the ornamental balls. Mantel ornaments were generally not offered in the production lines of most glass manufactories, but instead afforded the individual glassblower an outlet for experimenting with lively color combinations and innovative forms. Whimsical glass objects such as these, perhaps used as a decoration for a glassmaker's home or as a gift for a friend, are difficult to date, as their production remained a popular pastime for craftsmen throughout the nineteenth century. These examples, one of the rare pairs to have survived, illustrate the high skills of the bottle glassblower, exhibiting a charming sophistication in form, color selection, and proportion. MEM

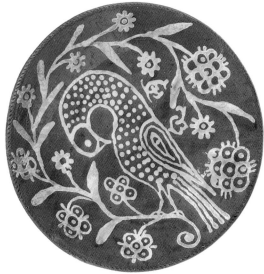

Plate
Attributed to Benjamin Bergey
(American, 1797–1854)
Made in Montgomery County,
Pennsylvania
1820–40
Glazed earthenware with slip
decoration, daubed with
copper oxide
Diameter 13¼"
Purchased with Museum funds. 1893-218

The rich clay deposits on Benjamin Bergey's farm in Franconia Township, Montgomery County, Pennsylvania, supplied several small local potteries, one of which likely produced this plate. The central motif may represent a mother pelican piercing her breast with her beak to feed her young with her blood, an ancient Christian symbol of maternal devotion that often figured in old German manuscripts. The design is executed in yellow slip, applied to the red clay body of the plate with a slip cup, a molded earthenware vessel fitted with goose quills through which the liquid slip was made to trickle over the surface of the ware to create the desired pattern. After the piece had dried sufficiently, the slip decoration was sometimes pressed into the body of the plate so that the surface was perfectly smooth to prevent the designs from wearing off with use or flaking away under heat. The flat treatment of the ornament on this plate, one of about one hundred in the Museum's comprehensive collection of Pennsylvania German ceramics, suggests that it was made for utilitarian rather than ornamental purposes. MCH

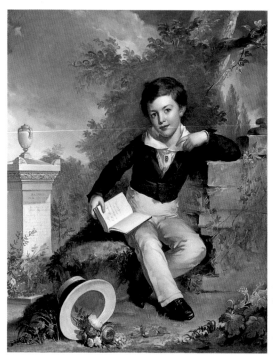

Manuel Joachim de França
American, born Portugal,
1808–1865
Portrait of Matthew Hinzinga Messchert, 1839
Oil on canvas
50⅛ x 40¼"
Gift of Dr. and Mrs. Harold Lefft
1965-214-1

Portuguese-born Manuel Joachim de França studied art in Lisbon before immigrating to the United States in the late 1820s, settling first in Philadelphia and then in Saint Louis, where he became the city's most fashionable portraitist. In its size and elaborate composition, this portrait of Matthew Hinzinga Messchert of Philadelphia is De França's most ambitious work, and its pleasing combination of bright pastel colors with more technical dash than is usually evident in his portraits suggests the influence of the artist's friend Thomas Sully, the city's most famous portrait painter. The charm and freshness of the picture momentarily distract us from observing that the cemetery monument at the left is dedicated to a woman of the Messchert family and that Matthew holds a book inscribed "a Remembrance from his Mother." This painting is thus a mourning picture, a popular art form that appealed to the romantic sentiment of the early nineteenth century. De França's portrayal of the young man as a living memorial to his dead mother is one of the largest and most touching examples of the genre. DS

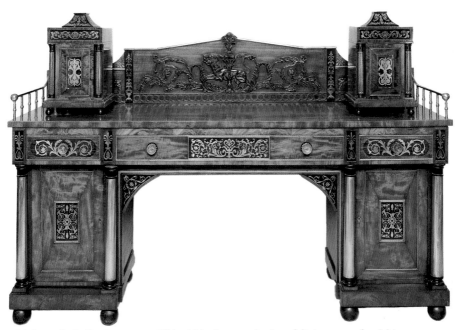

Sideboard, Knife Boxes, and Cellarette

Attributed to Joseph B. Barry
(American, born Ireland,
c. 1757–1839)
Made in Philadelphia
c. 1825–30
Mahogany and mahogany veneer
with brass and ebony inlay
50 x 91 x 27" (sideboard)
21⅝ x 13½ x 14½" (knife boxes)
29 x 28⅓ x 23" (cellarette)

Bequest of Miss Elizabeth Gratz
1909-2a–c (sideboard and knife boxes)
Gift of Simon Gratz in memory of
Caroline S. Gratz. 1925-76-2 (cellarette)

This richly decorated suite of dining room furnishings represents the highest development of ornamental inlay and carving found on Philadelphia furniture of the Empire style, which was popular in the first quarter of the nineteenth century. Made for Simon Gratz, a successful Philadelphia businessman, this sideboard with its two knife boxes (above) and the cellarette, or wine cooler (below), display an impressive scale and lavish design that demonstrate the stylistic sophistication and refined tastes of the city's leading families. The ornate panels of brass and ebony inlay were imported from Birmingham, England, and set into surrounding veneers to create decorative surfaces of a type rarely seen in American furniture. This group is attributed to Joseph B. Barry, who during the 1820s advertised his ability to produce such work from his extensive furniture warehouse at 134 South Second Street in Philadelphia. JLL

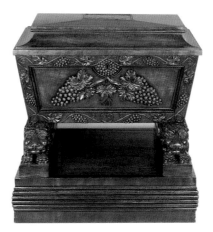

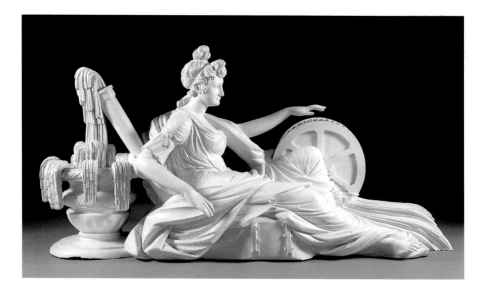

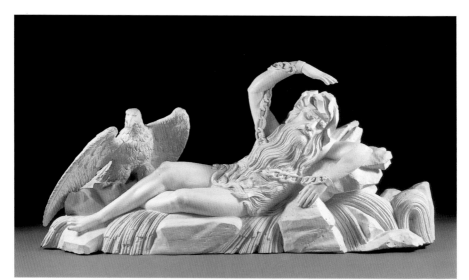

William Rush
American, 1756–1833
Allegory of the Waterworks (top)
*Allegory of the Schuylkill River
in Its Improved State* (bottom)
1825
Spanish cedar, painted
41³⁄₁₆ x 87¹⁄₁₆ x 30⁷⁄₁₆″ (*Waterworks*)
39³⁄₈ x 87¹⁄₄ x 26⁷⁄₁₆″ (*Schuylkill River*)
Commissioners of Fairmount Park,
Philadelphia

With the decline of ship construction early in the nineteenth century, the Philadelphian William Rush, who was famous for his carvings of ships' figureheads, began to make allegorical figures of wood painted white to complement the marble of the city's new Neoclassical buildings. A civic and cultural leader as well, Rush served on Philadelphia's city council and was particularly interested in the Watering Committee, which was responsible for the municipal water supply. Rush carved these allegorical figures of the Schuylkill River, the source of Philadelphia's water, for the city's second waterworks, a group of Neoclassical wooden pavilions that still stand on the bank of the river in Fairmount Park. The chained male figure represents the river being controlled by dams and locks, while the reclining female figure extends a graceful arm to power the waterwheel as she sits on the pumping mechanism and leans against a pipe from which water gushes into an urn symbolizing a reservoir. Both figures ultimately derive from antique sources as interpreted through the artist's characteristically bold and vigorous style. By combining his allegorical figures with machinery Rush created the first American monument to celebrate the triumph of engineering over nature. DS

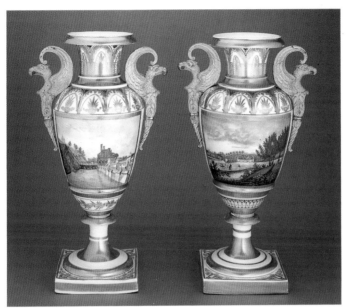

Pair of Urns

Made by the Tucker porcelain factory (Philadelphia, 1826–1838)
Painting attributed to William Ellis Tucker (American, 1800–1832)
c. 1830
Porcelain with underglaze and overglaze decoration, and gilded bronze handles
Height 21⅛″ (each)
Purchased with the Baugh-Barber Fund, the Thomas Skelton Harrison Fund, the Elizabeth Wandell Smith Fund, funds given in memory of Sophie E. Pennebaker, and with funds contributed by the Barra Foundation, Mrs. Henry W. Breyer, Mr. and Mrs. M. Todd Cooke, the Dietrich American Foundation, Mr. and Mrs. Anthony N. B. Garvan, the Philadelphia Savings Fund Society, and Andrew M. Rouse. 1984-160-1, 2

These elaborate urns painted with views of the Fairmount Waterworks (at the foot of the small hill on which the Philadelphia Museum of Art now stands) are the largest and most ornate objects produced by the first successful porcelain manufactory in the United States, which was established in Philadelphia in 1826 by the brothers William Ellis and Thomas Tucker. Although it was short-lived, the Tucker factory made a high-quality porcelain that rivaled popular French and German imports of the same date. Both brothers supervised all aspects of the company's production, although scenic decorations of this quality are generally attributed to William. The classically shaped urns, designed in imitation of Parisian porcelain, have gilded bronze handles in the form of griffins that were designed by John Frederick Sachse, a sculptor working for the Philadelphia lamp and chandelier factory of Cornelius and Company. Such close collaboration between manufacturers of domestic furnishings was uncommon during this period and rarely resulted in the successfully congruent designs that are evident here. JLL

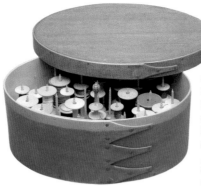

Spool Box
Made in Canterbury,
New Hampshire
c. 1825–40
Maple, pine, chestnut, copper tacks,
silk and cotton thread
3½ x 9¼ x 6⅞"
Gift of Mr. and Mrs. Julius Zieget
1963-160-54a,b

In their search for a perfect society, the religious group known as the Shakers rejected the world around them and established their own communities. As they pursued their spiritual vision, they devoted their lives to work and developed a unique sense of design as they fashioned objects that blended simplicity, harmony, and utility. This oval box, which is fitted with a removable rack with thirty-eight dowels for holding spools of thread, perfectly reflects the Shaker aesthetic: it is an unadorned, functional, and well-made object used for the productive task of sewing. Even the thread on the spools was made by the Shakers. The initials on the bottom of the box, which was acquired from the Shaker community in Canterbury, New Hampshire, suggest that it was used by Anna Carr (1776–1852), head nurse at the infirmary. The box may have been made by James Johnson, an elder and wood turner at Canterbury. MCH

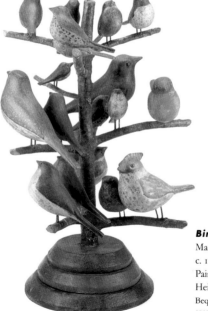

Bird Tree
Made in Pennsylvania
c. 1800–1830
Painted hardwoods, wire
Height 17⅜"
Bequest of Lisa Norris Elkins
1950-92-201

A long and rich tradition of decorative wood carving was brought to North America by the Germanic populations that settled in southeastern Pennsylvania. Carved motifs adorned many households, and whimsical creations, such as this colorful bird tree, were often presented as a part of the ritual of courtship or as other tokens of affection or esteem. Nature served as a powerful source of inspiration and reassurance among the predominantly agrarian Pennsylvania Germans. Depicted with great realism or with characteristic humor and wit, animals frequently served as decorative motifs while maintaining their strong spiritual or symbolic connotations within the community. Among the Pennsylvania Germans birds were a symbol of rebirth and renewal, and carvings such as this were often given to acknowledge the arrival of a child or to mark the coming of spring. JLL

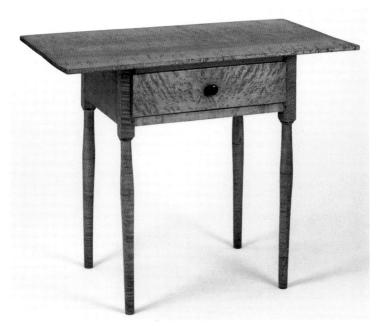

Table

Made in Canterbury,
New Hampshire
c. 1820–40
Maple
28 x 53 x 35″
Gift of Mr. and Mrs. Julius Zieget
1963-160-23

The United Society of Believers in Christ's First and Second Appearing, more commonly known as the Shakers, established a thriving and industrious community in Canterbury, New Hampshire, in 1792. This table, part of the Museum's extensive collection of objects made by the Shakers, epitomizes the refined simplicity and fine craftsmanship inspired by the religious tenets of their movement. Highly "curled," or grained, wood such as the maple used here was regarded by the Shakers as a gift from God, and thus was the preferred material for a number of the talented cabinetmakers within the Canterbury community. The natural pattern of the maple provides this table with its bold, visual presence, while its turning and form remain in the characteristically restrained Shaker style. Shaker craftsmen using more plainly grained woods often painted the finished piece a bright color, such as yellow or blue, to add beauty and interest, or included more pronounced turned or shaped elements in its design. JLL

Presentation Ewer

Made by Osmon Reed
(American, active 1833–63)
Made in Philadelphia
1843
Silver
Height 17¾"
Purchased with the Joseph E. Temple
Fund. 1902-6

This ornate ewer, bearing the mark of Osmon Reed, a Philadelphia silversmith and jeweler, was skillfully decorated with heavily chased, repoussé, and engraved motifs. It was commissioned by the Philadelphia Whig party for presentation to the Whig candidate James C. Jones upon his election as governor of Tennessee in 1843. The ewer shape, derived from antiquity, became popular for presentation silver objects in the first half of the nineteenth century. In this design Reed incorporated scenes from Jones's campaign surrounded by rocaille scrollwork interspersed with dogwood and rose blossoms, which grew in abundance in Tennessee. The purchase of this ewer in 1902 marked the beginning of the Museum's distinguished collection of American silver. JLL

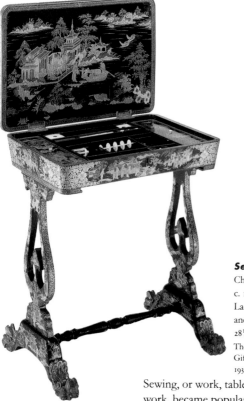

Sewing Table

China, for the American market
c. 1825–40
Lacquer on wood with turned
and carved ivory fittings
28½ x 24½ x 17³⁄₁₆"
The Mary Wilcocks Campbell Memorial
Gift, bequest of Betty Campbell Madeira
1931-42-6

Sewing, or work, tables, designed for use in domestic needlework, became popular in stylish American interiors during the

Federal period. This ornate example with lacquer decorations of Chinese motifs and an interior intricately fitted with ivory sewing implements was purchased in China by the Philadelphia merchant Benjamin Chew Wilcocks, who enjoyed such great success in the China trade that he was appointed United States consul there in 1813. Beginning in 1784, Philadelphia led the nation in the development of a regular and highly profitable trade with China. Wilcocks was just one of a number of Philadelphia merchants who amassed great fortunes importing a wide range of decorative objects as well as silk, tea, and opium for the American consumer. This sewing table is typical of the taste for "exotic" Chinese goods that seized many Philadelphians and influenced domestic decoration during the first half of the nineteenth century. JLL

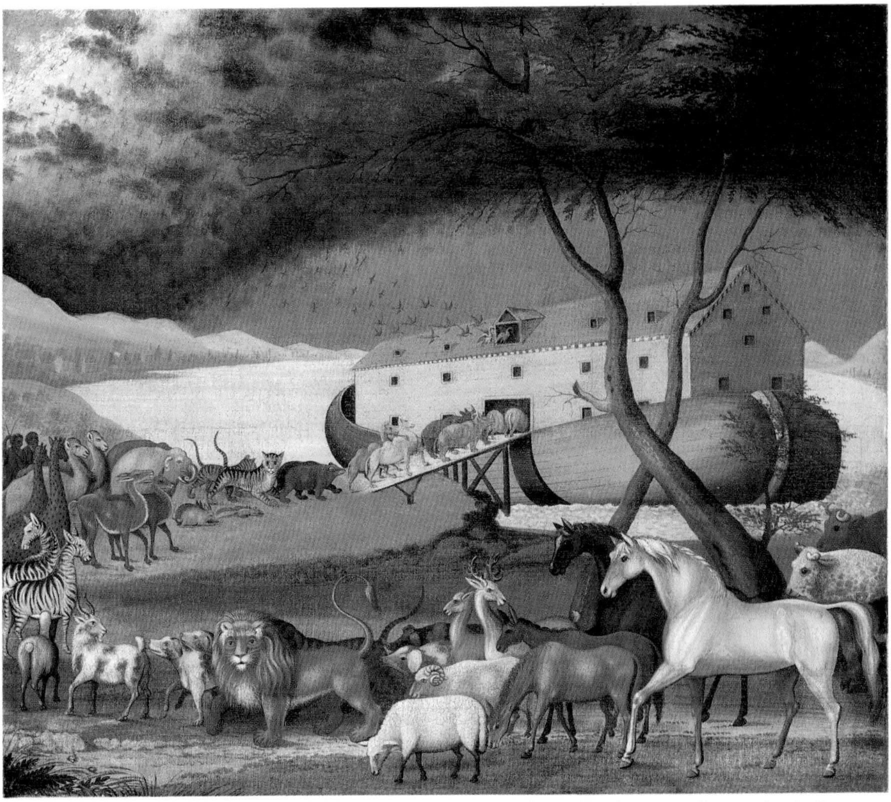

Edward Hicks
American, 1780–1849
Noah's Ark, 1846
Oil on canvas
26 5/16 x 30 3/8"
Bequest of Lisa Norris Elkins. 1950-92-7

For Edward Hicks, a zealous Quaker preacher and missionary, making a living by painting portraits or other symbols of self-indulgence was incompatible with his religious beliefs. Yet his greatest talent was as an artist, so to satisfy both his image-making impulse and his Quaker convictions, he made nearly a hundred paintings on the biblical theme of the Peaceable Kingdom, to which *Noah's Ark,* although a unique subject among his work, is clearly related. Hicks based the general composition of the scene on Nathaniel Currier's popular lithograph issued in 1844, but gave the pairs of animals a beauty and dignity lacking in the print. As a result, the calm procession of beasts has a stately rhythm that embodies the gravity of God's command that they enter the ark to escape the approaching flood. The grayish green horizon with black clouds looming above intensifies the drama of the impending cataclysm, and the dignified old lion staring directly at the viewer focuses attention upon this lesson of God's power to destroy and redeem. DS

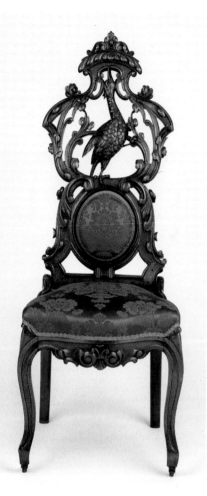

Side Chair
United States
1865–70
Mahogany
45½ x 16 x 18″
Gift of Pauline Townsend Pease
1979-108-5

This side chair, with its naturalistic foliate and C-scroll carvings and cabriole legs, is an unusual example of the Rococo Revival, a high-fashion style popular in the mid-nineteenth century, when it was known as the "Modern French style." Typical of the nineteenth-century tendency to borrow patterns from the past rather than creating completely new ones, Rococo Revival furniture combined contemporary forms with motifs popularized by the eighteenth-century English cabinetmaker Thomas Chippendale, interpreted in a manner that appealed to the newly affluent clientele of the industrial age. The most prominent design element of this chair, the large bird that is most likely a phoenix, an ancient symbol of immortality and rebirth, recalls a motif often found on the pediment of eighteenth-century looking glasses. An example of the Rococo Revival's ability to create styles that were almost always inventive adaptations of the past rather than reproductions, this revival work achieves a considerable distinction of its own. MCH

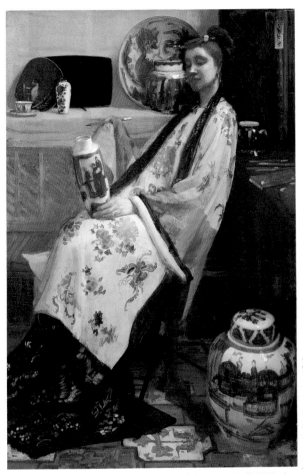

James Abbott McNeill Whistler
American, active England, 1834–1903
Purple and Rose: The Lange Leizen of the Six Marks, 1864
Oil on canvas
36¾ x 24⅛"
John G. Johnson Collection. Cat. 1112

James Abbott McNeill Whistler was a leading figure in the Aesthetic movement, which rejected the rich stuffiness of Victorian taste in favor of a style defined by spareness, delicacy, and refinement. Central to his concept of design were Asian objects from his own collection, such as the ceramics and the woman's embroidered Chinese robe in *Purple and Rose: The Lange Leizen of the Six Marks.* Following the names of the colors that set the painting's tone—Whistler's way of emphasizing that his works are primarily abstract compositions of colors—the title refers to the seventeenth-century Chinese porcelain jar that the young woman holds. *Lange Leizen,* a Dutch phrase that Whistler translated as "Long Elizas," refers to such ware decorated with elongated figures. The *Six Marks* are the potter's marks on the bottom of the jar. Although Whistler's depiction of a Chinese pottery shop is much more akin to contemporary genre scenes than to his later, more adventurous compositions influenced by Japanese prints, he carved the potter's marks into the gilded frame to enhance the exoticism of the subject. DS

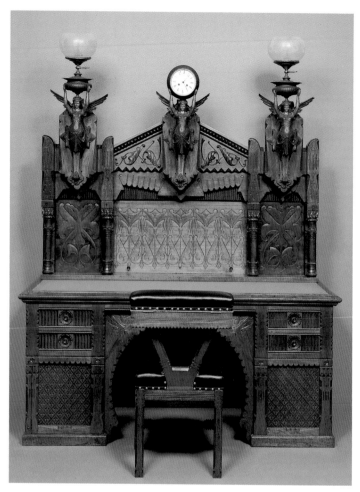

Desk and Chair

Designed by Frank Furness
(American, 1839–1912)
Made by Daniel Pabst
(American, born Germany,
1827–1910)
Made in Philadelphia
1875
Walnut, white pine, maple, poplar,
with clock and lamp mounts and
glass globes
71 x 62 x 32½" (desk)
30¾ x 17⅜ x 22¼" (chair)
Gift of George Wood Furness
1974-224-1, 2

Frank Furness, one of Philadelphia's most influential architects of the late nineteenth century, designed this desk and chair for his brother Horace in 1875. Strongly architectonic in form, the eclectic, highly stylized decorations of the desk reflect Furness's early training with the prominent American architect Richard Morris Hunt as well as his interest in the work of contemporary English designers such as William Morris. His collaboration with Daniel Pabst, a German-born Philadelphia cabinetmaker, resulted in some of the most imaginative furniture forms produced in the city during the period. Several of the naturalistic motifs included in the desk's design echo those found on a number of Furness's prominent buildings in the city. Perhaps his most important project was the school and galleries of the Pennsylvania Academy of the Fine Arts at Broad and Cherry streets, completed in 1876, which incorporate similar exotic motifs, all imbued with the architect's highly original sense of proportion, style, and historic revivalism. JLL

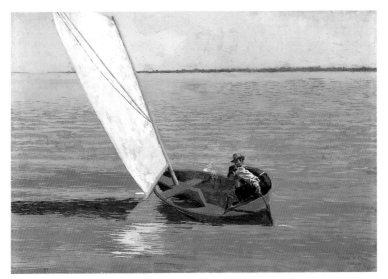

Thomas Eakins
American, 1844–1916
Sailing, c. 1875
Oil on canvas
31⅞ x 46¼"
The Alex Simpson, Jr., Collection
1928-63-6

When Thomas Eakins returned to Philadelphia in 1870 after four years of study in Paris, he immediately began to apply the rigorous training he had received at the Ecole des Beaux-Arts to local subjects in a series of paintings of his male friends engaged in sports that the artist himself enjoyed, such as rowing, sailing, and hunting. In works such as *Sailing* Eakins developed his skills by applying the fundamentals of academic art that he had learned: the solid, anatomically correct representation of the human figure and the meticulous construction of a scene using perspective drawings, which here capture the exact tilt of the boat. At this early point in his career, Eakins was still experimenting with his technique, and *Sailing* is unusual in that it was painted largely with a palette knife. He may have used this atypically broad treatment in response to criticism of another version of the same subject from Jean-Léon Gérôme, his teacher in Paris. DS

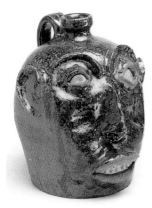

Face Vessel
Attributed to the Thomas J. Davies
pottery (Edgefield district,
South Carolina), c. 1862–70
Glazed stoneware
Height 9¾"
Gift of Edward Russell Jones. 1904-36

Early in the nineteenth century potters working in the Edgefield district of South Carolina began experimenting with new forms and techniques of alkaline-glazed stoneware that combined an unusual mix of European, Asian, and African ceramic traditions. A number of highly skilled slave potters influenced these new productions and developed a distinctive aesthetic style for face vessels such as this, which incorporated African folk traditions and belief systems in their design and manufacture. Working with indigenous clays, these craftsmen used a potter's wheel to create the vessel's basic form, onto which the hand-modeled face was added. Edwin AtLee Barber, the Museum's first curator of American ceramics, documented these African American traditions early in the 1890s and was responsible for the acquisition of several face vessels for the collection. His interviews with Thomas Davies, owner of one of the traditional potteries, identify this example as one of the earliest extant pieces from the Edgefield district. JLL

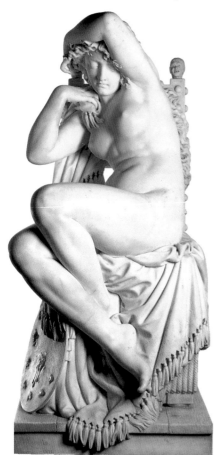

Howard Roberts
American, 1843–1900
La Première Pose, 1873–76
Marble
Height 51¼″
Gift of Mrs. Howard Roberts
1929-134-1

Howard Roberts, like his fellow Philadelphian Thomas Eakins, was among the first of two generations of Americans who flocked to Paris to study art. Although both he and Eakins mastered the French academic style of portraying the human figure, Roberts remained more closely tied to contemporary French art and, unlike Eakins, returned to Paris to work on major projects such as *La Première Pose.* When it was shown at the Centennial Exhibition in Philadelphia in 1876, this sculpture was acclaimed as an unequaled tour de force of American sculpture for the subtlety and realism of its modeling, a match in technique for any French work. Its subject, a young model overcome with shyness at posing nude for the first time, was considered, if anything, "too French" in conception. Critics claimed that it was a deliberately scandalous excuse to portray the female nude with sensual realism. Its defenders, however, argued that it was a chaste and sympathetic characterization of the model's predicament. In any case, *La Première Pose* brought a new sophistication of subject and technique to American sculpture. DS

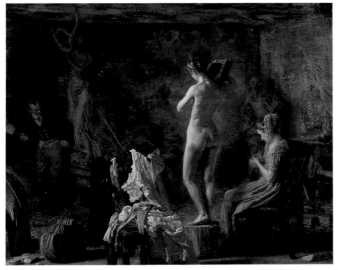

Thomas Eakins
American, 1844–1916
William Rush Carving His Allegorical Figure of the Schuylkill River, 1876–77
Oil on canvas on Masonite
20⅛ x 26⅛"
Gift of Mrs. Thomas Eakins and Miss Mary Adeline Williams. 1929-184-27

In this canvas Thomas Eakins shows William Rush carving one of his many public sculptures—an allegorical figure of the Schuylkill River done in 1808 for Philadelphia's first waterworks. Other works by Rush, including a life-size figure of George Washington and his *Allegory of the Waterworks* (see page 276), are visible in the dim background of the shop and constitute a survey of the venerable artist's career. Eakins made this painting just as he was beginning his years at the Pennsylvania Academy of the Fine Arts as a charismatic but controversial teacher, notorious for his insistence on the study of the nude as the basis for all art. It is highly unlikely that Rush had employed a nude model for his draped figure, but in this exquisite historical fabrication Eakins uses the impeccable reputation of the distinguished Philadelphia sculptor to justify his own practices. The unidealized but sympathetically observed and beautifully painted figure of the nude woman stands as a manifesto of Eakins's beliefs about the goal of art. DS

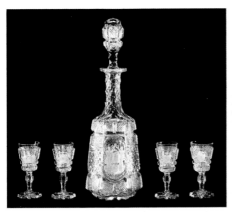

Wine Set
Made by the Dorflinger Glass Company (White Mills, Pennsylvania, 1865–1921)
1876
Lead glass
Height 16¼" (decanter),
5" (wineglass)
Gift of the Dorflinger Glass Company
1876-1693i,j,t,aa,cc,hh

In competition with wares submitted by both domestic and foreign manufacturers, this magnificent set of a wine decanter and glasses produced by the Dorflinger Glass Company won the highest honors for cut glass at the Centennial Exposition in Philadelphia in 1876, and in that same year became the first American glass acquired for the Museum's collection. The Dorflinger firm excelled in the manufacture of such high-quality lead glass with wheel-cut and hand-engraved decoration. This decanter has three engraved panels: one with the seal of the United States, one with the goddess of liberty, and one with the seal of the City of Philadelphia and the name of the mayor in 1876, William S. Stokely. Each footed wineglass represents one of the thirty-eight states in the union at the time of the Centennial, and is engraved with its crest, its motto, and the name of its governor. MEM

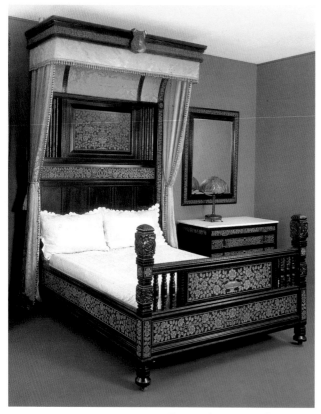

Bedroom Suite
Made by Herter Brothers
(New York, 1864–1906)
c. 1880–85
Ebonized cherry with mixed
wood inlay
112 x 77 x 88″ (bed with canopy)
Gift of Mrs. William T. Carter
1928-121-1

During the 1870s and 1880s the New York firm of Herter Brothers became one of the most influential decorating and design houses in the United States, producing innovative, high-quality "art furniture" in an eclectic range of revival styles that showed the impact of English design reformers such as William Morris. This suite, made for the Philadelphia coal investor William T. Carter, includes a bed with a canopy, wardrobe, chest of drawers, pier glass, and two side chairs. Its design, characteristic of much of the Herters' work, relies on rectilinear shapes richly ornamented with inlaid marquetry panels, shallow relief carving, and ring-turned vertical elements. Known for its fine craftsmanship and stylish innovations, the firm set the standard for domestic luxury among the new elite in the United States, such as the Vanderbilts and Rockefellers. JLL

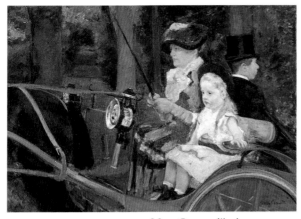

Mary Stevenson Cassatt
American, 1844–1926
A Woman and a Girl Driving
1881
Oil on canvas
35 5/16 x 51 3/8"
Purchased with the W. P. Wilstach
Fund. W1921-1-1

Mary Cassatt, like her contemporary Thomas Eakins, left
Philadelphia for study in Paris in 1866. As a woman, she was
ineligible for admission to the Ecole des Beaux-Arts, and perhaps because she was excluded from the official system, her
taste in art was much more adventurous than that of any other
young American expatriate artist. Cassatt was drawn to the
work of such antiestablishment figures as Gustave Courbet,
Edouard Manet, and the group derisively called the "Impressionists" after their first exhibition in 1874. Her friend and
artistic adviser Edgar Degas invited her to exhibit with the
Impressionists, and she was the only American to do so, beginning in 1879. *A Woman and a Girl Driving,* portraying the artist's
sister Lydia Cassatt with a young niece of Degas's in the Bois
de Boulogne in Paris, shows Cassatt's affinity with the Impressionists in the depiction of a scene of daily life with fresh colors
and loosely defined forms. The asymmetrical composition
and its abrupt truncation on all four sides are particularly reminiscent of the work of her friend Degas. DS

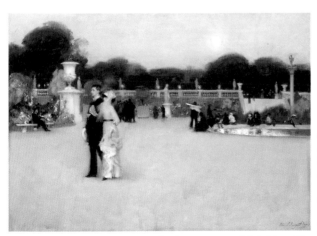

John Singer Sargent
American, active London,
Florence, and Paris, 1856–1925
In the Luxembourg Gardens
1879
Oil on canvas
25 7/8 x 36 3/8"
John G. Johnson Collection. Cat. 1080

Setting out to establish himself as a portrait painter with an
international clientele, John Singer Sargent developed a style
that was necessarily more conservative but more ostentatious
technically than the avant-garde productions of his contemporaries, the Impressionists. *In the Luxembourg Gardens,* set in

Paris's largest urban park, is one of the few landscapes from his early career. It shares the Impressionists' interest in the effects of light and color at a specific time of day and in every-day, middle-class subjects. Yet by scrubbing in the thin paint to create the opalescent areas of color for sky, gravel paving, and stone architecture at twilight and the dark, billowing forms of trees, Sargent created a study in tone and atmosphere more akin to the carefully adjusted harmonies of James Abbott McNeill Whistler. Each person, no matter how sketchy or distant, is characterized with a portraitist's eye for distinctive posture and attitude, and the touches of glowing color that define people and flowers are applied with a brio very different from an Impressionist's uninflected stroke. DS

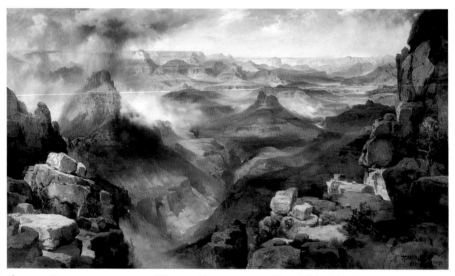

Thomas Moran
American, 1837–1926
Grand Canyon of the Colorado River, 1892 and 1908
Oil on canvas
53 x 94″
Gift of Graeme Lorimer. 1975-182-1

Thomas Moran was a well-established landscape painter and illustrator in Philadelphia before he accompanied a scientific expedition to the Yellowstone region in 1871 and made the first paintings of the spectacular scenery for which he would earn the nickname Tom "Yellowstone" Moran. Based upon his own meticulous sketches and photographs, his Western views were geologically accurate, but presented with dramatic effects of light and atmosphere reminiscent of the work of J.M.W. Turner. Moran's turbulent skies and glowing colors could convey a sense of place unequaled by a photograph, especially when he chose a canvas large enough to suggest the vast spaces that were as unimaginable to Eastern viewers as the spectacular geological features themselves. His monumental canvases were in fact influential in the establishment of national parks in the West. Although his paintings were always based upon his sketches, photographs, and direct experience, Moran did not hesitate to modify the landscape to enhance pictorial effect. The Museum's painting has two dates—1892 and 1908—which indicates that he changed the work to suit his own changing painting style. DS

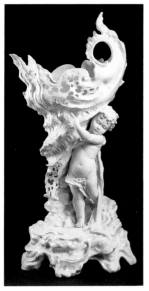

Centerpiece
Made by the Ohio Valley China
Company (Wheeling, West Virginia,
1891–1896)
1893
Bisque-fired and glazed porcelain
Height 25¼"
Gift of the Ohio Valley China Company[2]
1893-376

Although in operation for only five years, the Ohio Valley
China Company produced some of the best porcelains, or
"translucent china," made in the United States during the late
nineteenth century. The firm was most widely known for its
fine dinner and tea services, but in an effort to expand its clientele, the factory introduced a line of art porcelains in 1892. This
elaborate centerpiece, the only large-scale example from the
art line known to have survived, is attributed to the German-
born sculptor Carl Goetz, who was employed by the company.
Its subtly and finely modeled decorations are finished with
a combination of bisque and glazed surfaces. Edwin AtLee
Barber, the Museum's first curator of pottery and porcelain,
acquired this piece directly from the company in 1893, impressed by its beauty and superior quality. Barber's early scholarship and collecting efforts on behalf of the Museum formed
the core of its important holdings of American ceramics. JLL

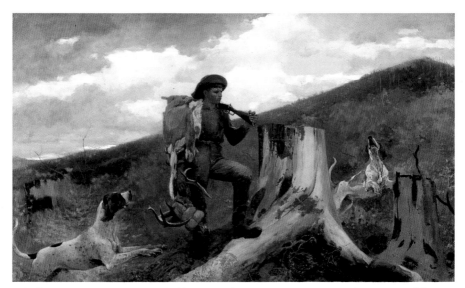

Winslow Homer
American, 1836–1910
A Huntsman and Dogs, 1891
Oil on canvas
28⅛ x 48"
The William L. Elkins Collection
E1924-3-8

Unlike most of his contemporaries, Winslow Homer did not
have academic training in Paris, and he also remained aloof
from Impressionism and various other artistic trends. However,
his personal interest in recreational hunting and fishing and in
natural scenery coincided with the growing nostalgia for the
American wilderness and rural life that accompanied the in-

creasing urbanization of the United States in the late nineteenth century, and Homer became one of the period's most popular and successful artists. Based upon studies he had made in the Adirondacks, *A Huntsman and Dogs* is characteristic of his unsentimental view of the conflict of humans and animals in a vast, overwhelmingly powerful natural world. In this overcast, late autumn landscape, only the hunter and his dogs are alive. All else is dead, the result of the inexorable working of the seasons and the depredations of man. The energetic movement of the barking dogs emphasizes both the hunter's isolation and his kinship with the silent, immutable landscape. DS

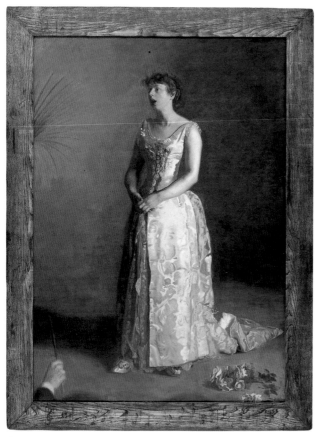

Thomas Eakins
American, 1844–1916
The Concert Singer, 1890–92
Oil on canvas
75⅛ x 54¼"
Gift of Mrs. Thomas Eakins and
Miss Mary Adeline Williams. 1929-184-19

Thomas Eakins's abrupt dismissal from the Pennsylvania Academy of the Fine Arts in Philadelphia in 1886 for his use of nude models in life classes for both men and women caused a marked change in his work. When he started to paint again, after a two-year period of depression, he began to concentrate on the penetrating studies of individuals that would comprise the majority of his works until his death. Eakins's paintings of musicians, for example, a favorite subject throughout his career, were no longer complete narratives but rather portraits of talented performers such as *The Concert Singer.* His laborious procedure for exactly representing the act of singing was described by his friend and model Weda Cook, who recalled that Eakins would have her sing the same phrase repeatedly as he watched the action of her mouth and throat. So that a music-loving viewer could judge the accuracy of his portrayal, Eakins carved the appropriate bars of music from Felix Mendelssohn's oratorio *Elijah* into the frame that he made for the painting. DS

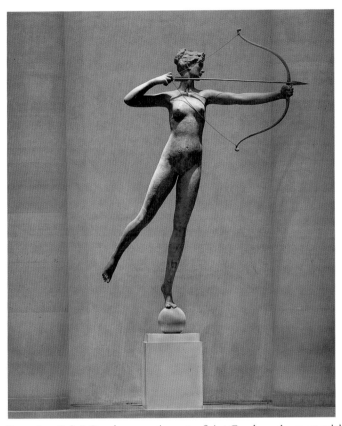

Augustus Saint-Gaudens
American, born Ireland, 1848–1907
Diana, 1892–94
Copper sheets
Height 14′6″
Gift of the New York Life Insurance Company. 1932-30-1

Augustus Saint-Gaudens, the most celebrated American sculptor of his day, created *Diana* as a weathervane for the tower of the first Madison Square Garden in New York, designed by his equally renowned friend and frequent collaborator, Stanford White. The lithe Roman goddess of the hunt, standing on tiptoe as she draws her bow, embodied the festive spirit of a building that was conceived as the "most magnificent amusement palace in the world." Like White's eclectic architecture, Saint-Gaudens's graceful young woman referred to the great art of past ages, and her presence now in the Museum's vast Neoclassical Stair Hall seems perfectly apt. Her undraped figure was historically correct, but her athletic fitness and elongated proportions were strikingly modern, and her nudity initially provoked indignant comments. Hammered from thin copper sheets for lightness, *Diana* originally was gilded and had a drapery billowing out behind to catch the wind. Gleaming in sunshine or in electric spotlights—then still a novelty—*Diana* on her three-hundred-foot tower was then the highest point in New York City, and she quickly gained respectability as a symbol of the sophistication of the growing metropolis. DS

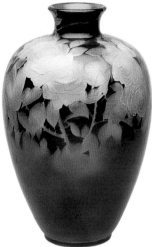

Vase

Made by the Rookwood Pottery
(Cincinnati, 1880–1967)
Decorated by Kataro Shirayama-
dani (Japanese, active United
States, 1865–1948)
1899
Earthenware with underglaze
decoration
Height 17⅜″
Gift of John T. Morris. 1901-15

This large vase is a masterpiece of the American art pottery
movement, which began at the Rookwood Pottery, where this
work was made, and was dedicated to the creation of ceramics
for purely aesthetic and decorative purposes. Always trying
to develop new styles of ware and decoration, by 1900 Rookwood's innovative designers and potters had perfected what
they called the "Black Iris" glaze, characterized by a brilliant
black ground painted with delicate floral motifs. This vase,
which was decorated by the Japanese-born Kataro Shirayama-
dani, who was brought to Rookwood in 1887 to inject the
influence of Japanese technique, was part of the "Black Iris"
line of ceramics that was introduced with great success at the
Exposition Universelle in Paris in 1900. It features a dark,
high-gloss black glaze combined with dark green and decorated
with yellow-green roses and green foliage executed in very
slight relief. MCH

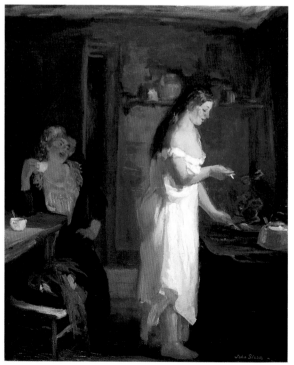

John Sloan

American, 1871–1951
Three A.M., 1909
Oil on canvas
32⅛ x 26¼″
Gift of Mrs. Cyrus McCormick
1946-10-1

Three A.M. reflects John Sloan's early artistic apprenticeship in
Philadelphia, where he worked as an illustrator for newspapers

and popular publications, and was a member of a group of artists who were united by their rebellion against the restrictions of academic technique and the idealized subject matter then favored in much of American art. Like his fellows of the Philadelphia "press gang," Sloan moved to New York City, where he painted this scene of what he described as "a poor, back, gas-lit room." Because of its unidealized portrayal of lower-class life and its deliberately rough painting style, Sloan's picture was rejected for exhibition at the Pennsylvania Academy of the Fine Arts in Philadelphia in 1910. In its celebration of the realities of everyday urban life in the United States, however, it is typical of the work of Sloan and other members of the so-called Ashcan School, which would provide a new direction for American art in the decades to follow. DS

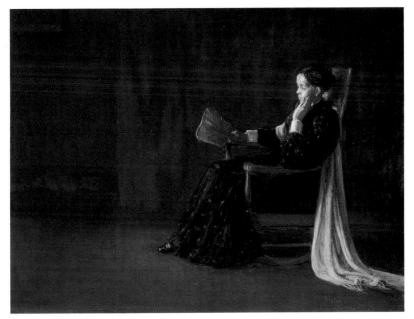

Henry Ossawa Tanner
American, active France, 1859–1937
Portrait of the Artist's Mother
1897
Oil on canvas
29¼ x 39½"
Partial gift of Dr. Rae Alexander-Minter and purchased with the W. P. Wilstach Fund, the George W. Elkins Fund, and with funds contributed by the Dietrich Foundation and a private donor
EW1993-61-1

Painted during a triumphant visit home from Paris in 1897, after the French government had purchased his *Resurrection of Lazarus,* Henry Ossawa Tanner's portrait of his mother is both a tribute to Sarah Elizabeth Miller Tanner, the central, stabilizing figure in her large and distinguished African American family, and a celebration of her son's recent professional success. In its composition Tanner's work refers to the world-famous image by another American: Whistler's *Arrangement in Gray and Black No. 1: Portrait of the Artist's Mother* of 1871 (Musée d'Orsay, Paris). That the gentle, reticent Tanner had symbolically placed himself in the company of the flamboyant and controversial Whistler is the kind of intellectual joke that would have been appreciated by his family. The painting also stands as a reminder of Tanner's success in his chosen career, in which he had persevered despite initial opposition from his parents. Tanner's portrait of his mother has none of the cool austerity of Whistler's picture, however. Instead it is an affectionate portrayal of a strong, sensitive, thoughtful personality. DS

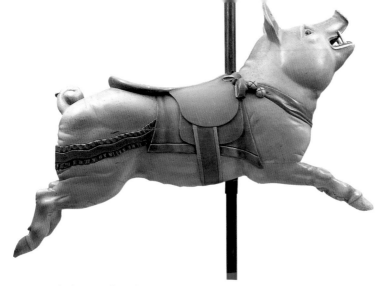

Carousel Figure of a Pig
Made by the Dentzel Carousel
Company (Philadelphia, 1867–1928)
c. 1903–9
Painted basswood
64 x 52 x 12″
Centennial gift of the Friends of the
Philadelphia Museum of Art. 1976-158-2

While the first "flying coaches and horse" in North America
were built in Philadelphia in the mid-eighteenth century, more
elaborate carousels composed of lavish, brightly painted figures
such as this pig grew in popularity later during the Victorian
era. One of the largest and most famous examples was built for
Woodside Park in Philadelphia by the Dentzel Carousel Company in the 1890s. Gustave A. Dentzel, an immigrant from
Kreuznach, Germany, established his shop at 155 Poplar Street
in Philadelphia in 1887, advertising his skills as a "steam and
horse power carousell [sic] builder." His reputation for supplying the finest amusements decorated with ornately carved
animals grew quickly, and his factory expanded into larger
quarters in the Germantown section of the city, where it oper-
ated until 1928. Dentzel employed a number of highly skilled
immigrant craftsmen from Germany and Italy to produce his
carousels. The Museum's pig is attributed to the Italian-born
Salvatoré Cernigliano, who is known to have made a number
of the more whimsical, animated figures incorporated into
the factory's assembled menageries. JLL

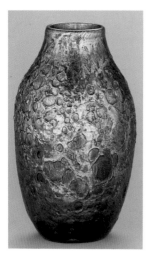

Vase
Designed by Louis Comfort Tiffany
(American, 1848–1933)
Made by the Tiffany Glass and
Decorating Company (Corona,
New York, 1892–1924)
c. 1900
Blown and iridized glass
Height 9⅜″
Purchased with the Joseph E. Temple
Fund. 1901-63

Inspired by the iridescence and irregular surfaces that resulted
from the mineral decomposition of ancient Greek and Roman
glass, Louis Comfort Tiffany began experimenting to achieve

similar effects on blown glass produced by his firm. By introducing acid fumes during the manufacturing, Tiffany was able to achieve the rich and variegated colors seen on this vase, called "Cypriote" glass to acknowledge his admiration for ancient prototypes. Shown in the Exposition Universelle in Paris in 1900, this piece was bought by the Museum as a superb example of the latest style and technique. Tiffany himself, who was largely responsible for the mature style of Art Nouveau glass in the United States, never actually made any of the glass produced by his company, but he worked closely with his chemists and technicians and supervised the myriad details of manufacturing such elaborately worked objects. MEM

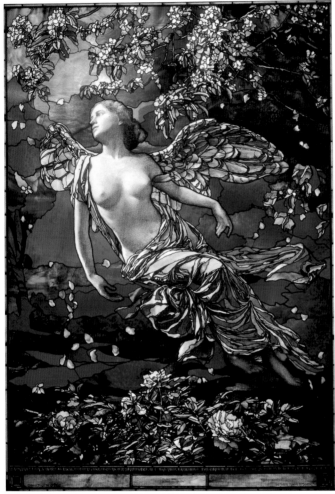

John La Farge
American, 1835–1910
Spring, 1900–1902
Opalescent glass, painted glass, lead
100 x 69½"
Gift of Charles S. Payson. 1977-33-1

One of the most renowned late nineteenth-century American artists, John La Farge began his career as a painter but is best remembered for his elaborate, richly colored stained-glass windows. As a friend of the architects and sculptors who developed the style known as the American Renaissance for its borrowings from fourteenth- and fifteenth-century Italian art, La Farge designed entire decorative schemes in painting, sculpture, and stained glass for many of the major architectural projects of his day, often in competition with his better-known contemporary Louis Comfort Tiffany. La Farge considered *Spring* his masterpiece in stained glass, and technically the window is a tour de force: the face and torso of the young woman are painted and fired on the largest single sheet of glass ever used in a stained-glass window, and the rich colors, including the milky, opalescent glass that was La Farge's invention, are his most varied and intricately designed. Few other works better express the combination of allegorical subject, realistic treatment of the figure, historical associations, and rich effect that characterized the American Renaissance style. DS

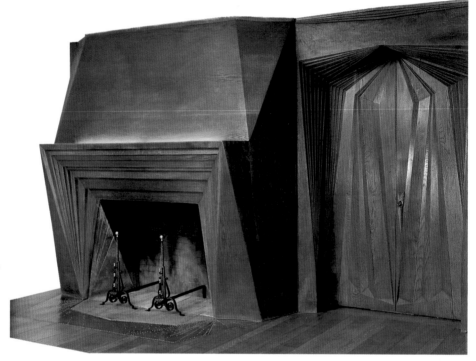

Fireplace and Doorway

Made by Wharton Esherick
(American, 1887–1970)
1936–37
White oak, stone, copper, brass
Acquired through the generosity of W. B. Dixon Stroud, with additional funds for its preservation and installation provided by Dr. and Mrs. Allen Goldman, Marion Boulton Stroud, and the Women's Committee of the Philadelphia Museum of Art. 1989-1-1, 2

Born in Philadelphia, where he was trained as a painter in the first decade of this century, Wharton Esherick had shifted his attention to wooden sculpture and furniture by the mid-1920s. His devotion to wood as a material and insistence upon hand-craftsmanship (although often using innovative production techniques) combined with his free-spirited personality to establish Esherick as a pioneer of the contemporary American craft movement. The commission to renovate the home of Judge and Mrs. Curtis Bok in Gulph Mills, Pennsylvania, offered him a rare opportunity to devise an overall scheme of dramatic wooden elements that would transform the interior spaces. As this fireplace and doorway from the library and music room of the Bok home demonstrate, Esherick used angular motifs in the contemporary "modern" style adopted by other designers and architects of the day, but the sensuous, hand-finished surfaces that emphasize wood grain and color, and the massive beams and planks, boldly carved and assembled into projecting and receding shapes, are unique to the artist. DS

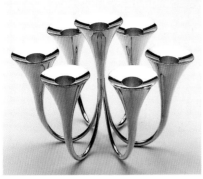

Olaf Skoogfors
American, born Sweden, 1930–1975
Candelabrum, 1957
Silver
Height 6"
Gift of Judy Skoogfors. 1986-102-1

An artist who quickly gained international renown during his tragically short career, Olaf Skoogfors spent his entire professional life in Philadelphia, where his reputation as a charismatic teacher and the formal innovation and technical mastery of his work in metal were important factors in establishing Philadelphia as a center for metalsmithing in the 1960s and 1970s. *Candelabrum* is an early example of Skoogfors's mature style, with an elegantly simple, unornamented form that shows the influence of contemporary Scandinavian design—an interest that he shared with many other craft artists and that, as he pointed out, he had acquired in the United States, not his native Sweden. Closer consideration of this functional object reveals a painstaking and thoughtful refinement of the form, sensitivity to the weight and malleability of the silver, and perfection of workmanship that are distinctly individual and characteristic of all of Skoogfors's art. DS

José Delores Lopez
American, active 1925–48
Saint George and the Dragon
c. 1930–40
Cottonwood, leather
18 x 22½ x 13¾"
Gift of an anonymous donor in memory of Elizabeth Wheatley Bendiner
1991-76-1

The sculptures of José Delores Lopez represent the twentieth-century survival of traditional eighteenth- and nineteenth-century wood carving in the Hispanic folk culture of the southwestern United States. As its local carvers supplied architectural woodwork, decorated furniture, and religious figures for ecclesiastical and domestic shrines, the New Mexican village of Cordova became a center for a number of these sculptural styles, which evolved from the tradition of the *santos,* or carved saints. Lopez expanded this genre to include subjects drawn from European beliefs and everyday village life. His *Saint George and the Dragon,* which represents a European theme rarely depicted in Hispanic art before this period, integrates the finely carved but undecorated surfaces, carefully rendered shapes, and haunting spirituality that are characteristic of his style. JLL

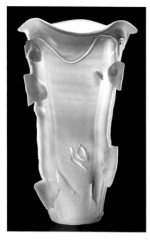

Rudolf Staffel
American, born 1911
Light Gatherer, 1981
Unglazed porcelain washed
with copper salts
Height 10"
Gift of the Women's Committee of the
Philadelphia Museum of Art. 1985-30-1

When Rudolf Staffel, a ceramist and professor of ceramics who is a seminal figure in the Philadelphia art community, began to work with porcelain in the early 1960s, he was accepting the challenge of an unusually difficult material. The fine, sticky porcelain clay is weak and difficult to shape into thin-walled forms, and it tends to melt and collapse in the high temperature at which it is fired. Yet Staffel completely mastered this intractable material to create the distinctive style for which he is known internationally. He calls many of his ceramics "Light Gatherers" to emphasize his interest in the translucency and crystalline luminescence of the porcelain. Because of their material and relatively small size, the works appear delicate at first glance, yet the record of shaping clearly evident in the clay surface shows that it has been manipulated with expert casualness by pinching, scoring, and denting to deny any preciousness and to stand as testimony to the material's remarkable plasticity as captured in the hard, strong body of fired porcelain. DS

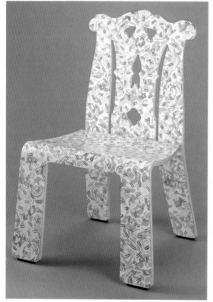

"Chippendale" Chair
Designed by Robert Venturi
(American, born 1925)/Venturi,
Scott Brown and Associates
Made by Knoll International
(New York, established 1955)
1979–84
Bent and laminated wood, plastic
Height 33¼"
Gift of COLLAB: The Contemporary
Design Group for the Philadelphia
Museum of Art. 1985-94-4

In his furniture for Knoll, Robert Venturi challenged the International Style dictum that form follows function, as he had in his provocative writings and postmodern architecture. All nine side chairs designed by this eminent Philadelphia-born architect conform to modern standards of elegance, comfort, and function, but each is shaped to suggest a specific historical furniture style. In this chair the silhouette of the back is an adaptation of the designs of the eighteenth-century English furniture designer

Thomas Chippendale. Popular in the colonies at the time of the American Revolution, this style carries all sorts of historical and patriotic associations. Another layer of complexity is added by the surface of plastic laminate in Venturi's pastel floral "Grandmother" pattern, a knowingly sentimental visual generalization about motherly good nature. Only the forceful rhythm of overlaid black parallel bars denies the blandness of the image and reminds us that, like the bent plywood construction of the chair itself, it is distinctly contemporary. DS

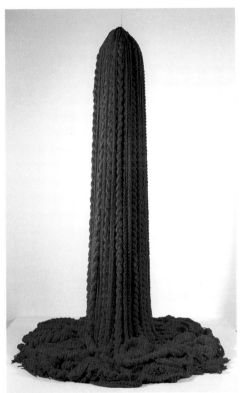

Claire Zeisler
American, 1903–1991
Private Affair II, 1986
Synthetic fiber
Height 10′
Gift of the Women's Committee of the
Philadelphia Museum of Art. 1987-49-2

Trained as a painter and sculptor, and with broad experience as an astute collector of pre-Columbian objects, Native American baskets, and contemporary art, Claire Zeisler did not begin to show her own fiber works until the early 1960s, when she was nearly sixty. She quickly was recognized internationally as a leader in the revolution in the fiber arts that occurred during that decade, when traditional weaving was replaced by wide-ranging experimentation with materials and techniques. Zeisler became famous for the boldness of her strikingly large, often freestanding forms in natural or primary colors, which gave mass and three-dimensionality to supple fiber by using the off-loom technique of knotting, often combined with luxuriant cascades of unworked fiber falling into an opulent tangle at the base. In *Private Affair II,* the ten-foot spill of red fiber is built up of individual elements created from a repertory of ancient techniques unique to fiber—twisting into rope, knotting, wrapping, braiding, and fringing. The dramatic result embodies Zeisler's goal of creating "large, strong, single images." DS

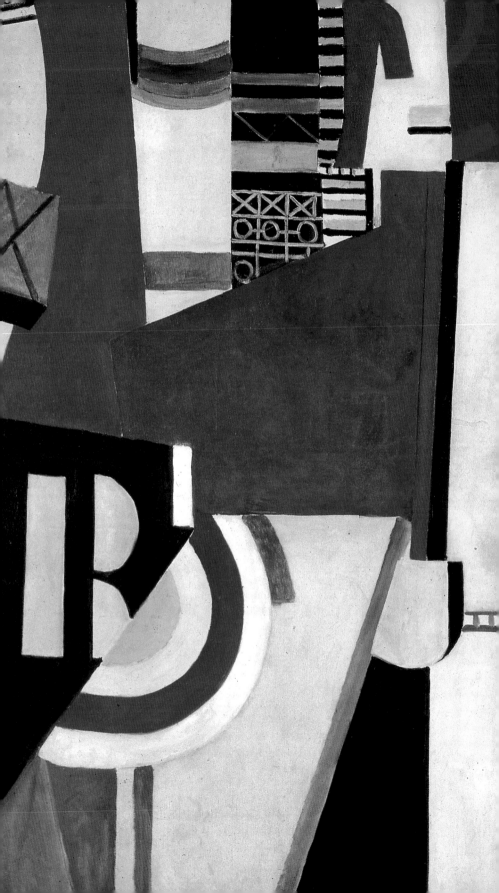

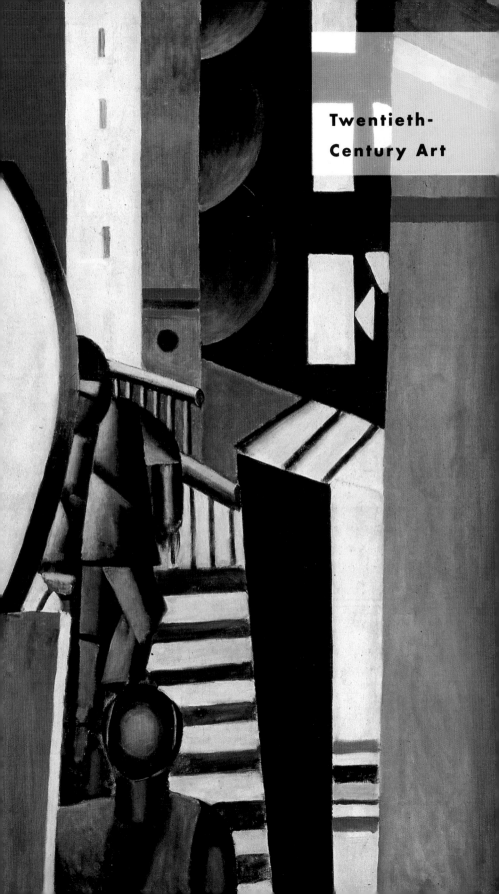

Twentieth-Century Art

Although the Department of Twentieth-Century Art was not established until 1971, the Museum has a long history of a strong and adventurous commitment to contemporary art that is unusual for a museum of encyclopedic nature. This emphasis was heralded by the first acquisitions of works by Constantin Brancusi and Pablo Picasso at the beginning of the 1930s. Fiske Kimball's commitment to the art of his time was proven by his ability to attract a series of important gifts of large collections and individual masterpieces over the following decades. Henry Clifford, who served as curator of paintings from 1941 to 1965, also played a major role in the Museum's early interest in twentieth-century art.

At the core of the holdings of modern art are the A. E. Gallatin and Louise and Walter Arensberg collections. Both were among the most significant collections of contemporary art formed during the 1920s and 1930s in the United States; together they establish this institution as one of the world's outstanding museums in which to see modern art. The Gallatin and Arensberg gifts determined the nature of this collection as one of especially rich concentrations of the work of particular artists, such as Picasso, Duchamp, Brancusi, and Miró. American modernists admired by Gallatin and the Arensbergs, including the Pennsylvanian Charles Demuth, were also represented in the selection from Alfred Stieglitz's collections accorded to the Museum by his widow, Georgia O'Keeffe.

Philadelphia's twentieth-century holdings represent an unusually close collaboration between artists and collectors. Gallatin, a serious painter as well as collector, was a central figure in the American Abstract Artists group in New York, where his collection was on view to the public for sixteen years as the "Gallery of Living Art" before it was transferred to Philadelphia in 1943. The Arensbergs formed their collection with the attentive help of their great friend Marcel Duchamp. The Museum is now home to the world's most important collection of Duchamp's work, most of it assembled by the Arensbergs over the course of four decades.

The tradition begun by Gallatin and the Arensbergs was followed by the development of the collection of contemporary art since the 1960s. The many important gifts presented by the Friends of the Museum, an association formed in 1964 with the aim of augmenting the meager funds for the purchase of works of art, include works by artists ranging from Robert Rauschenberg to Sigmar Polke. In recent years, a number of major purchases have made a striking impact on the collections and have represented important steps within the American museum community as a whole. These include the ten-part painting by Cy Twombly, *Fifty Days at Iliam* (1977–78), to which the Museum has devoted an entire gallery designed in collaboration with the artist.

The continuity between past and present is richly felt within the collection, with the work of many contemporary artists represented, such as Jasper Johns and Ellsworth Kelly, deeply rooted in the art found in the Gallatin and Arensberg collections. Philadelphia's historic role as a center of training for artists continues to encourage interaction between the Museum's collections and each new generation of students. Ongoing additions of new works by young artists, many of which overturn conventional assumptions about what art can be, play a central role in bringing the Museum into the future.

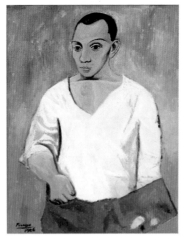

Pablo Ruiz y Picasso
Spanish, 1881–1973
Self-Portrait, 1906
Oil on canvas
36³/₁₆ x 28⁷/₈″
A. E. Gallatin Collection. 1950-1-1

This painting of 1906 was Pablo Picasso's first important self-portrait since 1901. In the intervening years, he had appeared in his works only in the guise of hungry beggars or scraggly performers, metaphorical representations of the outcast artist. Now he emerges as a proud and determined painter, his palette the only clue to the profession of this hardy, almost athletic figure whose power is concentrated in the right arm with clenched fist, a massive and richly volumed form that overwhelms the simply rendered body. The vitality in this arm acts in counterpoint to the stern inexpression of the artist's face, whose exaggerated eyelids and brows, oval face, and oversized ear give it the impression of a mask, separated from the body by both the hue and the pronounced line of the collarbone. In this painting, which reflects the stylistic influences of his recent encounters with Catalan art and prehistoric Iberian sculpture, Picasso appears as the painter without a brush, thus confidently and presciently ascribing to himself the "magic" he would continue to find in premodern and non-Western traditions. AT

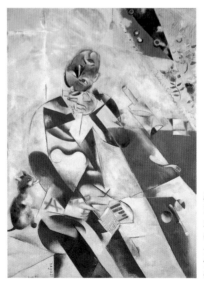

Marc Chagall
French, born Belorussia, 1887–1985
Half-Past Three (The Poet), 1911
Oil on canvas
77¹/₈ x 57″
The Louise and Walter Arensberg Collection. 1950-134-36

Arriving in Paris from Saint Petersburg in 1910, Marc Chagall rapidly assimilated the language of avant-garde European art and married it to the artistic traditions of his native Russia. Here Chagall puts the pictorial devices of Cubism and Futurism to the service of a poetic fantasy imbued with a dreamy lyricism far from the café scenes of contemporary French and Italian artists. The fragmentation of the body and background into faceted planes and diagonal shafts of color gives the composition a prismatic sensation, as if the poet of the title were lifted into the magic space of a kaleidoscope. The poet, who is thought to be Chagall's friend and neighbor, also serves as a generalized figure of all artistic inspiration: green head upturned on his neckless shoulders, affectionate feline muse by his side, friendly wine bottle floating off the red table, poem or letter in process. AT

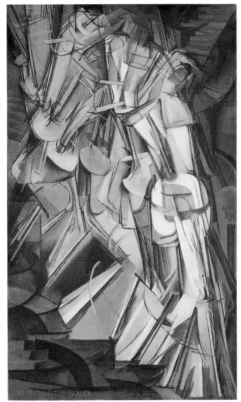

Marcel Duchamp
American, born France, 1887–1968
*Nude Descending a Staircase
(No. 2),* 1912
Oil on canvas
57⁷⁄₈ x 35¹⁄₈"
The Louise and Walter Arensberg
Collection. 1950-134-59

This painting created a sensation when it was exhibited in New York in February 1913 at the historic Armory Show of contemporary art, where perplexed Americans saw it as representing all the tricks they felt European artists were playing at their expense. The picture's outrageousness surely lay in its seemingly mechanical portrayal of a subject at once so sensual and time-honored. The *Nude*'s destiny as a symbol also stemmed from its remarkable aggregation of avant-garde concerns: the birth of cinema; the Cubists' fracturing of form; the Futurists' depiction of movement; the chromophotography of Etienne-Jules Marey, Eadweard Muybridge, and Thomas Eakins; and the redefinitions of time and space by scientists and philosophers. The painting was bought directly from the Armory Show for three hundred dollars by a San Francisco dealer. Marcel Duchamp's great collector-friend Walter Arensberg was able to buy the work in 1927, eleven years after Duchamp had obligingly made him a hand-colored, actual-size photographic copy. Today both the copy and the original, together with a preparatory study, are owned by the Museum. AT

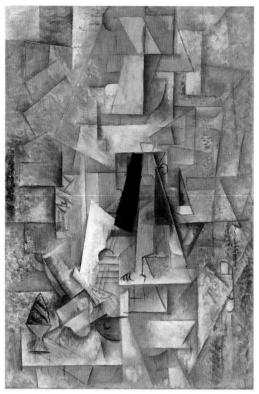

Pablo Ruiz y Picasso
Spanish, 1881–1973
Man with a Guitar, 1912
Oil on canvas
51 ¹³⁄₁₆ x 35 ¹⁄₁₆"
The Louise and Walter Arensberg
Collection. 1950-134-169

The Cubist language that Pablo Picasso and Georges Braque developed redefined the concept of painterly realism. Every picture confirms Picasso's insistence that his images were always grounded in reality and never conceived as abstract combinations of pictorial elements. The subject of this painting, for example, can be deciphered by situating the identifiable elements relative to one another within the rigorously shallow space of the composition, its volumes flattened into a scaffold-like system of lines and softly modeled planes. The vertical canvas refers the viewer to the traditional format for portraiture. The ivory trapezoid at upper center suggests a face, although all features are absent. Recognition of the guitar is aided by Picasso's familiar visual shorthand for the instrument: the key at its upper neck, the shaded arc of the sound hole, the vertical lines of the strings. The most recognizable element in the composition—the dish holding a swirled dessert—adds an unusual note of bright color to the relatively somber Cubist palette. AT

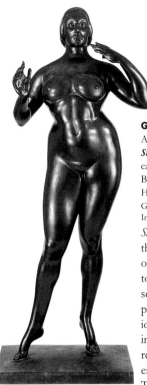

Gaston Lachaise
American, born France, 1882–1935
Standing Woman, begun 1912,
cast 1927
Bronze
Height 73″
Gift of R. Sturgis and Marion B. F.
Ingersoll. 1962-182-1

Standing Woman was Gaston Lachaise's first major rendering of the female nude, a subject that would provide his main source of inspiration. He began the work as a plaster in 1912, but had to wait until 1927 to cast it in bronze. Lachaise's wife Isabel served as the original model, but in the final sculpture he completely transcended any specific representation. Instead he has idealized and heroicized the female form, seeking to render an image of the universal and eternal essence of femininity. He represented this archetypal woman as a fully matured being, emphasizing the sensuality of her swelling hips and breasts. To counter this exaggerated sense of volume and weight, he balanced the figure on her toes, while she gestures gracefully toward herself. The emotional and erotic suggestion of this physical uplift is moderated by a feeling of spirituality evoked by the impassive face that turns inward in contemplative detachment. JBR

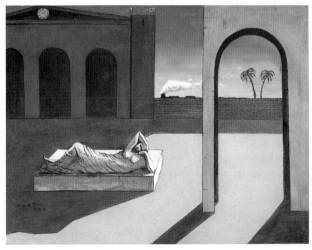

Giorgio de Chirico
Italian, born Greece, 1888–1978
The Soothsayer's Recompense, 1913
Oil on canvas
53⅜ x 70⅞″
The Louise and Walter Arensberg
Collection. 1950-134-38

Giorgio de Chirico embraced enigma as the central theme in his painting and writing. To this end, he collided styles and imagery from the past and present, fusing them into an art of evocative ambiguity. In *The Soothsayer's Recompense,* he employed a precise painting style and linear perspective, familiar since the Renaissance as a means of representing three-dimensional space. But rather than promoting legibility, here these devices are subverted, serving instead as instruments of poetic and philosophical suggestion. The tower, colonnades, and smokestack (which could belong to either a train or a factory) are frequent props in the artist's dream worlds. While together they evoke the melancholy that De Chirico associated with northern Italian cities, each refers to a different epoch—medieval, Renaissance, and industrial, respectively—thereby defying a stable location in time or place. The classical statue of Ariadne, darkened by a long shadow that dominates the foreground, underscores this melancholy, for she was the Greek princess deserted by Theseus after helping him to escape the Labyrinth. JBR

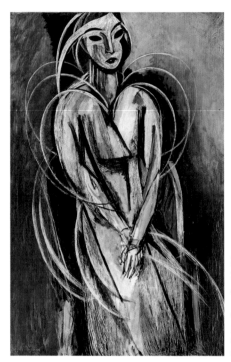

Henri Matisse
French, 1869–1954
Mademoiselle Yvonne Landsberg
1914
Oil on canvas
58 x 38⅜″
The Louise and Walter Arensberg
Collection. 1950-134-130

This painting is one of the most mysterious portraits of the twentieth century. Henri Matisse asked to paint the portrait of the young woman Yvonne Landsberg on the condition that he could do as he pleased; her family was under no obligation to buy the finished work. During the course of many sittings, Matisse lost interest in naturalistic resemblance, repeatedly painting over previous efforts and beginning anew. Toward the end of the final sitting, he reversed his brush and used its wooden end to scratch wide, arcing lines that radiated from the shoulders and hips of his subject. The force of these lines dominates the portrayal, symbolically likening the demure young woman to a budding flower. The heart-shaped lines seem to project an energy—of beauty, of sensuality, of feeling— that her body cannot yet contain, and suggest the state of becoming that defines adolescence. The family in fact chose not to purchase the portrait, and it was instead sent to New York for exhibition, where Louise and Walter Arensberg were bold enough to buy it in 1915. AT

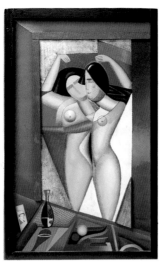

Alexander Porfirevich Archipenko
American, born Ukraine, 1887–1964
In the Boudoir (Before the Mirror)
1915
Oil, graphite, photograph, metal,
printed paper, and wood on panel
18 x 12″
Gift of Christian Brinton. 1941-79-119

Alexander Archipenko was a pioneering Cubist sculptor whose subjects were the traditional themes of heroic men and of women at their bath, but cast in the colorful, geometrized idiom of modernism. Working in Paris in the 1910s, he produced a number of compositions he called "sculpto-paintings"— brightly painted low-relief constructions using a variety of materials in which he sought to unify color and form. In *In the Boudoir,* Archipenko presents the private moment of a woman confronting her reflection. She exists in a complex space of sharp planes and jutting angles, in which the voids between objects have as much physical and chromatic reality as the objects themselves. Snippets of sheet metal create reflective surfaces, commercially printed paper forms a kind of table covering, and a collaged photograph of the artist himself sits on her dresser as both a visual signature and a sly insertion of the artist as idol. JBR

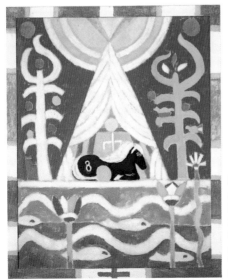

Marsden Hartley
American, 1877–1943
Painting No. 4 (A Black Horse)
1915
Oil on canvas
39¼ x 31⅝″
The Alfred Stieglitz Collection
1949-18-8

This painting was bequeathed to the Museum by Alfred Stieglitz, whose "291" gallery in New York was the focus of early modernism in the United States. It was Stieglitz who gave Marsden Hartley his first one-person show in 1909 and helped finance his trip to Europe in 1912. There Hartley came into contact with the works of Paul Cézanne, Pablo Picasso, and Henri Matisse as well as German Expressionists such as Wassily Kandinsky and Franz Marc. Hartley made *Painting No. 4* while in Germany at the outbreak of World War I. A part of his "Amerika" series, it combines the bright colors, flattened space, and simplified forms of French and German modern painting with symbols loosely drawn from Native American culture. While conveying Hartley's interest in representing spiritual values, the symbolism—such as the horse in front of the tepee flanked by plant forms—intentionally resists precise interpretation. In the face of his immersion in European modernism, his use of Native American motifs underscored Hartley's own American identity. He also spoke of the Native Americans as a gentle race, a counterbalance to European cultures preparing for a world war. JBR

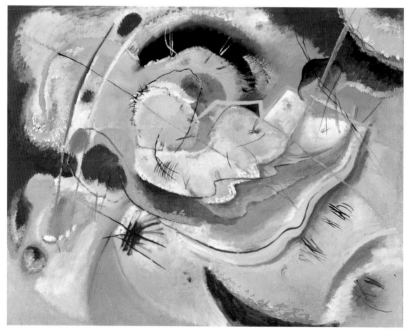

Wassily Kandinsky
Russian, active Germany,
1866–1944
*Little Painting with Yellow
(Improvisation),* 1914
Oil on canvas
31 x 39⅝"
The Louise and Walter Arensberg
Collection. 1950-134-103

Wassily Kandinsky, one of the founders of Der Blaue Reiter (The Blue Rider) group of Expressionist artists in Munich, is often considered to have made the earliest abstract paintings, which he called "Improvisations," in 1910. Kandinsky valued abstract shape, line, and color—liberated from their representational role—as carriers of spontaneous emotional and spiritual expression. In fact, however, his early works are neither totally abstract nor totally spontaneous, for many drawn studies exist for the paintings, and they themselves often contain recognizable, albeit schematic, biblical imagery. *Little Painting with Yellow,* although perhaps verging on complete abstraction, is often considered one of Kandinsky's later "Improvisations."

It was painted in Munich just months before the outbreak of World War I, which forced Kandinsky to return to Russia. Given this increasingly unstable political situation and the artist's belief in the imminence of the Apocalypse, the painting's whirlwind of explosive line and color suggests both the delirious and the terrifying qualities of a catastrophic event, a sublime moment of destruction and rebirth. JBR

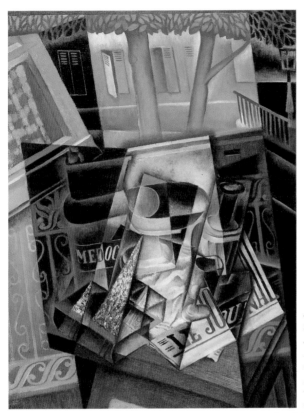

Juan Gris
Spanish, 1887–1927
Still Life Before an Open Window,
Place Ravignan, 1915
Oil on canvas
45⅝ x 35″
The Louise and Walter Arensberg
Collection. 1950-134-95

In early 1915, Juan Gris realized that at last his paintings were no longer the mere inventories of objects of which he long had despaired. His works now presented newly unified structures of interrelated pictorial elements, despite their densely complex compositions. Indeed, in *Place Ravignan,* Gris weds interior and exterior, still life and landscape, even day and night. The title refers to Gris's Paris address, and the painting presumably presents his own daily view from his studio. Traditional elements of still life—newspaper, glass, carafe, compote, bottle, and book—are arranged on a table, but refracted in great shafts of light from the window that bring the neighboring trees and houses into the composition. The umbrella of foliage on the trees and the wrought iron designs of the balcony gather background and foreground into one dreamlike sweep that revels in intense color, evoking the artist's close association with Henri Matisse. Gris, by nature an exacting artist, has here let calculation make room for a poetry and sensuousness rarely so explicitly revealed in his work. AT

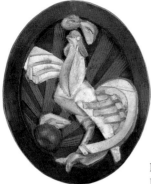

Raymond Duchamp-Villon
French, 1876–1918
Rooster (Gallic Cock), 1916–17,
cast 1919
Painted bronze
17½ x 14½ x 3"
Gift of Muriel and Philip Berman
1985-93-1

Raymond Duchamp-Villon was the middle brother of the artists Jacques Villon and Marcel Duchamp. During a career cut short by his death from typhoid fever during World War I, Duchamp-Villon produced a body of sculpture crucial to the development of early twentieth-century art. His emphasis on dynamic form and geometric structure perfectly expressed the advances of Cubism in three-dimensional form. Duchamp-Villon made the original plaster for *The Rooster* as a medallion for a temporary theater at the war's front. The stylized relief continued his exploration of animal images in geometric form, but here he restrained the level of abstraction in acknowledgment of the taste of his audience of enlisted men. The image of a rooster combined with the rising sun would have been understood as a clear reference to the heraldic and popular symbol for France. This bronze was cast from the original plaster as a memorial after the artist's death by John Quinn, his most devoted American collector. JBR

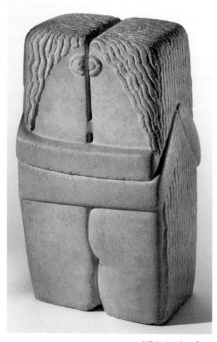

Constantin Brancusi
French, born Romania, 1876–1957
The Kiss, 1916
Limestone
Height 23"
The Louise and Walter Arensberg
Collection. 1950-134-4

This is the fourth of several stone versions of *The Kiss* that Brancusi would carve throughout his long career. The first, done in 1907, was one of the artist's earliest direct carvings in stone, a process newly popular among French sculptors that reflected their taste for the "primitive." The cutting away at stone or wood conveyed the immediacy and authenticity these sculptors sought as they eschewed the "refined" Western tradition of modeling and casting in plaster or bronze. The Philadelphia *Kiss* is the most geometric of all of Brancusi's versions. The tall block of stone is divided vertically down the center, the woman differentiated from the man by her rounded breast and the long hair falling down her back. But the flat horizontality of the arms, the overall regularity of the stone, the joined mouths, and the single arc of the two hairlines present a unified whole far more powerful than the two individuals within. *The Kiss* has come to be regarded as perhaps the quintessential representation of love in the art of the twentieth century. AT

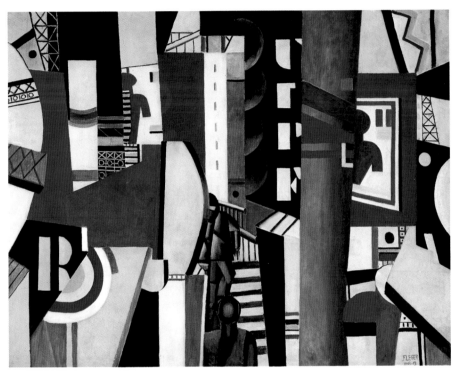

Fernand Léger
French, 1881–1955
The City, 1919
Oil on canvas
91 x 117½"
A. E. Gallatin Collection. 1952-61-58

Fernand Léger has been aptly called the preeminent painter of the modern city. He developed his brightly colored, machine-inspired style at a time when cities, including his native Paris, were taking shape as the dynamic complexes of sensation we experience today. *The City* is Léger's master statement celebrating the vitality of modern urban life. In it he has synthesized identifiable facts of the city's appearance—billboards, apartment buildings, scaffolding, billowing smoke, and a telephone pole—with irregular abstract shapes in vivid hues. The clash, overlap, and rapid jumps among the shapes and colors borrow from the cinematic technique of quickly cutting between scenes, and the inclusiveness of the composition resembles the panoramic sweep of a movie camera. This is not so much a particular city represented as the essence of the urban center as a site of overwhelming simultaneous impressions. JBR

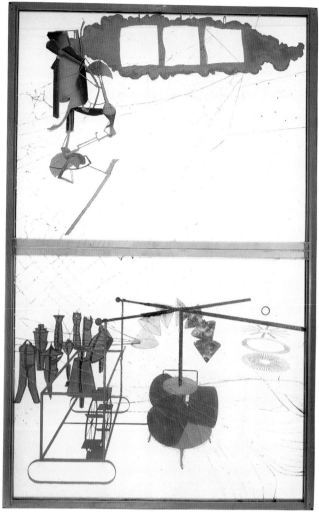

Marcel Duchamp
American, born France, 1887–1968
The Bride Stripped Bare by Her
Bachelors, Even (The Large
Glass), 1915–23
Oil, varnish, lead foil, lead wire,
and dust on two glass panels
109¼ x 69¼″
Bequest of Katherine S. Dreier
1952-98-1

Surely one of the most enigmatic works of art in any museum, *The Large Glass* dominates a gallery devoted to Marcel Duchamp's work from the exact location in which he placed it in 1954. Painstakingly executed on two large panes of glass with unconventional materials such as lead foil, fuse wire, and dust, the appearance of the *Glass* is the result of an extraordinary combination of chance procedures, carefully plotted perspective studies, and laborious craftsmanship. As for its metaphysical aspect, Duchamp's voluminous preparatory notes, published in 1934, reveal that his "hilarious picture" is intended to diagram the erratic progress of an encounter between the "Bride," in the upper panel, and her nine "Bachelors" gathered timidly below amidst a wealth of mysterious mechanical apparatus. Exhibited only once (in 1926 at the Brooklyn Museum) before it was accidentally broken and laboriously repaired by the artist, the *Glass* joined the Museum's collection in 1953 and has gradually become the subject of a vast scholarly literature and the object of pilgrimages for countless visitors drawn to its witty, intelligent, and vastly liberating redefinition of what a work of art can be. AD'H

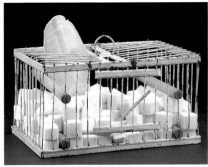

Marcel Duchamp
American, born France, 1887–1968
Why Not Sneeze, Rrose Sélavy?
1921
Painted metal birdcage,
marble cubes, porcelain dish,
thermometer, and cuttlebone
4⁷/₈ x 8³/₄ x 6³/₈″
The Louise and Walter Arensberg
Collection. 1950-134-75

Marcel Duchamp's concept of the "Readymade" suggested that an artist could select an ordinary object, present it as one's own, and declare it a work of art. His innovation was among the most scandalous and significant transformations to the history of modern art. This work is what Duchamp called an "assisted Readymade," in which the original object is altered by the artist. Its meaning is one of the most elusive among his many puzzling creations. The title, inscribed on the bottom of the cage in black adhesive tape, poses its enigmatic question in English. It is posed to, or perhaps by, Rrose Sélavy, the female alter ego Duchamp devised for himself (and a pun, in French, for "Eros is Life"). The painted metal birdcage is "assisted" by the addition of marble "sugar" cubes that almost fill it, a small porcelain dish, a mercury thermometer, and a cuttlebone. Its full delight only comes with use, as one is surprised by the weightiness of the marble, expecting the lightness of sugar. AT

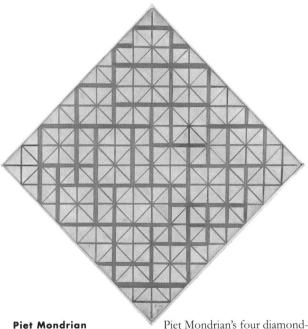

Piet Mondrian
Dutch, 1872–1944
Composition in Black and Gray
1919
Oil on canvas, 23⁵/₈ x 23¹¹/₁₆″
The Louise and Walter Arensberg
Collection. 1950-134-151

Piet Mondrian's four diamond-patterned paintings of 1918–19—of which this is the second—mark the artist's final step toward the abstraction of his mature style. *Composition in Black and Gray* is composed entirely of linear elements that diagonally divide the painting into 256 approximately equal triangular units. Mondrian thickened sections of the horizontal and vertical gray lines to create another pattern, an accent distinct from but in harmony with the overall grid. The canvas (now discolored by age) was rubbed with white paint, so that the grid of the woven fabric would remain apparent. The flickering optical effect of the intersections of the lines suggests their visual source in the starry sky. Mondrian, who began as a post-Impressionist painter working after nature and then integrated the Cubist vocabulary, remained committed to an art that retained a basis in nature. He spoke of these diamond paintings as the key to achieving this goal, as their abstract formal structure metaphorically corresponded to our experience of the sky at night, in which we supply harmony and equilibrium to a seemingly infinite, random field. AT

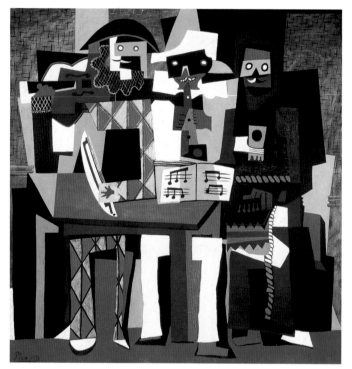

Pablo Ruiz y Picasso
Spanish, 1881–1973
Three Musicians, 1921
Oil on canvas
80½ x 74⅛″
A. E. Gallatin Collection
1952-61-96

Three Musicians provides a grand summation of Pablo Picasso's decade-long exploration of Synthetic Cubism, with its flat, patterned shapes, although painted in oil, echoing the cut and pasted papers of his collages of the period. Music was a favorite Cubist theme, and here Picasso equips Harlequin with a violin, Pierrot with a recorder, and the monk with an accordion. All three characters, which figure importantly in the history of painting and in Picasso's own earlier work, are derived from Italian, French, and Spanish popular theater and carnival traditions, but the artist had also encountered them more directly during recent visits to Italy as the set designer for Sergei Diaghilev's ballet. Indeed, the stagelike space of this monumental composition may be traced to Picasso's theatrical work. Quite probably a portrayal of Picasso himself (Harlequin) and two poet friends, the painting presents an allegory of the artist as performer, a major theme of Picasso's highly autobiographical work throughout his long life. AT

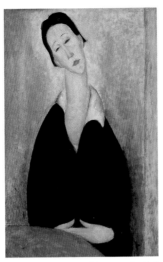

Amedeo Modigliani
Italian, 1884–1920
Portrait of a Polish Woman, 1919
Oil on canvas
39½ x 25½"
The Louis E. Stern Collection
1963-181-48

Portrait of a Polish Woman exemplifies Amedeo Modigliani's favorite choice of subject: the single figure, most often female, filling the frame, isolated from incidental detail, and directly confronting the artist and viewer. The unidentified sitter is most likely Hanka Zborowska, the aristocratic Polish wife of Modigliani's most devoted dealer, Leopold Zborowski. Zborowska, along with her close friend Luina Czechowska, another Polish woman who might also be the subject of this portrait, both posed frequently for Modigliani in the last years of his life. The use of friends for models, a practice that began out of financial necessity, resulted in a number of penetrating encounters for Modigliani, challenging him to achieve a balance between strong individual character and the emphatic imprint of his style. In this portrait, his propensity for fluid linearity, geometric simplification, and elongation and displacement of body parts—not unexpected for an artist sometimes described as an inheritor of the Italian Mannerist tradition—underscores the elegance and sophistication of his sitter. JBR

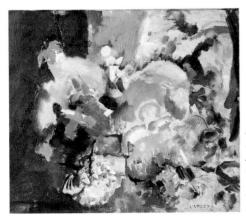

Arthur Beecher Carles
American, 1882–1952
Abstract of Flowers, c. 1922
Oil on canvas
21¼ x 25½"
The Samuel S. White 3rd and Vera White
Collection. 1967-30-14

Arthur Carles was one of the preeminent artists in Philadelphia during the first half of this century, known for his innovative painting as well as his teaching. Trained at the Pennsylvania

Academy of the Fine Arts, he arrived at his distinctive style through his travels to France, where the work of Henri Matisse had great impact on this American artist. The exuberance of color almost overpowers our reading of *Abstract of Flowers;* the choice of subject simply permitted the artist to celebrate his virtuosity in creating a complex interplay of reds, blues, pinks, greens, yellows, and, importantly, white. The painting was first exhibited under the title *Improvisation,* and the freedom manifest in Carles's apparently spontaneous application of paint is striking even today. This painting belonged to Samuel and Vera White, who were among the many prominent and adventurous Philadelphians who supported Carles with their patronage. AT

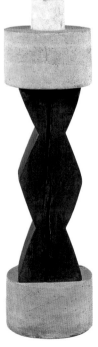

Constantin Brancusi

French, born Romania, 1876–1957
Bird in Space (Yellow Bird)
1923–24?
Marble with marble, limestone,
and oak base
Height 103″ (with base)
The Louise and Walter Arensberg
Collection. 1950-134-19

The bird is the predominant theme of Constantin Brancusi's work, forming the subject of over twenty-five marble or bronze sculptures that he made during the course of four decades, three of which are in the Museum's collection. It epitomized his search for an ideal form that triumphs over the imperfections of earthly existence. In *Bird in Space* all the parts of the creature become one soaring movement, with an elegance resulting from the slight swell of its chest and the graceful undulation of its slender footing. Brancusi considered his bases integral to his sculpture, and their contribution to the principles of balance, proportion, and combination was central to his aesthetic. Here the pedestal consists of a small marble cylinder, a limestone drum, a sawtooth form in oak, and a second limestone drum similar to the first. These rough textures and varieties of shape provide a counterpoint to the smooth unity of the yellow marble bird. The harmony of the whole achieves Brancusi's mystical goal of unifying opposites. AT

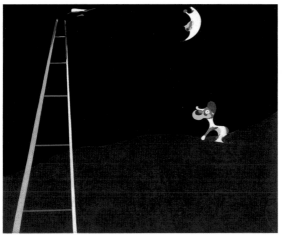

Joan Miró
Spanish, 1893–1983
Dog Barking at the Moon, 1926
Oil on canvas
28¾ x 36¼"
A. E. Gallatin Collection. 1952-61-82

At once engaging and perplexing, Joan Miró's *Dog Barking at the Moon* exemplifies his blend of sophisticated and enigmatic pictorial wit. In a sparse and stylized nighttime farm scene, the familiar elements of dog, moon, and ladder are endowed with intensified significance by their distortion and stark isolation against the balanced realms of earth and sky. Miró painted this work during a critical stage in his development, and one richly represented in the Museum's collection. In the 1920s and 1930s, he forged his mature style out of his contacts with Cubism and Surrealism in Paris, tempered by his allegiance to his roots in Catalonia, that distinctive province of Spain. In *Dog Barking at the Moon,* the precision of its structure owes much to the disciplined geometry of Cubism. Surrealism provided a liberating counterexample, with its inventive freedom born of memory, association, fantasy, and chance, while the energetic primitivism of Miró's Catalan heritage exerted an equally strong pull. JBR

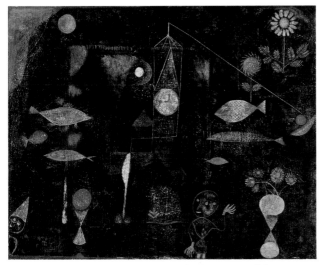

Paul Klee
Swiss, 1879–1940
Fish Magic, 1925
Oil and watercolor on canvas on panel
30⅜ x 38¾"
The Louise and Walter Arensberg Collection. 1950-134-112

Paul Klee is one of the greatest philosophers and theorists of twentieth-century art, particularly in the field of color, as well as one of its greatest fantasists. In paintings such as *Fish Magic* these two divergent gifts are reconciled, as intellect and imagination join forces. Klee has created a space that is not heavenly, earthly, or aquatic but rather exists elsewhere, in a realm where all forms of life intermingle. The painting is actually a collage, with a central square of muslin glued over the larger rectangular canvas surface. The sense of magic increases when one sees that a long painted line from the side seems ready to pull the square off to reveal something underneath. The dark palette and fragile muslin support give the picture a sense of silence that reinforces the mystery pervading the inky atmosphere. AT

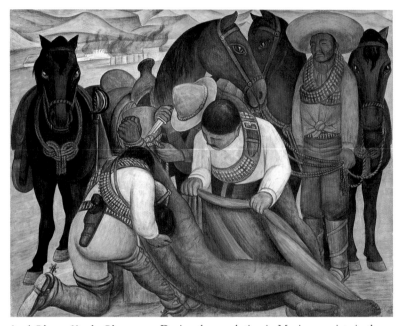

José Diego Maria Rivera
Mexican, 1886–1957
Liberation of the Peon, 1931
Fresco
73 x 94¼″
Gift of Mr. and Mrs. Herbert Cameron
Morris. 1943-46-1

During the revolution in Mexican society in the 1920s and 1930s, Diego Rivera was a leader among the core group of artists dedicated to creating a radical public art. Monumental murals for government buildings were ideally suited to these artists' socialist commitment to presenting a visual "people's history" of Mexico. For his mural commissions, Rivera revived the Italian Renaissance fresco tradition of applying pigments ground in water to a moist lime plaster wall surface. *Liberation of the Peon* is one of eight moveable frescoes that he created for his exhibition organized by the Museum of Modern Art in New York in 1931, which traveled to Philadelphia. Based on an image in the large decorative scheme Rivera painted for the Ministry of Public Education in Mexico City in 1923, it shows four revolutionary soldiers releasing a dying peasant from the stake where he had been tied and flogged. In an allusion to Christ's descent from the cross, the soldiers lower the naked, lacerated body and prepare to wrap it in a red robe. The tragedy is made more stark by the staring eyes of the horses, innocent witnesses to oppression. JBR

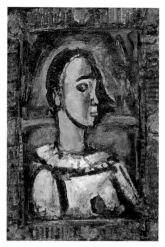

Georges Rouault
French, 1871–1958
Pierrot with a Rose, c. 1936
Oil on canvas
36½ x 24⁵⁄₁₆″
The Samuel S. White 3rd and Vera White
Collection. 1967-30-76

Georges Rouault is somewhat of an anomaly within twentieth-century modernism for having aimed to create a deeply religious art based on his strong Catholic convictions. Throughout his life he worked in solitude, using an intensely expressionist style characterized by the vigorous application of dark, thickly layered paint. Rouault's apprenticeship in a stained-glass workshop also seems to have left its mark in the heavy black outlines and glowing colors found here and in his other paintings. *Pierrot with a Rose* recalls the association typically made in nineteenth-century Romantic and Symbolist painting between the fate of marginal figures of society such as Pierrot, a character from French popular theater, and the martyrdom of Christ. This allusion is strengthened by the red rose, a long-standing symbol for the blood of Christ. This painting may plausibly be read as a self-portrait, in which the artist has romantically identified himself with the clown-martyr. AT

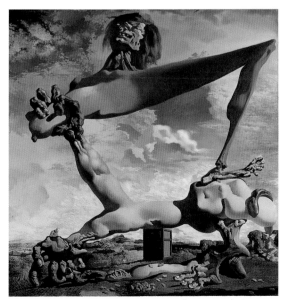

Salvador Dalí
Spanish, 1904–1989
Soft Construction with Boiled Beans (Premonition of Civil War), 1936
Oil on canvas
39⁵⁄₁₆ x 39³⁄₈″
The Louise and Walter Arensberg
Collection. 1950-134-41

Salvador Dalí developed his achingly precise version of Surrealism to achieve what he called a "concrete irrationality." This, he hoped, would lend credibility to images of the unconscious, which in turn would discredit the world of reality. In *Soft Construction with Boiled Beans,* however, Dalí applies his method to the very real and deeply troubling subject of the Spanish Civil War of 1936–39. Here a vast, grotesque body rips itself apart, its grimace registering the pain. Set against a technicolor sky and the parched landscape of northern Spain, the mutating figure dominates its environment. This disjunction of scale indicates its symbolic function—despite its hysterical concreteness—as a representation of the physical and emotional self-conflict in which Spain was both the victim and the aggressor. The little professor, wandering across the landscape at left, adds an odd counterpoint to the frenzied mass of flesh, as do the morsels of boiled beans that may refer to the ancient Catalan offering to appease the gods. JBR

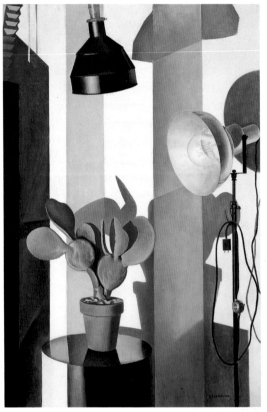

Charles Sheeler
American, 1883–1965
Cactus, 1931
Oil on canvas
45⅛ x 30¹⁄₁₆″
The Louise and Walter Arensberg
Collection. 1950-134-186

Beginning in the 1920s, Charles Sheeler played a central role in the development of Precisionism, a modernist movement characterized by a crisp, sharply defined style that united the desire for a distinctly American art with the lessons of the Parisian avant-garde. In *Cactus,* he continues the rigorous pursuit of clarity and order that had marked his Precisionist studies of such vernacular emblems of the United States as barns, Shaker furniture, and factories. As was often the case, Sheeler based this painting on one of his own photographs (here a set used for one of his commercial shoots), rendering the plant, pedestal, and lamps as well as the variations in light and shadow with photographic exactitude. Sheeler's early sympathy with Cubism also remains apparent, for he has transformed this seemingly straightforward document of his working life into a complex interplay of forms in a shallow, ambiguous space. Oddly, however, Sheeler's severe and analytic approach has produced a highly enigmatic image, as the denuded cactus, stripped of its spikes, sits forlornly beneath an unplugged light. JBR

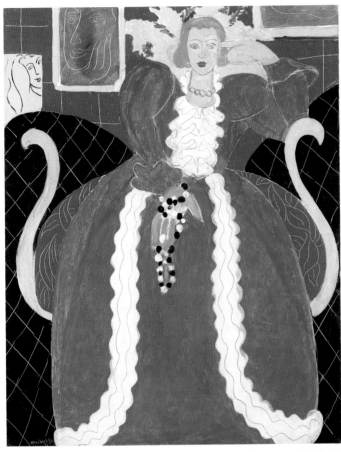

Henri Matisse
French, 1869–1954
Woman in Blue, 1937
Oil on canvas
36½ x 29″
Gift of Mrs. John Wintersteen
1956-23-1

The sitter for this painting was Lydia Delectorskaya, a Russian woman who had frequently posed for Matisse since the early 1930s. It is one of many portraits of the late 1930s in which Matisse focused on a dramatic costume rather than the personality of the model. The simplicity of the composition is striking, with a palette of only red, yellow, blue, black, and white. A seemingly casual harmony exists among the many billowing curves, the background grids, and the three drawings on the wall. Yet ten photographs taken over the three months that Matisse worked on the picture (now in the Museum archives) prove that this was a hard-won solution: the first version of the picture shows a relatively naturalistic composition of a woman leaning to her side, full of much greater detail and depth. Only gradually did the present state of the work evolve, with its absolutely flat picture plane, rather inexpressive portrayal, and the boldly exaggerated right hand encircled with beads. AT

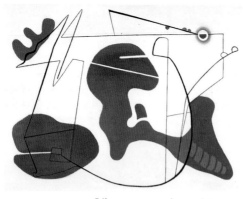

Alice Trumbull Mason
American, 1904–1971
Brown Shapes White, 1941
Oil on panel
23¹⁵⁄₁₆ x 31¾"
A. E. Gallatin Collection. 1952-61-76

Like many members of the generation of American artists
working between the two world wars, Alice Trumbull Mason
embraced the visual language of abstract art with unwavering
dedication in the face of a hostile public who viewed abstraction as a suspicious European import. In her own early work
she concentrated on irregular organic forms, but later focused
exclusively on what she called "architectural" abstraction. *Brown
Shapes White* represents a point between these poles with its
complex interplay between biomorphic shapes and linear geometric scaffolding. It has about it the intimacy of scale as well
as the precision and liveliness that are typical of Mason's work.
In her resolute focus on the immediate reality of the picture—
organizing relationships among shape, color, and line on the
two-dimensional surface—Mason considered herself a "true
realist." Albert Gallatin, himself a dedicated abstract painter,
bought this and many other works by his American contemporaries to join his collection of international modernism. JBR

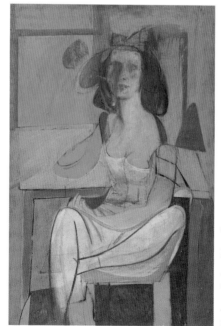

Willem de Kooning
American, born Netherlands,
born 1904
Seated Woman, c. 1940
Oil and charcoal on Masonite
54¹⁄₁₆ x 36"
The Albert M. Greenfield and Elizabeth
M. Greenfield Collection. 1974-178-23

This portrait signals the beginning of a long series of paintings
by Willem de Kooning that culminated in one of the most

aggressive revisions of the female figure in the art of this century. Here De Kooning's struggle to redefine the female form is presented explicitly in the painted outlines and charcoal underdrawing and overdrawing that emphasize the artist's re-arrangements, particularly of arms and legs. The intense greens, blues, pinks, and oranges comprise an acidic palette typical of De Kooning's work of this time. The woman is seated before a thin table within an environment of sufficient flatness and spatial ambiguity to recall the ancient Pompeian murals that De Kooning often visited at the Metropolitan Museum of Art in New York. By veiling the woman's face with layers of paint atop a wide, unfocused stare and bared teeth, De Kooning keeps the sitter at an unbridgeable distance from the viewer in both space and time. AT

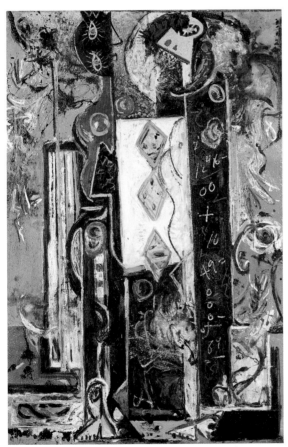

Jackson Pollock
American, 1912–1956
Male and Female, c. 1942
Oil on canvas
73 ¼ x 48 ¹⁵/₁₆"
Gift of Mr. and Mrs. H. Gates Lloyd
1974-232-1

Male and Female was the sole illustration to the catalogue of Jackson Pollock's first one-person exhibition, held in New York in 1943. It was a shocking painting in a shocking show that critics described as "volcanic" and "explosive." While the painting reveals Pollock's interest in contemporary European art, it introduces an unprecedented freedom with paint. This is particularly evident in the upper left, where a seemingly random burst of streaks and splotches foreshadows the "drip" painting that would become Pollock's signature style. The subject is an archetypal one, reflecting Pollock's desire to return painting to issues of primal significance. The female is identified by her bright red curvy torso and marvelous eyelashes, and the male by a column of numbers. These signifiers correspond to archetypes of the woman as sensual (nature) and the man as intellectual (culture). This painting thus seems to address both the unity of male and female, joined to form one blocky construction, as well as the interplay of their opposites. AT

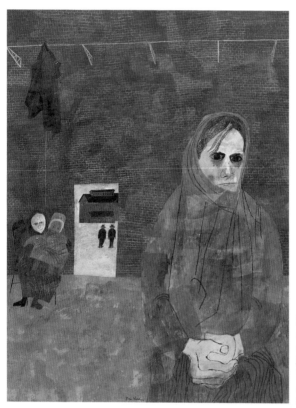

Ben Shahn
American, born Lithuania, 1898–1969
Miners' Wives, c. 1948
Tempera on panel
48 x 36″
Gift of Wright S. Ludington. 1951-3-1

Miners' Wives represents Ben Shahn's response to the death of over one hundred men in a mine explosion in Centralia, Illinois, in 1947. For an article on the disaster in *Harper's Magazine,* Shahn had provided numerous illustrations, four of which he used as the bases for paintings, including this powerful image. Shahn here shows two of the wives waiting near their husbands' street clothing in the mine's washhouse, as that would surely be the first place they would come if brought out alive. Based on an actual event, the scene makes a larger statement as well. The women's ashen faces, vacant stares, and clenched hands eloquently convey the isolation and suffering of working people that so often provided the central themes of Shahn's politically and socially committed art. JBR

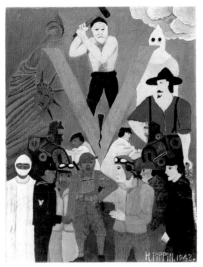

Horace Pippin
American, 1888–1946
Mr. Prejudice, 1943
Oil on canvas
18⅛ x 14⅛″
Gift of Dr. and Mrs. Matthew T. Moore
1984-108-1

Horace Pippin began to paint in earnest in the 1930s, combining the naïveté of the self-taught artist with an awareness of modern painting. World War I, in which he sustained a crippling arm wound, provided a frequent subject for his work, as did childhood memories and religious subjects. Human rights and social issues also often figure in this African American artist's work, but *Mr. Prejudice* is rare in its overt treatment of racism. In a style owing to the political poster, Pippin crowds a shallow space with symbols of the division of the races. Three black soldiers (including the artist's self-portrait with his dangling, useless arm) face off against their hostile white counterparts, as a black and a white machinist turn their backs to perform identical tasks. The masked and gowned black doctor counterbalances a hooded and cloaked Klansman, while the red-shirted white man holding a noose looks across to a brown-skinned Statue of Liberty. Surmounting the scene, the brutish Mr. Prejudice drives a wedge into the golden *V* of victory. JBR

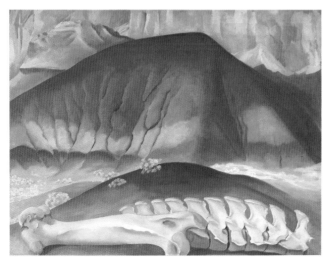

Georgia O'Keeffe
American, 1887–1986
Red Hills and Bones, 1941
Oil on canvas
29¾ x 40″
The Alfred Stieglitz Collection
1949-18-109

This painting came to the Museum from the Alfred Stieglitz Bequest, which Georgia O'Keeffe administered. O'Keeffe met the photographer in 1916, when he first became interested in showing her work at his "291" gallery in New York, an early center of avant-garde activity in the United States. Stieglitz soon became her dealer and, in 1924, her husband. *Red Hills and Bones* represents an actual location near O'Keeffe's New Mexico home, but in a number of ways she has distilled her personal experience of the landscape to extract a symbol of something larger and more permanent. No glimpse of sky nor even breath of air alleviates the intensity of these desolate but richly colored hills that fill the picture from edge to edge. The bleached animal bones looming in the foreground serve as monumental reminders of the struggle between animate and inanimate forces so keenly evident in the western desert; O'Keeffe in fact prided herself on being one of the few who were creating a truly American art. JBR

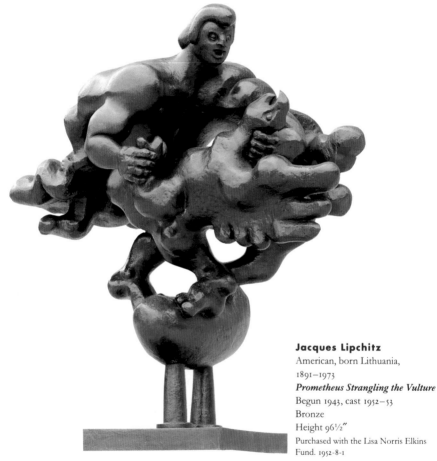

Jacques Lipchitz
American, born Lithuania,
1891–1973
Prometheus Strangling the Vulture
Begun 1943, cast 1952–53
Bronze
Height 96½"
Purchased with the Lisa Norris Elkins Fund. 1952-8-1

Jacques Lipchitz was a leading Cubist sculptor of the early twentieth century, applying the faceted, geometrizing manner he had learned primarily from Pablo Picasso and Juan Gris to such familiar Cubist subjects as sailors, musicians, and bathers. During the 1930s and 1940s, however, Lipchitz's style and subject evolved toward monumental depictions of mythological and biblical conflicts as he sought to respond to world events, particularly the rise and spread of Fascism, from which he himself had to flee. Philadelphia boasts a strong group of his monumental public sculpture, such as this one. In *Prometheus Strangling the Vulture,* Lipchitz represented the mythic Greek hero who brought fire to humans, here locked in deadly struggle with the winged beast sent by the gods as punishment for his independence. Balanced gracefully on a tiny cloud, the muscular Prometheus will clearly be the victor as he throttles the bird with one hand and fends off his talons with the other. Lipchitz's version of this ancient story, with its clear distinction between good and evil, was meant to warn contemporary society about the importance of its own struggles but is not without optimism. JBR

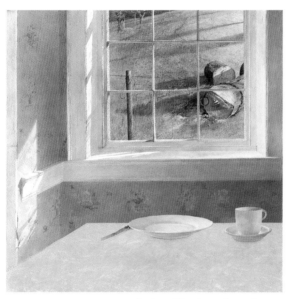

Andrew Newell Wyeth
American, born 1917
Groundhog Day, 1959
Tempera on Masonite
31 ⅜ x 32 ⅛″
Gift of Henry F. du Pont and
Mrs. John Wintersteen. 1959-102-1

Andrew Wyeth, perhaps the most widely known contemporary painter in the United States, is often seen as existing outside of his own time or any particular tradition. In his art, however, he maintains a strong continuity with the painters of the 1930s and 1940s who focused on typically American scenes of urban and rural daily life, and who sought to achieve a sense of permanence and authority in their work. Like these painters he turned to the medieval technique of egg tempera on gessoed panel and to the work of the old masters for inspiration. The exquisite clarity with which Wyeth here renders every detail of the light-flooded Pennsylvania farmhouse kitchen of his neighbor holds out the promise of great intimacy. Yet the dryness of the tempera technique and the restraint fostered by its painstaking application combine with the image of a solitary place setting to create a mood of overwhelming loneliness. The wire fence and massive log outside the window, held in place by the steeply rising hill that cuts off any glimpse of sky, compound this sense of isolation. JBR

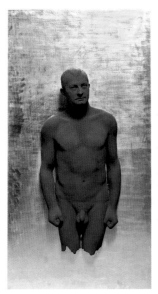

Yves Klein
French, 1928–1962
Portrait Relief I: Arman, 1962
Painted bronze on panel covered
in gold leaf
69 x 37″
Gift of Dr. and Mrs. William Wolgin
1978-174-1

Yves Klein molded the body of his artist-friend Arman in plaster and had it cast in bronze. The bronze was then painted with
"Yves Klein Blue," a mixture of dry pigment and clear binder
that Klein had patented in 1957, and the life-size sculpture was
placed against a gilded wooden panel. Klein's use of his trade-
mark blue was oddly ambivalent: the choice had spiritual and
poetic resonance, while the implications of trademarking a
color were richly ironic. This portrait relief continued Klein's
longtime interest in using the body to make art, exemplified
in his controversial series of large paintings in which he used
paint-covered women as his "brushes." The efficiency of direct
body casting parodies the classical sculptural tradition of meticulous hand-carving. The portrait of Arman, done shortly before Klein's premature death, was the first in what was to have
been a "Collective Portrait Relief" of several artists, including
Klein himself at the center, in contrasting tones of gold-covered
bronze projecting from an Yves Klein Blue panel. AT

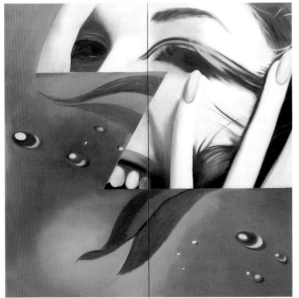

James Rosenquist
American, born 1933
Zone, 1961
Oil on two canvas sections
95 x 47¹¹⁄₁₆″ (each section)
Purchased with the Edith H. Bell Fund
1982-9-1

Zone, which James Rosenquist identified as his first successful
painting, is an entirely repainted composition, having originally
been a far busier assemblage of images ranging from three

cows to a suicide scene. Rosenquist finally reduced it to this iconic close-up of the left side of a woman's smiling face and two fingers (derived from a magazine advertisement for skin softener), placed above an image of a tomato with bracts and droplets of water. Rosenquist's exclusive use of photographic tones of gray unites the spliced composition, which is divided by a zigzag split as well as by the two vertical canvases that are joined to form the whole. The giant size of the imagery is owed to Rosenquist's earlier work as a billboard painter. It was with his billboard-like paintings such as *Zone* that he joined the ranks of those who would become known as Pop artists at the beginning of the 1960s. Like the others, Rosenquist rebelled against the sublime pretensions of Abstract Expressionism, instead exploiting the potential of concrete, everyday imagery to make pictures addressing real experience. AT

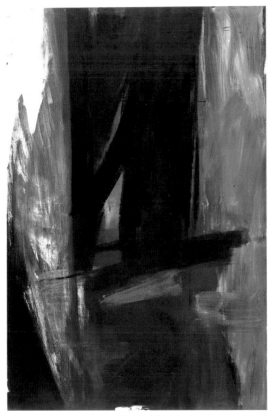

Franz Kline
American, 1910–1962
Torches Mauve, 1960
Oil on canvas
120⅛ x 81⅛″
Gift of the artist. 1961-223-1

Franz Kline is best known for his sweeping black-and-white strokes of paint that represent some of the purest examples of Abstract Expressionism during the 1940s and 1950s. By the late 1950s, however, Kline reintroduced color into his work as a way to extend and rearticulate the essential tensions between black and white. In *Torches Mauve,* the atmospheric haze of purple does not mitigate the sense of movement and pressure that arises between the two primary tones, but rather enriches it by creating a kind of plasmic environment in which the black exists. For all its suggestion of some elegiac ceremony illuminated by flames, *Torches Mauve* was in fact named for a brand of purple oil paint manufactured by Joseph Torch on Fourteenth Street in New York City. JBR

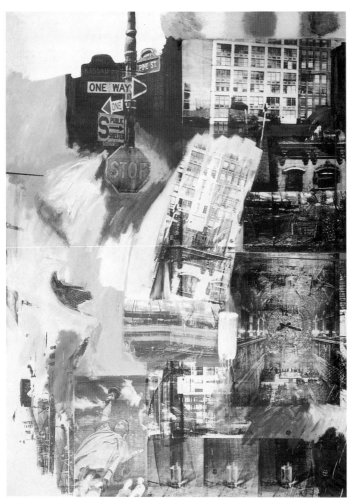

Robert Rauschenberg
American, born 1925
Estate, 1963
Oil and silkscreened inks
on canvas
96 x 69¹³⁄₁₆"
Gift of the Friends of the Philadelphia
Museum of Art. 1967-88-1

Estate is one of the first paintings in which Robert Rauschenberg used the commercial technique of the color silkscreen, in which photographic images are transferred onto paper or canvas by pushing paint or ink through specially prepared fine mesh screens on wooden stretchers. Rauschenberg exploited the silkscreen process in a deliberately casual fashion, provocatively combining the photographic images with expressive brushwork to create richly textured associative paintings. Several of the photographic images in *Estate,* including the Statue of Liberty, the glass of water, the Sistine Chapel, the diagram of a clock, the street sign from his New York neighborhood, and the launching rocket, recur frequently in Rauschenberg's seventy-nine color silkscreen paintings of 1963 and 1964. Although their combination does not lead to any clear reading, these widely ranging images have a persuasive sense of meaning that recalls Rauschenberg's 1963 reference to a very complex and random order that cannot be called accidental. AT

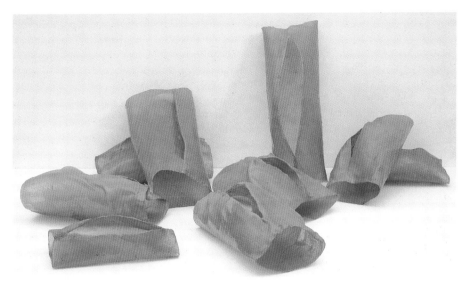

Eva Hesse
American, born Germany,
1936–1970
Tori, 1969
Fiberglass and resin on
wire mesh
47 x 17 x 15″ (largest unit)
Purchased with funds contributed by
Mr. and Mrs. Leonard Korman, Mr. and
Mrs. Keith Sachs, Marion Boulton
Stroud, Mr. and Mrs. Bayard T. Storey,
and other Museum funds. 1990-121-1–9

Eva Hesse belonged to a loosely associated group of New York artists who in the late 1960s rebelled against the harsh geometry and cool materiality of Minimalism, and began making works that came to be known as "antiform" or "process" art. This work was characterized by experimentation with flexible, fluid, and sometimes evanescent materials such as latex. Hesse's sculpture *Tori* consists of nine loosely wrapped podlike forms, hollow at the center and the ends. The armature is wire mesh, the surface a mixture of fiberglass and resin. The nine elements are to be arranged casually on the floor and against the wall. In any configuration, the sense of scarred surface, barren interior, and collapsed form is decidedly painful, yet the luminosity of the material and the delicacy of the shapes give this piece an unearthly beauty. The term *tori* itself generally describes smooth, rounded protuberances, with geometric, anatomical, architectural, and botanical references. AT

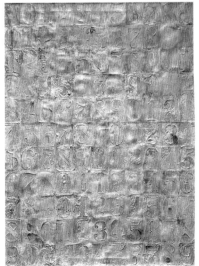

Jasper Johns
American, born 1930
Sculpmetal Numbers, 1963
Sculpmetal on canvas
57⅞ x 43⅞″
Centennial gift of the Woodward
Foundation. 1975-81-6

In his earliest paintings Jasper Johns depicted subjects that were familiar to everyone—"things the mind already knows," said the artist—such as numbers and letters as well as targets and the American flag. But numbers, which Johns first painted in 1955, are only apparently simple subjects, for these solid forms present the ultimate abstractions: manufactured signs for purely mental concepts. Here the numbers are standard commercial stencils used for labels or signage, presented in conventional order from 0 to 9 according to a grid that seems to proceed inevitably from the format of the canvas. The gray medium is Sculpmetal, a commercial aluminum putty, the use of which exemplifies the artist's investigation of the territorial blurring of sculpture and painting during the early 1960s. This painting likewise typifies Johns's deliberate removal of the standard indicators of personal expression: color, brushwork, and subject. In *Sculpmetal Numbers,* the stencils incorporated onto the canvas render the abstract concrete, and the texture and tones of the Sculpmetal sensualize the conceptual. Typically, Johns has made an entirely literal statement to introduce profound questions about subject and object, matter and thought, painting and seeing. AT

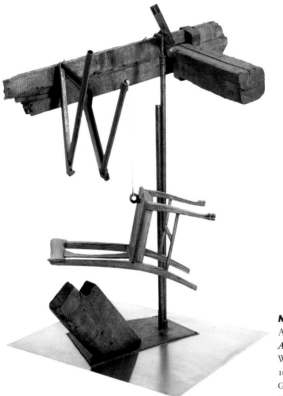

Mark di Suvero
American, born 1933
Amerigo for My Father, 1963
Wood, steel, iron, clothesline
102 x 78 x 60" (approximate)
Gift of Mr. and Mrs. David N. Pincus
1981-112-1

Mark di Suvero's wood and metal sculpture of the early 1960s is often described as painting in three dimensions. The jagged combinations of rough-hewn materials call to mind the rawness and energy of Abstract Expressionism, particularly the broad, slashing strokes of Willem de Kooning and Franz Kline. Yet Di Suvero's illogical juxtaposition of found materials, each possessing a history and reservoir of associations, connects him to a wider practice ranging from Dada and Surrealism to junk assemblage of the late 1950s and early 1960s. The title *Amerigo for My Father* conflates the experiences of the Italian explorer Amerigo Vespucci (1451–1512), for whom the Americas were named, with Di Suvero's father, an Italian soldier who brought his family to the United States at the outbreak of World War II. The sculpture's top-heavy structure pivots slowly on a tiny point, which adds to the dynamic interaction among its parts and with its environment. JBR

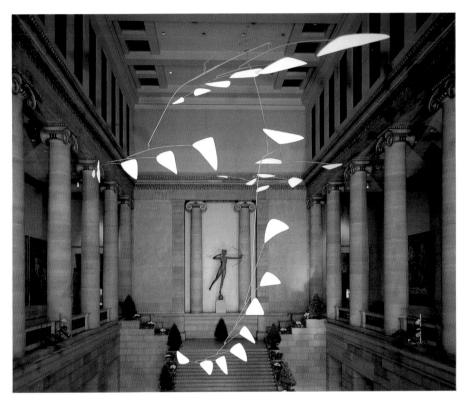

Alexander Calder
American, 1898–1976
Ghost, 1964
Metal rods, painted sheet metal
Length 34′
Purchased with the New Members Fund. 1965-47-1

Alexander Calder's mobiles are among the most often imitated works of art of the twentieth century and yet remain the most singular. Marcel Duchamp gave them their name, when Calder first began to make these constructions in the early 1930s. The mobiles reflect Calder's fascination with toys and his training as an engineer as well as his familiarity with the modern European art of Pablo Picasso, Piet Mondrian, and Joan Miró. Calder made *Ghost* for the central rotunda of the Solomon R. Guggenheim Museum in New York, on the occasion of an exhibition of his work in 1964. The white color of the sheet-metal panels, which gives the enormous mobile its name, probably was inspired by the all-white interior of Frank Lloyd Wright's Guggenheim building. Calder was delighted when the mobile was acquired by the Philadelphia Museum of Art, where it now hangs in the Great Stair Hall, with its view of the Logan Square fountain, made by his father, Alexander Stirling Calder, and the statue of William Penn atop City Hall, made by his grandfather Alexander Milne Calder. AT

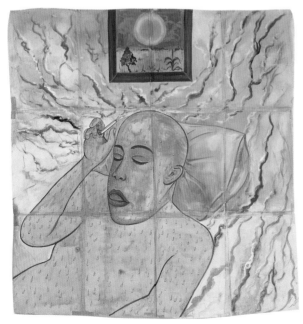

Claes Oldenburg

American, born Sweden, born 1929
Giant Three-Way Electric Plug
(Scale B), 1970
Cherry
Height 58″
Purchased with the Fiske Kimball Fund
and with funds contributed by the
Daniel W. Dietrich Foundation, Mr. and
Mrs. David N. Pincus, Dr. and Mrs.
William Wolgin, and anonymous donors
1983-74-1

Claes Oldenburg came to prominence in the early 1960s, along with a generation of fellow Pop artists, for drawn and sculpted renderings of everyday commercial products. He has continued to use these common functional objects, such as clothespins, lipstick, and toilet tank floats, as the basis for his art, manipulating the scale, shape, and material of the original sources to unleash a wealth of associations. Oldenburg first worked with the electric plug in 1965 and has since produced many variations. In *Giant Three-Way Electric Plug,* the acts of enlarging the plug to a gigantic scale, suspending it in the air, and making it out of cherry, a wood usually reserved for fine furniture, render this humble object nearly unfamiliar. Its affinity with architecture is revealed as the plug's form resembles a groin vault made by the crossing of two tunnels in a Romanesque church. As is characteristic of Oldenburg's embrace of multiple associations, the parallel with architecture here suggests confinement as much as shelter. JBR

Francesco Clemente

Italian, born 1952
Sun, 1980
Opaque watercolor on twelve
sheets of handmade paper, joined
by cotton strips
95 x 91″
Purchased with the Edward and Althea
Budd Fund, the Katharine Levin Farrell
Fund, and with funds contributed by
Mrs. H. Gates Lloyd. 1984-118-1

Francesco Clemente's unusual, often fantastical paintings and drawings helped usher in what was variously dubbed "the rebirth of painting" and "the return to the figure" during the late 1970s and 1980s. Working in a variety of traditional materials, including fresco, pastel, watercolor, and oils, Clemente creates expressive images of the human figure that range from the comic and scatological to the erotic and spiritual. Made in 1980 in Madras, India, where Clemente spends part of each year, and painted on twelve sheets of handmade local paper joined with cloth strips, *Sun* reflects Clemente's union of Eastern and Western traditions. The strangely androgynous man who lies sweating beneath a picture of the sun, cigarette slipping from his loosening grasp, seems as much the harem eunuch from countless tales and paintings as a contemporary European visitor suffering from the heat of South India. Clemente's images deliberately avoid facile or reductive interpretation, opting instead for more open-ended evocation, sometimes of mythic proportion. JBR

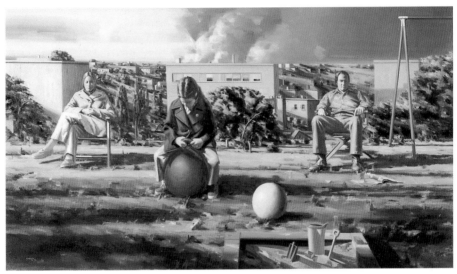

Sidney Goodman
American, born 1936
Figures in a Landscape, 1972–73
Oil on canvas
55 x 96"
Purchased with the Philadelphia Foundation Fund (by exchange) and the Adele Haas Turner and Beatrice Pastorius Turner Memorial Fund. 1974-112-1

The Philadelphia artist Sidney Goodman works in an expressive figurative style, synthesizing direct observation of the human form and landscape with prolonged study of European and American masters. Beginning with his first major showing in New York, at the Museum of Modern Art in 1962, he has received national recognition as an exemplar of contemporary realism. His work explores aspects of the human condition, often seen from an apocalyptic perspective. He is intrigued by issues ranging from mortality and suffering to desire and aspiration, frequently rendered on a monumental scale appropriate to such age-old, universal themes. In *Figures in a Landscape* Goodman paints himself and his first wife ensconced in lawn chairs in a suburban playground, while their daughter plays between them. The physical isolation of each family member, underscored by the storm clouds that gather only over the father, mirrors a seemingly unbridgeable emotional distance. No head or even building is allowed to break through the oppressive horizon line. Anxiety and quiet despair pervade the scene. JBR

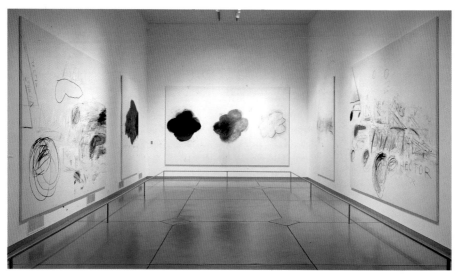

Cy Twombly

American, born 1928
Fifty Days at Iliam, 1977–78
Oil, oil crayon, and graphite on
ten canvases
118 x 193½" (largest canvas)
Gift (by exchange) of Samuel S. White
3rd and Vera White. 1989-90-1–10

Cy Twombly's *Fifty Days at Iliam* is a rare type of work for a twentieth-century artist—a painting cycle that illustrates a narrative. Long inspired by classical antiquity, Twombly here pays homage to what is perhaps the definitive narrative of Western literature: Homer's *Iliad,* the tragic story of the final fifty days of the Trojan War, probably written before 700 B.C. Twombly's series in ten parts progresses from the fiery moment when the Greek warrior Achilles is inspired to join the fight against Troy (Iliam) to an almost blank canvas filled with the silence of death. The installation develops in both diachronic and synchronic fashion: the story unfolds chronologically, while simultaneously one wall presents a predominantly Greek mood, passionate and explosive, as the facing wall depicts an essentially Trojan attitude, more contemplative and cool. Twombly uses the visual language that he had derived over twenty years earlier, full of scrawling marks, seemingly random brushstrokes, and legible numbers and letters, to create his own tribute to an anchor of Western culture. AT

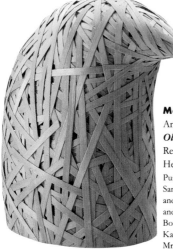

Martin Puryear

American, born 1941
Old Mole, 1985
Red cedar
Height 61"
Purchased with gifts (by exchange) of
Samuel S. White 3rd and Vera White,
and Mr. and Mrs. Charles C. G. Chaplin,
and with funds contributed by Marion
Boulton Stroud, Mr. and Mrs. Robert
Kardon, Mr. and Mrs. Dennis Alter, and
Mrs. H. Gates Lloyd. 1986-70-1

Old Mole exemplifies the work of this contemporary American sculptor in joining the traditions of woodworking with the forms of modernist sculpture. Over a wooden armature, Martin Puryear has wrapped layers of red cedar strips in a manner recalling basketry. The overall shape, however, is compact and simple, and responds to a history of abstract sculptural forms that embrace both geometric and organic allusions. This diversity of approach is typical of Puryear, whose background includes training in sculpture, painting, and printmaking as well as the study of contemporary and traditional crafts and carpentry in West Africa, Sweden, and Japan. Like much of Puryear's work, *Old Mole* presents a union of opposing tendencies. To the regularity of its cone shape—albeit deflated and bent—it adds the natural variations in its woven exterior. Occasional glimpses between the slats into the piece's interior pierce the work's apparent solidity and bulk. And the human scale and animal associations, suggested in part by the object's catchy title, give it a presence as mysterious and brooding as it is humorous. JBR

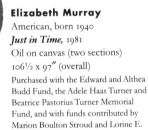

Elizabeth Murray
American, born 1940
Just in Time, 1981
Oil on canvas (two sections)
106½ x 97″ (overall)
Purchased with the Edward and Althea Budd Fund, the Adele Haas Turner and Beatrice Pastorius Turner Memorial Fund, and with funds contributed by Marion Boulton Stroud and Lorine E. Vogt. 1981-94-1a, b

Elizabeth Murray's vibrant, eccentrically shaped canvases are part of a reinvigoration of painting that began in the late 1970s after two decades of Minimalist and Conceptual art. Her paintings, which border on relief sculpture, combine abstraction and figuration in equal parts. She takes as her subjects the humble objects that form the fabric of her daily life, such as cups, paintbrushes, tables, and shoes. But by fragmenting, distorting, and monumentalizing these mundane forms, she casts them as the protagonists in animated and psychologically loaded domestic dramas. In *Just in Time,* a giant cup and saucer with rising cloudlike steam suggests the traditional metaphor of the female as a vessel. A second, smaller handle jutting off to the left transforms this lowly container into its more elevated, and masculine, counterpart—the trophy cup. The jagged gap between these two pits them as perennial alter egos caught in either tense détente or the beginning of continental drift. JBR

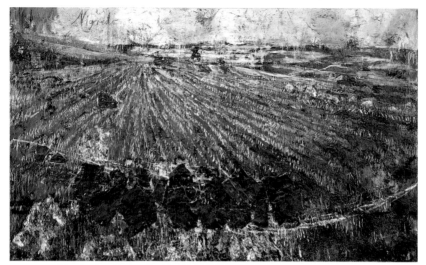

Anselm Kiefer
German, born 1945
Nigredo, 1984
Oil, acrylic, emulsion, shellac, and straw on photograph and woodcut, mounted on canvas
130 x 218½"
Gift of the Friends of the Philadelphia Museum of Art in celebration of their 20th anniversary. 1985-5-1

Anselm Kiefer's work has been interpreted as an exploration into the German nation and culture: a resurrection of symbols and memories taboo since the reign of the Nazis, and thus an evocation of a collective trauma that modern times have suppressed. This virtuosic landscape, a possible metaphor for the country as a whole, is built of thick layers of oil, acrylic, emulsion, shellac, and straw painted over a full-size photograph. The rocky field is ravaged, its heroic scale defeated and its symphonic music silenced. The title of the painting, however, provides an element of hope. "Nigredo" is a stage in the alchemical process of transformation of ordinary matter into gold; it is the moment of chaotic destruction that precedes purification. Despite the painting's primarily dark palette, its surface radiates a shimmering light that bears the promise of the transformation underway. AT

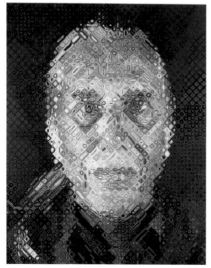

Chuck Close
American, born 1940
Paul, 1994
Oil on canvas
102 x 84"
Purchased with funds (by exchange) from the gift of Mr. and Mrs. Cummins Catherwood, the Edith H. Bell Fund, and with funds contributed by the Committee on Twentieth-Century Art
1994-166-1

Chuck Close has exclusively painted large-scale, full-face portraits for almost thirty years, beginning in an exacting photorealist manner. This is an example of Close's recent work, built on a far more freely organized network of painted units, buoyant blobs spilling from a diamond grid. The work coalesces into a grand portrait only when viewed from afar; up close, it is an ecstatic dance of color and shape. The painting is about perception, like many of the great paintings in history, a dramatization of the tension between paint's pure materiality and its power of illusionistic description. As if to emphasize this subject, Close has limited his recent work to portraits of painters. Here, "Paul" is Paul Cadmus, an artist ninety-two at the time of this painting and a charismatic figure on the New York scene for half a century. AT

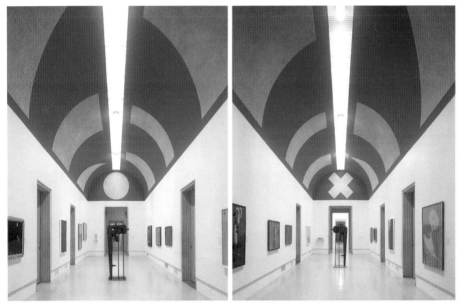

Sol LeWitt

American, born 1928

On a Blue Ceiling, Eight Geometric Figures: Circle, Trapezoid, Parallelogram, Rectangle, Square, Triangle, Right Triangle, X (Wall Drawing No. 351), 1981

Chalk and latex paint on plaster

15′6″ x 54′7″

Purchased with a grant from the National Endowment for the Arts and with funds contributed by Mrs. H. Gates Lloyd, Mr. and Mrs. N. Richard Miller, Mrs. Donald A. Petrie, Eileen and Peter Rosenau, Mrs. Adolf Schaap, Frances and Bayard Storey, Marion Boulton Stroud, and two anonymous donors (by exchange), with additional funds from Dr. and Mrs. William Wolgin, the Daniel W. Dietrich Foundation, and the Friends of the Philadelphia Museum of Art

1982-121-1

In the mid-1960s, Sol LeWitt emerged as a leading figure of Conceptual art, an international movement that emphasized a work's originating concept rather than the resulting object. Known initially for his geometric sculptures, in 1968 LeWitt began to draw directly on the wall, first in spare black pencil lines and later in washes of saturated colors. When a museum or a collector buys a piece of Conceptual art such as a wall drawing, the "object" the purchaser receives is a set of instructions for installing the work. The artist's role, as originator of the idea, is similar to that of the composer of a musical score. The wall drawing will vary with each installation, or "performance," as the characteristics of the work are adapted to the specific site. LeWitt welcomes this variability as a necessary part of his art. The "incarnation" of LeWitt's work at the Museum appears on the ceiling and end walls of a barrel vault. The happy convergence of the vaulted architecture, the lush blue hue, and the chalky white purity of the geometric forms evokes the orderly and contemplative mood of a frescoed chapel. It is perhaps no coincidence that LeWitt was living near Assisi in Italy when he conceived this work. JBR

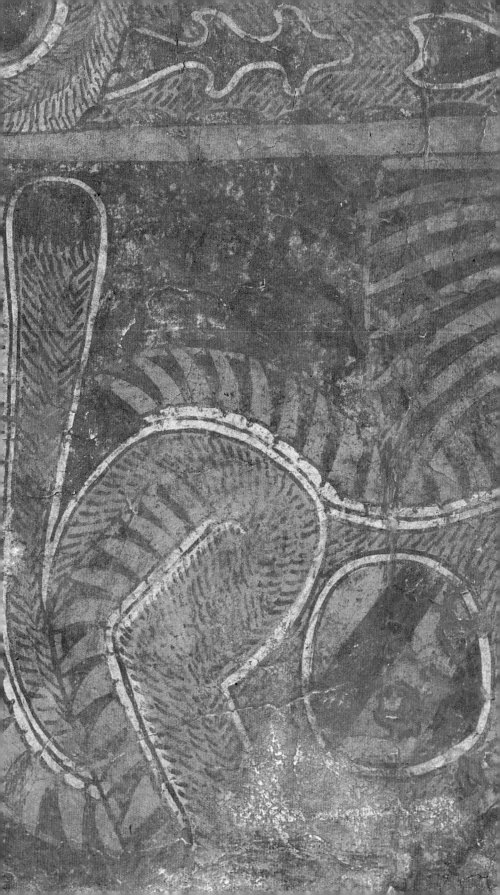